D1187910

International Marketing

International Marketing

VOLUME III

Edited by
Masaaki Kotabe

⑤SAGE Publications
London • Thousand Oaks • New Delhi

SAGE Publications Ltd
1 Oliver's Yard
55 City Road
London EC1Y 1SP

SAGE Publications Inc.
2455 Teller Road
Thousand Oaks, California 91320

SAGE Publications India Pvt Ltd
B-42, Panchsheel Enclave
Post Box 4109
New Delhi 110 017

British Library Cataloguing in Publication data

A catalogue record for this book is available from the British Library

ISBN: 10 1-4129-2830-3
ISBN: 13 978-1-4129-2830-4 (set of six volumes)

Library of Congress Control Number: 2006924629

Typeset by Star Compugraphics Private Limited, Delhi
Printed on paper from sustainable resources
Printed and bound in Great Britain by TJ International Ltd,
Padstow, Cornwall

Contents

Volume III

Section 2: Market Entry and Exit Decisions (*Continued*)

Section 3: Global Strategy

1. Competitive Strategy

1a. Conceptual Development

1b. Sources of Competitive Advantage and Performance Implications

1c. Regionalization of Global Strategy

SECTION 2

Market Entry and Exit Decisions (*Continued*)

2. Specific Modes of Entry (*Continued*)
3. Exit Strategies

Joint Ventures: Theoretical and Empirical Perspectives

Bruce Kogut

The study of joint ventures has attracted increasing interest in the popular press and academic literature. Though joint ventures are an important alternative to acquisitions, contracting, and internal development, the literature has not been consolidated and analyzed. This article provides a critical review of existing studies and new data in order to establish current theoretical and empirical directions. In particular, a theory of joint ventures as an instrument of organizational learning is proposed. In this view a joint venture is used for the transfer of organizationally embedded knowledge which cannot be easily blueprinted or packaged through licensing or market transactions.

The paper is divided into four sections. The first section develops three theories on joint ventures from the perspectives of transaction costs, strategic behavior, and organizational theory. The subsequent section reviews the literature on the motivations for joint ventures and empirical trends in their occurrence. Where possible, the findings are related to the three theoretical perspectives. Because there has been such considerable work in the area of international joint ventures, the third section summarizes some of the major findings regarding foreign entry and stability. The final section suggests some avenues for future research.

The theses of this article are essentially two. First, it will be argued that most statements on the motivations for joint ventures are reducible to three factors: evasion of small number bargaining, enhancement of competitive positioning (or market power), and mechanisms to transfer organizational knowledge. Second, it will be proposed that the cooperative aspects of joint ventures must be evaluated in the context of the competitive incentives among the partners and the competitive rivalry within the industry.

Joint Ventures

Source: *Strategic Management Journal*, Vol. 9, 1988, pp. 319–332.

Theoretical Explanations

Narrowly defined, a joint venture occurs when two or more firms pool a portion of their resources within a common legal organization. Conceptually, a joint venture is a selection among alternative modes by which two or more firms can transact. Thus, a theory of joint ventures must explain why this particular mode of transacting is chosen over such alternatives as acquisition, supply contract, licensing, or spot market purchases.

Three theoretical approaches are especially relevant in explaining the motivations and choice of joint ventures. One approach is derived from the theory of transaction costs as developed by Williamson (1975, 1985). The second approach focuses on strategic motivations and consists of a catalogue of formal and qualitative models describing competitive behavior. Though frequently these approaches are not carefully distinguished from one another, they differ principally, as discussed later, insofar as transaction cost arguments are driven by cost-minimization considerations, whereas strategic motivations are driven by competitive positioning and the impact of such positioning on profitability. A third approach is derived from organizational theories, which have not been fully developed in terms of explaining the choice to joint venture relative to other modes of cooperation.

Transaction Costs

A transaction cost explanation for joint ventures involves the question of how a firm should organize its boundary activities with other firms. Simply stated, Williamson proposes that firms choose how to transact according to the criterion of minimizing the sum of production and transaction costs. Production costs may differ between firms due to the scale of operations, to learning, or to proprietary knowledge. Transaction costs refer to the expenses incurred for writing and enforcing contracts, for haggling over terms and contingent claims, for deviating from optimal kinds of investments in order to increase dependence on a party or to stabilize a relationship, and for administering a transaction.

Williamson posits that the principal feature of high transaction costs between arms-length parties is small numbers bargaining in a situation of *bilateral governance*. Small number bargaining results when switching costs are high due to asset specificity; namely, the degree to which assets are specialized to support trade between only a few parties.[1] The upshot of this analysis is that a firm may choose, say, to produce a component even though its production costs are higher than what outside suppliers incur. Such a decision may, however, be optimal if the expected transaction costs of relying on an outside supplier outweigh the production saving.[2]

Because a joint venture straddles the border of two firms, it differs from a contract insofar as cooperation is administered within an organizational hierarchy.[3] It differs from a vertically integrated activity in so far as two firms claim ownership to the residual value and control rights over the use of the assets. An obvious question is why should either firm choose to share ownership? Clearly, the answer lies in the diseconomies of acquisition due to the costs of divesting or managing unrelated activities or the higher costs of internal development. Thus, a necessary condition is that the production cost achieved through internal development or acquisition is significantly higher than external sourcing for *at least one* of the partners.

If vertical (or horizontal) integration is not efficient, then an alternative is the market or contract. As described earlier, a transaction cost explanation for why market transactions are not chosen rests on potential exploitation of one party when assets are dedicated to the relationship and there is uncertainty over redress. Leaving aside integration as economically infeasible and market transactions as too fraught with opportunistic risk, the final comparison is between a joint venture and a long-term contract.

A transaction cost theory must explain what discriminates a joint venture from a contract, and in what transactional situations a joint venture is best suited. Two properties are particularly distinctive: joint ownership (and control) rights and the mutual commitment of resources. The situational characteristics best suited for a joint venture are high *uncertainty* over specifying and monitoring performance, in addition to a high degree of asset specificity.[4] It is uncertainty over performance which plays a fundamental role in encouraging a joint venture over a contract.

To clarify why uncertainty over peformance makes the properties of joint ownership and mutual contribution particularly valuable, consider first a joint venture designed to supply one of the parties, and second a joint venture serving as a horizontal extension of one or more links of each parent's value-added chain. In the case where the joint venture represents a vertical investment for one party and a horizontal for the other, the venture replaces a supply agreement. In this case the venture is the outcome of the production advantage of the supplier coupled with the transaction cost hazards facing one or both of the parties.

These hazards pose the problem of how an agreement to divide excess profits (sometimes called the problem of 'appropriability') can be stabilized over time. Transaction cost hazards can face either the supplier or the buyer. Such hazards are likely to stem from the uncertainty in a supply contract over whether the downstream party is providing information on market conditions, over whether both parties are sharing new technologies, or over whether the supplier is performing efficiently or with the requisite quality production. Each of these cases poses the issue of whether, in the absence of the capability to specify and monitor performance, a governance mechanism can be designed to provide the incentives to perform.

A joint venture addresses this issue by creating a superior monitoring mechanism and alignment of incentives to reveal information, share technologies, and guarantee peformance. Instrumental in achieving this alignment are the rules of sharing costs and/or profits and the mutual investment in dedicated assets, i.e. assets which are specialized to purchases or sales from a specific firm. Thus, both parties gain or lose by the performance of the venture.

It is by *mutual hostage positions* through joint commitment of financial or real assets that superior alignment of incentives is achieved, and the agreement on the division of profits or costs is stabilized. Non-equity contracts can also be written to provide similar incentives by stipulating complex contingencies and bonding. A joint venture differs by having both parties share in the residual value of the venture without specifying *ex ante* the performance requirements or behavior of each party. Instead, the initial commitments and rules of profit-sharing are specified, along with administration procedures for control and evaluation.

A more complex case is whether the joint venture represents a horizontal investment in order to supply both parties or sell in an outside market. The discriminating quality of a mutually horizontal joint venture is that the venture employs assets, such as one party's brand label reputation, which are vulnerable to erosion in their values. This latter aspect is particularly important if the joint venture has potential *externalities* which influence the value of the strategic assets of the parties, such as through a diffusion of technology, the erosion of reputation and brand labels, or the competitive effects on other common lines of business. It is, ironically, the initial complementarity between the parents' assets which both motivates joint cooperation and poses the transactional hazard of negative externalities, either through erosion or imitation of such assets as technology or reputation.

If two parties seek to resolve this dilemma by contracting to a third party, or to each other, the danger is that the agent will underinvest in complementary assets and free-ride the brand label or technological advantage. As a result the contracting party will undersupply, or mark up its price of, the inputs it contributes. A joint venture addresses these issues again by providing a superior alignment of incentives through a mutual dedication of resources along with better monitoring capabilities through ownership control rights. In summary, the critical dimension of a joint venture is its resolution of high levels of *uncertainty* over the behavior of the contracting parties when the assets of one or both parties are specialized to the transaction and the hazards of joint cooperation are outweighed by the higher production or acquisition costs of 100 percent ownership.

Strategic Behavior

An alternative explanation for the use of joint ventures stems from theories on how strategic behavior influences the competitive positioning of the firm. The motivations to joint venture for strategic reasons are numerous. Though transaction cost and strategic behavior theories share several commonalities, they differ fundamentally in the objectives attributed to firms. Transaction cost theory posits that firms transact by the mode which minimizes the sum of production and transaction costs. Strategic behavior posits that firms transact by the mode which maximizes profits through improving a firm's competitive position *vis-à-vis* rivals. A common confusion is treating the two theories as substitutes rather than as complementary.

Indeed, given a strategy to joint venture, for example, transaction cost theory is useful in analyzing problems in bilateral bargaining. But the decision itself to joint venture may stem from profit motivations and, in fact, may represent a more costly, though more profitable, alternative to other choices. The primary difference is that transaction costs address the costs specific to a particular economic exchange, independent of the product market strategy. Strategic behavior addresses how competitive positioning influences the asset value of the firm.

Potentially, every model of imperfect competition which explains vertical integration is applicable to joint ventures, from tying downstream distributors to depriving competitors of raw materials and to stabilizing oligopolistic competition. Of course, not every motive for collusive behavior is contrary to public welfare. Where there are strong network externalities, such as in technological compatibility of communication services, joint research and development of standards can result in lower prices and improved quality in the final market.[5] Research joint ventures which avoid costly duplication among firms but still preserve downstream competition can similarly be shown to be welfare-improving.[6]

Many joint ventures are, on the other hand, motivated by strategic behavior to deter entry or erode competitors' positions. Vickers (1985) analyzes joint ventures in research as a way to deter entry through pre-emptive patenting. In oligopolistic industries it might be optimal for the industry if one of the firms invested in patentable research in order to forestall entry. But given free-rider problems, encumbents would tend to underinvest collectively in the absence of collusion. Vickers shows that, for small innovations, a joint venture is an effective mechanism to guarantee the entry-deterring investment. For large innovations it is in the interest of each firm to pursue its own research, for the expected payoff justifies the costs. More generally, Vernon (1983) sees joint ventures as a form of defensive investment by which firms hedge against strategic uncertainty, especially in industries of moderate concentration where collusion is difficult to achieve despite the benefits of coordinating the interdependence among firms.

A strategic behavior perspective of joint venture choice implies that the selection of partners is made in the context of competitive positioning *vis-à-vis* other rivals or consumers. Though this area has not been investigated, the prediction of which firms will joint venture is unlikely to be the same for both transaction cost and strategic behavior perspectives. Whereas the former predicts that the matching should reflect minimizing costs, the latter predicts that joint venture partners will be chosen to improve the competitive positioning of the parties, whether through collusion or through depriving competitors of potentially valuable allies. Thus, two important differences in the implications of a transaction cost and strategic behavior analysis are the identification of the motives to cooperate and the selection of partners.

Organizational Knowledge and Learning

Transaction cost and strategic motivation explanations provide compelling economic reasons for joint ventures. There are, of course, other explanations outside of economic rationality. Dimaggio and Powell's depicture of mimetic processes of firms offers an interesting alternative point of view, for it is premature to rule out joint venture activity as a form of band-wagon behavior (Dimaggio and Powell, 1983). In other words, joint venture activity can be analogous to fashion trend-setting.[7]

There is, however, a third rational explanation for joint ventures which does not rest on either transaction cost or strategic behavior motivations. This explanation views joint ventures as a means by which firms learn or seek to retain their capabilities. In this view, firms consist of a knowledge base, or what McKelvey (1983) calls 'comps', which are not easily diffused across the boundaries of the firm.[8] Joint ventures are, then, a vehicle by which, to use the often-quoted expression of Polanyi (1967), 'tacit knowledge' is transferred. Other forms of transfer, such as through licensing, are ruled out – not because of market failure or high transaction costs as defined by Williamson and others, but rather because the very knowledge being transferred is organizationally embedded.

This perspective is frequently identified with a transaction cost argument, even though the explanatory factors are organizational and cognitive rather than derivatives of opportunism under uncertainty and asset specificity. An example of this confusion is the explanation for joint ventures, commonly embraced as a form of transaction cost theory, that the transfer of know-how in the market place is severely encumbered by the hazards which attend the pricing of information without revealing its contents. Because knowledge can be transferred at – so it is claimed – zero marginal cost, the market fails, as sellers are unwilling to reveal their technology and buyers are unwilling to purchase in the absence of inspection.

Yet, as Teece (1977) demonstrated, the transfer of technology entails non-trivial costs, partly because of the difficulty of communicating tacit knowledge. If knowledge is tacit, then it is not clear why markets should fail due to opportunistic behavior. It would seem, in fact, that knowledge could be described to a purchaser without effecting a transfer, specified in a contract, and sold with the possibility of legal redress. In this sense tacitness tends to preserve the market.

Rather, the market is replaced by a joint venture not because tacitness is a cost stemming from opportunism, but rather from the necessity of replicating experiential knowledge which is not well understood. More generally, tacitness is an aspect of the capital stock of knowledge within a firm. In this regard there is an important distinction between capital specific to individuals, and for which there may be an external labor market, and capital specific to organizations, or what Nelson and Winter (1982) call skills and routines, respectively. For transactions which are the product of complex organizational routines, the transfer of know-how can be severely impaired unless the organization is itself replicated.[9]

In this perspective a joint venture is encouraged if neither party owns each other's technology or underlying 'comps', nor understands each other's routines.[10] Or conversely, following Nelson and Winter (1982), a firm may decide to joint venture in order to *retain* the capability (or what they call 'remember-by-doing') of organizing a particular activity while benefitting from the superior production techniques of a partner. Even if a supply agreement were to operate at lower production and transaction costs a firm may choose a more costly joint venture in order to maintain the option, albeit at a cost, to exploit the capability in the future. What drives the choice of joint ventures in this situation is the difference in the value of options to exploit future opportunities across market, contractual, and organizational modes of transacting. Thus, a joint venture is encouraged under two conditions: one or both firms desire to acquire the other's organizational knowhow; or one firm wishes to maintain an organizational capability while benefitting from another firm's current knowledge or cost advantage.

The three perspectives of transaction cost, strategic behavior, and organizational learning provide distinct, though at times, overlapping, explanations for joint venture behavior. Transaction cost analyzes joint ventures as an efficient solution to the hazards of economic transactions. Strategic behavior places joint ventures in the context of competitive rivalry and collusive agreements to enhance market power. Finally, transfer or organizational skills views joint ventures as a vehicle by which organizational knowledge is exchanged and imitated – though controlling and delimiting the process can be itself a cause of instability.

Empirical Studies on Joint Venture Motivations

Despite a relatively long history of research on joint ventures there have been only a few empirical studies of their frequency and motivations. In part the paucity of cross-sectional studies on joint ventures has been due to the difficulty of acquiring information. There have been, however, sufficient studies to date to draw a picture of joint venture activity in the United States and, to a lesser extent, overseas for the case of American multinational corporations.

A summary of the broad sectoral findings of a number of studies is given in Table 1. All of the studies rely on the publication *Mergers and Acquisitions*, though a few of the studies had access to the data used for the journal directly from the Bureau of Economics of the Federal Trade Commission.[11] All the studies show a similar concentration of joint ventures in the manufacturing sector. Kogut finds, however, a higher percentage in manufacturing than the rest. Because joint venture activity appears to be cyclical, it is unclear whether his estimates are the result of the chosen period, the smaller sample, or the correction for announced ventures which were never realized. (The other estimates are based on announcements.)

A problem with the above data is that it is difficult to infer trends regarding the propensity to venture without normalizing for the size of the industry and of firms. Boyle (1968) discovered persuasive evidence that larger firms engage more frequently in joint ventures than do smaller firms. Ideally, therefore, the ratio of joint venture sales or assets to industry sales or assets would serve as a measure of intensity which would correct for size effects. Unfortunately, the data required for the calculations of this ratio are not available.

Berg and Friedman (1978a) attempt to normalize their sample by taking a ratio between the number of joint ventures in an industry and the total number of companies. The measure is conceptually faulty, as there is no reason to exclude parents outside of the industry. Moreover, as most publicly available data underreport joint ventures among small firms, the ratio tends to overstate joint venture participation of industries with large firms. On the other hand,

Table 1
Summary of Results on the Sectoral Distribution of Joint Ventures

	Manufac- turing Industries	Natural Resource Development	Services	Other	Source
Pate (1960–68) ($n = 520$)	53.5	7.9	16.9	21.7	Federal Reserve Bank of Cleveland, FTC, Mergers and Acquisitions
Boyle (1965–66) ($n = 275$)	66.1	15.3	5.8	12.7	FTC, Mergers and Acquisitions
Duncan (1964–75) ($n = 541$)	59.1	12.8	20.7	8.1	Bureau of Economics, FTC, Mergers and Acquisitions
Harrigan (pre-1969–84) ($n = 880$)	54.8	11.7	15.1	18.4	Mergers and Acquisitions, Funk & Scott
Berg and Friedman (1966–70) ($n = 1762$)	60.4	9.5	N.A.	30.1*	Bureau of Economics, FTC Mergers and Acquisitions
Kogut (1971–85) ($n = 148$)	67.1	12.8	11.3	8.7	Questionnaire based on Mergers and Acquisitions (U.S.-based only)

* Includes services.
Sources: Pate (1969), Boyle (1968), Duncan and Harrigan reported in Harrigan (1985), Berg and Friedman (1978a), and author's estimate.

they find that the ratio is correlated at 0.95 with the absolute number of joint ventures in an industry; moreover, their sample is dominated by ventures between two firms from the same industry as the joint venture. Joint venture incidence was especially predominant in mining, petroleum refining and basic chemicals, and low in textiles, paint and agricultural chemicals, specialty non-electric machinery. Electronics and computers were found to have a low ratio of joint ventures to the number of firms but a high absolute number. In general, then, their measure appears to provide a reasonable gauge of joint venture incidence except for a few industries. It is important, therefore, to check results using their measure against other ways of estimating joint venture incidence.

Another strategy to analyze joint ventures is to study one or a few selected industries in depth. Studies of this type have been specifically oriented to testing whether joint ventures increase efficiency or enhance market power. Whereas a finding which shows enhanced market power for all firms in the industry suggests strategic motivations for joint ventures, findings of efficiency are consistent with, but not confirmatory of, a transaction cost hypothesis, since strategic rivalry may reduce costs within any firm attaining a long-run competitive advantage. For this reason it has been easier to test strategic motivation explanations for joint ventures than transaction cost hypotheses.

Previous industry studies have found some support that joint ventures are a form of strategic behavior to increase market power. Fusfeld (1958) found 70 joint ventures in the iron and steel industry, 53 of which were supply agreements among firms within the industry. More strikingly, he found that the joint ventures created two industrial groups, in addition to U.S. Steel. Using a rich data set, Berg and Friedman (1977) tested for the impact of joint ventures on firm rates of return in the chemical industry. Controlling for other variables they found that firms which had engaged in one or more joint ventures earned lower rates of return. Based on this finding they argued that, since most joint ventures in this industry involved some form of technological exchange, upstream ventures did not increase the market power of the participants. On the other hand, as they admit elsewhere (1978a), they cannot reject the hypothesis that failing firms engage in joint ventures in order to stabilize competition.

Stuckey's (1983) investigation of the aluminum and bauxite industry is a particularly valuable contribution because it specifically analyzed whether joint ventures were motivated by transaction cost or strategic motivations. Having examined 64 joint ventures among the six major firms, he found that of 15 possible linkages, eight occurred, that each major had at least one joint venture with another and five had at least two. He also found a high number of joint ventures with new entrants and other industry members. Moreover, while Stuckey noted that many of the joint ventures resulted in more efficiency through achieving optimal scale economies, the ventures between the majors occurred 'in bauxite and alumina production, the stages where coordination on expansion is most vital' (Stuckey, 1983: 201). Hence he concluded that transaction cost explanations appear more relevant to aluminum production, whereas strategic behavior was more prevalent in the upstream stages.

A third strategy is to analyze the within-sample variation across industries among variables to test for the efficiency and market power characteristics of joint ventures by relating their incidence to structural characteristics of the industry or to the characteristics of the parents. Pate (1969: 18) looked at 520 domestic joint ventures during 1960–1968 and found that over 50 percent of the parents belonged to the same two-digit SIC level and 80 percent were either horizontally or vertically related. Similar results were found by Boyle (1968) for 276 domestic ventures, and by Mead (1967) who, after examining 885 bids for oil and gas leases, found only 16 instances where the joint venture partners competed on another tract in the same sale. Thus, the Pate, Boyle, and Mead studies all conclude that joint ventures are motivated by market power objectives.

Pfeffer and Nowak (1976a) investigated more directly the motivation of market power by analyzing transaction patterns across industries and the degree of industry concentration. Out of 166 joint ventures, 55.5 percent were between parents from the same industry. They found that parents from industries which have a high exchange of sales and purchase transactions, and which are technology-intensive, tend to have more joint ventures. Interestingly, they found that joint ventures occur more frequently when the two parents are from the same industry of intermediate concentration. Since it is beneficial, though difficult, to collude in industries of intermediate concentration, they conclude that joint ventures are used to reduce uncertainty when oligopolistic rivalry is difficult to stabilize. In investigating the relationship between parents and progeny they found that again transaction frequency and technology of the venture industry were significantly related to joint venture incidence at the industry level, though no significant relationship was found for industry concentration.[12]

A second study by Pfeffer and Nowak (1976b) found further that horizontal parent pairings were correlated with concentration of the venture's industry.

Both studies are, however, open to the problem that concentration and firm size are likely to be correlated; thus the result may be the outcome of the sampling bias discussed earlier. In fact, Berg and Friedman (1980) show that the correlation between concentration and joint venture incidence disappears when controlling for the size of the parent firms.

A number of studies have tried to analyze motivations by looking at the effect of joint ventures upon the profitability of the parents. McConnell and Nantell (1985) analyzed stock returns by an event study of 210 firms listed on the American and New York Stock Exchanges which entered into 136 joint ventures between 1972 and 1979. They found a significant and positive impact on the stock values of the parent firms, with an average increase of just less than 5 million dollars in equity value. Arguing that joint ventures were motivated by synergies, they concluded that the similarities in their findings to those for merger activity imply that both are carried out largely for efficiency reasons. Given, however, that they did not attempt to test further if the positive gains are related to measures of market power, their conclusion is unwarranted, especially given the evidence, as discussed earlier, that joint ventures are frequently used between parent firms in interdependent industries.

Berg and Friedman (1981) tested more explicitly the relationship between industry rates of industry returns, joint venture incidence, and potential market power. Their sample consisted of over 300 ventures (mostly at the three-digit level) and was divided into joint ventures which are and are not formed for knowledge-acquisition. Controlling for other variables, and correcting for auto-correlation in the data, they found that industry rates of return were negatively related to knowledge-acquisition joint ventures and positively related to non-knowledge-acquisition ventures. They conclude on this basis that knowledge-acquisition ventures do not enhance the market power of the firm, for the benefits of market coordination would be immediate whereas the payoff to R&D is long-term. No control was made for structural variables, such as concentration, to test for other market power effects. Their results are also consistent with the view that joint ventures are likely to be chosen to transfer organizational knowledge, as opposed to achieving market power.

In an important study, Duncan (1982) partitioned his sample as to whether the parents are from the same three-digit SIC industry and to whether the joint venture and the parents are from the same industry. He finds that, at the three-digit level, ventures with parents from different industries are more prevalent (73 percent of the sample). Thus, Duncan concludes that Pfeffer and Nowak's inference of market power for parent pairings at the two-digit level is not robust at a lower level of industry aggregation. Since two-digit SIC classifications are too broad to infer collusive motivations when parent firms are related at this level of aggregation, Duncan's findings are to be preferred over those of Pfeffer and Nowak. In addition, he found that non-horizontal pairings between parents or between parents and the venture are negatively related to industry rates of returns. However, Duncan did find support for higher industry rates of return when there is a horizontal relationship between the parents, suggesting that market power objectives may be the objective for these cases.

In summary, studies to date show that there is evidence both for a market power and efficiency argument for joint venture motivations. The Berg and Friedman (1981) study also provides support for the use of joint ventures as instruments for the transfer of organizational knowledge as opposed to means by which to enhance market power. However, these results must be taken as preliminary. None of the studies explicitly tested the effect of horizontal joint ventures between two firms from the same industry on firm rates of return.[13] Finally, whereas evidence of market power supports the strategic behavior perspective, the evidence of efficiency is consistent with, but not confirmatory of a transaction cost explanation. Future work should analyze directly the joint effect of joint ventures and industry structural characteristics on the valuation of the firm and specify more rigorous tests of transaction cost theories.

International Joint Ventures

Because the subject of how a foreign firm enters a country has been central in the literature on the international activities of the multinational enterprise, there is a longer history of studies on joint ventures in the field of international business. These studies are especially important because, unlike the domestic studies, a few have investigated the choice of joint ventures among other alternatives for entry. Many of these studies have examined the use of joint ventures as a response to governmental regulations, especially in developing countries, through an analysis of a few cases (Tomlinson, 1970; Friedman and Kalmanoff, 1961). Though the case studies are of unquestionable interest, we focus primarily upon studies statistically analyzing entry decisions.

Though, theoretically, there has been significant work in understanding entry decisions as a question of minimizing transaction costs, most studies have empirically investigated the strategic motivation hypothesis. Stopford and Wells (1972) conducted the earliest statistical analysis of the foreign entry decision for 155 American multinational corporations. They found that the use of joint ventures relative to wholly owned subsidiaries declined as the importance of technology and, especially, marketing and product standardization increased. Moreover, joint ventures were particularly prevalent in extractive industries. Of particular interest is their finding that if the entry entailed a product diversification, joint ventures were more likely, ostensibly for the reasons of acquiring local expertise in new areas.

Fagre and Wells (1982) tested to see if the value of a firm's intangible assets influenced its ability to bargain with governments to acquire control, and found that the greater the technological, marketing expense, need for intra-firm coordination, and product diversity, the greater the control (i.e. equity share) of the multinational corporation. The authors explained the positive relationship of product diversity to the preference for wholly owned subsidiaries – among other factors, the superior capability of the multinational corporation to manage multi-product subsidiaries, an argument which suggests a possible contradiction of the earlier Stopford and Wells finding on the need for local cooperation in new product entry. Another interpretation of their results is that multinational corporations will only transfer important resources if they attain control. That indeed the equity percentage reflects an outcome of a negotiation is supported by Gomes-Casseres (1985), who estimated that if constraints were to be removed, equity percentage of joint ventures would stabilize at wholly owned.

Despite a few studies on the choice of acquisition or wholly owned subsidiaries, only two studies to date have analyzed statistically the selection of joint ventures against other alternative entry modes. Caves and Mehra (1986) analyzed the acquisition and greenfield (i.e. startup investments) entry decisions of 138 foreign firms into the United States. Using joint ventures as a control they found that joint ventures and acquisitions served as subsitute, rather than as complementary, modes of entry, when controlling for other variables.[14]

Kogut and Singh (1986) analyzed explicitly the choice of acquisitions and joint ventures, focusing on country patterns.[15] They hypothesized that entry could be influenced by the cultural characteristics of a firm's country of origin in relation to the United States because of the difficulty of managing the post-acquisition process. In part, if cultural distance effects were to be found, it could be concluded that foreign firms respond to the *perceived* transactional costs of entry. They found that acquisitions were positively related to the size of the foreign firm and negatively related to the size of the American firm and cultural distance between the United States and the country of origin.

Another line of research has been to investigate the use of joint ventures when there is high need for intra-firm coordination across borders. If there are frequent intra-firm transfers of resources and potential export conflict, Franko (1971) found that joint ventures are more unstable, and Stopford and Wells (1972) found they are used less often. Hladik (1985) analyzed this indirectly by testing the determinants of whether an overseas venture would entail either R&D or export responsibilities. She found that a number of environmental variables (size of the market, technical competence of the partner, technological resources of the host country) were positively related to R&D ventures, whereas scale economies in R&D and the American firm's technological intensity were negatively related. In the case of exports she found that a joint venture was more likely to be allowed to export if the product was outside of, or peripheral to, the parent's product line.

The studies on international joint ventures have, in summary, found:

1. Equity share is influenced by the strategic importance of the R&D or marketing expenditures and product diversity (Stopford and Wells, 1972; Fagre and Wells, 1982).
2. The choice to enter by a joint venture is considered against other alternatives, and is influenced by the size of the targeted firm relative to that of the foreign firm, by the characteristics of the industry, and by the cultural characteristics of the foreign and home countries (Caves and Mehra, 1986; Kogut and Singh, 1986).
3. The responsibilities assigned to the joint venture are influenced by the capabilities of the foreign country and of both partners, in addition to possible conflict between the subsidiary and the foreign partner (Stopford and Wells, 1972; Hladik, 1985).

A Digression on Joint Venture Instability

The international business literature has also addressed the issue of instability. Beamish (1985) has recently summarized the findings of several studies regarding instability. My own findings have been added, and are given along with his summary in Table 2. Some care must be given in comparing the studies. Several authors have defined instability in terms of attitudinal data; others have looked at the dissolution of the venture; and still others have looked at dissolution, acquisition, or any change in ownership. A more complex obstacle to making a comparison is that one of the most potent causes of instability is the age of the venture; there is no correction for age differences of the ventures in the table.

Table 2
Summary of Results on Instability of Joint Ventures

Sample Size	Development Level of Country	Unstable* (%)	Unsatisfactory
1100	Primarily developed (DC) – Franko (1971)	24.1†	NA
36	Developed (DC) – Killing (1982, 1983)	30‡	36
168	Mixed (DC and LDC) – Janger (1980)	NA	37
60	Mixed (DC and LDC) – Stuckey (1983)	42‡	NA
66	Developing – Beamish (1985)	45‡	61
52	Developing – Reynolds (1984)	50	NA
149	United States – Kogut	46.3†	NA

*Franko defined a joint venture as unstable where the holdings of the MNE crossed the 50 percent or 95 percent ownership lines, the interests of the MNE were sold, or the venture was liquidated.
† Includes dissolutions and acquisitions. If major reorganizations added, instability is 28.3 percent and 51.7 percent for the Franko and Kogut samples, respectively.
‡ Includes major reorganizations.
Source: Table is adapted (with alterations) from Beamish (1985). Calculations of Kogut are from unpublished data.

Nevertheless, the table is of interest in providing some idea of the significance of instability. Based on this table, Beamish concluded that instability rates of joint ventures in less developed countries are significantly higher, even after correcting for the higher incidence of joint ventures with governments in LDCs which show the greatest rates of instability. The data from the study by Kogut (1987) show instability rates for domestic and international joint ventures in the United States to be roughly equivalent to those for LDCs in Beamish's study. At this time, therefore, it is premature to conclude whether joint venture instability varies across regions, especially in the absence of correcting for age.

Several explanations for joint venture termination have been offered. One destabilizing source is conflict between the parents and the joint venture. Stopford and Wells (1972), Franko (1971), and Holton (1981) discuss the trade-off between autonomy and parental control, and conclude that the conflict increases with the degree of coordination desired by the parents with their other operations. In summarizing his interesting work on control in joint ventures, Schaan (1985) concludes that satisfactory performance is more likely to the degree to which parents fit control mechanisms to their criteria for success, presumably because otherwise there is likely to be confusion over how each parent can exercise power to achieve its objectives without infringing upon its partner's authority.

There have been a few studies which have methodically examined stability rates in terms of the relationship of the parents.[16] Killing (1982, 1983) found that satisfactory performance was more prevalent in ventures with a dominant parent compared to those where control was shared. However, neither Janger (1980) nor Beamish (1984) found any relationship between dominant control and satisfactory performance. Beamish (1984, 1985) qualifies Killing's conclusion by finding that foreign majority ownership is not common in LDCs, and that shared control reveals better performance.[17]

One problem with the above studies is the failure to correct for the age distribution of the ventures. Using a hazard rate methodology, Kogut (1987) looked at the influence of cooperative and competitive incentives on instability while incorporating the age distribution directly into the estimation. The results showed that the health of the industry, the cooperative incentives among the partners, and the degree of competitive rivalry influenced stability.

A final way to examine instability among joint ventures is to analyze changes in the environment of strategy. It stands to reason that if the incidence of joint venture is related to industry characteristics or strategies, then changes in the values of these parameters should affect survival rates. Franko (1971) examined instability of foreign ventures of American firms in terms of changes in strategy, as proxied by changes in the organizational structure of the firm. He found higher instability for organizations which had divided divisions into world regional areas. Since firms organized along areas tend towards product standardization and high marketing expenses, joint ventures would obstruct. Franko concludes, the coordination of international trans-shipments of standardized goods and the control over brand labels and advertising.

Conclusions

In comparing the theoretical and empirical results it is clear that studies have advanced further in testing strategic behavior explanations. Transaction cost and organizational knowledge explanations involve microanalytic detail which is difficult to acquire for one firm, not to mention for a cross-section of joint ventures. For this reason it is likely that case studies of industries or a few ventures will be the most appealing methodology to provide initial insight into transaction cost and transfer of organizational knowhow motivations. Less difficult, but still formidable, will be the analysis of joint venture formation and stability in terms of the strategies of the parents. It is not surprising, therefore, that more headway has been made into the relationship of joint ventures to industry characteristics.

It should be expected that the theories and their derived hypotheses will fare differently depending on contextual factors and the type of research questions being pursued. A transaction cost explanation should fit reasonably well the choice of how to cooperate when the transaction has little effect on downstream competition. Strategic behavior explanations certainly provide a more informative framework for the investigation of how joint ventures affect the competitive position of the firm. Organizational learning should apply reasonably well to explain ventures in industries undergoing rapid structural change, whether due to emergent technologies which affect industry boundaries or the entry of new (and perhaps foreign) firms.[18]

There is the danger, however, that more profound reasons for the use of joint ventures may be obscured by focusing only on theoretical explanations for joint ventures at the cost of more substantive explanations. Two alternative views are worthy of attention. The first is a reformulation of strategic behavior but only writ large – namely, that joint ventures are a response of leading members of national oligopolies to coopt foreign entrants. It is easy to forget that interpenetration of firms from different national oligopolies is a relatively recent phenomenon. Some insight into the motives of joint ventures might be gained by comparing several of the recent pairings between international firms against the international cartel agreements in oil, steel, iron and other minerals in the 1920s and 1930s.

The coordination of international competition by joint ventures raises a second perspective on joint ventures as one expression of what Dimaggio and Powell (1983) see as the growing institutionalization of markets and the bureaucratic dominance of the economy. From this point of view, joint ventures are another mode by which markets are replaced by organizational coordination. In this sense, joint ventures are a means by which large corporations increase their organizational control through ties to smaller firms and to each other. In the need to develop a better understanding of the choice of joint ventures against other alternatives of transacting or effecting strategies, it would be a mistake to ignore the larger question of the role of joint ventures in the evolution of national institutional structures and international oligopolies.

Acknowledgements

I would like to acknowledge the helpful criticism of Erin Anderson, Dan Schendel, and the anonymous referees, as well as the research assistance of Bernadette Fox. The research for this paper has been funded under the auspices of the Reginald H. Jones Center of the Wharton School through a grant from AT&T.

Notes

1. Asset specificity is not a sufficient condition; uncertainty and frequency of the transactions are also necessary.
2. For a careful analysis of this problem, see Walker and Weber, 1984; for an analysis of the downstream choice of using a direct sales agent (employee) or representative, see Anderson and Schmittlein, 1984.
3. Subsequent to writing the earlier drafts of this paper, working papers by Hennart, and by Buckley and Casson (both forthcoming) came to my attention. The subsequent revisions have benefited from their work, though the substance of the argument has not changed.

4. It is frequently suggested that institutional choices can be linearly ordered from market to firm. Not only is this conceptually unfounded, but the interaction of asset specificity, uncertainty, and frequency is unlikely, to say the least, to result in a linear effect.
5. For an analysis of network externality, see Katz and Shapiro, 1985.
6. See Ordover and Willig, 1985. Friedman, Berg, and Duncan (1979) found, in fact, that firms which joint venture tend to lower R&D expenditures. Their findings, therefore, support the argument that research ventures substitute for internal development and are motivated by efficiency considerations.
7. Indeed, Gomes-Casseres (1987) has found that joint venture waves exist and are difficult to predict by reasonable economic causes.
8. It could be argued that there is no more sustainable asset over which there is, to paraphrase Rumelt (1984), an uncertainty of imitation, than an organizationally embedded source of competitive advantage.
9. Teece (1982) makes a similar point in explaining the multi-product firm.
10. Harrigan (1985) provides an excellent description by which firms seek to benefit from technological 'bleedthrough'. For example, internal R&D facilities are sometimes created which parallel the joint venture and staff is then rotated back and forth from the parent and joint venture organizations.
11. The Pate data are for joint ventures only between American firms; the Kogut data are for joint ventures located only in the United States.
12. It is hard to evaluate the results of this paper because the authors move back and forth from multiple regression to bivariate and partial correlations without stating why one test is preferred, and report in one place concentration as significant even though it only tested at 0.15 (Pfeffer and Nowak, 1976: 415).
13. Berg and Friedman (1981) and Duncan (1982) employed industry rates of return, which can be argued to be a good measure of the public good characteristic of collusion but is a poor measure of the efficiency implications of joint ventures and for competitive rivalry within industry.
14. It is unclear from the data whether this is the result of treating only greenfield as wholly-owned or jointly controlled.
15. Franko (1976) had shown that Europeans have a higher frequency for the use of joint ventures than American firms, and Wilson (1980) had found strong country patterns in his greenfield and acquisition study. Edstrom (1976) analyzed only Swedish joint ventures and acquisition.
16. This conflict is likely to be of a cultural nature as well, if the venture or subsidiary is overseas. See, for example, Peterson and Shimada (1978) and Wright (1979).
17. Both Killing's and Beamish's results await confirmatory statistical tests. Beamish has provided some tests in his thesis. See Beamish, 1984: 51–52 for the main results.
18. For speculations along these lines, see Westney, forthcoming.

References

Anderson, F.. and D. Schmittlein. 'Integration of the sales force: an empirical examination', *Rand Journal of Economics*, 1984, pp. 385–395.

Beamish, P. M. 'Joint venture performance in developing countries'. Unpublished doctoral dissertation, University of Ontario, 1984.

Beamish, P. M. 'The characteristics of joint ventures in developed and developing countries', *Columbia Journal of World Business*, 1985, pp. 13–19.

Berg, S. and P. Friedman. 'Joint ventures, competition and technological complementaries', *Southern Economic Journal*, 1977, pp. 1330–1337.

Berg, S. and P. Friedman. 'Joint ventures in American industry: an overview', *Mergers and Acquisitions*, **13**, 1978a, pp. 28–41.

Berg, S. and P. Friedman. 'Joint ventures in American industry, Part II: Case studies of managerial policy', *Mergers and Acquisitions*, **13**, 1978b, pp. 9–17.

Berg, S. and P. Friedman. 'Technological complementarities and industrial patterns of JV activity, 1964–1965', *Industrial Organization Review*, 6, 1978c, pp. 110–116.

Berg, S. and P. Friedman. 'Joint ventures in American industry, Part III: Public policy issues', *Mergers and Acquisitions*, **13**, 1979, pp. 18–29.

Berg, S. and P. Friedman. 'Causes and effects of joint venture activity', *Antitrust Bulletin*, **25**, 1980, pp. 143–168.

Berg, S. and P. Friedman. 'Impacts of domestic joint ventures on industrial rates of return: a pooled cross-section analysis', *Review of Economics and Statistics*, **63**, 1981, pp. 293–298.

Boyle, S. E. 'The joint subsidiary: an economic appraisal', *Antitrust Bulletin*, 1963, pp. 303–318.

Boyle, S. E. 'Estimate of the number and size distribution of domestic joint subsidiaries', *Antitrust Law and Economics Review*, **1**, 1968, pp. 81–92.

Buckley, P. and M. Casson. 'A theory of cooperation in international business', in Contractor, F. and Lorange, P. (eds), *Cooperative Strategies in International Business*, Lexington Books, Lexington, MA, forthcoming.

Caves, E. and K. Mehra. 'Entry of foreign multinationals into U.S. manufacturing industries', in Porter, M. E. (ed.), *Competition in Global Industries*, Harvard Business School Press, Boston, MA, 1986.

Dimaggio, J. and W. Powell. 'The iron cage revisited: institutional isomorphism and collective rationality in organizational fields', *American Sociological Review*, **48**, 1983, pp. 147–160.

Duncan, J. 'Impacts of new entry and horizontal joint ventures on industrial rates of return', *Review of Economics and Statistics*, **64**, 1982, pp. 120–125.

Edstrom, A. 'Acquisition and joint venture behavior of Swedish manufacturing firms', *Scandinavian Journal of Economics*, 1976, pp. 477–490.

Fagre, N. and L. Wells. 'Bargaining power of multinationals and host government', *Journal of International Business Studies*, Fall 1982, pp. 9–23.

Franko, L. G. *Joint Venture Survival in Multinational Corporations*, Praeger, New York, 1971.

Franko, L. G. *The European Multinationals*, Harper & Row, London, 1976.

Friedman, P., S. V. Berg and J. Duncan. 'External vs. internal knowledge acquisition: JV activity and and R&D intensity', *Journal of Economics and Business*, **31**, 1979, pp. 103–110.

Friedman, W. and G. Kalmanoff. *Joint International Business Ventures*, Columbia University Press, New York, 1961.

Fusfeld, D. 'Joint subsidiaries in the iron and steel industry', *American Economic Review*, **48**, 1958, pp. 578–587.

Gomes-Casseres, B. 'Multinational Ownership Strategies'. Unpublished DBA thesis, Harvard Business School, 1985.

Gomes-Casseres, B. 'Evolution of ownership strategies of U.S. MNEs', in Contractor, F. and Lorange, P. (eds), *Cooperative Strategies in International Business*, Lexington Books, Lexington, MA, forthcoming.

Harrigan, K. R. *Strategies for Joint Ventures*, Lexington Books, Lexington, MA, 1985.

Harrigan, K. R. *Managing for Joint Venture Success*, Lexington Books, Lexington, MA, 1986.

Hennart, J. F. 'A transaction cost theory of equity joint ventures', *Strategic Management Journal*, forthcoming.

Hladik, K. J. *International Joint Ventures: An Economic Analysis of U.S. Foreign Business Partnerships.* Lexington Books, Lexington, MA, 1985.

Holton, R. E. 'Making international JVs work', Otterbeck, L. (ed.), in *Management of Headquarters-Subsidiary Relationships in Multinational Corporations*, St. Martins Press, New York, 1981.

Janger, A. H. *Organizations of International Joint Ventures*, Conference Board Report 87, New York, 1980.

Katz, M. L. and C. Shapiro. 'Network externalities, competition, and compatibility', *American Economic Review*, **75**, 1985, pp. 424–40.

Killing, J. 'How to make a global joint venture work', *Harvard Business Review*, **60**, 1982, pp. 120–127.

Killing, J. *Strategies for Joint Venture Success*, Praeger, New York, 1983.

Kogut, B. 'Competitive rivalry and the stability of joint ventures', Reginald H. Jones Working Paper, Wharton School, 1987.

Kogut, B. and H. Singh. 'Entering the United States by acquisition or joint venture, country patterns and cultural characteristics', Reginald H. Jones, Working Paper, Wharton School, 1986.

McConnell, J. and J. Nantell. 'Common stock returns and corporate combinations: the case of joint ventures', *Journal of Finance*, **40**, 1985, pp. 519–536.

McKelvey, B. *Organizational Systematics: Taxonomy, Evolution, Classification*, University of California, Berkeley, 1983.

Mead, W. J. 'Competitive significance of joint ventures', *Antitrust Bulletin*, 1967.

Nelson, R. and S. Winter. *An Evolutionary Theory of Economic Change*, Harvard University Press, Cambridge, MA, 1982.

Ordover, J. A. and R. D. Willig. 'Antitrust for high-technology industries: assessing research joint ventures and mergers', *Journal of Law and Economics*, **28**, 1985, pp. 311–343.

Pate, J. L. 'Joint venture activity, 1960–1968', *Economic Review*. Federal Research Bank of Cleveland, 1969, pp. 16–23.

Peterson, R. B. and Shimada, J. Y. 'Sources of management problems in Japanese–American joint ventures', *Academy of Management Review*, **3**, 1978, pp. 796–804.

Pfeffer, J. and P. Nowak. 'Joint ventures and interorganizational interdependence', *Administrative Science Quarterly*, **21**, 1976a, pp. 398–418.

Pfeffer, J. and P. Nowak. 'Patterns of joint venture activity: implications for anti-trust research', *Antitrust Bulletin*, **21**, 1976b, pp. 315–339.

Polanyi, M. *The Tacit Dimension*, Doubleday, New York, 1967.

Reynolds, J. I. 'The "pinched shoe" effect on international joint ventures'. *Columbia Journal of World Business*, **19**, 1984, pp. 23–29.

Rumelt, R. 'Towards a strategic theory of the firm', in Lamb, R. B. (ed.), *Competitive Strategic Management*, Prentice Hall, New Jersey, 1984.

Schaan, J. L. 'Managing the parent control in joint ventures'. Paper presented at the Fifth Annual Strategic Management Society Conference, Barcelona, Spain, 1985.

Stopford, M. and L. Wells. *Managing the Multinational Enterprise*, Basic Books, New York, 1972.

Stuckey, A. *Vertical Integration and Joint Ventures in the Aluminum Industry*. Harvard University Press. Cambridge, MA, 1983.

Teece, D. 'Technology transfer by multinational firms', *Economic Journal*, **87**, 1977, pp. 242–261.

Teece, D. 'Towards an economic theory of the multiproduct firm', *Journal of Economic Behavior and Organization*, **3**, 1982, pp. 39–63.

Thompson, D. *Organizations in Action*, McGraw Hill, New York, 1967.

Tomlinson, J. W. L. *The Joint Venture Process in International Business*, MIT Press, Cambridge, MA, 1970.

Vernon, R. 'Organizational and institutional reponses to international risk', in Herring, R. (ed.), *Managing International Risk*. Cambridge University Press, New York, 1983.

Vickers, J. 'Pre-emptive patenting, joint ventures, and the persistence of oligopoly', *International Journal of Industrial Organization*, **3**, 1985, pp. 261–273.

Walker, G. and D. Weber. 'A transaction cost approach to make or buy decisions', *Administrative Science Quarterly*, **29**, 1984, pp. 373–391.

Westney, E. 'Domestic and foreign learning curves in managing international cooperative strategies', in Contractor, F. and Lorange, P. (eds), *Cooperative Strategies in International Business*, Lexington Books, Lexington, MA, forthcoming.

Williamson, O. E. *Markets and Hierarchies: Analysis and Antitrust Implications*, Basic Books, New York, 1975.

Williamson, O. E. 'The economics of organization: the transaction cost approach', *American Journal of Sociology*, **87**, 1981, pp. 548–577.

Williamson, O. E. *The Economic Institutions of Capitalism*, Free Press, New York, 1985.

Wilson, B. 'The propensity of multinational companies to expand through acquisitions', *Journal of International Business Studies*, **12**, 1980, pp. 59–65.

Wright, R. W. 'Joint venture problems in Japan', *Columbia Journal of World Business*, **14**, 1979, pp. 25–30.

36

The Development of Local Marketing Knowledge within Joint Ventures: An Analysis of the Performance of Belgian Multinationals in China

Daniel van den Bulcke and Haiyan Zhang

Introduction

The excellent performance of Belgian multinationals in China came out very distinctively when two of their five fully operational affiliates in China, Xi'an Janssen Pharmaceutical Ltd. (XJP) and Shanghai Bell Telephone Equipment Manufacturing Co. Ltd. (SBTEMC), topped the list of China's 10 'best sino-foreign joint ventures'[1] in 1993 as well as in 1994. The excellent results of these Belgian ventures in China and the positive evaluation by the Chinese authorities are probably due to two major factors. Firstly, the Belgian multinationals in China transferred quite advanced technologies and introduced relatively sophisticated products to their local production joint ventures (JVs). Secondly, the organizational knowledge that these companies accumulated over the years and the learning process they went through since the start-up of their operations in China allowed them to successfully cope with the rapid and frequent changes in the Chinese economy and its regulatory system.

Since the mid-1990s the increasing market mechanism and the booming demand situation in China have led Western MNEs to revise radically their view of China's opportunities and to reconsider their strategic position in order to become market leaders and long-term partners of the Chinese economy. The opportunistic and strategic investors of the early years become 'local players'. However, the challenge for managers of these 'second-generation MNEs' are quite different (Shaw & Meier, 1994:11), because they have not only to shape industry

Source: *Advances in International Marketing: Globalization, the Multinational Firm*, Vol.10, 2000, pp. 315–337.

structure and norms with their advanced technology, but also to build up an 'insider' position by the accumulation of local organizational knowledge.

This chapter intends to emphasize the main changes of Chinese market situation and to analyze the dynamic process of the development of new organizational capabilities of the international joint ventures (IJVs), especially with regard to the formulation and management of their local marketing strategy. The second part of the paper reviews the literature on IJVs' knowledge learning process and proposes a specific analytical framework for marketing strategy development within the Chinese context. The third part shows the empirical evidence by analyzing two survey results of five Belgian JVs in China. The case of XJP is used to illustrate the development of local marketing knowledge by IJV. The concluding part provides some managerial implications.

Theoretical Considerations

The vast literature on the management of IJVs is generally concerned with the assessment of the mutual needs and resource commitments of the partners in these collaborative arrangements (e.g. Beamish, 1988; Kogut, 1988; Harrigan, 1988; Contractor & Lorange, 1988; Contractor, 1994; Li & Shenkar, 1994). Most of these approaches focus exclusively on the creation of the IJV's core competitiveness on the basis of the transfer of specific assets from both the multinational enterprises (MNEs) and the local partners and rarely look at the acquisition process of the organizational knowledge by the IJVs as such i.e. as ongoing operations, Yet, the dynamic process for the overseas subsidiaries themselves to develop new organizational knowledge is essential for the parent company to build up an 'insider position' in foreign markets and to upgrade its competitiveness in a global value-added chain.

Recently, the organizational learning and corporate self-renewal approaches have become prominent and applied to IJVs' management (Hamel, 1991; Osland, 1994). They are considered as the 'core capabilities' of the firm-specific advantages (FSAs) of MNEs, which provide the basis for their competitive strength and the capacity to earn monopoly rents (Hedlund, 1992). Thus, the organizational learning approach is significantly different from the earlier literature on IJVs. On the one hand, the FSAs were taken as created rather than given (Fladmoe-Lindquist & Tallman, 1992:3). On the other hand, the organizational resources and capabilities, in particular the 'tacit' knowledge, of foreign subsidiaries were regarded as bounded by the local market situation and the relevant industry cluster and tended to be developed within host national boundaries (Cantwell, 1989; Zander & Sölvell, 1992; Heldlund, 1992).

To illustrate the development of organizational knowledge within IJVs, several theoretical arguments can be advanced to show the extent of the organizational learning process. First, it has to be assumed that the organizational knowledge of IJVs can be separated into two distinctive types, i.e. codifiable and non-codifiable technology. The former kind of knowledge resides in 'information, blueprints and formulae' and is tradable in the sense that it can be easily transferred from the parent companies to the local jointly owned subsidiaries. Product and process technology, technical assistance, production support, brand names, marketing resources (information and infrastructure), management systems, inventory and quality control systems are examples of codifiable know-how. The latter kind of knowledge is mainly based on the ability and capability of firms to 'process, integrate and deploy' new flows of knowledge (Li & Shenkar, 1994) and is concerned with skills and operational procedures developed for a particular market environment, such as beneficial government treatment, 'uncontractual' privileges and political links.

Secondly, the accumulation of these two forms of knowledge within IJVs consists of two very different processes. In fact, the first type is more concerned with the transfer of codifiable intangible assets by the IJV's parents as their contribution to its equity capital and the technology transfer, while the second type is more involved in the creation of knowledge by the IJVs themselves. Due to their specific features, neither of these forms can be neglected.

Thirdly, the development of less codifiable and local market bound capabilities and resources by the IJVs themselves is the result of a continuing process of knowledge exchange between both the foreign and local partners. It has to be emphasized that the possibility and cost for creating such knowledge within IJVs are affected not only by the degree of resource commitment from the investing partners, their commonality of objectives, their mutual understanding and trust, but also by the geographical proximity, the similarity of language and culture and the political relations between the home and host country (Zander & Sölvell, 1992).

Extending the above-mentioned theoretical approaches, this paper proposes an analytical framework about the development process of the local marketing knowledge within Belgian JVs in China (Figure 1).

Resource Commitment by the IJV Partners

The resource commitment of foreign and local partners in the creation of local manufacturing JVs relics both on their investment motives and core competence on the one hand and on the local market situation of the host country on the

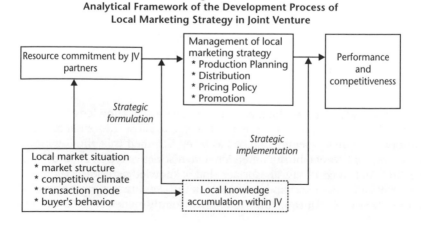

Figure 1
Analytical Framework of the Development Process of
Local Marketing Strategy in Joint Venture

other hand. The set-up of the IJVs' initial FSAs in emerging market, consists generally of the transfer of new products and manufacturing technology from the foreign partner and the contribution of local marketing know-how from the local partner.

Market Situation

Certain specific features of the local market, such as the market structure, the competitive situation, the transaction mode and the general behavior and frequent changes in the attitudes of the customers, put a limitation for the IJV to use the standardized resources and well-articulated production and marketing know-how from the parent companies.

Knowledge Accumulation within IJVs

The limitation of the FSAs provided by the IJV's parent companies make it necessary to consider the development of local organizational knowledge by the IJVs themselves as the key factors to build up of a competitive position vis-à-vis local rivals. This upgrading process and the complementarity of the assets will provide IJVs with their real competitive strengths. However, the organizational learning process of IJVs cannot be regarded as a 'stand-alone' operation. It must be considered as the result of a continuing process of knowledge exchange between both the foreign and local partners.

Marketing Strategy

The development of marketing strategy consists of the decision-making and implementation of the marketing mix and includes items such as the production planning, the distribution networks, the pricing policy and the promotion activities. As the Belgian IJVs surveyed in this chapter are almost all dealing with institutional or governmental consumers, the organizational buying process, i.e. decision making, personal motivation, multiple organizational influence, etc. are particularly relevant.

Performance and Competitiveness

The contribution of the local marketing knowledge by the IJVs needs to be measured not only by the market share and the rate of profitability of the IJVs themselves, but also by the success of the IJVs in creating a real 'insider' position for their foreign parent companies in the local host market.

Empirical Considerations

The empirical evidence of this study was derived from a set of interviews conducted by the authors during 1989–1994 and two questionnaire surveys (1990, 1993) of four Belgian multinational enterprises operating five manufacturing joint ventures in China. Eleven top managers of both parent companies (four) and subsidiaries (seven) were interviewed, of which five were expatriates from

Belgian parent companies. Several Chinese marketing and production managers of two Belgian JVs were also contacted in order to obtain information about managerial perspectives. The first questionnaire survey was carried out in 1990 and mainly focused on investment motivation, partner selection, negotiation process, transfer of technology and the initial strategic positioning of these enterprises in China. The second survey was organized in 1993 in order to check out the changes these companies went through since the first study and to compare their initial strategic options with their subsequent business situation. The central focus of this chapter is to illustrate the dynamic process of Belgian joint ventures to develop new organizational capabilities within the Chinese market. In particular the case of the XJP, will be studied in more detail against the background of the Chinese pharmaceutical sector, in which it is active.

Table 1 shows the main profile of the five surveyed Belgian JVs and their Belgian parent companies in terms of employment, sales, profits before taxes, ratio of profits to sales, etc. While the first Belgian joint venture in China began its operation in 1985, the most recent one included in the sample, started production in 1991. As to be expected, the size of the Belgian JVs in China was smaller than their parent company in Belgium both in terms of employment and total sales. However, the profitability of the Chinese JVs was much higher, as the ratio of profits to sales averaged more than 26%, as compared with 11.95% in their Belgian parent companies. Yet, productivity per employee of these Chinese ventures, as measured by the ratio of sales per employee, was always much lower, although the proportion of personnel involved in the direct production was much higher than in their parent companies because of differences in capital intensity.

It has to be noted that three of the four Belgian based MNEs in the sample are actually foreign owned. The fact that these highly multinationalized companies themselves belong to a larger foreign (i.e. non-Belgian) group provides them with more global strategic options and a stronger competitive position. Yet, these Belgian companies are multinationals in their own right and are fully involved with their own foreign subsidiaries (Van Den Bulcke, 1986; Van Den Bulcke & Zhang, 1992). Therefore, the experience of these companies in operating on the one hand as a relatively independent "dynamic community" (Schwartz, 1989:41) and on the other hand as a 'subsidiary' within a large multinational group may have inspired them to apply for their own foreign affiliates a management system that is more flexible and local market oriented. This more flexible attitude may even have developed into a firm specific competitive advantage.

Resource Commitment by the Parent Companies

The principal motive for Belgian multinationals to establish local production facilities in China relates to the size of the market, while the Chinese partners which entered into JV agreements were seeking Western products and new technology (Van Den Bulcke & Zhang, 1992). Although the entry mode of the equity joint venture was not regarded by Belgian multinationals as a cost saving device in establishing production facilities in China, they wanted to involve Chinese state owned enterprises and governmental organizations as local partners

Table 1
Profile of Belgian Multinationals and Their Joint Ventures in China (1992)

		Joint Ventures in China				Belgian Parent Companies			
Products	Start-Up of Production	Number of Employees	Sales (US$ Mil.)	Profits before Taxes (US$ Mil.)	Ratio Profits to Sales (%)	Number of Employees	Sales (US$ Mil.)	Profits before Tax (US$ Mil.)	Ratio Profits to Sales (US$ Mil.)
A Digital telephone switchers	1985	1,300	229.30	57.89	25.25	5,967	27,125.96	2,640.69	9.73
B Large-scale integrated circuits	1991	400	55.00	19.00	34.55				
C* Pharmaceuticals	1988	600	126.32	37.40	43.50	2,976	24,356.33	8,127.64	33.37
D Light equipment for public utilities	1988	32	1.93	0.18	9.33	200	872.37	17.47	2.00
E Fibre cement sheets	1987	350	9.00	1.30	20.00	1,303	5,933.33	160.02	2.70

Source: Belgian National Bank (CD-Rom) and Annual reports of individual companies.
Note: *Profits before taxes and ratio of profits to sales for 1991.

in order to have better relations with the Chinese bureaucratic system and to get access to the state controlled purchasing and distribution channels. Among the eleven Chinese partners involved in the five surveyed Belgian JVs in China, seven were governmental institutions which were responsible for regulation policies, resource allocation and product distribution in the related industrial ministry (or department) of the central and/or local government.

The products that the Belgian multinationals introduced into their IJVs in China as well as the manufacturing technology they transferred were nearly the same as their products and technology in the home market. The 1990 survey showed that different aspects of the JVs' products, such as quality, packaging and brand names were quite similar with those of the Belgian parent companies. However, the product range in China was significantly lower than in Belgium, while the price level was generally lower. From the point of view of the product life cycle, the products of the Belgian JVs could be assumed to be at the growth or the maturity stage in the international markets. Yet, they were almost unknown in the Chinese market at the time of their introduction by the Belgian parent companies. Thus, the main objective of the Belgian parent companies was to stimulate local demand for the new products they introduced into China.

The scale of production of some of the Belgian JVs in China was originally quite limited, mainly because the local business climate and investment regulations seemed still unclear at that time. It was considered too risky to engage into large scale production activities, e.g. because of the difficulties for balancing foreign exchange. On the other hand, the rapid and enormous increase in the expansion of local demand for their products was not sufficiently anticipated.

The transfer of technology from the Belgian parent companies to the JVs was not only based on new products and the introduction of production design, manufacturing engineering, technical assistance, quality control, but consisted also of management participation and special training programs, which have allowed their JVs to absorb and upgrade foreign technology in an efficient way. In 1992 the surveyed Belgian JVs in China employed more than 40 expatriates, representing 1.5% of the total employment in the JVs. Since the production activities were launched, the proportion of expatriates came down from 2.7% in 1988 to 2.3% in 1990. Two out of five expatriates take up operational management positions, while the others are responsible for technical assistance. Thirteen out of 33 key management posts in the sampled Belgian JVs are assured by expatriates. In three out of five Belgian JVs, the expatriates are general managers and production managers. In two out of five JVs the marketing managers are expatriates, while two of the four firms with a R&D department have an expatriate director. On the other hand, most Belgian JVs have established a permanent training program that became operational at the time of the construction of the factory. On average almost 60% of the local employees of the surveyed Belgian JVs had received some kind of training. Twenty percent of the personnel was trained in the Belgian parent companies, sometimes in programs which were partly financed by the Belgian government.

Broadly speaking, the FSAs of Belgian joint ventures in China were initially expected to be related, on the one hand, to the product characteristics (i.e. quality, brand name, design, etc), the manufacturing technology, the export networks and the production management skills of the Belgian multinationals, and on the other hand, to the local marketing resources (market information and distribution system) of the Chinese partners as well as their access to the local bureaucracy, their political links and administrative connections. Nonetheless, some of the initial advantages of Belgian JVs in China were lost over the years as a result of the radical changes in the Chinese market situation. The contribution of the Chinese partners to the JVs, particularly with regard to the marketing knowledge, became less important than originally assumed.

Changes in the Chinese Market Situation

The transition of the Chinese industry since 1984, especially from a centrally planned to a market regulated system, has gradually changed the local market situation in terms of the market structure, business transaction mode, competitive environment and the behavior of the Chinese institutional buyers (Table 2).

For the industrial enterprises, the bureaucratic command system has to a large extent been replaced by a real market situation. Also their marketing policy has become more customer oriented. With regard to the market structure, the decentralization of the Chinese economic system has led local governments, in particular at the provincial level, to set-up all kinds of trade and non-trade barriers in order to shield their own markets from outside competition. Because of these local protectionist motives, the market for both consumer and industrial goods in China has become quite fragmented. There is less and less coordination, which results in many inter-regional and inter-ministerial conflicts. On the other hand, the competitive pressures have increased tremendously and are sometimes unfair because of the underdeveloped legal system.

Table 2
Major Characteristics of the Market and Business Situation
in China under Different Economic Systems

	Under Bureaucratic Governance Oriented Economy	Under Quasi-Market Oriented Economy
Market structure	• Production driven by bureaucratic command • Centralized and unified structure	• Production driven by market demand • Decentralized and fragmented structure
Competitive climate	• Almost no market competition • Bureaucratic regulation and coordination	• Considerable competition both from domestic and foreign markets • Unfair competitive climate and high transacting risks due to underdeveloped legal system
Transaction mode	• Direct command from administrative authorities • Planned and unified pricing system	• Planning dominance in a few areas • Weak, but extending market mechanism • Pricing as a function of cost of production and market demand
Behavior of institutional buyers	• Centralized and hierarchical decision-making • Authority of administration over operational units	• Decentralisation and delegation • Transacting without involvement of ownership constituency

Source: Adapted by the authors on the basis of Dong, Zhang & Larson (1992: 25–48).

Most business transactions no longer rely on state controlled distribution and purchasing channels but make use of the marketplace. Also the former planned and unified pricing system has been largely liberalized (sometimes still monitored by the government) in function of market demand and production costs. However, laws related to the normal conduct of business transactions have not yet been sufficiently developed, such as legal procedures for governing company registration, securities trading, banking, bills of exchange, sale/purchase of real estate, unfair competition and product liability (Björkman, 1994). Therefore, the incomplete market mechanism may to some extent increase the complexity, costs and risks of doing business in China.

The authority which is linked to state ownership has been gradually separated from the regular decision of the operational units. The decentralization of economic decision-making has created industrial markets which are more influenced by decision-making of the individual customer that is characteristic in the Western system. Although certain large industrial purchase decisions may still be centralized within the key ministries, most other purchases are now primarily determined by local governments (McGuinness, Campbell and Leontiades, 1991). The decision-making process for the institutional buyer has been shortened. Yet, the forces influencing the buying behavior as such became more complex and less identifiable, as the relationship among the different organizations frequently changes and sometimes even varies according to the characteristics of specific business deals (Björkman, 1994). Thus, the development of strong customer relationships and political connections have become more important than before.

Upgrading of Production and Marketing Strategies

Facing the new market situation and the specific industrial patterns, the marketing strategies of the Belgian MNEs went through some significant changes as compared to their initial JV agreement, in particular with regard to the issues of the production planning, distribution, advertising and promotion.

The sampled companies were asked to rank a number of items in their marketing policy on a 5 point scale (from 1–very limited to 5–very important) to measure and rank the respective importance of the different factors. Highly ranked factors were: high quality (4.0), brand names (4.0), own sales branches (3.4), excellent product design (3.2) and own sales capabilities (3.2), while the low selling price (1.4) and state distribution channels (2.2) scored less well (Table 3).

Production Planning

While the demand in the institutional market (e.g. for telecom equipment and building materials) increased rapidly as a result of the political priority which was given to infrastructural development projects in the domestic market, the sampled Belgian JVs practically all (4 out of 5) extended their original production capacity by adding new product lines and/or engaged in subcontracting arrangements with local enterprises. Four out of five firms also widened their product range and two out of five introduced new products into the Chinese market.

Table 3
Marketing Policy of Belgian Joint Ventures in China (1992)

Marketing Tools	Belgian Joint Ventures in China	Chinese MNEs
High quality of products	4.0	4.3
Brand names	4.0	3.1
Own sales branches	3.4	4.0
Excellent product design	3.2	2.5
Advertising	2.6	1.9
Attractive payment terms	2.2	1.6
State distribution channels	2.2	3.0
Low selling price	1.4	3.5

Source: 1993 Survey and Zhang & Van Den Bulcke (1994) for Chinese MNEs.
Note: The importance of each factor is ranked on a 5 point scale: 1 = very limited, 2 = limited, 3 = moderate, 4 = important, 5 = very important.

However, the so-called 'localization' of production (or degree of local-content) by Belgian JVs has not greatly improved (Table 4) over the years, except for SBTEMC which established a subsidiary to locally manufacture components (see further). The Belgian JVs continued to import raw materials and intermediate products from their Belgian parent companies (about 30% of their total purchases) or other foreign suppliers (18%). According to all the responding companies local supplies were either not available, while 3 out of 5 firms added that the production standards could not be achieved by the domestic firms. One company even reported that the export of raw materials by the Belgian parent company contributed to a large extent to its return on investment in China. In 1992 the Belgian JVs exported only about 7% of total sales. In one particular case a limited quantity of some very new products of the parent company were manufactured in China for export to relatively sophisticated markets in South East Asia. The export by Belgian JVs from China is generally intended to provide more international credibility to their domestic reputation rather than the realization of specific commercial targets abroad.

Distribution

The product distribution of the sampled Belgian JVs in China went through several radical changes. First, all Sino-Belgian JVs replaced the state controlled

Table 4
Sales of Western Pharmaceutical Products in China (1988–1992)

	1988	1989	1990	1991	1992	Growth Rate 1988–1992
Total value (US$ billion)	2.7	3.0	2.6	2.9	3.5	29.63
Annual growth rate (%)	n.a.	11.1	–13.3	11.5	20.7	n.a.
Proportion of imports (%)	6.4	4.4	7.3	8.2	6.9	41.2
Proportion of local production (%)	93.6	95.6	92.7	91.8	93.1	28.90

Source: RCI Research Consultants AG, (1993: 95–98).
Notes: Market values were estimated by RCI on the basis of the factory price for local products and CIF for imported products.
n.a. = not available.

distribution channels by their own sales networks. While their initial marketing options had mainly been based on the access to the state controlled distribution channels (Van Den Bulcke & Zhang, 1992), the JVs built up their own marketing infrastructure and capabilities. Second, while the economic decentralization and regionalization of the Chinese economy provided the institutional buyers with more decision-making authority and opened up state distribution channels at different levels (e.g. XJP), the marketing policy of the Belgian JVs aimed for the local market (in particular at the provincial level) and the final customers much more directly. Consequently Belgian JVs established a large number of local and regional marketing and sales offices in different cities and increased the number of employees working in these direct sales and promotion outlets.

Pricing Policy

The low sales price was not considered as much of a marketing tool by Belgian IJVs as by Chinese multinational firms (Table 3). The price of Belgian JVs' products has been estimated to be nearly equal or lower (from 10 to 25%) to that of their Belgian parent companies by two out of five responding firms. According to the detailed information provided by one company, the price of its main product was increased with about 15 to 20% per year during the period 1991–1993, while the prices for comparable Chinese products only went up by 3.4% in 1991 and 9% in 1992 on average. The main reason for the price rise was that the devaluation of the Chinese currency had significantly increased the cost of imported raw materials.

Two out of five Belgian JVs reported that they were able to balance their foreign currencies without any difficulties, mainly because their products were considered as import substitutes. The other three companies used the swap market to obtain foreign currency. However, the requirement to balance foreign exchange has become easier to cope with recently. The facility to obtain foreign exchange and the liberalization of the foreign exchange control are considered by the Belgian JVs as two of the factors that most improved the operational environment in China during the last few years.

All Belgian JVs enjoyed a lower corporate tax rate. Two out of five JVs were granted special exemptions as producers of import substitutes, as compared with 4 out of 5 as technologically advanced enterprises. Enterprises also benefited from other special incentives, when they were located in the special economic zones (2 out of 5), concluded a joint production arrangement for more than 10 years (2 out of 5) or operated in a low profit sector (1 out of 5).

Promotion

With regard to their promotion policy, advertising in the media (except XJP, see further) was not considered by Belgian JVs as an important way to sell their products in the Chinese market, because of the specific features of the market segment. For introducing and promoting their products to different governmental, institutional and industrial users, most of Belgian JVs recognized that public relations (e.g. political links, strong relationship with bureaucratic institutions, etc) might be an efficient channel to promote their products.

Case Illustration-XJP

XJP was established in 1985 by the Belgian group Janssen Pharmaceutica together with four Chinese partners: Shaanxi Pharmaceutical Industry (local subsidiary of CNCPI)[2], Hanjiang Pharmaceutical Company, national CNCPI and CNCPFT. The joint venture of XJP followed upon a successful cooperation agreement between Janssen Pharmaceutica and Hanjiang Pharmaceutical Company in the field of technology transfer and compensation trade in the early 1970s.

Resource Commitment

The equity capital of XJP was completely made up by the contributions in cash from the foreign and Chinese partners. The transfer of technology and the purchasing of the land, machines and equipment were negotiated separately in order to reduce the length of the negotiation period. The agreement about the technology included the transfer of manufacturing know-how and a training program. A range of eight of Janssen's products were to be produced in China. More than 200 people were trained in the Belgian parent company with financial support of the AGCD, the Belgian governmental administration for development cooperation.

As the access to the domestic market and the need to balance foreign exchange were considered as the two main barriers to XJP's success, the Chinese partners were asked to commercialize the products via their state owned distribution channels. On the other hand, the Belgian parent company agreed to import Chinese pharmaceutical products (particularly raw materials) in order to balance its foreign currency transactions. However, neither the Chinese partners nor Janssen Pharmaceutica carried out their original agreement because of the changes that occurred in the Chinese pharmaceutical market.

Changes in the Chinese Pharmaceutical Market

In 1992, the Chinese market for drugs was estimated at US$5.4 billion, of which US$3.5 billion was spent on Western pharmaceutical products as opposed to the traditional Chinese drugs (RCI Research, 1993). The market size of China for pharmaceuticals is still limited, especially when compared to the size of the world market, i.e. US$226 billion of which 33.4% in the North America, 32.7% in Western Europe and 16.3% in Japan (Hamelink, 1994:5). The growth rate for pharmaceutical products in China was quite impressive, however. The sales of Western pharmaceutical products in 1992, measured in US$, were 30% higher than their level in 1988. The annual growth rate during this period amounted to 6.7% (Table 4). When the growth rate is expressed in local currency units, it was much higher, i.e. 92% between 1988 and 1992, because of the depreciation of the local currency.

The growth of the Chinese Western pharmaceutical market can be attributed not only to the increased production in the manufacturing plants of the IJVs, but also to the effectiveness of the sales promotion effects and the introduction of new products. The pharmaceutical industry of China consists of more than 2,000 enterprises employing about 860,000 people. Given the current level of consumption and the existing product range in China, the Chinese pharmaceutical industry would be able to meet demand with less than 7% of the products to be imported. However, because of the outdated technology in dosage forms, the shortage of raw materials and the lack of research capability, the government encourages foreign investment in this sector, especially in the form of IJVs. Several leading pharmaceutical multinationals, such as, e.g. Ciba-Geigy, Pfizer, SmithKline Beecham, Squibb, Johnson & Johnson, Otsuka, etc, have established joint venture manufacturing plants in China. The entry of these and other foreign companies has resulted in a significant intensification of competition in the Chinese pharmaceutical market. This increase in competition is not only related to the introduction of new products, but also to the marketing techniques and strategies used to promote their products. Consumers can buy practically all medicines directly, i.e. without any doctor's prescription, which is of course very different from the practices in Western countries. Media promotion can put two different products in direct market competition, as was the case of XJP's Motilium and Tagamet of Tianjin SmithKline.

The distribution system of pharmaceutical products in China has changed immensely. Before 1990, the distribution in the domestic market was totally controlled by STAC through CNCM. The distribution network was hierarchically structured and consisted of five levels of wholesalers from central to local supply stations. Since most pharmaceutical enterprises belonged to the central (first level) or provincial (second level) STAC, their products had to be delivered to the first and second supply station. From there products would be distributed to hospitals and drug stores for retail sale or to third-level wholesalers which covered hospitals and medicine stores at the country level.

While XJP involved both the national STAC (via CNCPFT and CNCPI) and provincial STAC (via Shaanxi CNCPI) at the start of its operations, it had expected that all sales of the joint venture could easily be integrated from the second level (i.e. CNCM of Shaanxi province) to the national CNCM and from there distributed to different provinces through the state distribution networks. Thus, the planned employment for the sales department of XJP was only about 10 persons whose main function it would be to follow up on the purchasing and sales targets fixed by the STAC plan.

In fact this hierarchical structure has actually been replaced by about 2,600 wholesalers of different sizes since 1990. The pharmaceutical manufacturers now take care of their own distribution and sell directly to hospitals, retail pharmacies or the wholesale network of CNCM. The single price policy has also been abandoned as the manufacturers can use now a more flexible approach with cash or quantity discounts, or other elements of price strategy.

The Chinese pharmaceutical market was to a certain extent an institutional market, as about 90–95% of imported products and 75 to 80% of the local products were distributed via hospitals in 1992. While drug purchases have become decentralized, hospital doctors have been granted the authority to decide about both products to be bought and suppliers to be involved. However, the extensive networks of relationships with significant interaction between people, the influence of 'outsiders' (such as, e.g. bureaucrats in related institutions and political leaders) on decision-making has become more important. On the other hand, since the individual consumers can buy pharmaceutical products without any doctors' prescription and can influence the prescriptive behavior of the doctors by suggesting particular products, the pharmaceutical market is also directly affected by the individual consumers themselves. This is why media advertising takes a more preponderant place in drug promotion than in most Western nations.

Changes in the XJP's Marketing Strategy

The new marketing strategy of XJP was conceptualized by its managers as a triangle divided in three parts. The top of this triangular marketing model is based on the reputation of some twenty famous scientists who are opinion makers in the domain of Chinese medicine and pharmacy. They are university professors, members of the Academy of Medical Sciences, senior technocrats of SPAC, etc. These 'VIP' are nominated by XJP as members of the Janssen Research Council and are granted special grants for their research programs and academic activities. In return the company hopes to benefit from them their political links and academic standing and to obtain useful marketing information. The main function of this upper level is to focus on the company's global marketing policy as a sort of 'pull' strategy. The 'bottom' of the triangle deals directly with the individual consumers who make their purchases in the retail pharmacies or may influence the doctors' prescriptions. The marketing function at this lower level is to 'push' institutional buyers (i.e. hospitals and pharmacies) by stimulating and orienting consumer demand.The advertising expenditures of XJP amounted to RMB11 million (US$2.3 million) in 1990 and RMB30 million (US$5.5 million) – i.e. about 5.5% of its total sales – in 1992.

The middle part of the triangle is represented by the hospital doctors who are the principal 'market target' of the company, because of their 'right of prescription'. Up to 1992, XJP hired and trained about 150 persons (nearly 25% of its total employees) to work in the sales department, although they had envisaged less than 10 salesmen in their initial JV plan. All their employees in the sales department obtained a university degree in pharmacy or medicine and were in company training for sales techniques and promotion activities during at least three weeks. Each sales employee is supposed to contact about 15–20 hospital doctors per day by organizing technical seminars, paying personal visits, etc. The main marketing function of this intermediate level is on the one hand to provide the doctors with the necessary knowledge about XJP's products and on the other hand to collect systematic data from them that may be useful for marketing or production purposes.

Although the distribution channels of XJP apparently have not changed over the years as they still distribute through the state owned network, the approach used to get access to governmental networks is totally different from the initial marketing plan. When the centrally controlled plan in the Chinese economic system was abandoned, the entry of state pharmaceutical distribution channels at the second-level procurement and supply stations (controlled by provincial governments) by administrative command became more and more difficult. As XJP faced the increasing fragmentation of the market and the opening of state distribution channels, the company established several regional marketing offices which covered cities and provinces with a higher population density, such as Shanghai in 1989, Beijing in 1990 and Guangdong in 1991. Later, these 'regional marketing offices' have been further 'decentralized' as marketing offices were established in nearly every province. Also the 'marketing headquarter' of the company was moved to Beijing and has taken over all the marketing functions which were previously carried out from Xi'an. The relocation of the marketing tasks was inspired by the re-consideration of Beijing's geographical position and the growing importance of the business and political connections. Actually the financial department and the general manager's office were also moved to Beijing. Xi'an remains the production location of the joint venture.

Performance and Competitiveness

The Belgian JVs have developed a strong competitive position in their particular subsectors in China, as they have established non negligible shares in the vast Chinese market. SBTEMC, for instance, has increased its market share of digital switches from less than 5% in 1988 to more than 40% in 1992, while other leading telecom MNEs, such as Ericsson, NEC and AT&T, have only 16%, 13% and 3% (Westlake, 1993). When the competitiveness of Belgian JVs vis-à-vis other foreign subsidiaries and local enterprises is evaluated by the JV's top managers, the mean scores on a 5 point scale are highest for the quality of their products (4.8), brand names and company reputation (3.8), economies of scale (3.4), parent company's support (3.4), high productivity (3.4), efficiency of distribution and product adaptation (3.2). Yet the distinctive competitive position of the Belgian multinationals in the Chinese market – especially for the two top performers in the Chinese JV's 'hit parade' – are likely to be attributed to the organizational knowledge that was successfully developed within the local joint ventures themselves because of the high commitment of and continual exchanges between both the Chinese and Belgian partners. Table 5 shows the main factors which were ranked by the top managers of Sino-Belgian JVs in 1990 and 1993 as having a positive influence on their performance. It can be

Table 5
Positive Factors Influencing the Performance of the
Belgian Joint Ventures in China (1990, 1993)

	1993 Survey		1990 Survey	
	Average Score	Ranking	Average Score	Ranking
Common objective	4.33	1	4.00	1
Mutual understanding	3.67	2	3.50	2
Favorable tax policy	3.00	3	2.50	3
Shared management	2.67	4	4.00	1
Adapted product	2.67	4	4.00	1
Export success	1.67	5	1.00	4
Favorable measures of Chinese authorities	1.67	5	3.50	2

Source: 1990 and 1993 Survey.
Note: The importance of each factor is ranked on a 5 point scale: 1 = very limited, 2 = limited, 3 = moderate, 4 = important, 5 = very important.

emphasized that both in 1990 and 1993, the 'common objective' and 'mutual understanding' were quoted as the most important factors. The significance of the favorable measures of the Chinese authorities decreased during this period. The relative importance of shared management system declined, as the operational management of one JVs was completely taken over by the Belgian partner, while in another case it was confided to the Chinese managers after the first survey was conducted.

Conclusions

Table 6 attempts to summarize the main features and the extent of the transfer of know-how as well as the creative responsiveness of Belgian JVs in China, in particular with respect to the marketing issues. Each '+' sign in the table represents one of the five companies in the sample, of which the knowledge accumulation process in the indicated field was positively evaluated.

Table 6
**The Process of Organizational Knowledge Accumulation
by Belgian Joint Ventures in China**

Technology and Know-How	Transfer of Organizational Knowledge by		Upgrading and Development of Knowledge by the Joint Ventures
	Belgian MNEs	Chinese Partners	
Product and process related:			
Product design and innovation	+++++		++
Process design	+++++		
Production control	+++++		+
Inventory control	+++++		+
Quality control	+++++		
Local supply capabilities	+	++	+++
Technique assistance	+++++		+
Training	++++		+++
Experienced manpower		+++	+++++
Marketing related:			
Brand names	+++++		
Distribution infrastructure		+++	+++++
Export channels	++		
Market information		+++++	+++++
Sales force			+++++
Customer relationship		++	+++++
Government contracts		++	
Marketing techniques	+++		+++++
Bureaucratic support	++	+++	

In all five surveyed JVs the product and process technology was transferred from the Belgian parent companies, i.e. product design, production engineering, process planning, operation, quality and inventory control, technical assistance, etc. The products and the product technology (e.g. quality and range) did not need to be modified or upgraded in order to meet the local market and supply conditions, because on the one hand in almost all cases they are industrial goods with an established international quality standard and norm (e.g. telecom equipment and electronic components), or on the other hand the firms took the necessary steps to maintain their product prestige and image (e.g. drugs), even when they were mainly sold in the local market.

The limited activities undertaken by two sampled JVs in the fields of product design and innovation were the result of the fact that they were more particularly concerned with the development of additional or auxiliary products that did not really relate to their main production scope. One Belgian parent company ensured local supply capabilities by transferring the manufacturing technology of components to its subsidiary, while two other JVs used the suppliers of their Chinese parent companies. Recently, three of these firms developed their own supply capabilities in the Chinese marketplace after the state purchasing system was abolished.

Three of the five surveyed Belgian JVs benefited in a significant way from the skilled manpower (workers or engineers) which was put at their disposal by the Chinese partners when the IJVs were established. Although these Chinese employees had no previous direct experience with the Belgian products and process technology, the experience they had acquired in related engineering and manufacturing activities allowed them to rapidly absorb and successfully convert the foreign technology. Also the training provided by Belgian parent companies (sometimes subsidized by the Belgian government) and the JVs themselves represented an important aspect of the accumulation of local production knowledge.

With regard to marketing issues, it is logical to expect that market oriented MNEs tend to use the local partners' marketing resources and capabilities, especially when they operate in an unfamiliar marketing environment, which China undoubtedly is for most Western firms. Especially at the beginning, the Belgian JVs in China relied upon their Chinese partners for market information, distribution channels, government contacts and the interventions of the bureaucratic system. However, because of the rapid introduction of the market mechanism and the decentralization of the Chinese economy, the marketing contribution of the Chinese partners proved to be less relevant, in particular with regard to their direct influence on the decision-making by the institutional customers. Some Belgian parent companies therefore decided to introduce certain Western marketing techniques (e.g. direct product advertising and promotion, market research) in order to cope with the new market situation.

However, the development of local marketing capabilities and distribution channels by Belgian JVs in China can be considered as knowledge accumulation bound by the local marketing environment. The 'quasi-market' mechanism that the JVs had to cope with is different from both a market and a command system (Lu & Child, 1994) with which neither the Belgian nor the Chinese parent companies had experience with. The marketing knowledge the Belgian JVs had to develop consisted of special marketing and sales networks, strong relationships with final customers and with separate bureaucracies in different provinces and cities, the training of a special sales force, the adoption of Western promotion and advertising methods to the Chinese social and cultural environment, etc.

Thus, the strong 'insider' position acquired by Belgian JVs in China cannot be solely attributed to the product and process technology transferred by the Belgian parent companies. Of great importance was the marketing expertise developed by the local JVs themselves, especially as the contribution by the Chinese partners was lacking. Although the evidence presented in this chapter is based on a very small sample of Belgian companies, it is hoped that future contributions will be able to highlight the role of local joint ventures, especially in the context of China, the second largest host for foreign direct investment in the world.

Notes

1. This national 'competition' is organized yearly by the 'Economic Daily' of China on the basis of 8 performance criteria, such as pre-tax profit to total assets, depreciation, sales per employee, expenses to gross profits, fixed assets per employee, percentage of sales in foreign currency, revenue in foreign currency per employee and foreign exchange balance (Han & Chen, 1993:346).
2. The Chinese pharmaceutical trade (domestic and foreign) and industry were totally controlled by the State Pharmaceutical Administration of China (STAC) until 1990 through its four production and trading enterprises: China National Corporation of Pharmaceutical Industry (CNCPI), China National Corporation of Pharmaceutical Foreign Trade (CNCPFT), China National Corporation of Medicine (CNCM) and China National Corporation of Medical Instrument Industry (CNCMII).

References

Adonis, A. (1994). Chinese telecoms move towards free competition, *Financial Times*, July 21.

Beamish, P. W. (1988). *Multinational Joint Ventures in Developing Countries.* London and New York: Routledge.

Björkman, I. (1994). The Organization of Industrial Sales in China: the Experience of Western Exporters, *Paper presented at the conference 'Management Issues for China in the 1990s'.* University of Cambridge, March 23–25.

Cantwell, J. (1989). *Technological Innovation and Multinational Corporation.* Oxford: Basil Blackwell.

Chen, Y. (1993). Driving Forces Behind China's Explosive Telecommunications Growth. *IEEE Communications Magazine, 31*(7): 20–22.

Clifford, M. (1994). Pressure for Change: Technology brings a wide array of growth options. *Far Eastern Economic Review*, April 7: 36–50.

Contractor, F.J., & Lorange, P. (1988). *Cooperative Strategies in International Business.* Lexington MA: Lexington Books.

Contractor, F. J. (1994). The Varied Modalities of Interfirm Cooperation: Negotiations and Strategy Implications. *Paper presented at the Second Conference on Joint Ventures in East Asia.* Organized by the Kellstadt Center Department of Marketing, DePaul University, Bangkok, December 16–17.

Dong, S., Danian, Z., & Larson, M. R. (1992). *Trade and Investment Opportunities in China: the Current Commercial and Legal Framework.* London: Quorum Books.

Fladmoe-Lindquist, K., & Tallman, S. (1992). Resource-based strategy and competitive advantage among multinationals, *Paper presented at the AIB Annual Meeting.* Brussels, November 21–22.

Gorham, S., & Chadran, A. M. (1993). Telecom Races Ahead. *The China Business Review.* March–April 18–30.

Gu, R. (1993). Shanghai Bell: A Successful Example of Sino-Foreign Joint Ventures. *Paper presented at the European-Chinese Entrepreneurs Symposium*, organized by the European Commission and CCPIT, Antwerp, December 7.

Hamelink, V. (1994). Deux Secteurs de Croissance en Belgique: L'Industrie Pharmaceutique et les Télécommunications. *Notes Economiques-Banque Paribas Belgique*, mai, 5: 3–31.

Harrigan, K. R. (1984). Joint Ventures and Global Strategies. *Columbia Journal of World Business*, Summer, 7–14.

Harrigan, K. R. (1988). Joint Ventures and Competitive Strategy. *Strategic Management Journal, 9*, 141–158.

Harris, Ph., & Yau, K. K. (1994). Understanding Chinese Buying Behavior-a cross cultural interaction model. *Paper presented at the Conference 'Management Issues for China in the 1990s'.* University of Cambridge, March 23–25.

Hedlund, G. (1992). A Model of Knowledge Management and The Global N-Form Corporation. *Paper presented at the EIBA Annual Meeting*, University of Reading, December, 13–15.

Jussawalla, M. (1994). Le Dynamisme de la technologie des télécommunications et son transfert à l'Asie du Sud-Est'. *Revue Tiers Monde, 138*: 297–312.

Keller, J. J., & Brauchli, M. W. (1994). Job of Wiring China Sets Off Wild Scramble By the Telecom Giants: Going After Huge Contracts. *The Wall Street Journal*, April 5.

Kogut, B. (1988). Joint Ventures: Theoretical and Empirical Perspectives'. *Strategic Management Journal, 9*: 319–332.

Kogut, B., & Zander, U. (1993). Knowledge of the Firm and the Evolutionary Theory of the Multinational Corporation. *Journal of International Business Studies*, Fourth Quarter: 625–645.

Li, J., & Shenkar, O. (1994). In Search of Complementary Assets: Cooperative Strategies and Knowledge Seeking by Prospective Chinese Partners. *Paper presented at the conference 'Management Issues for China in the 1990s'.* University of Cambridge, March 23–25.

Lin, S. (1993). Funding Telecom Expansion. *The China Business Review*, March–April.

Lu, Y., & Child, J. (1994). Decentralization of decision making in China's state enterprises. *Paper presented at the conference 'Management Issues for China in the 1990s'.* University of Cambridge, March, 23–25.

McGuinness, N., Campbell, N., & Leontiades, J. (1991). Selling Machinery to China: Chinese Perceptions of Strategies and Relationships. *Journal of International Business Studies*, Second Quarter: 187–207.

MOFTEC (1993). Foreign Trade and Economic Relations between China and Belgium. *International Business*, May 15 (in Chinese).

RCI Research Consultants AG (1993). *China: A New Beginning-A Strategic assessment of the dynamic Chinese pharmaceutical market.*

Rothmaier, K., & Verhille, H. (1987). System 12: A Pan-European Products. *Electrical Communication, 61*(2): 153–159.

Schwartz, H. (1989). *Breakthrough: the Discovery of Modern Medicines at Janssen.* New Jersey: The Skyline Publishing Group.

Smith, P. L., & Staple, G. (1994). Telecommunications Sector Reform in Asia: Toward a New Pragmatism. *World Bank Discussion Papers*, 232.

The Economist (1993) *Alcatel in China: the biggest prize*, January 16: 68–69.

Van Den Bulcke, D. (1986). Role and structure of Belgian Multinationals. In: K. Macharzina & W. Staehle (Eds.), *European Approaches to International Management*. W. De Gruyter: New York.

Van Den Bulcke, D. & Zhang, H. (1992). Belgium Equity Joint Ventures in China, Some Consideration and Evidence. In S. Stewart (Ed.), *Joint Ventures in the PRC, Advances in Chinese Industrial Studies*, Volume 4, JAI-Press.

Westlake, M. (1993). Millions Calling. *Far Eastern Economic Review*, April 8, 48–54.

Zander, I., & Sölvell, O. (1992). Transfer and Creation of Knowledge in Local Firm and Industry Clusters-Implications for Innovation in the Global Firm. *AIB Annual Meeting*, Brussels, November 21–22.

Zhou, H., & Kerkhofs, M. (1987). System 12 Technology Transfer to the People's Republic of China. *Electrical Communication*, *61*(2): 187–193.

37

Factors Influencing International Joint Venture Performance: Theoretical Perspectives, Assessment, and Future Directions[1]

Matthew J. Robson, Leonidas C. Leonidou
and Constantine S. Katsikeas

Introduction

Intensified technological and competitive challenges accompanying market globalization have resulted in the upsurge of international joint ventures over the past two decades (Beamish/Delios 1997a).[2] Despite the risk of greater resource commitment, IJV arrangements provide potentially better long-term financial payback in comparison with less resource-laden foreign market entry and expansion modes such as exporting, licensing, and contract manufacturing. The strategic importance of an IJV operation lies in that a firm can maintain more control over international business and enhance experiential knowledge, critical for further overseas commitments (Berdrow/Beamish 1999). Moreover, it may be neither feasible nor wise to compete in foreign markets via wholly owned production subsidiaries, as environmental risk or protectionist legislation may require local involvement (Blodgett 1992).

Examination of the international business and strategic management literatures reveals that the identification of factors influencing IJV performance has received focal empirical attention. These studies have been stimulated by two major trends. First, the proliferation of IJVs as critical elements in an organization's business network and strategic weapons for competing within core markets (Harrigan 1986). Second, there is substantial evidence reporting unsatisfactory IJV performance (e.g., Beamish 1993, Hill/Hellriegel 1994); in fact, Beamish and Delios (1997b) reveal that an average of two in five IJVs are perpetual

Source: *Management International Review*, Vol. 42, No. 4, 2002, pp. 385–418.

strugglers or outright failures. Thus, understanding IJV performance dynamics is vitally important to managers interested in developing and maintaining this type of cross-cultural strategic partnership.

Notwithstanding both the theoretical and pragmatic contributions of empirical IJV performance research, study findings are distinguishable by a certain degree of fragmentation and inconsistency. This is due to: (1) the different theoretical underpinnings adopted by IJV studies; (2) the fact that many studies were conducted in isolation, with little regard for the findings of previous research; (3) the tendency to investigate simultaneously just a few of the many factors linked to IJV performance; (4) the use of disparate construct operationalizations and research designs; and (5) disregard for the influence of contextual externalities on IJV behavior and success (Geringer 1998, Parkhe 1993a). And in spite of the volume of research on the drivers of IJV performance, as yet there has been no systematic attempt to analyze, assimilate, and project existing knowledge. Earlier reviews of the IJV literature have offered valuable insights into performance issues and identified areas worthy of empirical investigation, but they centered on particular aspects – for instance, the control – performance relationship (Beamish 1985, Geringer/Hebert 1989) or IJV instability (Yan/Zeng 1999).

This article provides a methodical, analytical, and focused review of those empirical studies examining the factors affecting IJV performance, with a view to isolating fruitful avenues of future empirical investigation. The *raison d'être* for such an exercise is that the lack of a comprehensive synthesis and evaluation of the research findings on the performance drivers of these complex, high-risk strategic arrangements limits theory development and management practice in this important area of international business (Parkhe 1993b, Yan/Zong 1999). Our intent is thus to facilitate theory building on the subject by consolidating disaggregated extant knowledge, and to provide practitioners with insights into IJV management practices pinpointing key success factors and elements threatening operational longevity.

The present study has five objectives to accomplish, also serving as the basis for organizing the remainder of the article: (1) examine the main theoretical paradigms used to explain IJV operation and performance; (2) develop a classificatory framework that integrates the scattered theoretical knowledge on IJV performance and its determinants; (3) aggregate and analyze all pertinent empirical findings utilizing the integrated framework; (4) draw conclusions from the analysis of the empirical findings, and derive implications for management; and (5) highlight directions for future research and make suggestions for their implementation.

IJVs and Theory

An examination of the IJV literature identifies several major theoretical paradigms that have been employed to explain the organization, operation, and outcomes of IJVs. To some extent this can be attributed to developments in the wider collaborative strategy field that offer valuable input in gaining an understanding of IJVs, together with the fact that IJVs represent a multifaceted organizational phenomenon (Kogut 1988a). Table 1 summarizes the underlying logic, focal aspects, and areas of concern for each paradigm, while these are described in the following.

The principal theoretical approach to explaining IJV formation and development is based on *transaction cost economics* (TCE) (Hennart 1988). Proponents of TCE argue that alliances occur because the sum of production and transaction costs associated with joint ownership is lower than that for sole ownership or market transactions (Kogut 1988a). As regards foreign market entry, an IJV may be preferable to the former because of the difficulties and costs involved in managing overseas employees, and to the latter as the local partner's equity stake lowers opportunism and monitoring costs and the local partner can contribute valuable market knowledge (Hennart 1988). During collaboration, each side assesses constantly costs accruing from its participation, especially those associated with inter-partner competition, the value of proprietary knowhow passed to the partner, and the risk of partner opportunism (Kogut 1989, Ramanathan/ Seth/Thomas 1997). If at some point costs are deemed too high, the firm may choose to organize the particular boundary activity in a different way and withdraw from the IJV.

A second theoretical approach from the organizational economics tradition is *agency theory*, which attributes a divergence of interests between shareholders (principals) and managers (agents) to the separation of ownership and control in modern businesses (Hoskisson/Hitt/Wan/Yiu 1999). From this perspective, the IJV management team may be regarded as the agent of the parent companies and, hence, the venture's business structure would reflect the parents' efforts to minimize risks they associate with the IJV's agenda (Kumar/Seth 1998). The foreign partner, in particular, is likely to discern potential difficulties in assessing the abilities and actions of the IJV executive committee due to physical and cultural distance (Contractor/Kundu 1998). Any differences in the local partner's goals for the IJV may cause the foreign firm to suppose that IJV managers will engage in activities that would neglect or compromise its own interests. Alternatively, according to the stakeholder management perspective (Barringer/ Harrison 2000), agency problems arise in the IJV context where a parent firm's shareholders become concerned that the alliance venture and partner will compete for the attention of the parent's executives (Reuer/Miller 1997).

Another popular approach has its roots in the *resource-based view* of the firm, which suggests that valuable firm resources – comprising tangible and intangible elements – are usually scarce, imperfectly imitable, and lacking in direct substitutes (Barney 1991). From this viewpoint, IJVs are formed to create bundles of strategic and social resources not otherwise available to either partner, which in turn can generate competitive advantage and improve performance (Mjoen/ Tallman 1997). It is about producing the most value from one's existing capabilities and resources by combining these with others' sources of advantage and, in this, ensuring complementarity is paramount. Venturing firms achieve positional advantages when they pursue a value creating strategy not followed by competing organizations; the reason competitors often find it difficult to implement a similar strategy is that they may not possess all the necessary resources themselves or be able to locate a partner willing and able to contribute the extra resources required (Das/Teng 2000).

Table 1
Alternative Theories for Researching IJVs

Organization Theories	Underlying Logic	Focal Aspects	Areas of Concern	Examples of Studies
Transaction costs economics	The sum of production and transaction costs associated with joint ownership is lower than that for sole ownership of the venture or market transactions.	The size and division of exchange and production costs incurred, mitigation of the hazards of partner opportunism, the use of administrative procedures for control, and the alignment of financial incentives.	No account is taken of the fact that IJVs are intrinsically strategic and can embody many different parental motives. Lack of attention to the social fabric of IJV partnerships.	Hennart 1988 Kogut 1988b Ramanathan et al. 1997
Agency theory	IJVs act as agents through which parent organizations (the principals) aim to increase their business activities and success. The principals act to control costs they attribute to the agency relationship.	Principal and agent agendas may differ, leading to future conflict; this is exacerbated by cultural distance and avoided via parent-initiated control mechanisms.	Agency hazards constitute just one difficulty amidst the many facing IJV managers. The assumption that IJV managers serve their own purposes before those of the parent firm may not be pragmatic.	Reuer/Miller 1997 Contractor/Kundu 1998 Kumar/Seth 1998
Resource-based view	IJVs form to create bundles of strategic and social resources that serve as a source of competitive advantage and, in turn, superior performance.	Achieving positional advantages on the basis of interfirm resource complementarity, the scarcity of valuable firm resources, the coalitional nature of organizations, and the resource interface in IJVs.	A comprehensive set of sources of advantage has not yet been isolated in the general management literature; little has been determined in the case of collaborative strategy. Difficulty in testing an IJV performance model for this dynamic perspective using cross-sectional data.	Eisenhardt/Schoonhoven 1996 Mjoen/Tallman 1997 Das/Teng 2000

(Table 1 continued)

(Table 1 continued)

Organization Theories	Underlying Logic	Focal Aspects	Areas of Concern	Examples of Studies
Behavioral perspective	The development and successful evolution of IJVs depends largely on behavioral interactions and the presence of goodwill among the parties involved.	Relational and interactional characteristics – such as trust, commitment, cooperation, and forbearance – and processes within the interfirm partnership.	Softer aspects should not always be placed before structural factors in developing IJV businesses, let alone be treated as an 'end' rather than a 'means'. Problems exist in the quantification of relational variables; the extant research is too general and diffuse.	Inkpen/Birkenshaw 1994 Eroglu/Yavas 1996 Inkpen/Currall 1997
Organizational learning/ knowledge	IJVs represent a conduit through which firms can obtain tacit organizational knowledge embedded in others. Firms form partnerships to capitalize on opportunities to acquire particular new skills.	How organizational knowledge possessed by the partners and IJV is used and managed; procedures for information transfer, transformation, and harvesting.	Learning is not a key factor for many firms engaged in IJVs; hence, learning outcomes may have little effect on IJV business performance. Quantitative study on the topic has not been able to elucidate how learning processes unfold over time.	Inkpen/Crossnan 1995 Lyles/Salk 1996 Inkpen/Dinur 1998
Political economy	A sponsoring firm's level of control and performance in an IJV business is contingent on bargaining power it accrues from resources and capabilities.	The interplay of power between the partners, their resources, goals, decision making control, and perceptions of equality, and the concept of productive exchange.	Firms recognize that power play does not increase the size of the pie for each partner and enable the most to be made from the joint opportunity. Problems with the quantification of power/dependence.	Lecraw 1984 Yan/Gray 1994 Lee/Beamish 1995
Strategic management	IJVs are motivated by strategic behavior in response to environmental conditions, and their performance hinges on whether a mutual coalignment/fit between parent strategy and venture structure is achieved.	Formative and structural aspects of the IJV are attributable to a focal parent's competitive position/strategy along with important traits of its industry.	Lack of attention to the interactive relationship existing between partner firms. Firm homogeneity is unrealistically assumed.	Harrigan 1988 Lyles/Baird 1994 Millington/Bayliss 1997

Criticism that past empirical work on IJVs does not adequately recognize the inseparability of the outcome (e.g., survival, control) from the process has given rise to a *behavioral research* paradigm. On this basis, critical issues pertaining to the relationship process, such as commitment, trust, and satisfaction, have been placed at the heart of voluntary IJV cooperation (Madhok 1995, Parkhe 1993b). The social dimension within which these arrangements are embedded can be nurtured to increase the partners' goodwill and flexibility regarding the IJV and generate operational efficiencies based on mutual orientation toward the partnership (Ring/Van de Ven 1992). In such cases IJV development is likely to be integrative, as each party would be committed to involving the other in areas where it can provide impetus for alliance development and success. Relationship-oriented exchange behaviors might even result in lucrative ends outside the original IJV agreement.

The quest for *organizational learning* or *knowledge* is another theoretical explanation for firms cooperating and continuing to engage in IJV partnerships. A growing body of research suggests that venturing firms may enhance their competitive positions through acquiring new skills and capabilities from partner firms (Shenkar/Li 1999). Based on this school of thought, IJVs are a repository of valuable information and provide a platform for acquiring a partner's tacit experiential knowledge or even obtaining new knowledge developed by the IJV itself (Berdrow/Beamish 1999). This knowledge can be useful to parent firms in three ways: (a) it can strengthen the strategic, operational, and tactical aspects of their businesses; (b) it can enhance experience in the design, implementation, and management of IJV businesses; and (c) it can be embedded in specific processes and outputs of the IJV and benefit the venture itself, but otherwise be of limited value (Inkpen/Dinur 1998). Proponents of the learning perspective consider IJV behaviors in terms of how managers should be cognizant of knowledge types, manage learning states and connections, and regulate knowledge transfer processes.

The *political economy* paradigm has also been employed to explain the functioning of IJVs, emphasizing particularly the interplay of power between the venture parties, goals of the power wielders, and the concept of productive exchange (Buchanan/Tollison/Tullock 1984). Advocates of this paradigm contend that a major motive for a firm to participate in an IJV is the superior bargaining power accrued from its resources and capabilities (Gray/Yan 1992). Firms controlling 'irreplaceable' IJV resources or inputs would be best placed to dominate proceedings and establish overall management control (Mjoen/Tallman 1997). Nonetheless, the expectations, strategic missions, urgency and commitment, and strengths and weaknesses of the partners would also impact the bargaining process and appearance of conflict throughout the lifespan of the IJV deal (Yan/Gray 1994). Power differences would result in positive ownership and control positions; the latter transpires at two different levels, strategic (e.g., overall business strategy) and tactical (e.g., production technology), for which each party's degree of control depends on its prevailing strengths (Mjoen/Tallman 1997).

A final approach to understanding IJVs is derived from the *strategic management* perspective, which stresses strategic goals and objectives pursued through the venture, along with the various policies, structures, and plans developed to achieve them (Hofer/Schendel 1978). The importance of this theory can be attributed to the fact that firms utilize complex modes of interorganizational collaboration, such as IJVs, in their efforts to increase competitiveness and maximize profits (Kogut 1988a). In expanding abroad firms often pair with local businesses in foreign markets to obtain particular competitive advantages (e.g., product-market access), following a carefully made strategic decision (Barringer/Harrison 2000). During IJV development, emphasis is placed on achieving success through matching the strategy of the parent organization with the structure by which the venture is controlled (Franko 1971). Further, attention is devoted to establishing strategic symmetry between the sponsoring firms, in terms of company missions, resources, management skills, and allied attributes, critical in building a complementary and equitable business relationship (Harrigan 1986).

A number of observations can be made regarding the preceding overview of IJV research paradigms. First, each theory tries to explain IJVs from a different perspective, although several of the constructs employed are common to some of them due to overlapping theoretical domains. For example, knowledge acquisition and agency problems could be contemplated together within the TCE framework.[3] Identifying the many connections and overlaps among the various theories is beyond the scope of the present assessment exercise. Second, the applicability of each theory depends on situation specific factors – for instance, the resource-based view is better suited to IJVs operating in highly competitive business environments. Third, while certain theories place emphasis on the establishment and structuring of IJVs (e.g., TCE), others focus more closely on management and performance outcomes (e.g., political economy). Finally, although the theoretical perspectives are all relevant to developing a deeper understanding of IJVs, no single paradigm provides an adequate foundation for a general theory explaining the economic and social outcomes of IJVs.

An Integrated Approach to IJVs

What is needed is the adoption of a paradigmatic pluralism which would help develop a theoretically integrated model of IJV performance that will put together the different constructs studied in IJV theories and establish relationships between them (Ramanathan et al. 1997). Such paradigmatic eclecticism may provide more creative, innovative, and insightful ideas, facilitating new theory generation and enhancing the level of disciplinary maturity in the field. Accordingly, an attempt is made to synthesize the scattered knowledge on IJV performance determinants into an integrated organizing framework, in order to enable an unambiguous taxonomy of the various constructs studied. Drawing heavily on the coding method used in grounded theory, a procedure was undertaken that conceptualizes, categorizes, compares, and associates textual data obtained from various sources (Corbin/Strauss 1990). This is essentially an analytical process facilitating the identification and development of concepts that can be used as basic building blocks for theory advancement (Strauss/Corbin 1990). Here, three sequential steps were taken.

First, all factors with a potential impact on IJV performance and performance measurement modes were identified and their frequency of appearance established by each author independently, through systematic content analysis of the literature under review (Krippendorff 1980). These analyses were merged to reveal 120 determinants and ten approaches to IJV performance assessment. Variables were then examined for overlaps and evaluated on the basis of their theoretical and practical meaning, resulting in a total of 74 determinants and seven performance measurement approaches.

Second, variable categorization was also performed separately by each author, based on a procedure where broad variable sets are developed and successively subdivided until reaching parsimony (Strauss/Corbin 1990). Following Singleton, Straits, Straits, and McAllister (1988) these categorizations were consolidated after an extensive discussion among the authors, yielding 16 groups of determinants and three categories of IJV performance indicators, each of which was assigned a mutually agreed label. To ascertain the validity of the emerging categories, two independent teams of academic researchers (1) matched unlabelled sets of variables against group definitions and (2) allocated group definitions across unclassified list variables (Kidder/Wrightman/Cook 1981). Consequently, certain independent variables had to be reallocated among groups, resulting in 14 categories.

Finally, to establish the relative position of each variable group and their interrelationships a focus group composed of academics and practitioners specializing in IJVs was conducted by the lead investigator, during which a broad exchange of ideas and views was stimulated (Sharp/Howard 1996). Informed by a purpose statement and a definition and brief exposition for each variable, which revealed group placement, participants identified five principal construct types – background, antecedent, core, external, and outcome – and established their order and priority within the context of an IJV performance framework (see Figure 1). This framework is genuinely pluralistic and provides a meaningful tool for assessing the factors affecting IJV performance. The nature and underpinnings of each constituent part of this framework are discussed below.

Background Variables

This set contains factors shaping the domain of the venture partners – foreign investor(s) and host country firm(s) – and comprises two variable subsets: *intrapartner characteristics* and *interpartner fit*. The former category includes factors found exclusively within the foreign investor's organization that demonstrate its ability to successfully undertake an IJV (e.g., international business experience). The latter category holds elements relevant to partner choice, with the emphasis placed on ascertaining whether it possesses: trustworthiness credentials (e.g., relational history); affinities conducive to cooperation (e.g., sociocultural); adequate resources (e.g., resource complementarity); and the drive to work toward achieving common benefits (e.g., goal congruence).

Figure 1
Organizing Framework of Factors Influencing IJV Performance

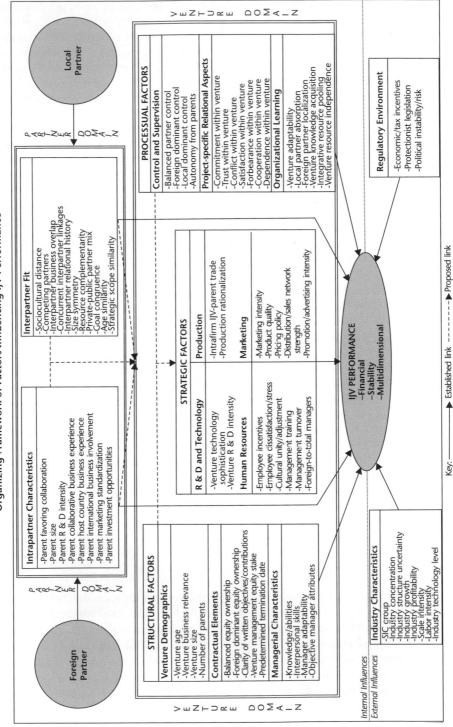

Antecedent Variables

This group concerns structural and processual aspects of IJV development. Structural variables include: (1) *venture demographics,* i.e., the age and parental status of the IJV; (2) *contractual elements*, governing the formal IJV agreement such as ownership participation and clarity of objectives and obligations; and (3) *managerial characteristics*, objective attributes of IJV managers, as well as subjective qualities such as their experiential knowledge and interpersonal skills. Processual factors also comprise three groups: (1) *control and supervision*, variables concerning the locus of parental control and IJV autonomy; (2) *project-specific relational aspects*, relating to the atmosphere of the interpartner arrangement (e.g., trust); and (3) *organizational learning*, elements indicating the partners' ability and willingness to adjust to the IJV's requirements (e.g., resource integration).

Core Variables

This group is also in the venture domain and contains strategic factors pertaining to enterprise functions at the forefront of the IJV's efforts to attain a high level of performance. *R & D* strategy refers to the IJV's potential to develop products that are both technologically sound and commercially suitable. Here attention is given to R&D intensity and technological sophistication. *Production* strategy may play a crucial role in IJV performance through the provision of adequate supply and goods of appropriate quality. In this context, extant research has examined parent firm-IJV product/materials flow and production rationalization. *Marketing* strategy has been emphasized in the literature; sound product, pricing, distribution, and promotion strategies are expected to favorably affect IJV performance. Likewise, *human resource* strategy has been recognized, with attention to issues such as unity of the IJV's employees and the recruitment, development, and turnover of IJV managers.

External Variables

Variables over which executives have little or no control fall into two categories: *industry characteristics* and *regulatory environment*. Relevant industry characteristics include growth rate, technology status, and labor and scale intensity. Consideration of such attributes can provide insight into foreign market entry and expansion barriers confronting an IJV, the nature and intensity of competition facing IJV operations, and the IJV's future competitive position, development, and success. The regulatory environment consists of all those forces shaping the host country politico – legal framework within which the IJV must operate. Potentially important factors are financial and allied incentives for foreign investors, legislation protecting indigenous manufacturing firms, and political stability.

Outcome Variables

Three distinct IJV performance measurement approaches are identified in the literature. The first is *financial* assessment, where performance is usually appraised on the basis of objective indicators (e.g., profitability, sales growth) that constitute the dominant model of empirical strategy – performance research (Hofer 1983). A number of recent studies have operationalized financial performance using perceptual measures based on managerial assessment of IJV economic goal attainment (e.g., Luo/Chen 1997), or company share-price reaction to the public announcement of an IJV strategy (e.g., Koh/Venkatraman 1991). The second approach is also unidimensional and involves assessing IJV *stability*, in terms of operational survival (e.g., rate of unexpected dissolution) or specific signs of instability (e.g., unplanned equity renegotiation).[4] Stability measurement has the benefit of being fully objective, insofar as it is based on systematic tracking, whereas financial indicators may be inaccurate or difficult to interpret (Anderson 1990).

The third approach is *multidimensional* assessment, where diverse IJV performance facets (i.e., market and financial outcomes together with inputs and throughputs such as employee morale and knowledge acquisition) are incorporated into the measurement (Anderson 1990). The rationale for this approach lies in that unidimensional performance measures may not adequately capture the extent to which an IJV has achieved its objectives (Luo 1999) – these may be unrelated to venture longevity or economic fulfilment (e.g., access to new markets). Multidimensional assessment of IJV performance is customarily based upon managers' perceptual judgements, whereby respondents are asked to self-rate performance to: (1) give an overall viewpoint on satisfaction with performance or goal achievement, and/or (2) provide indications along multiple, specific outcome dimensions. Here the level of detail varies considerably across studies. Olk (1997), for example, asked managers to evaluate IJV performance on 31 outcome-specific criteria, whereas Zeira, Newburry, and Yeheskel (1997) employed only four indicators of this kind. Occasionally, the informants are also asked to attach weights to the importance of the criteria used in order to tie performance measurement to the achievement of objectives (e.g., Ding 1997).

Empirical Assessment

Having developed the classificatory framework, we now proceed to aggregate and analyze empirical findings pertinent to the subject. Our investigation focuses on studies examining factors related to IJV performance and, thus, does not cover research considering IJV performance in absolute terms, such as market entry mode appraisal papers. Studies eligible for inclusion had to: (1) be empirical in nature, based on the collection and analysis of primary and/or secondary data; (2) concentrate on IJVs involved in the manufacture of products, as they constitute the overwhelming majority (Hu/Chen 1996);

(3) concentrate on the corporate level as the unit of analysis;[5] (4) clearly state and operationalize both determinants and indicators of IJV performance; and (5) document explicitly new research findings. Eligible studies were identified using three types of literature sources: *primary*, journal articles, conference proceedings, and working papers; *secondary*, review papers in journals, textbooks, and subject abstracts; and *tertiary*, handbooks and subject bibliographies (Sharp/Howard 1996). The literature search was based on both computerized and manual methods. While the former method was effective in identifying subject abstracts and bibliographies, journal articles, and working papers, the latter was more practical in scanning books and conference proceedings. In total, ninety-one articles appearing before the end of 2000 were identified, published in 36 literature sources – most commonly *Journal of International Business Studies, Management International Review*, and *Academy of Management Journal*.[6]

The thrust of IJV performance research occurred in the 1990s, while relatively few studies were conducted in the 1970s and 1980s. Performance analysis usually occurs at the microbusiness level; mesoeconomic approaches were used in one-fifth of the studies reviewed.[7] Emphasis was placed on ventures involving only two parent firms and those based in developing or newly industrialized countries, frequently in South East Asia; this trend is attributable to microbusiness research, whereas mesoeconomic analysis is commonly used to examine geographically spread IJV populations. Some studies set a lower bound on IJV operating duration to ensure availability of normalized IJV performance data, often favoring the two-year stabilization period suggested by Beamish (1984). However, the majority of studies did not impose a minimum operating duration. Study samples ranged from only one to as high as 2,442 cases, with many falling below 50.

In 31 studies IJV performance data collection schemes included more than one point in time. Mesoeconomic research designs are accountable for this, considering that barely 20 percent of microbusiness studies assumed a temporal dimension. With few exceptions mesoeconomic studies were based on secondary data or firsthand documentary evidence; microbusiness studies most often relied on personal interviews. Although the 1980s witnessed the widespread use of managerial informants from parent organizations, studies reported in the 1990s more frequently used an IJV manager as the key informant. The independent factors most commonly studied relate to the domain of the venture and, to a lesser extent, that of the partner. Environmental influences are examined infrequently, and relatively few studies include factors from all three domains. In the majority of cases, the performance construct was operationalized using multidimensional measures. The analysis usually involved multivariate methods, although few studies employed structural equations modeling.

Empirical findings extracted from the studies were aggregated to determine the relative importance of factors identified as influencing IJV performance. Subsequently, the accumulated effect of each variable on performance (in terms of financial, stability, and multidimensional assessments, see Table 2) and the extent to which this effect varies in relation to IJV operating period and geographic location and study analytical level,[8] were examined. The nature of association (positive, negative, or not significant) between each independent factor and IJV performance is thus illustrated across all variable groups.[9]

Table 2
IJV Performance Determinants by Method of Performance Assessment[a], [b]

Determinants of Performance	Total	Overall Performance (n = 95)[c]			Financial Performance (n = 26)			Stability Performance (n = 25)			Multi-dimensional Performance (n = 44)		
		[+]	[0]	[−]	[+]	[0]	[−]	[+]	[0]	[−]	[+]	[0]	[−]
Internal Influences													
Intrapartner Characteristics													
Parent favoring collaboration	3	3						1			2		
Parent size	10		6	4	4	4		1				1	
Parent R&D activity	4	1	3		1	1		1			1		
Parent collaborative business experience	7	3	4		1	1			2		2	1	
Parent host country business experience	7	3	3	1		3	1	2				1	
Parent international business involvement	7	2	4	1	1	3	1	1	1				
Parent marketing standardization	2	1		1				1		1			
Parent investment opportunities	1	1			1								
Interpartner Fit													
Sociocultural distance	24	4	11	9		4		1	2	7	3	5	2
Competing partners	3	1		2	1					2			
Interpartner business overlap	6	2	2	2	1	1	1				1	1	1
Concurrent interpartner linkages	2	2						2					
Interpartner relational history	7	4	2	1	2		1	1	1		1	1	
Size symmetry	8		6	2		1	1	4				1	1
Resource complementarity	5	3	2		1			1			2	1	
Private-public partner mix	4		1	3	1					1			2
Goal congruence	2	2						1			1		
Age similarity	1		1					1					
Strategic scope similarity	1		1					1					
Venture Demographics													
Venture age	22	11	10	1	4	4		2	2		5	4	1
Venture business relevance	10	5	4	1	4	1		1		1	3		
Venture size	15	5	9	1	2	6	1	1	1		2	2	
Number of parents	5	3	1	1	1			1	1		1		1
Contractual Elements													
Balanced equity ownership	14	2	10	2	1	1	1	1	6			3	1
Foreign dominant equity ownership	12	2	7	3		4	2	1			1	3	1
Precise objectives/contributions	5	4	1					1			3	1	
Venture management equity stake	1	1									1		
Predetermined termination date	1	1									1		

(Table 2 continued)

(Table 2 continued)

Determinants of Performance	Total	Overall Performance (n = 95)[c]			Financial Performance (n = 26)			Stability Performance (n = 25)			Multi-dimensional Performance (n = 44)		
		[+]	[0]	[−]	[+]	[0]	[−]	[+]	[0]	[−]	[+]	[0]	[−]
Managerial Characteristics													
Knowledge/abilities	3	2	1								2	1	
Interpersonal skills	1	1									1		
Manager adaptability	2	2									2		
Objective manager attributes	1		1									1	
Control and Supervision													
Balanced partner control	12	2	7	3					1		2	6	3
Foreign dominant control	18	5	10	3	2	1			1		4	7	2
Local dominant control	9	2	6	1					1		2	5	1
Autonomy from parents	4	1	3								1	3	
Project-specific Relational Aspects													
Commitment within venture	7	5	2								5	2	
Trust within venture	9	7	2					3			4	2	
Conflict within venture	12		2	10			1			3		2	6
Satisfaction with agreement	4	4						2			2		
Forbearance within venture	1	1									1		
Cooperation within venture	6	6									6		
Dependence within venture	3	2		1						1	2		
Organizational Learning													
Venture adaptability	3	1	1	1							1	1	1
Local partner absorption	3	1	1	1	1							1	1
Foreign partner localization	3	1	1	1				1		1	1		
Venture knowledge acquisition	4	2	2					1			1	2	
Integration resource pooling	3		3						2			1	
Venture resource independence	1			1									1
R&D and Technology													
Venture technology sophistication	9	2	4	3		3	1			1	2	1	1
Venture R&D intensity	6	3	3		2	2		1	1				
Production													
Intrafirm IJV-parent trade	6	3	2	1	1			1	2			1	1
Production rationalization	1		1						1				
Marketing													
Marketing intensity	9	2	3	4	1	2			1	3	1		1
Product quality	2	2			2								
Pricing policy	1			1			1						
Distribution/sales network strength	4	3	1		1	1						2	
Promotion/advertising intensity	3	1	2			2						1	
Human Resources													
Employee incentives	2	2									2		
Employee dissatisfaction/stress	1	1									1		

(Table 2 continued)

(Table 2 continued)

		Overall Performance (n = 95)[c]			Financial Performance (n = 26)			Stability Performance (n = 25)			Multi-dimensional Performance (n = 44)		
Determinants of Performance	Total	[+]	[0]	[–]	[+]	[0]	[–]	[+]	[0]	[–]	[+]	[0]	[–]
Cultural unity/adjustment	2	1		1							1		1
Management training	4	2	2			1					2	1	
Management turnover	2			2									2
Foreign-to-total managers	6		3	3	1	1					2		2
External Influences													
Industry Characteristics													
SIC group	8	3	5		2	2		1	2		1		
Industry concentration	4		2	2		1	1		1	1			
Industry structure uncertainty	2	1		1	1								1
Industry growth	4	2	2		1	1		1			1		
Industry profitability	2	2			1						1		
Scale intensity	1			1						1			
Labor intensity	2		2		1						1		
Industry technology level	1	1									1		
Regulatory Environment													
Economic/tax incentives	5	4	1		2						2	1	
Protectionist legislation	6	2	3	1		2		1		1	1	1	
Political instability/risk	5		4	1	2				2				1

Notes: (a) [+], positive association reported; [0], no association reported; [–], negative association reported. (b) Numbers indicate the frequency of association between individual independent factors and IJV performance. (c) The studies of Inkpen and Makino (1995), Lee and Beamish (1995), Makino (1995), and Makino and Beamish (1998) each employed two performance measurement systems.

Intrapartner Characteristics

Because of many conflicting findings, it is difficult to clarify the effect of this subset of background variables on IJV performance. A parent firm's *positive attitude toward collaborative modes of business* is the only intrapartner factor with consistent results – a positive association (e.g., Beamish 1984). The effect of a parent firm's *size* on the performance of its IJVs is uncertain: results are negative in six studies (e.g., Isobe/Makino/Montgomery 2000), whereas four others (e.g., Barkema/Vermeulen 1997) reveal nonsignificant findings. In this context, analytical level appears to have an important effect in that the performance of large firms' IJVs is weak only in microbusiness study. There is less evidence linking parent firm *R&D intensity* to IJV performance: Nakamura (1991) alone finds a significant positive association, while Franko (1971), Isobe et al (2000), and Makino and Delios (1996) assert no relationship.

Confusion has arisen over the importance of a parent firm's *prior collaborative experience*. Three studies (e.g., Sim/Ali 1998) indicate that this background factor is linked positively to IJV performance, whereas four others (e.g., Barkema/Shenkar/Vermeulen/Bell 1997) find no significant association.

A parent firm's level of *host country business experience* is associated positively with IJV performance when performance is gauged multidimensionally (Artisien/Buckley 1985) or in terms of stability (e.g., Barkema/Vermeulen 1996). Four studies employing financial measures (e.g., Chen/Hu/Shieh 1991) cast doubt on the existence of an overall positive effect by exhibiting either negative or nonsignificant findings. Consideration of the operating period reveals that, while pre-1990 attempts to link host country business experience to IJV performance show a positive association, later studies provide contradictory findings. Research on the *international business involvement* of a parent firm also gives conflicting results, positive (e.g., Makino/Delios 1996), negative (Hu et al. 1992), and not significant (e.g., Reuer 2000). Similar variation exists in the case of studies examining the correlation between a parental policy for *international marketing standardization* and IJV performance: Millington and Bayliss (1997) observe a positive effect, while Franko (1971) identifies an inverse relationship. Finally, favorable parent *investment opportunities* may effect superior IJV performance (Chen/Ho/Lee/Yeo 2000).

Interpartner Fit

The impact of *sociocultural distance* on IJV performance is unclear, whether assessed multidimensionally or simply through partner nationality. This is apparent even when discounting from the discussion those studies unable to identify performance differences among IJVs involving various western investors (e.g., Beamish 1984). Except for the work of Park and Ungson (1997) and Sim and Ali (2000) – the former actually finding improved IJV stability – there is consensus that partners' cultural distance is related inversely to this performance measure (e.g., Barkema et al. 1997). There is also consensus that no significant link exists between sociocultural distance and financial IJV performance (e.g., Luo 1997). By contrast, there is considerable incongruence in the findings where multidimensional IJV performance measures are utilized. Only Lin and Germain (1998) advocate the importance of sociocultural similarity, while others find no association (e.g., Mjoen/Tallman 1997) or report a paradoxical positive association (e.g., Hu/Chen 1996). Further, studies with a pre-1990 IJV operating period or focusing on developing country settings are more likely to suggest a negative relationship.

The importance of ensuring similarity between partner business interests was investigated in eight studies, with various and contradictory findings. Two stability-based performance studies (e.g., Park/Ungson 1997) showed that a prospective parent should avoid *collaborating with direct competitors*, while Park and Kim's (1997) market valuation findings suggest the opposite. Similarly, findings by Awadzi (1987) and Koh and Venkatraman (1991) indicating that partners should have a general *business domain overlap*, are negated by the work of others (e.g., Zeira et al. 1997). Two partner selection factors were found to improve performance by removing the threat of defection from an IJV project: the presence of *concurrent long-term relational ties* (e.g., Kogut 1989) and a *history of collaborative strategy* (e.g., Luo 1997) between partners. An established relationship might nevertheless have no positive effect on IJV performance (e.g., Park/Kim 1997).

Partner *size symmetry* is revealed relatively unimportant to managers concerned with partnership options (e.g., Kogut 1988b). Only Crutchley, Guo, and Hansen (1991) and Osland and Cavusgil (1996) identify a link, negative in nature, between this variable and IJV performance. A more consequential matter lies in ensuring *resource complementarity* (e.g., Sim/Ali 1998). When partners' resource contributions are combined with the development of relevant skills, resource similarity was found to facilitate greater coordination and better IJV management (Olk 1997). Perplexingly, Sim and Ali's (2000) performance study was unable to prove any kind of association involving this fit construct. In spite of Luo's (1997) nonsignificant findings, major problems may arise in IJVs that involve a *state-owned local business entity* (e.g., Beamish 1984). *Goal congruence* exhibits a positive association with IJV performance (e.g., Simiar 1983). Two interpartner factors, partners' *age* and *strategic scope similarity*, were considered only once each and found to be of no importance (Park/Ungson 1997).

Venture Demographics

Considerable performance research suggests that IJVs are subject to a positive *duration dependence* (e.g., Lin/Germain 1998). Still, many studies do not support this link (e.g., Beamish 1984). The contention that IJVs become more successful over time only holds true for developing country settings, microbusiness studies, and studies conducted in the 1990s. With the exception of one nonsignificant result (Merchant/Schendel 2000), the financial performance of an IJV improves where its *business is related*, horizontally or vertically, to that of the focal parent (e.g., Park/Kim 1997). Multidimensional IJV performance measurement approaches consistently yield nonsignificant findings (e.g., Sim/Ali 1998), while related IJV projects are found to be more (Reuer 1998) or less (Park/Ungson 1997) stable than unrelated projects. Excluding Chen et al (1991), research into the relative effect of *IJV size* on performance suggests either a positive (e.g., Hu/Chen 1996) or no significant (e.g., Makino/Delios 1996) correlation. Of the studies testing the relationship between *number of parent firms* and IJV performance, those using pre-1990 data assert a positive association (e.g., Hu/Chen 1996), whereas post-1990 investigations reveal either an inverse (Olk 1997) or no significant (Beamish/Kachra 1999) association.

Contractual Elements

The distribution of equity ownership is the only contractual item studied in depth. Except for Blodgett's (1992) and Park and Kim's (1997) findings that IJVs with *balanced equity ownership* perform better than those unilaterally-dominated, and Lecraw's (1984) and Ramaswamy et al's (1998) evidence to the contrary, extant research repudiates the existence of any significant link (e.g., Park/Ungson 1997). Geographic location is germane to this issue: balanced equity ownership is more likely to negatively affect performance among developing country-based IJVs. There is considerable variation in empirical findings regarding the impact of *foreign dominant equity ownership* on IJV performance. Several researchers find no relationship (e.g., Lee/Beamish 1995); two studies support foreign dominant ownership (Makino 1995); and three others hold that such ownership lowers performance (e.g., Beamish 1984). IJVs without explicit *goals and parental contributions* encounter performance difficulties (Lyles/Salk 1996); however, Lyles, Sulaiman, Barden, and Kechik (1999) detect no relationship. Although studied only once each, two other contractual elements may also increase IJV effectiveness: the sale of *equity to key managerial stakeholders* (Beamish 1984); and a definite venture *lifespan and endpoint* (Killing 1983).

Managerial Characteristics

Despite the unique managerial challenges posed by these interorganizational entities (Shenkar/Zeira 1992), only a few studies have explored associations between managerial attributes and IJV performance outcomes. Two of the three studies investigating the correlation between *experiential knowledge and abilities* and performance identify a positive relationship (e.g., Killing 1983), while no significant association is established in the study of Parker, Zeira, and Hatem (1996). Two studies found *interpersonal skills* (Parker et al. 1996) and managerial *adaptability* (Killing 1983, Parker et al 1996) to be important IJV performance determinants. Parker et al.'s (1996) study also examines the effect of managers' *demographics* on venture performance; here, nationality, gender, and allied objective attributes prove to be of little significance.

Control and Supervision

Dominant parental control over IJV operations correlates positively to performance in three studies (e.g., Lin/Germain 1998). However, other studies oppose unilateral dominance suggesting that split control IJVs exhibit superior performance (e.g., Beamish 1984), or find no clear association (e.g., Hebert 1994). Similarly, findings are inconsistent regarding the importance of relative partner decision making authority. Research indicates that a *foreign partner's dominant influence on decision making* enhances IJV performance (e.g., Ding 1997), has no impact on performance (e.g., Yan/Gray 1994), or even lowers it (e.g., Lyles/ Baird 1994). For this factor, studies based in the 1990s are more likely to find a positive association. *Local dominant control* is shown to augment IJV performance in two studies (e.g., Beamish 1984), while several others suggest little impact (e.g., Eroglu/Yavas 1996). Finally, the idea of granting complete *autonomy* to the IJV business is also contentious: Demirbag and Mirza (2000) connect performance benefits with greater venture autonomy, while Awadzi (1987) and Hebert (1994) can find no relationship.

Project-Specific Relational Aspects

The relationship between partner *commitment* and IJV performance is considered in seven studies, five of which report a positive correlation (e.g., Hu/Chen 1996), while the other two find no correlation (e.g., Lee/Beamish 1995). The impact of *trust* development is in like manner clear: seven studies (e.g., Hebert 1994) conclude that trust is a key factor in IJV success, although Inkpen and Currall (1997) and Lyles et al. (1999) find no significant association. In contrast, substantial evidence suggests that dysfunctional *conflict* is related inversely to venture performance (e.g., Ding 1997); however, Eroglu and Yavas (1996) and Lyles et al (1999) detect no relationship. Links between other relational dimensions and IJV performance also appear straightforward. Performance is higher where partners remain *satisfied with the venture agreement* (e.g., Zeira et al. 1997), *forbear* for each other (Inkpen/Currall 1997), and *cooperate* fully (e.g., Sim/Ali 1998). The same positive effect may transpire as a result of interpartner *dependence* (e.g., Beamish 1984) despite evidence to the contrary reported by Chen and Boggs (1998).

Organizational Learning

The relationship between learning and IJV performance remains indeterminate. Positive, negative, and nonsignificant findings were found for IJV *adaptiveness* (e.g., Berdrow/Beamish 1999), *local partner absorption* (e.g., Luo 1997), and *foreign partner localization* (e.g., Beamish/Inkpen 1995). Further, in opposition to results proving high performance is attributable to *IJV knowledge acquisition* (e.g., Lyles/Salk 1996), other pertinent research concludes there to be no relationship (e.g., Lyles et al. 1999). Of the two resource status factors, *resource integration* is found to have little bearing on IJV performance (e.g., Tiessen/Linton 2000), while venture *resource independence* is shown to trigger poor performance (Zeira et al. 1997).

R&D and Technology

The *technological sophistication* of an IJV may signify that it is to serve as a channel for technology transfer. In light of this supremacy of unilateral goals over mutual designs and greater coordination, performance suffers (Park/Ungson 1997). However, four microbusiness studies find technology level not to be significant (e.g., Luo/Chen 1997), and two others discover a positive association (e.g., Isobe et al. 2000). Three studies highlight the positive effect the magnitude of an IJV's *R&D involvement* has on performance (e.g., Kogut 1989). Nonetheless, further evidence attests that R & D-intensive IJVs are no more likely to perform well than other venture types (e.g., Luo 1995).

Production

Only six studies endeavor to explore aspects of production. The performance effect of *parent – child materials flow* remains unclear: Nakamura (1991), Nakamura, Shaver, and Yeung (1996), and Yan (1997) offer proof that this

Interstakeholder product exchange benefits IJV performance, Killing (1983) detects a negative association, and Franko's (1971) and Sim and Ali's (2000) findings downplay any correlation. Franko (1971) also examines the effect of cost-cutting *specialization/rationalization* on IJV performance, but finds no significant relationship.

Marketing

Several aspects of IJV marketing strategy have received empirical attention, albeit relatively limited. Four studies suggest that IJV projects with extensive *downstream operations* perform poorly (e.g., Kogut 1988b). Five others refute this association, indicating average (e.g., Merchant/Schendel 2000) or strong (e.g., Liu/Pak 1999) performance of marketing-driven IJVs. The finding that IJV marketing intensity negatively influences performance only holds true for ventures established in developed countries and mesoeconomic studies. Certain elements of the marketing mix can positively affect venture performance: the *quality of the IJV's product* (e.g., Luo/Chen 1997); offering products at a *low price* (Luo 1995); and *salesforce budget size and sales network development* (e.g., Luo 1995). However, Good's (1972) research finds that the sales network is not an important IJV marketing strategy constituent. Further research is also needed to clarify whether an intense *promotional campaign* underpins IJV success, as findings are inconsistent: Fey (1995) finds a positive correlation, while Luo (1995) and Luo and Chen (1997) find no association.

Human Resources

Attention has been devoted to human resource complexities resulting from the high level of partner interaction in IJVs. Variables pertaining to *employee well-being*, such as incentives offered (Lyles/Baird 1994) and empowerment (Fey 1996), improve IJV performance. Notwithstanding this, other research indicates paradoxically that IJV performance increases as *job dissatisfaction and stress* increase (Cartwright/Cooper 1989). While Cartwright and Cooper (1989) conclude that the presence of a *unitary work culture* impedes IJV performance, Zeira et al (1997) find foreign partner cultural adjustment to be related positively to IJV performance. *Training* of the workforce and managerial staff has been researched in four studies: Fey (1995) and Lyles et al (1999) find that insufficient training causes performance problems, whereas Good (1972) and Lyles and Salk (1996) identify no relationship. Two other management issues were studied: manager *turnover* (e.g., Isobe et al. 2000) and the *proportion of foreign managers* within the IJV (e.g., Beamish 1984) have both been found to adversely affect IJV performance. While the latter finding reflects the strategic necessity of leveraging a local partner's knowledge of market conditions, three other studies could not establish any relationship between this variable and IJV performance (Lyles/Baird 1994).

Industry Characteristics

Limited emphasis has been given to the impact of industry factors on IJV performance. Of the studies considering the importance of *SIC category*, those with a pre-1990 IJV operating period consistently find no significant association (e.g., Beamish 1984), whereas more recent evidence identifies a definite link (e.g., Beamish/Kachra 1999) or, again, no link (Anand/Khanna 2000). The importance of industry *concentration* is unclear: results are negative in two studies (e.g., Kogut 1988b), Kogut (1989) identifies a relationship where performance is high at both extremes of concentration, and Good (1972) signifies no association of any kind. Similarly, Luo's (1999) finding that industry *structure uncertainty* actually enhances IJV performance obscures whether there is a negative effect (Inkpen/Currall 1997). Although two studies (e.g., Luo 1997) assert that industry *growth rate* positively affects performance, two others (e.g., Kogut 1989) demonstrate that this external factor plays no role in influencing venture performance. The significance of industry *profitability* appears more straightforward, in that both Luo (1999) and Tiessen and Linton (2000) reveal a positive link between this factor and IJV performance. Three industry factors were considered only once each: industry *scale intensity* is shown to have a negative influence on IJV performance (Kogut 1989); and *labor intensity* and *technology level* are both found to be of no significance (Hu/Chen 1996).

Regulatory Environment

Research within this subset concentrates on the availability of financial incentives and intensity of government legislation. *Tax and economic incentives*, possibly as a result of location within LDC special economic zones, assist parent firms in improving IJV performance (e.g., Osland/Cavusgil 1996). Only Hu and Chen (1996) conclude that economic advantages yield no discernible benefits. *Protectionist regulation* within a national setting has only a moderate bearing on IJV performance (e.g., Makino 1995). In contrast, such influence may be marked: Blodgett (1992) and Osland and Cavusgil (1996) reveal a positive association, while Makino (1995) suggests a negative association. *Prima facie* a positive link here is surprising, given that a risky *political environment* leads to unsatisfactory IJV performance (e.g., Barkema/Vermeulen 1997). On the other hand, there are research findings that downplay the significance of political uncertainty (Merchant/Schendel 2000).

Conclusions and Implications for Management

IJV performance research constitutes the largest stream of empirical inquiry within the collaborative strategy field, yet it remains chaotic and to a large extent ambiguous. This is indicated by the fact that studies often: (1) lack a sound framework that would yield a comprehensive set of both determinants and indicators of IJV performance; (2) fail to contemplate the various theoretical perspectives; (3) define, operationalize, and categorize IJV performance determinants in different, and sometimes contradictory, ways; (4) are conducted in isolation, leading to a fragmented body of knowledge; and (5) fall short of connecting empirical findings to a rigorous future research program. This situation is echoed in our endeavor to synthesize and analyze the empirical results of this stream of research. Studies were found to be spread thinly across multifarious IJV performance determinants, rendering the extraction of conclusions dangerous and potentially misleading. What is more, for most independent factors that did attract considerable research attention, the consolidated results are inconclusive.[10]

Despite these limiting considerations, this sphere of research has been instrumental in our understanding of the complexities underlying IJV performance characteristics. The present assessment reveals important trends that should prove useful to international management practitioners and scholars. Of the 12 groups of controllable factors, interpartner fit is the most widely researched, with particular emphasis on the effects of sociocultural distance. Another well-investigated area concerns venture demographics, with much attention given to IJV age and size. The factors least studied represent production, technology, and R & D strategies and managerial characteristics, notwithstanding that these issues are considered important to the development and management of joint ventures in the broader collaborative strategy literature. Compared to internal determinants of IJV performance, external influences were virtually neglected. This also is counter-intuitive, since IJVs are often subject to complicated competitive and institutional pressures (Lu/Bjorkman 1997).

Several factors demonstrate a consistent pattern of association with overall IJV performance and should be a high priority from a global management perspective. In the *background* variable groups, success factors include a parent's positive attitude toward collaborative forms of business, avoiding partnerships with state-owned organizations, simultaneous development of additional ties with the partner, and ensuring interpartner goal congruence. In terms of *antecedents*, firms should clarify objectives and contributions, stress managerial adaptability, and heed interpartner relational variables such as commitment, trust, conflict, cooperation, and satisfaction with the alliance agreement. Concerning *core* factors, it is important that IJV marketing strategies are framed around product quality and strong distribution and sales networks, sound incentives are offered to employees, and management turnover is minimized. Finally, the significance of two *external* factors, industry profitability and the realization of economic/tax incentives, has been established by extant research.

While these performance drivers encompass many different considerations in IJV development, it can be observed that all key background and antecedent factors reflect the development of either strategic (rather than cultural/fundamental) fit between the partners, or behavioral aspects within partnerships. Hence, as well as attending to the alignment of venturing firms' project objectives and expectations, managers formulating IJV strategies should pay close attention to the social bases of alliance establishment.

Despite the scarcity of research across many determinant groups, differences can be noted for a number of performance drivers when considering the IJV's operating period, its geographic location, and the study's level of analysis. As regards *operating period*, the strategic importance of four elements, host country business experience, sociocultural distance, resource complementarity, and number of parent firms, lessened in the 1990s, whereas the opposite is true of venture age, foreign dominant control, and SIC group. With regard to *geographic location*, three variables only affect the success of IJV operations located in developing countries: these are sociocultural distance, balanced equity ownership, and venture age. A further factor, marketing intensity, has a marked, but opposite, impact on performance in the cases of IJVs in less-developed and advanced countries. A set of variables are also susceptible to the influence of *analytical level*; these are venture age and marketing intensity, once more, plus parent firm size and venture technology sophistication.

Multidimensional measures of IJV performance were the most frequently used, particularly in relation to managerial characteristics, control and supervision, relational aspects, organizational learning, and human resources. However, this measurement system exhibited consistently high correlations only with respect to relational aspects. Unidimensional IJV performance assessment approaches (*financial* and *stability*) were more commonly employed to test the effects of intrapartner and industry characteristics, and here results vary considerably. Further, there is substantial incongruity in empirical findings where it is possible to compare different IJV performance measurement approaches. For instance, sociocultural distance is found to have a dramatic negative effect on stability, whereas no relationship is established with financial performance and the multidimensional effect is unclear. Parent firms facing manifest psychic distance should therefore focus on manipulating venture and partnership characteristics that play an important role in moderating instability (e.g., concurrent interpartner relational linkages). Consequently, despite evidence that perceptual and objective IJV performance measures correlate (e.g., Lyles/Baird 1994), it may not be proper to treat them as equivalent modes of assessment.

Future Research Directions

Future research may pursue several directions that would make this body of knowledge theoretically more grounded, methodologically more robust, and empirically more coherent. These are discussed below.

Encouraging Paradigmatic Pluralism

The preceding review has amply demonstrated the positive impact of paradigm pluralism on knowledge discovery, generation, and development in this important field of research. Despite paradigmatic differences in the studies examined, there is considerable complementarity in their theoretical underpinnings with functional consequences for theory building. Empirical attempts melding together different theories should be encouraged in future research, as they can facilitate the development of richer, more insightful explanations of IJV performance (Kogut 1988a). Nonetheless, the fact that relational parameters alone were found to be consistently associated with IJV performance implies that the behavioral paradigm and associated perspectives, such as social exchange theory (e.g., Blau 1964), warrant focal attention in model building efforts. However, drawing simultaneously from knowledge developed within other theoretical domains, where feasible, would attach a holistic view to explanations of IJV phenomena.

Expanding the Set of Independent Variables Tested

Although a variety of background, antecedent, and core variables have proven consistently significant in IJV performance research, few studies test the importance of a comprehensive but varied set of factors. Such endeavors would facilitate a simultaneous examination of associations between diverse independent variables and IJV performance indicators and permit identification of the interrelationships involved. Further, although a large number of independent variables are identified in the literature, there are additional variables with a possible determining effect on IJV performance that should be considered. For instance, there is a need to study the effects of other strategic factors across IJV settings, especially those relating to production, R&D, and technology, as well as for more research into managerial capabilities.

Controlling for Contingent Forces

Because of huge diversity in the way IJVs are employed, researchers in the field may need to include contingency factors that potentially have an impact on empirical findings. To capture such effects, performance study could assess the role of different IJV goal types and categories of IJV business-resource focus. For instance, there might be subtle, but important differences in performance drivers for narrow purpose IJVs versus those that span multiple value chain links, or for foreign market entry IJVs versus technology development IJVs. Here, it may be enlightening to isolate performance determinants for those organizations within hightech business that, as a distinct strategic group, proactively pursue growth through partnering and develop new structures to accommodate the growing role of IJVs. In addition, making a distinction between IJVs that (are to) provide parent firms with much needed resources and those that furnish parent firms with the opportunity to exploit their valuable resources may prove constructive. For example, it can be theorized that relational aspects play a greater role in the case of IJVs sponsored by entrepreneurial organizations that do not have a strong base of social resources (Eisenhardt/Schoonhoven 1996).

Accounting for External Factors

Despite the fact that alliance strategies can be undermined by uncontrollable events (Inkpen 1995), there is a lacuna of knowledge regarding the impact external parameters have on IJV performance. Examining a wider range of both macroenvironmental (e.g., economic, political) and microenvironmental (e.g., market structure, competitive intensity) factors would allow more efficacious IJV performance study. Researchers might, for instance, acknowledge that governments, as extensions of their respective societies, can be key players in the creation of viable IJV strategies. Further, it would be enlightening to compare and contrast the role controllable independent factors play in influencing performance in: (a) centrally planned versus market-driven economies; (b) low- versus high-context cultural settings; (c) developing versus developed countries; (d) low- versus high-tech industries; and (e) buyers' versus sellers' markets.

Improving IJV Performance Conceptualization and Operationalization

One weakness of this stream of research is the use of diverse, and sometimes improper, measures of IJV performance, which may explain inconsistencies in empirical findings. To alleviate this problem, it is essential that theoretically anchored and methodologically robust measures be developed, drawing from the literatures of organizational effectiveness (e.g., Lewin/Minton 1986), management (e.g., Venkatraman/Ramanujam 1987), international business (e.g., Hitt/Hoskisson/Kim 1997), and strategy (e.g., Chakravarthy 1986), where the topic of business performance has received heightened conceptual and empirical attention. Researchers could benefit particularly from a recently developed evaluative framework of performance assessment, consisting of eight criteria: performance dimensions, frame of reference, stakeholder perspective, unit of analysis, scope of analysis, time horizon, data source, and assessment mode (Katsikeas/Leonidou/Morgan 2000). Future research may also find advantage in the conceptualization of IJV performance as a dynamic process (cf. March/Sutton 1997), in line with Anderson's (1990) input – output continuum of IJV business performance.

Enhancing Methodological Rigor

Notwithstanding the methodological standards maintained in this stream of research, certain research design and implementation improvements could be made in an effort to enhance the level of disciplinary maturity in the field. First, more studies should involve case-research, as the complex, dynamic, and intangible nature of several IJV performance determinants necessitates collection of qualitative data (Berdrow/Beamish 1999). Second, although a relative lack of comprehensive longitudinal studies is apparent in most fields of international management, the fact that such an absence exists within the IJV performance area may be particularly damaging since these business entities evolve through multiple life-stages (Reuer 1998). Third, an efficient means of testing a wider range of pre- and post-incorporation variables would be to combine mesoeconomic examination of IJV failure and microbusiness IJV performance analysis, despite the difficulties inherent in such an undertaking; these approaches have generally proven effective in examining different independent factors. Fourth, the complex causal associations between determinants of IJV performance and its outcomes, as well as among variables within these groups, require sophisticated analytical approaches (e.g., structural equation modeling) that are utilized rarely in extant study.

Alleviating Implementation Hurdles

Syndicated research teams with cross-cultural, multidisciplinary, and academic/practitioner foci should be established to overcome conceptual (e.g., inconsistent definitions and categorizations) and methodological (e.g., minimum IJV operating duration, sample development) difficulties inhibiting empirical IJV performance study. A team's cross-cultural character would facilitate the development of universally acceptable conceptual frameworks, employing common research frames and making time and cost efficiencies. Team multidisciplinary orientation would provide expertise on various IJV management functions and introduce creative new concepts, methods, and techniques. And an academic/practitioner interface would ensure a balance between theory and practice in IJV research, by isolating hidden pragmatic aspects associated with, and enriching the applied usefulness of, IJV performance models.

Notes

1. The constructive comments and suggestions of Roger Mansfield (Cardiff University), Saeed Samiee (University of Tulsa), and Neil Morgan (University of North Carolina at Chapel Hill) are gratefully acknowledged.
2. An IJV is defined on the basis of three characteristics: (1) it is a separate corporate entity, where two or more legally distinct organizations contribute assets, own the venture to some degree, and share associated business risks (Harrigan 1988); (2) each partner participates deliberately because of a need to take advantage of the skills, resources, and strategies of the other member(s) (Singh 1997); and (3) at least one parent is headquartered outside the venture's country of operation (Geringer/Frayne 1993), or the venture is owned by two or more parents of different nationality (Beamish/Inkpen 1995).
3. We are grateful to an anonymous MIR Reviewer for raising this particular point.
4. Although IJV instability has been viewed as distinct from IJV performance in some recent work (Beamish/Delios 1997b, Yan/Zeng 1999), the fact that many empirical studies have explicitly treated this variable as a performance outcome has led us to position it as such for review purposes.
5. Two studies (Berg/Friedman 1981, Duncan 1982) adopting an industry performance focus were excluded.
6. A complete list of the 91 IJV performance studies included, along with tables presenting their key characteristics and summarizing their methodological approaches, are available from the lead author.
7. Although the unit of analysis in all studies under review is the company, either as a whole or in terms of SBUs, IJV performance determinants are studied from two different perspectives: the microbusiness and the mesoeconomic. The former examines

managerial and business dynamics of the individual firm. The latter centers on the subject from the standpoint of the industry(ies) considered and generates results mainly through econometric testing (Randoy 1997); the term "meso" – implying in-between – is used as there are higher levels at which to examine the business process, e.g., government and society (Toyne/Nigh 1997).

8. A table exhibiting findings across IJV operating periods (pre- and post-1990), geographic locations (developed countries, developing countries/NICs, and cross-region), and study analytical levels (microbusiness and mesoeconomic) are available from the lead author.

9. A meta-analytical study of the available empirical findings was deemed inappropriate mainly for the following reasons: the link between many variables and IJV performance was examined in only one or two studies; construct operationalizations, measurement scales, and statistical methods were commonly diverse; and exact *p*-values resulting from testing for the effects of factors on IJV performance were in many cases undisclosed.

10. In primarily summarizing issues with regard to the contradictory empirical findings of prior IJV performance research, this article provides a sound base for future work focused on developing theory to explain the confusion surrounding particular factors.

References

Anand, B. N./Khanna, T., Do Firms Learn to Create Value? The Case of Alliances, *Strategic Management Journal*, 21, 2000, pp. 295–315.

Anderson, E., Two Firms, One Frontier: On Assessing Joint Venture Performance, *Sloan Management Review*, 31, Winter 1990, pp. 19–30.

Artisien, P. F. R./Buckley, P. J., Joint Ventures in Yugoslavia: Opportunities and Constraints, *Journal of International Business Studies*, 16, Spring 1985, pp. 111–134.

Awadzi, W. K., *Determinants of Joint Venture Performance: A Study of International Joint Ventures in the United States*, Unpublished doctoral dissertation, Louisiana State University 1987.

Barkema, H. G./Shenkar, O./Vermeulen, F./Bell, J. H. J., Working Abroad, Working with Others: How Firms Learn to Operate International Joint Ventures, *Academy of Management Journal*, 40, 2, 1997, pp. 426–442.

Barkema, H. G./Vermeulen, F., What Differences in the Cultural Backgrounds of Partners are Detrimental for International Joint Ventures? *Journal of International Business Studies*, 28, Fourth Quarter 1997, pp. 845–864.

Barney, J., Firm Resources and Sustained Competitive Advantage, *Journal of Management*, 17, 1991, pp. 99–120.

Barringer, B. R./Harrison, J. S., Walking a Tightrope: Creating Value Through Inter-organizational Relationships, *Journal of Management*, 26, 3, 2000, pp. 367–403.

Beamish, P. W., *Joint Venture Performance in Developing Countries*, Unpublished doctoral dissertation, University of Western Ontario 1984.

Beamish, P. W., The Characteristics of Joint Ventures in Developed and Developing Countries, *Columbia Journal of World Business*, 20, Fall 1985, pp. 13–19.

Beamish, P. W., The Characteristics of Joint Ventures in the People's Republic of China, *Journal of International Marketing*, 1, 2, 1993, pp. 29–48.

Beamish, P. W./Delios, A., Incidence and Propensity of Alliance Formation, in Beamish P. W./Killing, P. J. (eds.), *Cooperative Strategies: Asian Pacific Perspectives*, San Francisco: New Lexington Press 1997a.

Beamish P. W./Delios, A., Improving Joint Venture Performance Through Congruent Measures of Success, in Beamish, P. W./Killing, P. J. (eds.), *Cooperative Strategies: European Perspectives*, San Francisco: New Lexington Press 1997b.

Beamish, P. W./Inkpen, A. C., Keeping International Joint Ventures Stable and Profitable, *Long Range Planning*, 28, 3, 1995, pp. 26–36.

Beamish, P. W./Kachra, A., Number of Partners and Joint Venture Performance, *Richard Ivey School of Business Working Paper Series*, University of Western Ontario 1999.

Berdrow, I./Beamish, P. W., Unfolding the Myth of IJV Learning, *Richard Ivey School of Business Working Paper Series*, University of Western Ontario 1999.

Berg, S. V./Friedman, P., Impacts of Domestic Joint Ventures on Industrial Rates of Return: A Pooled Cross-Section Analysis, 1964–1975, *The Review of Economics and Statistics*, 63, 2, 1981, pp. 293–298.

Blau, P., *Exchange and Power in Social Life*, New York: John Wiley & Sons 1964.

Blodgett, L. L., Factors in the Instability of International Joint Ventures: An Event History Analysis, *Strategic Management Journal*, 13, 1992, pp. 475–481.

Buchanan, J. M./Tollison, R. D./Tullock, G., *Toward a Theory of the Rent-Seeking Society*, College Station: Texas A&M Press 1984.

Cartwright, S./Cooper, C. L., Predicting Success in Joint Venture Organizations in Information Technology, *Journal of General Management*, 15, 1, 1989, pp. 39–52.

Chakravarthy, B. S., Measuring Strategic Performance, *Strategic Management Journal*, 7, 1986, pp. 437–458.

Chen, H./Hu, M. Y./Shieh, J. C. P., The Wealth Effect of International Joint Ventures: The Case of U. S. Investment in China, *Financial Management*, Winter 1991, pp. 31–41.

Chen, R./Boggs, D. J., Long Term Cooperation Prospects in International Joint Ventures: Perspectives of Chinese Firms, *Journal of Applied Management Studies*, 7, 1, 1998, pp. 111–126.

Chen, S.-S./Ho, K. W./Lee, C.-F./Yeo, G. H. H., Investment Opportunities, Free Cash Flow and Market Reaction to International Joint Ventures, *Journal of Banking and Finance*, 24, 2000, pp. 1747–1765.

Contractor, F. J./Kundu, S. K., Modal Choice in a World of Alliances: Analyzing Organizational Forms in the International Hotel Sector, *Journal of International Business Studies*, Second Quarter 1998, pp. 325–358.

Corbin, J./Strauss, A., Grounded Theory Research: Procedures, Canons, and Evaluative Criteria, *Qualitative Sociology*, 13, 1, 1990, pp. 3–21.

Crutchley, C. E./Guo, E./Hansen, R. S., Stockholder Benefits from Japanese–U. S. Joint Ventures, *Financial Management*, Winter 1991, pp. 22–30.

Das, S./Sen, P. K./Sengupta, S., Impact of Strategic Alliances on Firm Valuation, *Academy of Management Journal*, 41, 1, 1998, pp. 27–41.

Das, T. K./Teng, B.-S., A Resource-Based Theory of Strategic Alliances, *Journal of Management*, 26, 1, 2000, pp. 31–61.

Demirbag, M./Mirza, H., Factors Affecting International Joint Venture Success: An Empirical Analysis of Foreign – Local Partner Relationships and Performance in Joint Ventures in Turkey, *International Business Review*, 9, 2000, pp. 1–35.

Ding, D. Z., Control, Conflict, and Performance: A Study of U. S.–Chinese Joint Ventures, *Journal of International Marketing*, 5, 3, 1997, pp. 31–45.

Duncan, J. L., Impacts of New Entry and Horizontal Joint Ventures on Industrial Rates of Return, *The Review of Economics and Statistics*, 64, 1, 1982, pp. 339–342.

Eisenhardt, K. M./Schoonhoven, C. B., Resource-Based View of Strategic Alliance Formation: Strategic and Social Effects in Entrepreneurial Firms, *Organization Science*, 7, 2, 1996, pp. 136–150.

Eroglu, D./Yavas, U., Determinants of Satisfaction with Partnership in International Joint Ventures: A Channels Perspective, *Journal of Marketing Channels*, 5, 2, 1996, pp. 63–80.

Fey, C., Important Design Characteristics for Russian – Foreign Joint Ventures, *European Management Journal*, 13, 4, 1995, pp. 405–415.

Fey, C., Key Success Factors for Russian – Foreign Joint Ventures, *The International Executive*, 38, 3, 1996, pp. 337–357.

Franko, L. G., *Joint Venture Survival in Multinational Corporations*, New York: Praeger 1971.

Galunic, D. C./ Eisenhardt, K. M., Renewing the Strategy – Structure – Performance Paradigm, in Staw, B. M./Cummings, L. L. (eds.), *Research in Organizational Behavior*, 16, Greenwich, CT: JAI Press 1994.

Geringer, J. M., Assessing Replication and Extension. A Commentary on Glaister and Buckley: Measures of Performance in U. K. International Alliances, *Organization Studies*, 19, 1, 1998, pp. 119–138.

Geringer, J. M./Frayne, C. A., Self-Efficacy, Outcome Expectancy, and Performance of International Joint Venture General Managers, *Canadian Journal of Administrative Sciences*, 10, 4, 1993, pp. 322–333.

Geringer, J. M./Hebert, L., Control and Performance of International Joint Ventures, *Journal of International Business Studies*, 20, 2, 1989, pp. 235–254.

Good, L., *United States Joint Ventures and Manufacturing Firms in Monterey, Mexico: Comparative Styles of Management*, Unpublished doctoral dissertation, Cornell University 1972.

Gray, B./Yan, A., A Negotiations Model of Joint Venture Formation, Structure and Performance: Implications for Global Management, *Advances in International Management*, 7, 1992, pp. 41–75.

Harrigan, K. R., *Managing for Joint Venture Success*, Lexington, MA: Lexington Books 1986.

Harrigan, K. R., Joint Ventures and Competitive Strategy, *Strategic Management Journal*, 9, 1988, pp. 141–158.

Hatfield, L./Pearce, J. A., Goal Achievement and Satisfaction of Joint Venture Partners, *Journal of Business Venturing*, 9, 5, 1994, pp. 423–449.

Hebert, L., *Division of Control, Relationship Dynamics, and Joint Venture Performance*, Unpublished doctoral dissertation, University of Western Ontario, Canada 1994.

Hennart, J.-F., A Transaction Costs Theory of Equity Joint Ventures, *Strategic Management Journal*, 9, 1988, pp. 361–374.

Hill, R. C./Hellriegel, D., Critical Contingencies in Joint Venture Management – Some Lessons from Managers, *Organization Science*, 5, 4, 1994, pp. 594–607.

Hitt, M. A./Hoskisson, R. E./Kim, H., International Diversification: Effects on Innovation and Firm Performance in Product-Diversified Firms, *Academy of Management Journal*, 40, 4, 1997, pp. 767–798.

Hofer, C. W., ROVA: A New Measure for Assessing Organizational Performance, *Advances in Strategic Management*, 2, 1983, pp. 43–55.

Hofer, C. W./Schendel, D., *Strategy Formulation: Analytical Concepts*, St Paul: West 1978.

Hoskisson, R. E./Hitt, M. A./Wan, W. P./Yiu, D., Theory and Research in Strategic Management: Swings of a Pendulum, *Journal of Management*, 25, 3, 1999, pp. 417–456.

Hu, M. Y./Chen, H., An Empirical Analysis of Factors Explaining Foreign Joint Venture Performance in China, *Journal of Business Research*, 35, 1996, pp. 165–173.

Hu, M. Y./Chen, H./Shich, J. C., Impact of U. S.–China Joint Ventures on Stockholders' Wealth by Degree of International Involvement, *Management International Review*, 32, 2, 1992, pp. 135–148.

Inkpen, A., *The Management of International Joint Ventures: An Organizational Learning Perspective*, New York: Routledge 1995.

Inkpen, A./Crossnan, M. M., Believing is Seeing: Joint Ventures and Organizational Learning, *Journal of Management Studies*, 32, 1995, pp. 595–618.

Inkpen, A./Currall, S. C., International Joint Venture Trust, in Beamish, P. W./Killing, J. P. (eds.), *Cooperative Strategies: North American Perspectives*, San Francisco: New Lexington Press 1997.

Inkpen, A./Dinur, A., Knowledge Management Processes and International Joint Ventures, *Organization Science*, 9, 4, 1998, pp. 454–468.

Isobe, T./Makino, S./Montgomery, D. B., Resource Commitment, Entry Timing, and Market Performance of Foreign Direct Investments in Emerging Economies: The Case of Japanese International Joint Ventures in China, *Academy of Management Journal*, 43, 3, 2000, pp. 468–484.

Kidder, L. H./Wrightman, S./Cook, *Research Methods in Social Relations*, Japan: Holt-Saunders International Editions 1981.

Killing, J. P., *Strategies for Joint Venture Success*, New York: Praeger 1983.

Katsikeas, C. S./Leonidou, L. C./Morgan, N. A., Firm-Level Export Performance Assessment: Review, Evaluation, and Development, *Journal of the Academy of Marketing Science*, 28, Fall 2000, pp. 493–511.

Kogut, B., Joint Ventures: Theoretical and Empirical Perspectives, *Strategic Management Journal*, 9, 1988a, pp. 319–332.

Kogut, B., A Study of the Life Cycle of Joint Ventures, in Contractor, F. J./Lorange, P. (eds.), *Cooperative Strategies in International Business*, Lexington, MA: Lexington Press 1988b.

Kogut, B., The Stability of Joint Ventures: Reciprocity and Competitive Rivalry, *Journal of Industrial Economics*, 38, 2, 1989, pp. 183–198.

Koh, J./Venkatraman, N., Joint Venture Formations and Stock Market Reactions: An Assessment in the Information Technology Sector, *Academy of Management Journal*, 34, 4, 1991, pp. 869–892.

Krippendorff, K., *Content Analysis: An Introduction to its Methodology*, U. S. A.: SAGE Publications 1980.

Kumar, S./Seth, A., The Design of Coordination and Control Mechanisms for Managing Joint Venture–Parent Relationships, *Strategic Management Journal*, 19, 1998, pp. 579–599.

Lasserre, P., Joint Venture Satisfaction in Asia Pacific, *Asia Pacific Journal of Management*, 16, 1999, pp. 1–28.

Lecraw, D. J., Bargaining Power, Ownership, and Profitability of Transnational Corporations in Developing Countries, *Journal of International Business Studies*, 15, Spring/Summer 1984, pp. 27–43.

Lee, C./Beamish, P. W., The Characteristics and Performance of Korean Joint Ventures in LDCs, *Journal of International Business Studies*, 26, Third Quarter 1995, pp. 637–654.

Lewin, A. Y./Minton, J. W., Determining Organizational Effectiveness: Another Look, and an Agenda for Research, *Management Science*, 32, 5, 1986, pp. 515–538.

Lin, X./Germain, R., Sustaining Satisfactory Joint Venture Relationships: The Role of Conflict Resolution Strategy, *Journal of International Business Studies*, 29, 1, 1998, pp. 179–196.

Liu, H./Pak, K., How Important is Marketing in China Today to Sino-Foreign Joint Ventures, *European Management Journal*, 17, 5, 1999, pp. 546–554.

Lu, Y./Bjorkman, I., International Joint Venture Decision Making, in Beamish, P. W./Killing, J. P. (eds.), *Cooperative Strategies: Asian Pacific Perspectives*, San Francisco: New Lexington Press 1997.

Luo, Y., Linking Strategic and Moderating Factors to Performance of International Joint Ventures in China, *The Mid-Atlantic Journal of Business*, 31, 1, 1995, pp. 5–23.

Luo, Y., Partner Selection and Venturing Success: The Case of Joint Ventures with Firms in the People's Republic of China, *Organization Science*, 8, 6, 1997, pp. 648–662.

Luo, Y., The Structure–Performance Relationship in a Transitional Economy: An Empirical Study of Multinational Alliances in China, *Journal of Business Research*, 46, 1999, pp. 15–30.

Luo, Y./Chen, M., Business Strategy, Investment Strategy, and Performance of International Joint Ventures, in Beamish, P. W./Killing, J. P. (eds.), *Cooperative Strategies: Asian Pacific Perspectives*, San Francisco: New Lexington Press 1997.

Lyles, M. A./Baird, I. S., Performance of International Joint Ventures in Two Eastern European Countries: The Case of Hungary and Poland, *Management International Review*, 34, 4, 1994, pp. 313–329.

Lyles, M. A./Salk, J. E., Knowledge Acquisition from Foreign Parents in International Joint Ventures: An Empirical Examination in the Hungarian Context, *Journal of International Business Studies*, 27, Special Issue 1996, pp. 877–903.

Lyles, M. A./Sulaiman, M./Barden, J. Q./Kechik, A. R. H. B. A., Factors Affecting International Joint Venture Performance: A Study of Malaysian Joint Ventures, *Journal of Asian Business*, 15, 2, 1999, pp. 1–20.

McConnell, J. J./Nantell, T. J., Corporate Combinations and Common Stock Returns: The Case of Joint Ventures, *Journal of Finance*, 40, 2, 1985, pp. 519–536.

Madhok, A., Revisiting Multinational Firms' Tolerance for Joint Ventures: A Trust-Based Approach, *Journal of International Business Studies*, First Quarter 1995, pp. 117–137.

Makino, S., *Joint Venture Ownership Structure and Performance: Japanese Joint Ventures in Asia*, Unpublished doctoral dissertation, University of Western Ontario 1995.

Makino, S./Beamish, P. W., Local Ownership Restrictions, Entry Mode Choice, and FDI Performance: Japanese Overseas Subsidiaries in Asia, *Asia Pacific Journal of Management*, 15, 1998, pp. 119–136.

Makino, S./Delios, A., Local Knowledge Transfer and Performance: Implications for Alliance Formation in Asia, *Journal of International Business Studies*, 27, Special Issue 1996, pp. 905–927.

March, J./Sutton, R. I., Organizational Performance as Dependant Variable, *Organization Science*, 8, 6, 1997, pp. 698–706.

Merchant, H./Schendel, D., How Do International Joint Ventures Create Shareholder Value? *Strategic Management Journal*, 21, 2000, pp. 723–737.

Millington, A. I./Bayliss, B. T., Instability of Market Penetration Joint Ventures: A Study of U. K. Joint Ventures in the European Union, *International Business Review*, 6, 1, 1997, pp. 1–17.

Mjoen, H./Tallman, S., Control and Performance in International Joint Ventures, *Organization Science*, 8, 3, 1997, pp. 257–274.

Nakamura, M., Modelling the Performance of U. S. Direct Investment in Japan: Some Empirical Estimates, *Managerial and Decision Economics*, 12, 1991, pp. 103–121.

Nakamura, M./Shaver, J. M./Yeung, B., An Empirical Investigation of Joint Venture Dynamics: Evidence from U. S.–Japan Joint Ventures, *International Journal of Industrial Organization*, 14, 1996, pp. 521–541.

Olk, P., The Effect of Partner Differences on the Performance of R&D Consortia, in Beamish, P. W./Killing, J. P. (eds.), *Cooperative Strategies: Asian Pacific Perspectives*, San Francisco: New Lexington Press 1997.

Osland, G. E./Cavusgil, S. T., Performance in U. S.–China Joint Ventures, *California Management Review*, 38, 2, 1996, pp. 106–130.

Park, S. H./Kim, D., Market Valuation of Joint Ventures: Joint Characteristics and Wealth Gains, *Journal of Business Venturing*, 12, 1997, pp. 83–108.

Park, S. H./Ungson, G. R., The Effect of National Culture, Organizational Complementarity, and Economic Motivation on Joint Venture Dissolution, *Academy of Management Journal*, 40, 2, 1997, pp. 279–307.

Parker, B./Zeira, Y./Hatem, T., International Joint Venture Managers: Factors Affecting Personal Success and Organizational Performance, *Journal of International Management*, 2, 1, 1996, pp. 1–29.

Parkhe, A., Strategic Alliance Structuring: A Game Theoretic and Transaction Cost Examination of Interfirm Cooperation, *Academy of Management Journal*, 36, 4, 1993a, pp. 794–829.

Parkhe, A., 'Messy' Research, Methodological Predispositions, and Theory Development in International Joint Ventures, *Academy of Management Review*, 18, 2, 1993b, pp. 227–268.

Ramanathan, K./Seth, A./Thomas, H., Explaining Joint Ventures: Alternative Theoretical Perspectives, in Beamish, P. W./Killing, J. P. (eds.), *Cooperative Strategies: North American Perspectives*, San Francisco: New Lexington Press 1997.

Ramaswamy, K./Gomes, L./Veliyath, R., The Performance Correlates of Ownership Control: A Study of U. S. and European MNE Joint Ventures in India, *International Business Review*, 7, 1998, pp. 423–441.

Randoy, T., Toward a Firm-Based Model of Foreign Direct Investment, in Bjorkman, I./Forsgren, M. (eds.), *The Nature of the International Firm*, Handelshojskolens Forlag, Copenhagen Business School 1997.

Reuer, J. J., The Dynamics and Effectiveness of International Joint Ventures, *European Management Journal*, 16, 2, 1998, pp. 160–168.

Reuer, J. J., Parent Firm Performance Across International Joint Venture Life-Cycle Stages, *Journal of International Business Studies*, 31, 1, 2000, pp. 1–20.

Reuer, J. J./Miller, K. D., Agency Costs and the Performance Implications of International Joint Venture Internalization, *Strategic Management Journal*, 18, 6, 1997, pp. 425–438.

Ring, P. S./Van de Ven, A. H., Structuring Cooperative Relationships Between Organizations, *Strategic Management Journal*, 13, 7, 1992, pp. 483–498.

Sharp, J. A./Howard, K., *The Management of a Student Research Project*, U. K.: Gower Publishing Limited 1996.

Shenkar, O./Li, J., Knowledge Search in International Cooperative Ventures, *Organization Science*, 10, 2, 1999, pp. 134–143.

Shenkar, O./Zeira, Y., Role Conflict and Role Ambiguity of Chief Executive Officers in International Joint Ventures, *Journal of International Business Studies*, 23, First Quarter 1992, pp. 55–75.

Sim, A. B./Ali, Y., Performance of International Joint Ventures from Developing and Developed Countries: An Empirical Study in a Developing Country Context, *Journal of World Business*, 33, 4, 1998, pp. 357–377.

Sim, A. B./Ali, M. Y., Determinants of Stability in International Joint Ventures: Evidence from a Developing Country Context, *Asia Pacific Journal of Management*, 17, 2000, pp. 373–397.

Simiar, F., Major Causes of Joint Venture Failures in the Middle East: The Case of Iran, *Management International Review*, 23, 1, 1983, pp. 58–68.

Singh, K., The Impact of Technology Complexity and Interfirm Cooperation on Business Survival, *Academy of Management Journal*, 40, 2, 1997, pp. 339–367.

Singleton, R./Straits, B. C./Straits, M. M./McAllister, R. J., *Approaches to Social Research*, New York: Oxford University Press, 1988.

Steensma, H. K./Lyles, M. A., Explaining IJV Survival in a Transitional Economy Through Social Exchange and Knowledge-Based Perspectives, *Strategic Management Journal*, 21, 2000, pp. 831–852.

Strauss, A./Corbin, J., *Basics of Qualitative Research: Grounded Theory Procedures and Techniques*, U. S. A.: SAGE Publications 1990.

Tiessen, J. H./Linton, J. D., The JV Dilemma: Cooperating and Competing in Joint Ventures, *Canadian Journal of Administrative Sciences*, 17, 3, 2000, pp. 203–216.

Toyne, B./Nigh, D., Foundations of an Emerging Paradigm, in Toyne, B./Nigh, D. (eds.), *International Business: An Emerging Vision*, Columbia, South Carolina: University of South Carolina Press 1997.

Venkatraman, N./Ramanujam, V., Measurement of Business Performance in Strategy Research: An Examination of Method Congruence, *Journal of Management*, 13, 1, 1987, pp. 109–122.

Yan, A./Gray, B., Bargaining Power, Management Control, and Performance in United States–China Joint Ventures: A Comparative Case Study, *Academy of Management Journal*, 37, 6, 1994, pp. 1478–1517.

Yan, A./Zeng, M., International Joint Venture Instability: A Critique of Previous Research, a Reconceptualization, and Directions for Future Research, *Journal of International Business Studies*, 30, 2, 1999, pp. 397–414.

Yan, Y., *Ownership and Control in International Joint Ventures: A Study of Sino-Foreign Joint Ventures*, Unpublished doctoral dissertation, Cambridge University, UK, 1997.

Zeira, Y./Newburry, W./Yeheskel, O., Factors Affecting the Effectiveness of Equity International Joint Ventures in Hungary, *Management International Review*, 37, 3, 1997, pp. 259–279.

38

Closure and Divestiture by Foreign Entrants: The Impact of Entry and Post-Entry Strategies

José Mata and Pedro Portugal

Introduction

In one of the few studies which has analyzed exit of foreign entrants, Li (1995) convincingly showed that the longevity of foreign presence depends on the strategic choices at entry, namely the choice between starting a new company and acquiring an existing one and the choice between running a joint venture and running a fully-owned business.

This work extends previous research by studying the survival of foreign entrants while recognizing that there are also different ways of exiting from foreign markets. Exit may occur through liquidation of the subsidiary firm or simply through divestiture. The two processes are likely to be governed by different forces and understanding the reasons that determine each of them is important to improving our knowledge of the process of international expansion. The analysis is conducted with reference to over 1000 foreign-owned firms that started operating in Portugal during the period 1983–1989.

The topic is not of mere academic interest, and should attract considerable attention from the practitioners as well. Managers considering going into international markets are interested in evaluating the chances of their success. Since the two alternative modes of exit may be determined by different forces, managers should benefit from knowing under which circumstances each type of exit is more likely to occur.

The plan is as follows. First, we present the hypotheses to be tested. The following section discusses methodological issues, including the description of the data source, the methods used in computing the variables, and the statistical

Source: *Strategic Management Journal*, Vol. 21, No. 5, 2000, pp. 549–562.

methodology employed. Next, we give an overview of the sample characteristics and exit patterns, followed by the presentation of the results. Finally, in the last section we discuss the contribution of the study and offer concluding comments.

Hypotheses

The framework employed in the analysis is the following. In each period, foreign subsidiaries confront two risks, the risk of closure and that of divestiture, which are assumed here to be independent. In each period, therefore, three outcomes are possible. The firm may continue its operations under foreign ownership, it may be divested or it may close. These outcomes are produced by two separate decisions, represented in Figure 1. One is the decision to divest or not to divest. The other is decision to shutdown or not to shutdown. The common theme of the hypotheses developed below is that the strategies followed by foreign entrants may exert disparate effects upon the two decisions.

Figure 1
Exit Decisions

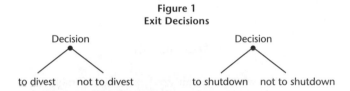

Entry Mode

One of the crucial decisions when deciding to expand into a new market is the decision on whether to set up a new venture or to acquire an existing firm (Yip, 1982, Zejan, 1990, Woodcock, Beamish and Makimo, 1994). In a recent paper, Shaver (1998) suggested that the choice of entry mode may be endogenous, being determined by the firm's prospects of failure. While we do not investigate the endogeneity issue, we acknowledge that the choice of entry mode may have different effects upon the probabilities of closure and divestment. The different patterns of dissolution and divestiture experienced by start-ups and diversifying entrants have been investigated by Mitchell (1994), but this has not been studied in the context of foreign entry.

The theory of the multinational corporation emphasizes that the possession of ownership advantages is a key factor in explaining why firms do business abroad, despite the increased costs they incur due to their poorer knowledge of the local conditions (Dunning, 1993). The choice of the entry method is largely determined by the nature and extent of these ownership advantages. Acquisition may be the preferred method of entry when the acquired firm possesses some intrinsic advantage such as location, and the advantage of the acquiring firm rests elsewhere than in production technology, for example in marketing. However, if the advantage of the multinational firm rests on the superiority of its production-specific assets, for example, because it has access to a proprietory technology, it may not be easy to find an ongoing business suitable for acquisition, and starting a new company from scratch may be the best alternative.

To the extent that acquisition signals the predominance of non-specific assets while greenfield entry indicates the need to develop a tailored production facility, we would expect that firms that had been once acquired would be more suitable to other potential buyers. Also, if a foreign firm entered by greenfield because it owns some proprietary technology, it is very unlikely that it wants to let others use its technology. Therefore, we would expect acquisition entrants to be more likely to be resold than firms that have been created from scratch. Thus, our first hypothesis is formulated as follows (where the letters *D* and *C* after the hypothesis number indicate that the hypothesis refers to divestiture and closure, respectively).

Hypothesis 1D: Foreign firms entering by acquisition are more likely to divest from their subsidiaries than are those entering through greenfield entry.

Furthermore, studies on multinational firms have generally found that, although new ventures promise a higher rate of return, their profits are more variable than those from acquisitions (Caves, 1996). The reason why profits from acquisitions are less risky is that those firms which are acquired have already gone into a process of developing procedures and routines that enable them to deal effectively with their environment (Hannan and Carroll, 1992). They are, therefore, typically less subject than new ventures to those unforeseen contingencies that may lead to the closure of the productive facility. This leads us to hypothesize that

Hypothesis 1C: Foreign firms entering by acquisition are less likely to be shutdown than are those entering through greenfield entry.

Ownership Advantages

Ownership advantages are typically associated with the ability of firms to develop firm-specific assets, which cannot be imitated by competitors and provide the basis for their competitive advantage (Wernerfelt, 1984). Firms with such assets are normally those which conduct R&D activities, spend considerably on advertising, and possess large amounts of human capital. Recent studies on entry, post-entry penetration and survival show that the ability to develop and exploit such assets is crucial for the post-entry performance of firms (Burgelman, 1994; Bogner, Thomas and McGee 1996; Chang, 1996). We thus expect that firms using larger amounts of human capital will experience higher chances of success in operating in a foreign country. Because human capital is directly related to the extent of the firm's ownership advantages, we expect it to be influential in the firm's decision to leave the foreign country, regardless of the mode of exit. Therefore, we hypothesize that

Hypothesis 2C: New firms with a larger human capital endowment experience a lower probability of closure.

Hypothesis 2D: New firms with a larger human capital endowment experience a lower probability of divestment.

Ownership Structure

Joint Ventures

Transaction costs theory contends that joint ventures are a response to failures in markets for particular assets held by different companies. A good example of such assets in the context of multinational investment is tacit knowledge about technology from the potential foreign investor and about the host country from the local partner. The market failure emerges because local firms find it difficult to acquire knowledge about the unspecified details of the technology and foreign firms find it difficult to buy knowledge about the *modus operandi* of local markets. It thus becomes cheaper for the parties to share both assets through a common endeavor than to trade them through the market. On the other hand, joint ventures also have costs. By making both parties residual claimants on firm's profits, they create in both parties incentives to free-ride, which makes these ventures highly unstable.

This instability of joint ventures has been widely recognized in the literature. As the cooperative venture ages, and firms learn about the other party's assets, the benefits of joint ventures are often offset by their costs and the likelihood of joint venture dissolution increases. For example, Hennart (1991) found that Japanese subsidiaries in the U.S. are less likely to be joint ventures, the greater the age of the subsidiary. Kogut (1989) observed that in some circumstances firms may be able to develop strategies to reduce the likelihood of dissolution. He observed that partner firms which had established several simultaneous cooperative agreements, thereby increasing the punishment cost of breaking any particular agreement, were significantly less likely to dissolve a joint venture, than those which had a single common venture. As a consequence of this greater instability, Yamawaki (1997) found that fully-owned subsidiaries of Japanese multinationals were less likely to exit than joint ventures. This leads us directly to our next hypothesis.

> *Hypothesis 3D: Fully-owned subsidiaries are less likely to be divested than joint-ventures.*

Minority Holdings

Joint ventures differ with respect to the degree of control exerted by the foreign party. Although the foreign share can vary in a continuous scale between 0 and 100, two thresholds are of particular importance. The first threshold distinguishes portfolio investments from joint ventures in a narrow sense. The second distinguishes majority from minority joint ventures. The distinction between portfolio investments and joint ventures is important because portfolio investments typically do not confer controlling rights. In this study, we are not concerned with this type of investments and will not include firms with such type of foreign ownership (foreign equity below 10%) in our sample.

We are, however, interested in the distinction between minority joint-venture, in which foreign firms have some degree of control rights, and joint ventures in which foreign firms have the majority of the votes. Minority holdings are a risky strategy, since control escapes to the foreign firm, and it may be subject to opportunistic behavior. In fact, the literature comparing the choice of multinationals with respect to the type of control they possess over their subsidiaries has found that the propensity to hold minority stakes in the subsidiary increases with the size of the parent firm (Gatignon and Anderson, 1988, Blomstrom and Zejan, 1989) and with its degree of diversification (Alzona, Rondi and Vitali, 1993; Blomstrom and Zejan, 1989). These findings have been interpreted as a consequence of the greater willingness of large parent firms to take risks abroad. Moreover, Gatignon and Anderson (1988) found that the degree of control over subsidiaries varies positively with the intensity of R&D and advertising expenditures. This suggests that minority positions are less likely to be held when asset specificity is important and entry involves a strong commitment to the market.

These arguments lead naturally to our next hypothesis, which posits that

Hypothesis 4D: Minority holdings are more likely to be divested than are majority holdings.

Legal Form

The reason why there are several legal forms under which firms can operate is to allow for different limitations on the degree of liability incurred by firms' owners. While in unlimited liability firms the owners are personally accountable for the firm's debts, the liability of the owners of a limited liability firm is restricted to the value of their equity in the company. Because the liability of firms is reduced with increases in the degree of complexity of the legal form, the requirements in terms of organization and formalization of the firms' financial reports also increase. There are also minimum requirements to form a limited liability firm (amount of equity capital, number of equity owners) which do not apply to unlimited liability venture. Thus, limited liability companies involve significantly higher set-up and fixed operating costs than do unlimited liability firms. On the other hand, the transaction of one's stake in the firm is easier for limited liability firms than for their unlimited liability counterparts. For example, only limited liability firms can go public and have their shares publicly traded, while the ownership of unlimited liability firms can be changed only with the explicit agreement of all owners.

Legal form may thus have an opposite effect on divestment and closure. The more limited the liability of firms, the easier is the transfer of propriety rights and thus, holding everything else constant, the more likely the firm is to be divested. On the contrary, the more limited the liability of firms, the less likely it is that they will be shut down. On the one hand, given their higher set-up costs, they have a higher option value in waiting and are likely to remain open longer than firms with lower set-up costs (Dixit and Pindyck, 1994). On the other hand, because the personal responsibility of the owners decreases with liability, the owners of unlimited liability firms are likely to be more conservative with respect to exit decisions than the owners of limited liability firms. Therefore, they will exit before the moment where a similar decision would be taken by the limited liability firms, who have less to lose in case of bankruptcy. The effect of the choice of legal firm on the survival of firms has been examined by Brüdel, Preisendörfer and Ziegler (1992) and Harhoff, Stahl and Woywode (1996), who found the company legal form to be associated with the chances of success. Harhoff *et al.* (1996), in particular, found that limited liability companies are more prone to insolvencies, but less likely to undergo voluntary liquidation, than are other companies.

Thus, we will test the following hypotheses.

Hypothesis 5C: The likelihood of closure decreases with the limitation of liability.

Hypothesis 5D: The likelihood of divestment increases with the limitation of liability.

Control Variables

Other variables need to be taken into account in our empirical analysis. At the firm level, we include size, growth, the extent of diversification and of multiplant operations.

Many studies have found a positive relationship between firm size and the probability of survival (Dunne, Roberts and Samuelson, 1989; Mitchell, 1994; Mata, Portugal and Guimaraes, 1995). This has been rationalized as resulting from firms having a high degree of uncertainty about their own capabilities when they start (Jovanovic, 1982). Because of the irreversibility inherent to most investments, it is optimal for firms to start at a small scale and grow only if they find that they have been successful in the past (Cabral, 1995). A second reason why firms may start small and expand afterwards is because their entry size is partially determined by cash constraints. Firms which are not part of a large multinational organization, where cash constraints are less important, may find it difficult to raise enough money to finance entry at their most preferred scale (Evans and Jovanovic, 1989). Therefore, large firms are less likely to exit than their small counterparts. The relationship between size and the likelihood of divestiture is less obvious and the empirical studies that have analyzed exit by divestment have not found any significant relationship between divestment and the size of firms (Schary, 1991; Mitchell, 1994).

Most studies that have analyzed the impact of foreign firm diversification upon exit have examined primarily the proximity between the parent firm and the subsidiary main activities. These studies have found that unrelated subsidiaries are more likely to exit than subsidiaries operating in the same activity as the parent firm (Li, 1995, Yamawaki, 1997). To our knowledge, only Bane and Neubauer (1981) have looked at the effect of subsidiary's internal diversification, finding that narrowly focused branches experienced a lower failure rate than did more diversified ones. This result can be due to the fact that specialized firms experience a greater degree of commitment to their activity and management is less dispersed. On the other hand, the number of plants operated by the firm was found to have a positive impact on firms' prospects of survival by Mata and Portugal (1994). This result can be rationalized by noting that multiplant firms can accommodate the failure of one of their plants without failing themselves, while single plant firms cannot. To the extent that this argument depends on the correlation between the success of different business units in a firm, it also applies to the extent of diversification. We will accommodate these two aspects in our empirical analysis, without making any specific predictions about the relationships.

Furthermore, the environment in which entry occurs is also likely to affect the survival prospects of the firm. We will use a number of industry characteristics to control for the different environments in which firms operate.

The first of such variables is the degree of industry concentration. Based on an Industrial Organization argument, the degree of competition in the market has been hypothesized to increase the likelihood of survival. The argument here is that concentration facilitates collusion among incumbents and hence aggressive responses to entry. Market concentration has been found to negatively affect the chances of survival of new firms by Audretsch and Mahmood (1994), but it has been found to be insignificant by Romanelli (1989) and by Mata and Portugal (1994). Focusing on foreign firms, Li (1995) and Mitchell, Shaver and Yeung (1994) found a positive effect of concentration on new firm survival, although this effect was barely significant.

We will also control for the entry and growth rates in the industry. Dunne, Roberts and Samuelson (1988) found that there is a strong positive cross-sectional correlation between entry and exit, and this finding has been further corroborated by a number of scholars (see Cable and Schwalbach 1991, for example). This has been explained in terms of symmetry between entry and exit barriers by Eaton and Lipsey (1980), an hypothesis which received empirical confirmation by Shapiro (1993) in the context of multinational firms.

Industries which are growing quickly are likely to be environments in which the probability of exit of new firms is lower. One of the stylized facts established by Schmalensee in his survey of empirical work on Industrial Organization (1989: 972) is that profits are in general larger in growing than in otherwise identical industries. This makes survival easier, as new firms do not have to attract customers away from incumbents. Both Audretsch and Mahmood (1994) and Mata and Portugal (1994) found a positive and significant effect of industry growth upon the survival of new firms.

Survival is also likely to be correlated with the extent of economies of scale in the industry. Firms which operate at a scale smaller than the minimum efficient scale incur a cost disadvantage *vis-à-vis* efficiently scaled firms. This cost disadvantage puts firms in a fragile position, as they have to develop alternative competitive strategies that enable them to cope with competitive pressures. Therefore, for a firm of a given size, the larger the extent of economies of scale in an industry, the more likely it is that such a firm is smaller than the minimum efficient scale, and thus will suffer a cost disadvantage. Everything else being identical, the chances of survival will thus be higher in industries where economies of scale are not very important than in those where they are significant. Audretsch and Mahmood (1994) present empirical evidence supporting this hypothesis.

Finally, the survival of the new foreign owned firms is likely to be related to the previous presence of foreign firms in the market. Shaver, Mitchell and

Yeung (1997) found that foreign presence mostly affects the survival of foreign entrants if entrants are already operating in the country, but in a different industry than that in which entry is attempted. They argue that firms which are already in the country are in the best position to benefit from the learning spillovers generated from foreign presence, and that those which do not possess direct information about the industry will benefit the most from these spillovers. We do not have information on previous experience, and therefore, we will not be able to take this qualification into account. As a consequence, if such qualification is indeed important, we will obtain weaker results than if we could control for previous experience. In an earlier study, the same authors present evidence that foreign presence affects the survival of foreign entrants, but they argue that one should expect an inverse U-relationship between foreign presence and survival (Mitchell *et al.*, 1994). They claim that foreign survival at the earlier stages of foreign presence should be more difficult due to lack of market knowledge, while at the latter stages it should again be more difficult due to congestion effects. This argument is developed in a time-series context, in which the same market is observed over time. In our case, we have essentially a cross-section variation. We thus expect previous foreign presence to signal the presence of those characteristics which make foreign survival more likely.

Methods

Data

Our data were obtained from a survey conducted by the Portuguese Ministry of Employment (*Quadros de Pessoal* hereafter QP). This is a comprehensive survey covering all firms with wage earners in Portugal, which has been conducted every year since 1982. Moreover, its longitudinal capacity, i.e., firms are identified through a unique number, allows firms to be followed over time. What makes this data source really unique and particularly valuable from the point of view of the analysis of foreign entry and exit is that, among other data, the survey records the share of equity held by non-residents. Taken together with its longitudinal characteristic, this allows us to compute measures of entry of foreign capital and to establish the longevity of these investments in Portugal.

We identified changes in foreign capital participation with a three step procedure. First, we identified all firms which held foreign capital in at least one year from 1983 to 1989 and which did not have foreign capital in the previous year. This enabled us to date the moment of entry of foreign capital. Second, we searched for the existence of the firm itself in the year before entry in order to be able to classify foreign entry as acquisition *versus* greenfield. This could be easily done because firms' identifiers are numbers supplied sequentially when firms first report to the survey. Identification of new firms can thus be achieved by comparing firms' identifiers with the highest identification number in the file in the previous year. Finally, the last step was the establishment of the life span of foreign capital. For this we had to be able to identify the moment in which the foreign participation ceased. As previously discussed we are interested in distinguishing two alternatives: foreign firm closure, where the foreign owned firm ceases its operations, and foreign capital divestiture, where the firm continues to operate, but no longer with foreign capital participation. To identify the moment of divestiture we searched for the first year when the firm reported foreign participation below 10%, while for identifying closure we searched for the moment when the firm ceased to report to the survey.

The data base has limitations that should be made clear. First, we do not know the identity of the foreign owners. This is unfortunate because it prevents us from using the parents' characteristics to explain the exit of subsidiaries, and because we are not able to identify the sale of a foreign equity participation by one foreign firm to another. Another potential limitation of our data set is that we cannot tell mergers from true exits. What typically happens when one of such movements occurs is that one of the identifiers of the firms involved in the merger is transmitted to the resulting firm, while the others disappear, and are counted as exits in our data. Furthermore, with such a large data base, one can never be sure that no coding errors are made.

We took special care to minimize the number of false foreign entries and exits that were included in our sample. In the sake of economy, we do not describe here all the procedures employed to check the reliability of the data base, which consisted in comparing our data with data from other sources and in double-checking the moment of exit. In summary, we were able to conclude that the measurement of the entry and exit flows is quite reliable, and that mergers and changes in ownership due to simultaneous investment and divestment by foreign owners are not significant. The details of all the procedures employed to perform these checks are described in a methodology appendix, which is available from the authors upon request.

Statistical Model

The key concept in duration analysis is the hazard rate, that gives the probability that a unit exits within a particular time interval, given that it survived until then. In our context, we will work with two distinct hazard rates, corresponding to the two types of exit we are interested in. Rather than imposing a parametric functional form for the hazard function, a simple flexible hazard model (Kalbfleisch and Prentice, 1980) was employed

$$h(m) = \lambda_m \quad m = 1, 2, \ldots, M \quad 0 < \lambda_m < 1,$$

where λ_m is just the hazard rate for the time interval m. Thus, the sequence from λ_1 to λ_M exhibits the yearly evolution of the exit probabilities for a given firm.

The effects of the explanatory variables (some of which may vary over time) are incorporated by allowing the hazard function to be influenced proportionally by the covariates, as suggested by Cox (1972):

$$h(m) = exp(\beta X_m) \lambda_m,$$

where X_m is the vector of independent variables observed at m, and β is the corresponding vector of regression coefficients.

In this model it is assumed that, at each period, the firm decides whether to continue, to divest or to shutdown. Technically, this is known as a competing risks model. In this setup, there are two latent durations: time until divestment and time until closure. The observed duration is the minimum value between those two latent durations, which are governed by two distinct hazard functions. Accordingly, when a foreign firm is observed to close down, this observation is treated as censored in the divestment equation. Conversely, when divestment is observed, this observation is treated as censored in the closure equation.

Estimation is performed by maximum likelihood methods. In writing the likelihood function, a distinction has to be made between firms that exited and those firms that survived until the end of the survey. To the former, we can assign both a lower and an upper interval for the corresponding durations (interval censored durations). To the latter, all we know is that their duration exceeds a given limit (censored durations). The derivation of the likelihood function that accommodates our sampling plan is provided in the Appendix, which is available upon request.

Following the discussion of the hypotheses, the following explanatory variables were computed.

Entry Mode: Greenfield – Dummy variable which takes the value 1 if entry is greenfield, 0 if entry is by acquisition.

Human Capital – Proportion of college graduates in the firm's work force.

Size – Logarithm of the number of employees.

Fully-Owned Subsidiaries – Dummy variable which takes the value 1 if foreign capital has a 100% stake in the company, 0 otherwise.

Majority Joint-Ventures – Dummy variable which takes the value 1 if the foreign capital's stake in the company is greater or equal to 50% but less than 100%, 0 otherwise.

Limited Liability – Dummy variable which takes the value 1 if the firm is a limited liability company, 0 otherwise.

Plants – Logarithm of the number of plants operated by the firm.

Diversification – 1 minus the Herfindahl index of firm specialization. The shares of the firm's activities in different industries were used to compute this index.

Concentration – Herfindahl index of industry concentration.

Scale Economies – Logarithm of the estimate of the Minimum Efficient Scale in the industry, computed as suggested by Lyons (1980).

Entry – Share of the employment in new firms in total employment in the industry.

Industry Growth – Growth rate of industry employment, computed as the difference in the logarithms of the employment in the industry in two consecutive years.

Foreign Presence – Share of industry employment in foreign owned firms.

With the exception of *Greenfield*, which refers to the conditions at the time of entry, all variables are time-varying. That is, they may assume different values over the lifespan of firms. In some cases, these variables reflect post-entry decisions, in others they simply reflect the evolution of the environment. As we observe firms on an annual basis, we are able to measure all of these variables annually. Our empirical model assumes the most recent observations of these variables to be the determinants of the exit decisions, that is, we specify exit between moment $t - 1$ and t as a function of the independent variables observed at moment $t - 1$.

Sample

Our sample includes 1033 foreign firms, which entered during the period 1983–89, which were identified using the procedures previously discussed. The sample is described in Table 1.

Table 1 shows that almost 60% of our entrants are greenfield entrants. Almost one half of the total number of entrants are fully-owned by foreign owners while, among the remaining, majority owned firms are slightly more than minority holdings. The vast majority of our foreign entrants are established as limited liability firms, only 8% operating under unlimited liability. On average, entrants employ 57 persons, of which around 10% hold a college degree (the employment figure cannot be read from the table, as the size variable is in logarithms). Most firms operate a single establishment at the time of entry, but a significant number (175) operate more than one, resulting in an average of 1.64 per firm (as with size, the figures reported in the table are in logarithms). The subsidiaries in our sample tend to be relatively specialized as well, and the diversification index is rather small. The statistics on the industry variables presented in Table 1 are less straightforward to interpret than the data on firm variables, as these averages refer to industries but come from a sample of firms. For completeness Table 1 also presents the correlations between the independent variables.

Patterns of Exit

Figure 2 plots the failure rates over the first years after entry, that is, the proportion of firms that have already exited by a given year. In the first plot, the failure rates for the whole set of foreign entrants is displayed. It is clear that the two types of exit display quite identical levels and a rather similar pattern over time. While exit by firm closure experiences an average yearly rate of 5.9% over the period, the corresponding rate for divestiture is 5.7%. The timing of the two types of exit seems to be different, however. Exit by divestiture is lower than exit by closure during the first years, but it increases at such a pace that it is greater than exit by divestiture in the fifth year.

The distinction between types of entrants produces more contrasting results. For example, while for greenfield entrants the probability of closure is always greater than that of divestment, the opposite result holds (at least from the second year onwards) for acquisition entrants. Although for greenfield entrants this result changes at the eighth year, there is no reason to make a strong case based on this single figure. One should keep in mind that our estimates for the

Table 1
Independent Variables at Entry ($N = 1033$)

	Average	S.D.	(1)	(2)	(3)	(4)	(5)	(6)	(7)	(8)	(9)	(10)	(11)	(12)
(1) Entry Mode: Greenfield	0.59	—	—											
(2) College	0.11	0.20	0.14	—										
(3) Size	2.61	1.61	-0.38	-0.27	—									
(4) Plants	0.20	0.53	-0.24	-0.11	0.46	—								
(5) Diversification	0.01	0.07	0.14	0.06	-0.25	-0.43	—							
(6) Limited Liability	0.92	—	0.02	-0.11	0.04	0.02	0.00	—						
(7) Majority Joint Ventures	0.32	—	0.01	-0.07	-0.02	-0.01	0.01	0.15	—					
(8) Fully Owned Subsidiaries	0.47	—	0.06	0.01	-0.03	-0.02	0.04	-0.24	-0.65	—				
(9) MES	3.51	1.04	-0.09	-0.16	0.44	-0.05	-0.02	0.00	0.01	-0.04	—			
(10) Concentration	0.05	0.12	-0.05	0.04	0.04	0.06	-0.05	-0.02	-0.01	0.00	-0.02	—		
(11) Entry	0.07	0.08	0.19	0.11	-0.11	-0.07	0.03	0.02	-0.02	0.05	-0.21	0.21	—	
(12) Industry Growth	0.06	0.18	0.11	0.05	0.01	-0.02	0.02	-0.03	-0.04	0.02	0.02	0.07	0.54	—
(13) Foreign Presence	0.15	0.17	-0.05	0.09	0.18	0.13	-0.10	0.03	-0.01	0.01	0.09	0.37	0.13	0.15

Figure 2
Failure Rates of Foreign Entrants, by Exit Mode

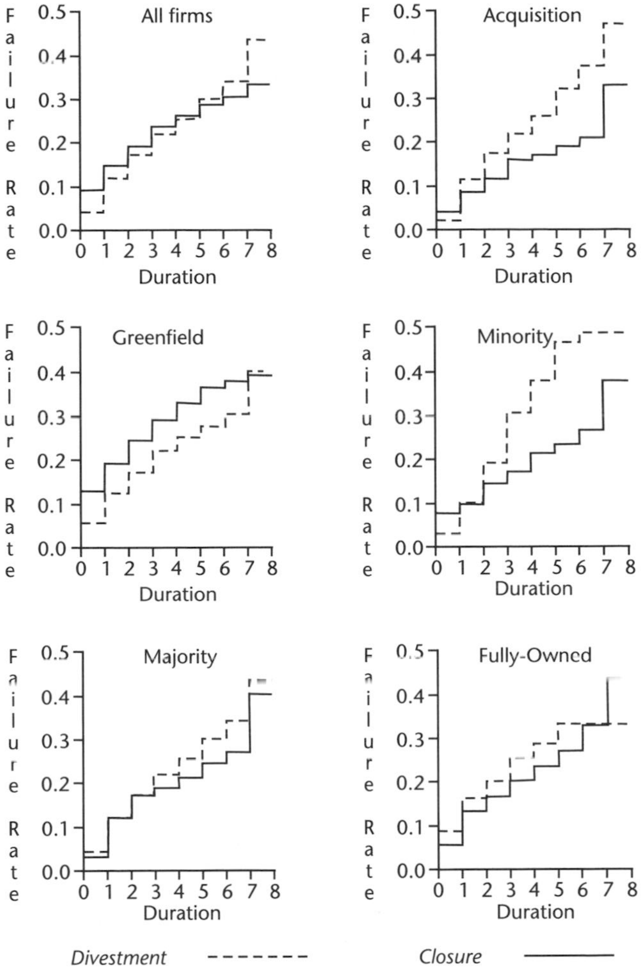

Divestment — — — — — —   Closure ————————

last year are produced using the survivors of a single cohort. Those correspond to a very small number of observations, and thus the estimates are much less precise. Moreover, comparing the two plots, one also sees that while acquisition entrants face a higher probability of divestment than do greenfield ones, these experience a higher probability of closure.

The split of the sample according to the type of ownership arrangement is also instructive. For majority and fully-owned subsidiaries, the probability of closure is always lower than that of exit by divestment (again this changes at the eighth year for fully-owned subsidiaries). However, the evolution of these probabilities over time displays a rather similar pattern. In contrast, during the first year, minority holdings are less likely to be divested than closed. However, in subsequent years their probability of being divested increases quite dramatically, and the evolution of the two probabilities is quite disparate. As a consequence, after the third year, these firms experience a much higher probability of divestment than majority and fully-owned subsidiaries do.

Results

Table 2 presents the results of the estimation of our empirical model for the two modes of foreign exit. For each exit mode the second column excludes those variables which were not statistically significant in the first column, thus constituting our preferred parsimonious specification.

Table 2
The Determinants of Exit by Divestment and Closure ($N = 3766$)

	Capital Divestiture		Firm Closure	
	(1)	(2)	(3)	(4)
Entry Mode: Greenfield	-0.151	-0.162	0.278	0.266
	(0.147)	(0.147)	(0.160)	(0.160)
Human Capital	-0.922	-0.919	-0.896	-0.908
	(0.505)	(0.503)	(0.384)	(0.383)
Size	-0.054	-0.059	-0.479	-0.487
	(0.061)	(0.061)	(0.058)	(0.063)
Plants	-0.322	-0.295	-0.437	0.072
	(0.183)	(0.170)	(0.233)	(0.215)
Diversification	-0.372		-0.266	
	(0.997)		(1.328)	
Limited Liability	0.918	0.916	0.135	-0.453
	(0.424)	(0.424)	(0.204)	(0.233)
Majority Joint Ventures	-0.513	-0.506	0.062	0.148
	(0.186)	(0.186)	(0.200)	(0.203)
Fully Owned Subsidiaries	-0.281	-0.283	-0.365	0.060
	(0.171)	(0.171)	(1.244)	(0.200)
Scale Economies	-0.051	-0.046	0.207	0.214
	(0.084)	(0.084)	(0.078)	(0.081)
Concentration	0.468		0.707	
	(0.633)		(0.545)	
Entry	0.172	0.169	2.773	3.122
	(1.560)	(1.570)	(0.928)	(0.893)
Industry Growth	0.167		0.108	
	(0.128)		(0.172)	
Foreign presence	-1.669	-1.601	-0.755	-0.588
	(0.517)	(0.518)	(0.469)	(0.462)
χ^2	99.234	97.337	145.773	143.892

Notes: Figures in parentheses are asymptotic standard errors. Annual time dummies and age dummies (not required in the table) were also included in all regressions.

The results indicate that the determinants of exit are different for the two destinations. Most variables attract opposite signs in the two equations or are significant in only one. One variable (*Human Capital*), however, is an unsurprising exception. The proportion of college graduates in the labor force exerts a sizeable negative effect upon the exit decision in both equations. This effect is significantly associated with lower failure rates for both types of exit, which

indicates that the extent of ownership advantages (broadly considered) determines the decision to leave the country.

On the contrary, the entry mode exerts an opposite effect on firm closure
and capital divestiture. Greenfield entrants are more likely than acquisitions
to be closed, but they are less likely to be sold, although the statistical significance
of this latter effect is only marginal. From the estimated coefficients associated
with *Greenfield* in Table 2, one can estimate that the conditional probability of
closure is 30% higher for greenfield entrants than for acquisition ones, while
the conditional probability of divestment is 15% lower. This discrete rate of
change in the probability of exit is simply calculated by $exp(\hat{\beta}) - 1$, where $(\hat{\beta})$
is the corresponding instantaneous rate displayed in Table 2. This confirms
our hypothesis that the acquisition of an ongoing business reflects the existence
of some business-specific advantage, which makes it less likely to shut down.
On the other hand, the fact that it has been acquired also signals that the business
is not owner specific to any great extent, which makes it more likely to be sold.

The ownership structure and internal organization seem to affect mostly the
likelihood of divestiture rather than closure. The coefficients of both *Majority
Joint-Venture* and *Fully-Owned Subsidiaries* are negative in the firm closure
equation, which indicates that these ownership arrangements experience a lower
probability of failure than does the omitted category, minority holdings. The
coefficient associated with *Majority Joint-Venture* in the capital divestiture
equation is, however, greater (in absolute values) than the one associated with
Fully-Owned Subsidiaries. This suggests that the probability of divestiture is
higher for fully owned firms than it is for majority holdings, which is contrary
to our expectations, but the difference is not statistically significant.

The legal form variables have the expected signs. In the firm closure equation,
the omitted category (unlimited liability) is the most likely type of firm to be
closed, the probability of being shut down varying inversely with the complexity
of the legal form. In the capital divestiture equation, the opposite result holds,
reflecting the greater difficulty inherent in selling an unlimited liability business.

Firm size is clearly significant in the closure, but not in the divestiture
equation. This indicates that it is not the amount of money invested that deters
divestment by foreign firms; rather, the size of the firm seems to summarize a
number of relevant characteristics that affect their ability to compete and
survive.

The last comment on the effects of firm variables goes to the variables reflecting internal organization. Firms with a larger number of plants are less likely
to be sold, but after controlling for the number of plants, the coefficient
associated with firm's diversification is not significant.

With respect to industry variables, the overall impression is that industry
structure matters for the survival of firms, but not for capital divestiture. However, concentration does not capture the industry effect. Rather, the minimum
efficient scale and the entry rate in the industry are the two variables which come
out to be important. Foreign presence in the industry is the only variable that
exerts a similar effect on the two modes of foreign capital exit. Foreign firms
are more likely to survive and to remain foreign owned in those industries which

were already more heavily populated by foreign firms. This is not surprising, since foreign firm presence signals the existence of location conditions that attract foreign ownership.

A final comment goes to the evolution of the probabilities of exit over time. As an outcome of our estimation procedures, we obtain estimates of the baseline hazard parameters, which measure the probability of closure/divestiture at each moment. Figure 3 depicts such estimates for a firm with average character- istics and compares them with the estimates obtained without controlling for the characteristics of firms. For computing the estimates reported here, we have used our preferred specifications in columns (2) and (4) of Table 2. For making both sets of estimates comparable, in both cases the estimates are re- ported as if the overall conditions of the economy were kept constant. That is, in both cases the estimates are obtained when one particular annual dummy is set to one and the others to zero. The reported estimates are for the case where the 1987 dummy is set to one.

Two substantive comments are in line here. First, as a consequence of the flexibility in our estimation procedure, our estimated baseline hazard rates conform quite closely to the observed pattern (that is, the estimates without covariates). Second, the evolution of baseline hazard rates appears to be very different for the two types of exit. While the parameters of the closure equation display a decreasing pattern over time, reflecting the learning process that follows entry, the parameters of the capital divestiture are remarkably constant, except at the second year, when it peaks.

In reading Figure 3, we should remember that the hazard rate in the last year is estimated with a very small number of observations and being, therefore, estimated with much less precision. Accordingly, we should not put much em- phasis on the fact that the hazard rate for the divestment in this year is quite out of line with the previous ones. However, despite these apparently divergent patterns of exit over time, a comparison of the estimated baselines against the hypothesis of a constant baseline over the period, does not allow one to reject the null in any of the equations.

Figure 3
Hazard Functions

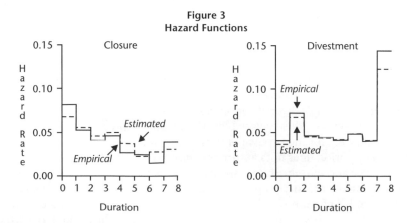

Conclusion

This work contributes to the literature on the survival of foreign owned firms by analyzing two alternative forms of exit by foreign entrants. The analysis distinguishes between the closure of foreign owned businesses and foreign capital divestiture, interpreted here as the end of the match between firms and foreign owners. The study shows that the decisions to shutdown and to divest are governed by different factors.

We find that the entry mode and the extent of the firm's liability exert opposite effects upon the two modes of exit. Being a greenfield entry increases the likelihood of closure while reducing that of divestiture. Limited liability firms are more likely to divest, but less likely to shutdown than unlimited liability ones. Furthermore, ownership arrangements and organizational structure affect the likelihood of capital divestment, but have little effect on the survival of firms. Only the human capital in the firm and the previous presence of foreign firms exert a similar effect upon both modes of exit. Moreover, while the probability of closure seems to decline with experience, the probability of divestment is roughly constant over time.

Our results provide important insights for managers considering entry into a foreign market, by showing to what extent the decisions taken during the entry and post-entry periods may affect the likelihood of exiting by one and the other exit modes. In attempting to learn from our study, however, managers should be careful in drawing prescriptive measures. One should keep in mind that, in many circumstances, exit is the best decision, if that option is available. Actions that create that option may thus be valuable, especially if the firm has little experience with international operations in general, or with that country in particular. In our context, this suggests that firms with little previous experience should avoid making highly specific investments, as this may decrease the chances of finding a suitable buyer, enabling them to leave the country.

The results of our study can also be of interest from an economic policy perspective. Some countries have policies of attracting foreign direct investment. Such policies are pursued in the belief that foreign investment creates spillovers to the rest of the economy and, therefore, will be the more valuable the longer the foreign firm remains in the country. Our study shows that greenfield investments are likely to have a longer lasting presence in the host country than investments by acquisition of ongoing concerns, which may lead policy makers to handle the two types of investment differently.

For scholars interested in the survival of foreign owned firms, our work creates new challenges. Most of the literature on survival in foreign countries implicitly identifies exit with the failure of the foreign subsidiary. However, exit may be due to reasons other than failure. In the finance literature, the acquisition of companies followed by its reorganization and subsequent sell-off has been clearly identified as a means of making a profit (Kaplan and Weisbach 1989). In the context of international business, Tsetekos and Gombola (1992) and Ghertman (1988) noted that divestment of foreign subsidiaries does not necessarily indicate problems in the subsidiary, nor in the parent company. Rather, it may be due to strategic reorientation of the parent company and to the perception that the subsidiary no longer fits with the parent. All of these reasons suggest that the two modes of exit may be associated with different pre-exit performances of the exitors.

Measuring the performance of subsidiaries of foreign companies is tricky, not least because of the problems associated with transfer pricing. However, evaluating the extent to which the performance of these two types of exitors differs in the pre-exit period is crucial for knowing the magnitude of the costs involved in the trade-off between the adequacy of the productive facilities to the foreign firm and the specificity of capital, which leads to the subsequent increased difficulty in exiting from the country. Our understanding of the entry and post-entry performance in foreign countries would benefit greatly from such knowledge.

Acknowledgements

We are grateful to Conference audiences in Barcelona (SMS), Lisbon (SPIE) and Oporto (IFTA), two reviewers, and the Associate Editor Will Mitchell for helpful comments and to Lucena Vieira for computational assistance. The usual disclaimer applies.

References

Alzona, G., L. Rondi and G. Vitali (1993). 'New forms of international involvement, competition, and competitiveness: The case of Italy'. In K. Hughes (ed.), *European Competitiveness*. Cambridge University Press, Cambridge, U.K. pp. 29–59.

Audretsch, D. and T. Mahmood (1994). 'The rate of hazard confronting new firms and plants in U.S. manufacturing', *Review of Industrial Organization*, **9**, pp. 41–56.

Bane, W. and F.-F. Neubauer (1981). 'Diversification and the failure of new foreign activities', *Strategic Management Journal*, **2**(3), pp. 219–233.

Blomstrom, M and M. Zejan (1989). 'Why do multinational firms seek out joint ventures', NBER Discussion Paper no. 2987.

Bogner, W., H. Thomas and J. McGee (1996). 'A longitudinal study of the competitive positions and entry paths of European firms in the U.S. pharmaceutical market', *Strategic Management Journal*, **17**(2), pp. 85–107.

Brüdel, J., P. Preisendörfer and R. Ziegler (1992). 'Survival chances of newly founded organizations', *American Sociological Review*, **57**, pp. 227–242.

Burgelman, R. (1994). 'Fading memories: A process theory of strategic business exit in dynamic environments', *Administrative Science Quarterly*, **39**, pp. 24–56.

Cable, J. and J. Schwalbach (1991). 'International comparisons of entry and exit'. In P. Geroski and J. Schwalbach, *Entry and Market Contestability: An International Comparison*. Basil Blackwell, Oxford, pp. 257–281.

Cabral, L. (1995). 'Sunk costs, firm size and firm growth', *Journal of Industrial Economics*, **43**, pp. 161–172.

Caves, R. (1996). *Multinational Enterprise and Economic Analysis* (2nd edn.). Cambridge University Press, Cambridge, U.K.

Chang, S. (1996) 'An evolutionary perspective on diversification and corporate restructuring: Entry, exit and economic performance during 1981–89', *Strategic Management Journal*, **17**(8), pp. 587–611.

Cox, D. R. (1972). 'Regression models and life tables (with discussion)', *Journal of the Royal Statistical Society, series B*, **34**, pp. 187–220.

Dixit, A. and R. Pindyck (1994). *Investment Under Uncertainty*. Princeton University Press, Princeton, NJ.

Dunne, T., M. Roberts and L. Samuelson (1988). 'Patterns of firm entry and exit in U.S. manufacturing industries', *Rand Journal of Economics*, **19**, pp. 495–515.

Dunne, T., M. Roberts and L. Samuelson (1989). 'The growth and failure of U.S. manufacturing plants', *Quarterly Journal of Economics*, **104**, pp. 671–698.

Dunning, J. (1993). *Multinational Enterprises and the Global Economy*. Addison-Wesley, New York.

Eaton, B. and R. Lipsey (1980). 'Entry barriers are exit barriers: The durability of capital as a barrier to entry', *Bell Journal of Economics*, **11**, pp. 721–729.

Evans, D. and B. Jovanovic, (1989) 'An estimated model of entrepreneurial choice under liquidity constraints', *Journal of Political Economy*, **97**, pp. 808–827.

Gatignon, H. and E. Anderson (1988). 'The multinational corporation's degree of control over foreign subsidiaries: An empirical test of a transaction cost explanation', *Journal of Law, Economics and Organization*, **4**, pp. 305–336.

Ghertman, M. (1988). 'Foreign subsidiary and parents' roles during strategic investment and divestment decisions', *Journal of International Business Studies*, Spring, pp. 47–67.

Hannan, M. and G. Carroll (1992). *Dynamics of Organizational Populations*. Oxford University Press, Oxford, U.K.

Harhoff, D., K., Stahl and M. Woywode (1996). 'Legal form, growth and exit of West German firms', CEPR Discussion Paper n. 1401.

Hennart, J.-F. (1991). "The transaction costs theory of joint ventures: An empirical study of Japanese subsidiaries in the United States', *Management Science*, **37**, pp. 483–497.

Jovanovic, B. (1982). 'Selection and evolution of industry', *Econometrica*, **50**, pp. 649–670.

Kalbfleisch, J. and R. Prentice (1980). *The Statistical Analysis of Failure Data*. Wiley, New York.

Kaplan, S. and M. Weisbach (1989). 'The success of acquisitions: Evidence from divestitures', *Journal of Finance*, **47**, pp. 107–138.

Kogut, B. (1989). 'The stability of joint ventures: Reciprocity and competitive rivalry', *Journal of Industrial Economics*, **38**, pp. 183–198.

Li, J. (1995). 'Foreign entry and survival: Effects of strategic choices on performance in international markets', *Strategic Management Journal*, 16(5), pp, 333–351.

Lyons, B. (1980). 'A new measure of minimum efficient plant size in U.K. manufacturing industry', *Economica*, **17**, pp. 19–34.

Mata, J. and P. Portugal (1994). 'Life duration of new firms', *Journal of Industrial Economics*, **42**, pp. 227–246.

Mata, J., P. Portugal and P. Guimarães (1995). "The survival of new plants: Entry conditions and post-entry evolution', *International Journal of Industrial Organization*, **13**, pp. 459–482.

Mitchell, W. (1994). 'The dynamics of evolving markets: The effects of business sales and age on dissolutions and divestitures', *Administrative Science Quarterly*, **39**, pp. 575–602.

Mitchell, W., J. Shaver and B. Yeung (1994). 'Foreign entrant survival and foreign market share: Canadian companies' experience in United States medical sector markets', *Strategic Management Journal*, **15**(7), pp. 555–567.

Romanelli, E. (1989). 'Environments and strategies at start-up: Effects on early survival', *Administrative Science Quarterly*, **34**, pp. 369–387.

Schary, M. (1991). 'The probability of exit', *Rand Journal of Economics*, **22**, pp. 339–353.

Schmalensee, R. (1989). 'Inter-industry studies of structure and performance'. In R. Schmalensee and R. Willig (eds.), *Handbook of Industrial Organization*. North-Holland, Amsterdam, pp. 951–1010.

Shapiro, D. (1983). 'Entry, exit and the theory of multinational corporation'. In C. Kindleberger and D. Audretsch (eds.), *The Multinational Corporation in the 1980s*. MIT Press, Cambridge, MA, pp. 103–122.

Shaver, J. M. (1998). 'Accounting for endogeneity when assessing strategy performance: Does entry mode choice affect survival', *Management Science*, **44**, pp. 571–585.

Shaver, J., W. Mitchell and B. Yeung (1997). 'The effect of own-firm and other-firm experience on foreign entrant survival in the United States, 1987–92', *Strategic Management Journal*, **18**(10), pp. 811–824.

Tsetekos, G. and M. Gombola (1992). 'Foreign and domestic divestments: Evidence on valuation effects of plant closings', *Journal of International Business Studies*, 2nd Quarter, pp. 203–223.

Wernerfelt, B. (1984). 'A resource-based view of the firm', *Strategic Management Journal*, **5**(2), pp. 171–180.

Woodcock, C., P. Beamish and S. Makimo (1994). 'Ownership-based entry strategies and international performance', *Journal of International Business Studies*, 2nd Quarter, pp. 253–273.

Yamawaki, H. (1997). 'Exit of Japanese multinationals in U.S. and European manufacturing industries'. In P. Buckley, and J.-L. Mucchielli (eds.), *Multinational Firms and International Relocation*. Edward Elgar, Cheltenham, pp. 220–237.

Yip, G. (1982). *Barriers To Entry: A Corporate-Strategy Perspective*. Lexington Books, Lexington, MA.

Zejan, M. (1990). 'New ventures or acquisitions. The choice of Swedish multinational enterprises', *Journal of Industrial Economics*, **38**, pp. 349–355.

39

Do Exits Proxy a Liability of Foreignness? The Case of Japanese Exits from the US

Jean-François Hennart, Thomas Roehl and Ming Zeng

1. Introduction

One of the central tenets of the theory of the multinational enterprise (MNE) is that MNEs are at a disadvantage compared to native firms when they enter foreign markets (Hymer, 1960; Hennart, 1982), a disadvantage that has been subsequently called the "liability of foreignness" (Zaheer and Mosakowski, 1997). Hymer (1960, p. 34) gives three main reasons for such a liability: (1) foreign firms have less information than local firms on how to do business in a foreign country, (2) foreign firms are exposed to discrimination by governments, consumers and suppliers and (3) foreign firms are exposed to foreign exchange risk.

The liability of foreignness plays a central role in the theory of the MNE because it explains why only a select set of international interactions are handled through foreign direct investment. The theory argues that coordination within MNEs occurs when it yields greater rents than coordination through prices and when these rents are sufficient to offset the additional costs of operating abroad (the liability of foreignness). Hence, the level of the costs caused by the liability of foreignness determines in part whether a given international interdependence will be organized by an MNE, by the market, or not at all (Hennart, 1982). Yet, despite its theoretical importance, there has been only limited study of this concept (Mezias, 2002; Pennings et al., 1994; Zaheer and Mosakowski, 1997). Do foreign firms systematically incur a liability of foreignness when they enter foreign markets? What are the main causes of this liability? How do we measure it?

In this paper, we argue that foreign firms do face a liability of foreignness, but that the way scholars have tested for its existence, i.e., by looking at exit rates, has clear limitations. As a result, the empirical evidence on the existence

Source: *Journal of International Management*, Vol. 8, No. 3, 2002, pp. 241–264.

and impact of the liability of foreignness has been mixed. Inferring the existence of a liability of foreignness from exits is fraught with difficulties, as exit is a complex and ambiguous phenomenon. That point is made first theoretically by surveying the literature on exits and then empirically by analyzing the reasons why 32 Japanese manufacturing affiliates exited from the US. We show directly how the liability of foreignness led to the exit of some Japanese affiliates from that country. However, our study also highlights the danger of inferring the presence of such a liability from exits, as there were many other reasons for exits.

2. The Liability of Foreignness

The key argument of the liability of foreignness is that foreign firms wanting to do business in a foreign country face additional costs compared to their local competitors. Foreigners must collect information on local conditions that come to a large extent free to local firms. They may also be subject to discrimination by host-country governments, suppliers and consumers.[1] They also face foreign exchange risks that are not faced by their purely local counterparts.

While the above seems intuitively true, what is its importance in practice? Do firms doing business abroad experience greater difficulties than firms operating at home? Do these difficulties translate into lower profitability for foreign affiliates and do they lead to their exit? As we will see, the empirical evidence on this point is mixed.

With the exception of Mezias (2002) who showed that foreign firms had more US labor lawsuits judgments than US-owned firms, the few studies that have tried to answer these questions have tested for the existence of a liability of foreignness facing foreign investors by looking at the survival rates of their foreign affiliates. The argument is that coping with a liability of foreignness will depress profits and that this in turn will cause affiliates to exit. Hence, one way to establish that there is a liability of foreignness is to show that foreign firms have a lower survival rate than their domestic counterparts. As we will show below, for this argument to hold, a number of conditions must be present. First, exits must be correlated with poor profitability. If firms also exit when they are profitable, then exits are a poor proxy for poor performance. Second, there must be a tight link between liability of foreignness and exits. If exits are caused by other factors, then we cannot infer the presence of a liability of foreignness from exits. For example, if a foreign affiliate closes not because it experiences discrimination from local suppliers, customers or governments but because its industry is in a slump, then one should not assign its exit to a liability of foreignness.

2.1. Differences in Exit Rates between Domestic and Foreign Firms

Zaheer and Mosakowski's (1997) pioneering article illustrates the difficulties that arise when using exits to measure the liability of foreignness. The two authors looked at the survival of market-making foreign exchange trading rooms.

They hypothesized that such trading rooms established outside the country of the parent (foreign trading rooms) would face a liability of foreignness and would exhibit lower survival than those established in the country of the parent (local trading rooms). They therefore ascertained whether a particular trading room was listed as a market-making trading room in a particular place and considered that it had exited if it was not listed for 2 consecutive years. Implicit in their analysis is that delisting occurs when the trading room has profitability problems and that these problems are caused by a liability of foreignness. As expected, they find that after 20 years the survival rate of foreign rooms is (statistically) significantly lower than that of local rooms (both are around 40% of the initial population). They conclude therefore as to the presence of a liability of foreignness.

As we will see below, delistings (i.e., exits) do not necessarily result from poor profitability. According to the authors, there are low barriers to entry and exit to being a market-maker.[2] To be listed as such only requires a commitment to always being ready to buy and sell the same currency. It is therefore unclear how (temporarily) withdrawing from being a market-maker in a given location means failure, as, given the low transportation and communication costs in the market for foreign exchange, a firm that exits can probably serve the market from another location. MNEs, being present in many markets, may be indifferent as to where they buy and sell foreign exchange. Exits may also result from strategic change. A firm may have chosen to no longer be a market-maker in a particular location because it has decided to concentrate on a different set of currencies. Because in this industry both the direct and opportunity costs of exit are low, exit may take place for these and possibly other reasons unrelated to poor profitability.

Another study that compared the exit rate of domestic versus foreign firms is that by Mata and Portugal (2002). The authors analyzed the survival patterns of two samples of domestic and foreign-owned units operating in Portugal. After controlling for a number of firm and industry characteristics, such as technological intensity, unit size and legal form at entry, parent diversification and growth rate and concentration ratio of the industry entered by the unit, they did not find any differences in gross exit rates between foreign and domestic units.

Pennings et al.'s (1994) research setup is slightly different, because they compared the survival of the domestic and international subsidiaries of a set of Dutch firms. They found that subsidiaries established in the Netherlands had lower exit rates than those established overseas, but they looked at gross exits (i.e., they did not distinguish by form of exit, that is, whether exits took the form of sell-offs or liquidation of the affiliate) and they did not control for economic conditions in the target markets. Worse conditions abroad (impacting both native and foreign firms) may have accounted for the difference.

2.2. Difference in Exit Rates between Foreign Affiliates

As we have seen, one of the purported causes of a liability of foreignness is the foreign investor's lack of knowledge of the local economy. That lack of knowledge should vary with the cultural distance between the home country of the parent and the foreign country where its affiliate is doing business (Johanson and Vahlne, 1977). Hence, another way of testing for the presence of a liability of foreignness is to compare exit rates of foreign affiliates located in countries that are at varying cultural distance from the investor's home country.

This approach has been used in a number of studies, with mixed results. Barkema et al. (1996) looked at the gross exit rates of 225 foreign affiliates of Dutch firms. They found that affiliates located in culturally farthest countries were more likely to exit.[3] Park and Park (2000) analyzed the gross exit rates of 2090 foreign affiliates of Korean firms. After controlling for a variety of factors that affect exits, such as mode of entry, economic conditions in the target market and parent characteristics, affiliates in culturally distant countries did not have statistically greater gross exit rates than those in culturally closer markets. Larimo (2000) studied the gross exit rates of more than 2600 foreign affiliates of Danish, Finnish, Norwegian and Swedish firms in over 50 countries. After controlling for the usual variables, he found that being located in a culturally distant country actually reduced the probability of gross exit.

A third way to test for the presence of a liability of foreignness is to look at the survival *in a given country* of affiliates of parents based in countries that are situated at varying cultural distance from that country. If there is a liability of foreignness, then that liability should be greater for the affiliates of parents based in countries that are culturally farthest from the target country. Li (1995) looked at the gross exit rate of the US affiliates of foreign pharmaceutical and computer firms. He hypothesized that, everything else constant, Japanese affiliates, whose parents are at a high cultural distance from the US, should experience higher gross exit rates than the other foreign affiliates in his sample. After controlling for various factors, he found that gross exit rates for Japanese firms were not statistically higher than those for the other firms in his sample.

Hennart et al. (1997) looked at exits by liquidation and sale of a sample of North Europeans and Japanese affiliates in the US. They hypothesized that Japanese affiliates, whose parents are at a greater cultural distance from the US than their North European counterparts, should experience higher gross exit rates. After carefully controlling for a large number of factors that affect exits, they found no statistical difference between exit rates of Japanese and North European affiliates, whether exits took the form of sell-offs or of liquidations.

McCloughan and Stone (1998) analyzed a sample of foreign affiliates in Northern England. Again, the nationality of the parent had no impact on gross exit rates, even when controlling for industry and mode of entry.

A conclusion that can be drawn from this survey is that the evidence for the presence of a liability of foreignness that would seriously handicap foreign investors is mixed. The reason, as we will now see by surveying the literature on exits, is that gross exit rates are a rather noisy index of poor performance and that the mixed evidence on the liability of foreignness is due to improper use of exits as an indicator for this key concept.

3. The Literature on Exits of Business Units

The literature on exits can be partitioned into two, that on exits of domestic units and that on exits of foreign affiliates.

3.1. Exits of Domestic Units

Duhaime and Grant (1984) asked the managers of 40 large American firms why they divested their affiliates. Sixteen percent of the 59 divested affiliates had, according to their parents, acceptable profitability. The same question was put by Hamilton and Chow (1993) to the CEOs of New Zealand's 98 largest companies that had sold or liquidated 208 of their units (three-fourths of them were sell-offs). They were asked to rank (from 1 = *unimportant* to 5 = *very important*) the reasons why they had closed their domestic affiliates. "Low return of units" was ranked at 4.2, but need to "focus on core activities" and to "meet corporate liquidity requirements" were not far behind with 3.8. Kaplan and Weisbach's (1992) study of the characteristics of units sold off by US firms found that poor profitability was cited for only 22% of the affiliates, while accounting measures showed that only half of the divested units were making losses when divested. The findings of these three studies were basically consistent in suggesting that not all divestments were failures. While divested affiliates were typically poorly performing, a significant number were in fact profitable. Profitable affiliates were divested because of factors affecting the parents, principally worsening financial situation and changes in strategy (accounting for 31% and 42%, respectively, for Kaplan and Weisbach's sell-offs). Affiliates that were less dependent on the rest of the firm (Duhaime and Grant, 1984) and less central to its business (Hamilton and Chow, 1993) were more likely to be let go.

Besides these survey-type studies, two recent econometric analyses have looked at the determinants of domestic exits. Sharma and Kesner (1996) analyzed the factors that affect the survival of diversifying entries made by American Fortune 500 firms. They found that industry factors (selling and advertising intensity of the entered industry, scale of entry and interaction of scale and seller concentration) tended to have a stronger effect on survival than firm-level variables (firm size and liquidity) or the relatedness between the unit and the parent. They noted the presence of a large number of small-scale entries that were quickly reversed within a few years. Chang (1996) looked at the determinants of exit from a given line of business for all publicly traded manufacturing firms in the US. He found that the most important variable explaining exit was the scale of entry, with small stakes more likely to be let go. Relative performance and dissimilarity of the affiliate's business from the parent were additional factors. Chang noted that the firms in his sample were continuously changing their product configurations by divesting affiliates.

3.2. Exits of Foreign Affiliates

As discussed above, scholars have used two strategies to study exits of foreign affiliates. They have either concentrated on the exits of the foreign affiliates of parents based in a given country (or group of countries) or looked at the exits of foreign firms investing in a given host country. Gomes-Casseres (1987), Barkema et al. (1997), Park and Park (2000) and Larimo (2000) are examples of the first strategy, while Li (1995), Mata and Portugal (1998), Hennart et al. (1998), Hennart et al. (1997) and McCloughan and Stone (1998) have taken the second approach.

3.3. Exits of All Affiliates Based in One Country

Gomes-Casseres was one of the first to look at exits of foreign affiliates. He found that most of them did not take the form of liquidations/bankruptcies but of sell-offs (the unit was sold to another firm). Sell-offs made up more than three-fourths of the 610 exits of affiliates of American MNEs that took place between 1900 and 1975. Gomes-Casseres argued that the predominance of sell-offs among exits suggested caution when interpreting them as failure.

Larimo (2000) found that exits of the foreign affiliates of Nordic MNEs were affected by characteristics of the affiliate, by those of the parent and by those of the environment. Affiliates that had higher exit rates were those (1) which were joint ventured (as opposed to wholly owned), (2) which manufactured products not manufactured by their parents, (3) which were owned by inexperienced parents (for which this was their first investment in that country), (4) which belonged to diversified parents and (5) which were operating in slow-growing countries.

Park and Park's (2000) results basically support those of Larimo. Like him, they found that affiliates, which were joint ventured and which manufactured a product different from those of their parents, were more likely to exit. However, they found that this was also true for affiliates created through acquisitions and for those of small parents. Like Larimo, they found that the probability of exit was lower in fast-growing markets.

3.4. Exits of Affiliates Located in a Given Country

A second way to study the determinants of exits is to compare the survival of affiliates of various parents in a single foreign host country. McCloughan and Stone (1998) focused on the gross exits of foreign-owned subsidiaries in Northern England. Their results broadly support those reported above, with acquired affiliates having higher exit rates and some industry dummies significant.

Li's (1995) findings on the determinants of the gross exits of the US affiliates of foreign computer and pharmaceutical firms are similar to those of Larimo and Park and Park. Like them, he found that exit rates were affected by characteristics of the affiliate (mode of entry, size at entry and diversification), of the parent (affiliates of inexperienced parents had higher exit rates) and of the environment (lower exit rates in fast-growing US markets). Li concluded his article by recommending that, given the differences in motivation between sell-offs and liquidations, these two forms of exit should be separately analyzed in the future.

Following Li's recommendation, both Mata and Portugal (1998) and Hennart et al. (1998) separated exits into their two main components, liquidations/ bankruptcies and sell-offs. Hennart et al. (1998) used event history analysis to identify the reasons why 288 Japanese affiliates established in the US in 1980 had exited by 1991. They argued that the two types of exit, sell-offs and liquidations, were likely to have different motivations. An affiliate that is liquidated or goes bankrupt ceases to exist as an entity. Its assets are sold piecemeal. In contrast, an affiliate that is sold by its parent continues to exist, but under different owner-ship. Because the affiliate continues to operate, one would think that its perform-ance was good enough to attract interest from another firm. Hence, while one would expect affiliates that are liquidated or go bankrupt to have had low profitability, a higher proportion of those that are sold should be profitable. As predicted, Hennart et al. (1998) found that their models of exits had a better fit when liquidations and sell-offs were analyzed separately. Paradoxically, the variables used to explain gross exits did a better job explaining sell-offs than liquidations. In other words, their results show that the reasons generally given in the literature for gross exits apply instead to sell-offs. Hennart et al. found sell-offs to be explained by characteristics of the affiliate (joint ventures, acquisitions and affiliates manufacturing a product not manufactured by their parents were more likely to be sold but not liquidated). Large parents were also more likely to sell their US affiliates (but not to liquidate them). A high rate of growth of demand in the industry entered reduced the chances that the affiliate would be sold or liquidated. Similar results were found in Hennart et al. (1997) for a sample of Japanese and North European affiliates in the US.

Mata and Portugal (2000), who analyzed exits of 1033 foreign affiliates that entered Portugal between 1983 and 1989, also found that exits through liquid-ations and those through sell-offs had separate determinants. Minority joint ven-tures, for example, had a higher probability of being sold but not liquidated. The same was true for affiliates that had been established through acquisitions. Large affiliates were less likely to be liquidated (but this had no impact on sell-offs).

3.5. What Can We Conclude from this Literature?

As we have seen, the liability of foreignness has often been tested by looking at exit rates. Implicit is the assumption that the liability of foreignness causes poor profitability and that poor profitability leads to exits.

The literature on exits we have just reviewed paints a more complex picture. It shows that the view that exits are caused by poor profitability is an oversimpli-fication. This for a number of reasons. First, surveys of why firms divest show that a significant number of exits are undertaken for strategic reasons and in-volve profitable units (Duhaime and Grant, 1984; Hamilton and Chow, 1993; Kaplan and Weisbach, 1992). Exits result from a continuous process by which firms readjust their product portfolio and close down small stakes taken as options (Chang, 1996; Sharma and Kesner, 1996). The fact that most exits take the form of sales, as opposed to liquidations, seem to suggest that the affiliates that are let go can be profitably operated by other firms (Gomes-Casseres, 1987; Hennart et al., 1998; Mata and Portugal, 2000). The literature also shows that the probability of exits depends on barriers to exit (Benito, 1997). Affiliates that are relatively easy to hive off tend to have higher exit rates. Hence, small affiliates and those whose products differ from those of their parents have a higher prob-ability of exiting (Chang, 1996). Likewise, acquired and joint-ventured foreign affiliates have a higher probability of exit than greenfield and wholly owned ones because they are easier to sell (Hennart et al., 1998; Park and Park, 2000). Acquired affiliates have already been carved off once, hence can be severed again. By contrast, plants which are set up de novo by their parents (greenfield entries) are more customized to their present owner. Likewise, joint ventures have low exit costs. Their contracts sometimes contain clauses that oblige one partner to buy the other partner's stake, thus facilitating exit through sale (Nanda and Williamson, 1995). Partners in joint ventures have also good knowledge and an existing interest in the business and hence provide ready buyers. As expected, the higher probability of exit of acquired and joint-ventured affiliates is only found for exit through sale but not for exit through liquidation (Hennart et al., 1998). This suggests that a significant number of sell-offs result from strategic realignment or the winding down of options. This view is confirmed by the fact that international sell-offs and liquidations have different determinants (Mata and Portugal, 2000; Hennart et al., 1998).

What this suggests is that the correspondence between exits and poor performance is likely to be clouded by the sale of entries made to "test the water" and by those which fall victims to the parent's strategic changes. This is especially likely when barriers to exit are low.

The literature also shows that the causes for exit are varied and that they must be sought at three levels – the affiliate, the parent and the environment. Hence, besides being caused by a liability of foreignness, exits depend on the economic and political conditions facing the affiliate and the parent and on parent strategies. When testing for the presence of a liability of foreignness, it is therefore important to separate the additional risk caused by that liability from the baseline risk facing all units, foreign as well as domestic. One way to deal with this is by using matched samples of foreign and domestic firms or by carefully controlling for all these factors. A difficulty will remain, however, if there are some systematic differences between foreign and domestic firms in the strength of the causal link between poor profitability and exit.

One can think of two such differences. The first one is that multinational firms have often the additional option of exiting a given market and serving it from another affiliate in a different country. A second difference is that the foreign affiliate has an overseas corporate parent and that, in contrast to domestic units, exits of foreign affiliates may be affected by events affecting the parent and hence may have little to do with a liability of foreignness facing the affiliate. These two differences mean that a larger proportion of exits of foreign-owned than of domestic units may be caused by other factors than poor profitability.

Are those caveats overdone? Can they be safely dismissed as statistical noise or should they be seen as significant concerns that might have invalidated most empirical tests of the liability of foreignness? The answer to this question requires a careful look at the circumstances and causes of exits. Because we need to bring to light not only the variety of causes that lead to exit but also their relative importance, we have chosen a strategy that is midway between reporting one or two detailed case studies on one hand and doing a large sample statistical study on the other. A few detailed case studies would provide us with rich insights as to the causes of exits but would not tell us their relative importance. On the other hand, it is difficult for researchers using large samples to obtain detailed data on the causes of exit. Hence, we propose to look in detail at a limited number of cases of exit and to find out their causes.

4. Case Studies of Japanese Exits

Our goal is to ascertain the extent to which exits of foreign affiliates are caused by a liability of foreignness. An ideal population for that purpose is one where the investor is relatively inexperienced in managing in a foreign country that is culturally distant from his home base and one in which the costs of exit are significant. We chose therefore to look at the exits (to 1998) of the cohort of all Japanese manufacturing affiliates active in the US in 1980. There are great differences in culture between Japan and the US. Prior to the 1980s, Japanese firms had a very limited knowledge of the US. Manufacturing requires substantial investments (usually greater than those in sales or services) and the US is such an important market for Japan that exit costs are significant. We cross listed many separate sources and are confident that we are close to the total population of all Japanese-owned manufacturing plants that were operating in the US in 1980. Our population is characteristic of the early phase of Japanese investment in the US (Wilkins, 1990), with a higher proportion of trading company investments and of ventures in food and metals than in subsequent Japanese investment in the US.

Our unit of observation is the manufacturing plant. An ownership link between a Japanese firm and a US affiliate counts as one observation. Hence, there are, for example, 10 observations in our database for the two plants (each owned by five parents) of Alaska Lumber and Pulp (ALP).

There were 411 ownership links between Japanese firms and their US manufacturing subsidiaries in 1980. We endeavored to find out for each of these links whether it had survived to the end of 1998 or whether it had exited. We count as exits (1) the liquidation of the affiliate, (2) the full sale of the parent's stake in the affiliate to another firm, American, Japanese or third country and (3) the cessation of manufacturing (without closing the affiliate). In contrast to much of the work on exits that infers exits from not being on a list of affiliates, we positively verified all exits (through secondary sources and telephone interviews) and the form they took.

How many of these links were surviving at the end of 1998? We have data on 392 of our 411 links (95% of our population). About 57% (or 225 of the 392 links for which we have information) was still in existence in 1998, while 167 links had been dissolved. In 7 cases (1.7% of 392), the affiliates were still in business but had ceased manufacturing. In 55 cases (14% of 392), the affiliates had been closed or liquidated. In 105 cases (27% of 392), the affiliates had been sold. Of these 105 cases, 62 had been sold to their joint venture partners and 43 to third parties. As in the case of US firms, sell-offs made up the majority of the exits (63%) and the largest part was to joint venture partners.

We also tried to ascertain why these 167 ownership stakes came to an end. This proved to be remarkably difficult. Firm memory seems to be highly selective, with exits more easily forgotten than entries. Annual reports are short on the former but long on the latter. We used secondary sources such as books, press articles, company Web sites and interviews with industry observers and existing or former employees of the affiliate, of its partner(s) or of its parents. From these 167 ownership links that were dissolved, there were 83 (or about half of the dissolved links) for which we could reconstruct a reasonably good story, thus giving us a representative sample of the overall population of exits.[4] Because some exits involved multiple plants and Japanese owners, these 83 links correspond to 32 affiliate exits. Table 1 provides summary data on these affiliates, their parents and their reasons for exit. Fourteen were greenfield entries (seven wholly owned by Japanese firms, six joint ventures between Japanese and US firms and one joint venture between Japanese firms). Eighteen entries were acquisitions of US firms (8 full and 10 partial). Fifteen affiliates were liquidated and 17 were sold. Appendix A gives a short history of each of the 32 cases.

What do these 32 exits show? We can make a first distinction between exits due to poor profitability (whether caused by the liability of foreignness or not) and those for which poor profitability did not seem to have been involved. Twenty-seven affiliates belong to the first group (Alaska Lumber and Pulp, Alpha Therapeutic, the Catalyst Company, Ceradyne, Daitom, Denka Chemical, Dorchester Fabrics, Everett Piano, Feltloc, Fletcher Oil and Chemical, Hitachi Consumer Products, Honeylon, Kodiak Lumber, Marcrest Pacific, Matsushita, Micro Power Systems, Mitsubishi Aircraft, Mount Pleasant Chemicals, Neptune Packing, New England Drawn Steel, Oki Electric, Rosewood Knitting Mills, Sakura Noodle, Southern Metal Service, Topri, Transco Textiles and West Virginia Flat Glass) and five in the second (Alumax, Firestone Vineyards, Key Pharmaceuticals, Nachi Bearings and Olga).

In Alumax's case, the Japanese parents, Mitsui and Nippon Steel, sold their aluminum assets back to Amax and replaced them with a long-term contract for aluminum. In both the Firestone Vineyards and Olga cases, the American joint venture partners exercised their option to buy back their Japanese partner's stake. Mitsubishi Kasei sold its minority stake in Key Pharmaceuticals when that firm was acquired by Schering-Plough. Nachi Bearing closed due to changes in the location of customers. None of these exits appear to have been due to management difficulties caused by a liability of foreignness.

We can further split the first category of 27 affiliates for which exit was a consequence of poor performance into two groups: those which exited due to the poor performance of the parent and those which exited due to the poor performance of the subsidiary. The first group, for which exits were *not* due to the poor performance of the affiliate, consists of two affiliates, Alpha Therapeutic and Sakura Noodle. Alpha Therapeutic's parent, Green Cross, was acquired by Yoshitomi after Green Cross was tainted by the scandal of HIV-contaminated blood. Sakura Noodle's parent, Yoahan, went bankrupt due to over-diversification and lax controls.

The remaining 25 affiliates can again be divided into two main groups: those which exited following difficulties that can be ascribed to a liability of foreignness and those which exited due to problems that could have affected all firms, foreign or domestic. We put 10 affiliates in the second category (The Catalyst Company, Daitom, Dorchester Fabrics, Fletcher Oil and Refining, Honeylon, Kodiak Lumber Mills, Marcrest Pacific, Neptune Packing, Rosewood Knitting Mills, Southern Metal Service, Topri and Transco Textiles). Some of these affiliates floundered because of the unexpected increase in costs (for example, following the oil crisis) or because of declines in the demand for their products due to changes in tastes or technology. An example is the Catalyst Company, a

Table 1
Exits of Japanese Manufacturing Affiliates from the US

Affiliate Name	Japanese Parent(s)	Type at Entry	Type of Exit	Reason(s) for Exit
Alaska Lumber and Pulp	Teijin, Toray, Mitsubishi, Marubeni, Mitsui and others	J–JG	L	Change in US regulations
Alpha Therapeutic	Green Cross	J A	S	Parent acquired
Alumax	Mitsui and Nippon Steel	J–J–US PA	S	Replaced by contract
Catalyst Company	Nippon Shokubai	J–US G	L	Lost its market
Ceradyne	Kyocera	J A	S	Discrimination by Pentagon
Daitom	Daiichi Seiyaku	J–US G	L	High costs due to oil price hike
Denka Chemical	Denki Kagaku Kogyo	J A	S	Labor problems
Dorchester Fabrics	Tomen	J–US PA	S	Poor performance
Everett Piano	Yamaha	J A	L	Labor problems
Feltloc	Dynic	J–G	L	Poor marketing
Firestone Vineyards	Suntory	J–US G	S	US partner buys back
Fletcher Oil and Refining	Mitsubishi Trading	J–US PA	S	Change in US regulations
Hitachi Consumer Products	Hitachi	J G	L	Labor problems
Honeylon	Honey Fiber and Bedding	J–US G	L	Supply problems
Key Pharmaceuticals	Mitsubishi Kasei	J–US PA	S	Mission accomplished
Kodiak Lumber Mills	Mitsui Trading	J–G	L	Change in market and US regulations
Marcrest Pacific	Marubeni	J–US PA	L	Change in market
Matsushita Industrial	Matsushita Electric	J A	L	Labor problems
Micro Power System	Seiko Epson	J–US PA	S	Labor problems
Mitsubishi Aircraft	Mitsubishi Heavy Industries	J–A	S	Change in US regulations/ exchange rate
Mount Pleasant Chemicals	Sumitomo Chemical	J–US G	L	Deficient marketing
Nachi Bearing	Nachi Fujikoshi, Kanematsu Gosho, Nissho-Iwai, Shima Trading	J–J A	S	Bad location
Neptune Packing	Mitsui Trading	J A	L	High labor costs
New England Drawn Steel	Azuma Steel, Oh-Esu, Nittetsu Trading	J–J A	S	Labor problems
Oki Electronics	Oki	J G	L	Poor marketing
Olga	Wacoal	J–US PA	S	US partner buys back
Rosewood Knitting Mills	Toyobo	J–US PA	S	Change in market
Sakura Noodle	Yaohan Department Store	J G	S	Parent went bankrupt
Southern Metal Service	Kanematsu Gosho	J–US PA	L	Change in US regulations
Topri	Tokyo Print Industry	J–G	S	Customer defects
Transco Textiles	Seiren, Toyobo, Nichida Tsusho	J–J–US G	S	Change in market
West Virginia Flat Glass	Asahi Glass	J–US PA	S	Labor/technical problems

J = Japanese parent, US = US parent, G = greenfield, PA = partial acquisition, A = full acquisition, S = sell-off, L = liquidation.

joint venture of Nippon Shokubai and American Cyanamid. Its main customer, General Motors, decided to switch to a new type of catalyst, the manufacture of which laid outside the mission and competence of the joint venture. The partners chose therefore to dissolve it. The cases of Southern Metal Service and Topri are slightly more ambiguous. Southern Metal Service is a Gulfport, MS steel service center that was set up by Kanematsu Gosho, a Japanese general trading company, and an American partner to process hot bands and related products from hot-rolled steel imported from Mexico, Brazil, South Africa and other sources. In 1986, the US imposed so-called voluntary restraint agreements on these countries, thus shutting off Southern Metal Service from its steel suppliers. Kanematsu then decided to close its (by then fully owned) subsidiary. It seems that Southern Metal's supply sources and location made it particularly vulnerable to the imposition of these voluntary restraint agreements. Because these measures affected all steel processors, regardless of nationality, it is difficult to ascribe the failure of Southern Metal Service to a liability of foreignness.

Topri was invited by the Delco Electronics division of General Motors to supply it with printed circuit board. Three years later, Delco opened its own captive plant, thus forcing its Japanese parent to sell Topri to a US firm. We have no evidence that Delco's behavior was caused by Topri's Japanese ownership.

The remaining 13 exits can be ascribed to a liability of foreignness. In seven cases, the Japanese experienced difficulties in human resource management. In five affiliates, Denka Chemical, Matsushita, Everett, New England Drawn Steel and West Virginia Flat Glass, the Japanese owners did not realize the difficulty of transferring their "lean production" advantages to an acquired affiliate. Lean production techniques consist mainly in better human resource management and they require significant shifts in worker behavior, shifts that are difficult to implement, especially in acquisitions. This is the story of Matsushita. The firm purchased Motorola's Quasar television division but was unsuccessful in its effort to reorganize the plant along "lean production" lines (Kenney, 1999).

At Hitachi Consumer Products, the Japanese managers, faced with a very diverse labor force, ran the plant using US management techniques, even though they had set it up as a greenfield and ended up with poor productivity and product quality (Kenney, 1999). At Micro Power Systems, a semiconductor manufacturer in which Seiko Epson had taken a majority stake, the managers, unhappy with Seiko's lack of understanding of the business, persuaded their Japanese bosses to sell them the affiliate.

A second cause of failures that can be ascribed to a liability of foreignness is overoptimistic market forecasts, apparently due to a poor understanding of the target market. This is the story of Feltloc, Oki Electric and Mount Pleasant Chemicals. In the Mount Pleasant Chemical case, a joint venture set up by Sumitomo Chemicals and Stauffer Chemical to manufacture Sumitomo's brand of forest insecticide, Sumitomo underestimated the strength of its established US competitors.

The remaining three cases of exit, Mitsubishi Aircraft, Alaska Lumber and Pulp and Ceradyne, involve the Japanese firms' dealing with the U.S. Government. Kyocera bought Ceradyne, a custom maker of ceramic packages, but found that its ownership of the firm was making it difficult to sell to the Pentagon. It then decided to spin off the firm to one of its cofounder. The two other cases, Mitsubishi Aircraft and ALP, are less clear-cut but suggest that the Japanese firms either did not have the skills to deal with Uncle Sam or faced additional hostility in doing so.

Mitsubishi Heavy Industry entered the US in 1967 to sell its MU-2 turboprop business jet and then followed up with a jet-engine plane, the Diamond One. Part of the plane was to be built in Japan and part at a manufacturing plant Mitsubishi bought in Texas (Kujawa, 1983). As the Diamond One was going through FAA certification, a door fell off a DC 10 at the Paris Air Show, leading to a tightening of regulations. This forced Mitsubishi to redesign the plane and delayed its launch. In the meantime, the yen has appreciated so much that making part of the plane in Japan was no longer competitive. Mitsubishi ended up selling the plans and technology for the Diamond One to Beech Aircraft, which had excess manufacturing capacity in the US. The Texas plant was liquidated. While it is clear that the direct cause of liquidation was an unexpected change in exchange rates, an additional reason were delays due to Mitsubishi's inexperience with FAA procedures.

In the 1950s, the U.S. Government offered attractive long-term timber supply contracts to encourage the exploitation of Alaska's more isolated forests. The beneficiaries of these 50-year contracts were to build processing facilities. Two firms, Louisiana-Pacific and Alaska Lumber and Pulp (ALP) responded to this offer. ALP, a consortium of Japanese synthetic fiber and general trading companies, built a pulp mill in Sitka and a lumber mill in Wrangell. In 1993, ALP decided to close its pulp mill because of low pulp prices and to convert the plant to the production of medium density fiberboard. Under pressure from environmentalists, the U.S. Forest Service responded by canceling ALP's favorable 50-year timber supply contract, forcing ALP to close its two mills. Louisiana-Pacific's contract was not affected (the company closed its pulp plant in 1997 anyhow due to the need for pollution control investments and to difficulties encountered in negotiating the extension of its timber supply contract beyond 2004). In May 2000, a federal court ruled that the U.S. Government had no legal basis for canceling ALP's contract and awarded damages. There is some evidence here that ALP's Japanese status made it more exposed to political risk than its domestic rival. Though US courts eventually supported the company's positions, ALP was apparently not able to defend its contractual rights in the political arena.

Our analysis of our 32 cases of exit shows the rich variety of causes we had predicted earlier. While a significant number of exits (13 out of 32) can be attributed to a liability of foreignness, there are also many other reasons for exit that have little to do with it. Hence, one has to be very cautious when using exits to measure the liability of foreignness.

5. Conclusions

The liability of foreignness is a crucial concept in the theory of the MNE, for it explains why, in spite of significant market transaction costs, some international interactions are not handled by MNEs. In spite of its theoretical importance, the phenomenon has been underresearched. The major approach taken by the literature has been to infer the presence of such a liability from higher exit rates.

That literature has come up with mixed results and one of the reasons, we argued, has been that the relationship between poor profitability caused by a liability of foreignness on one hand and exits on the other is not as straightforward as most researchers have implicitly assumed. Our survey of the literature on exits shows that a significant number of exits are not due to poor profitability but rather to parents restructuring their portfolios or winding down their options. Does this invalidate studies that attempt to measure by exit rates the existence and level of a liability of foreignness? To find out, we analyzed the exits to 1998 of 32 Japanese-owned affiliates that manufactured in the US in 1980. This is a good sample to evaluate the presence of a liability of foreignness, as liquidating a manufacturing affiliate is relatively costly and the US market is a strategic one for Japan. Many of our affiliates were also their parent's first investment in the US. Hence, the liability of foreignness should have been high for these firms. After carefully documenting the causes of exit, we find that 13 cases out of 32 can be ascribed to a liability of foreignness. In seven cases, Japanese investors experienced difficulties with managing their American employees. In two (and possibly three) cases, they seemed to have had trouble with the U.S. Government. In another three cases, they appear to have made overoptimistic market forecasts.

What these results show is that relatively inexperienced Japanese investors did incur serious difficulties in managing in the US, difficulties that, not surprisingly, had primarily to do with the most country-specific aspects of management, i.e., that of human resources. Our findings are thus consistent with those of Mezias (2002) and with an abundant literature on the difficulties Japanese managers have had with their US employees (e.g., Lanier, 1992).

That Japanese firms experienced difficulties in their relationships with the U.S. Government and in their understanding of the US market is also not surprising. Marketing know-how is often tacit and difficult to transfer across countries. Dealing with host governments is also a challenge for foreign investors because the way a country's political system is set up is a subtle reflection of its values and style. The rules of the political game are often tacit and hence very hard for foreigners to understand.

A second conclusion of our study is that exits are due to many factors besides a liability of foreignness and that to test the theory it is important to isolate the additional impact of the liability over the baseline exit rate. Failure to perform the test on matched samples or to carefully control for the factors that affect all exits will give misleading results.

In that context, our findings must be considered with caution, because we do not have a matched sample of domestic American firms. This would have helped us better separate exits due to a liability of foreignness from those due to hazards affecting both foreign and domestic firms. Another limitation comes from the difficulty of ascertaining causes for exit from secondary sources and from interviews with protagonists. Yet, given the complexity of both the liability of foreignness and of exits, we believe that it is quite possible to misinterpret statistical results. Examining in sufficient detail a large enough sample of exits over a long period and finding out the causes of such exits can provide an important reality check to make sure that we understand what lies behind the data.

Acknowledgements

We thank Bas Daamen, Jim Hagen, Georgine Kryda, Candace Martinez, Danchi Tan, Yueming Wu and Dixie Zietlow for help with data collection.

Appendix A. Short History of Exits
A.1. Alaska Lumber and Pulp (ALP)

In the 1950s, the U.S. Government offered attractive long-term timber supply contracts to encourage the exploitation of Alaska's more isolated forests. The beneficiaries of these 50-year contracts had to promise to build processing facilities in that state. One US company, Louisiana-Pacific, and a Japanese consortium, ALP, made up of 240 Japanese firms, including two Japanese man-made textile manufacturers (Teijin and Toray) and three trading companies (Marubeni, Mitsui and Mitsubishi), decided to accept the contracts and to build a pulp mill in Sitka. The pulp was shipped to Japan used by the textile firms for their own synthetic fiber production, while the trading companies sold it to Japanese paper companies. As the price of lumber increased, ALP also built a major sawmill in Wrangell.

This project became less and less popular as Alaska's oil-derived wealth led to an increased concern for its environment. In 1993, ALP decided to close its pulp mill because of low pulp prices and to convert the plant to the production of medium-density fiberboard. Under pressure from environmentalists, the U.S. Forest Service responded by canceling ALP's favorable 50-year timber supply contract, forcing the firm to close its two mills. Louisiana-Pacific's contract was not affected (the company closed its pulp plant in 1997 anyhow due to the need for pollution control investments and to difficulties encountered in negotiating the extension of its timber supply contract beyond 2004). In May 2000, a federal court ruled that the U.S. Government had no legal basis for canceling ALP's contract and awarded damages. There is some evidence here that ALP's Japanese status made it more exposed to political risk than its domestic rival.

A.2. Alpha Therapeutic

Green Cross acquired Alpha Therapeutic in 1978. Green Cross got caught in the HIV-tainted blood scandal in Japan, in which the Japanese health ministry delayed the use of foreign AIDS blood tests while waiting for Green Cross to develop its own. Many people died as a result and Green Cross was forced to merge with (be acquired by) Yoshitomi, thus breaking the ownership link between Alpha Therapeutic and Green Cross.

(Appendix A continued)

(Appendix A continued)

A.3. Alumax Joint Venture

The Mitsui Group found itself in 1945 without an aluminum plant. As a result, Mitsui & Co., the Group's trading arm, was at a disadvantage in an important product area. Mitsui saw its chance when Amax was looking for an outside investor to help finance an expansion in capacity. By taking a 50% stake in Amax's aluminum business (renamed Alumax), Mitsui secured access to low cost ingot at a time where the Japanese aluminum industry use of oil-based electricity made it uncompetitive. Mitsui provided a secure outlet for Alumax's aluminum and Alumax a secure source of supply for Mitsui (Tsurumi, 1976). By 1986, the market for aluminum had considerably developed and Mitsui sold its Alumax share to Amax and replaced its investment by a series of long-term contracts with Amax. There is some indication that Mitsui's divestment did not involve hard feeling, since 2 years later Mitsui was back into partnership with Amax after buying Pechiney's share in the Intalco and Eastalco smelters.

A.4. The Catalyst Company

The Catalyst Company was a joint venture set up in 1973 by American Cyanamid and Nippon Shokubai in response to new U.S. Environmental Protection Agency regulations for car exhausts. Both firms were already selling catalytic converters when General Motors, a major customer, suggested that it would favor a joint venture between the two competitors as one was strong in pellet substrate formation and the other in noble metal deposition. Each parent held a 50% share in the venture that was active until 1982. In 1982, automobile manufacturers switched to monolithic catalysts and the joint venture went inactive rather than to switch to a technology that did into fit the original rationale of the joint venture and for which the partners had no special competence (Tyebjee, 1988). The joint venture was officially liquidated in 1987.

A.5. Ceradyne

Ceradyne, a firm making custom ceramic packages, was acquired by Kyocera in 1978. According to Moskowitz, Ceradyne's cofounder, the acquisition was not synergistic, because the company made custom parts while Kyocera mass-produced. Ceradyne was sold back to its management in 1983. The sale was given added impetus by Ceradyne's attempt to win large military contracts. As long as the firm only sold small quantities to the military, its affiliation with Kyocera was not an obstacle. However, the Pentagon frowned on handing out large amount of classified work to a non-American company, so Kyocera agreed to spin off Ceradyne to Moskowitz for 2.3 million plus a royalty equal to 3% of sales over the next 10 years.

A.6. Daitom

The company was set up in 1979 as a greenfield joint venture between Daiichi Seiyaku and Thomson-Hayward Chemical to manufacture vitamins for animals.

(Appendix A continued)

(Appendix A continued)

Oil price hikes caused production costs to skyrocket. In 1984, the joint venture was dissolved.

A.7. Denka Chemical

Denka Chemical was established in 1977 when Denki Kagaku Kogyo bought a plant in Houston to manufacture synthetic rubber in response to a US lawsuit against dumping. The company could not adjust to the vertical division of labor practiced at the plant and operated in the red. After an accident at the plant, the parent sold the firm in 1984 to its American managers.

A.8. Dorchester Fabrics

In 1980, the Japanese general trading firm Tomen took at 80% share in Dorchester Fabrics, a company owned by an American entrepreneur. Tomen came later to the conclusion that Dorchester did not keep up with market trends, so it sold its stake in 1985 to a Korean firm.

A.9. Everett Piano

In 1973, Yamaha acquired Everett Piano, a medium-caliber piano maker located in South Haven, Michigan. Immediately after the purchase, Everett's employees went on 3-month long strike. The strike turned ugly, with shots reportedly fired at the house of the American president and threatening calls made to those of Japanese expatriate managers. Yamaha kept the Everett line of pianos and added its own Yamaha line. In 1977, it closed the plant. The official reason was "declining piano sales." However, labor problems seem to have played a major role, because Yamaha did not subsequently reduce its output. Instead, it moved the manufacture of its Yamaha line of pianos to its Georgia organ manufacturing plant and contracted with Baldwin to continue the production of the Everett piano line. This suggests that demand for pianos may not have been the main problem.

A.10. Feltloc

Feltloc was set up by Dynic in 1974 to manufacture all-cotton nonwoven cloth for the graphic arts, hospital and industrial markets. The subsidiary never seems to have sold enough cloth to make a profit. After being continuously in the red, it was liquidated in 1982.

A.11. Firestone Vineyards

In the early 1970s, younger members of the Firestone family decided to start a vineyard on family land in the Santa Ynes valley, an area not previously used for wine-quality grapes, but soon found out they could not get financing. The family had good personal relations with the president of Suntory, a Japanese spirits company, so they asked Suntory for financing. Suntory set up a joint venture with the

(Appendix A continued)

(Appendix A continued)

Firestone family to carry out the project. The vineyard prospered, helping to establish this valley as a prime-growing region. The Firestones had put into the joint venture contract an option to buy back the 31% share that Suntory owned, and they exercised it in 1994, without apparent resistance from Suntory.

A.12. Fletcher Oil and Refining

In 1979, Mitsubishi Trading acquired a 20% stake in Fletcher Oil and Refining, a small Carson, California oil refinery, and obtained the right to market 70% of its output. However, the worsening economics of oil refining in California persuaded Mitsubishi to sell its stake in 1987.

A.13. Hitachi Consumer Products

The plant was initially set up by Hitachi in Compton/Anaheim to assemble TV sets. It was nonunionized and the labor force was extremely diverse ethnically and linguistically, an attribute that Japanese managers considered an impediment to management. According to Kenney (1999), the plant was managed along US lines, with no effort to incorporate Japanese labor management techniques. The plant's high cost and low productivity persuaded Hitachi to close it and move its production of projection TVs to its Tijuana maquiladora and that of videocassette recorders to Malaysia.

A.14. Honeylon

Honeylon was set up in 1974 by Honey Fiber and Bedding (now Honeylon) and National Novelty Brush, a US company, to manufacture nonwoven cotton fabrics. The joint venture was liquidated in 1992 because it could not find raw materials at competitive prices in the US.

A.15. Key Pharmaceuticals

In 1979, Mitsubishi Kasei bought a 10% stake in Key Pharmaceuticals to learn about the American market. Mitsubishi argues that by 1986 they had achieved their objectives and this was the reason they sold back their share (at a $20 million profit) when Key Pharmaceuticals was acquired by Schering-Plough.

A.16. Kodiak Lumber Mills

Kodiak Lumber Mills was set up in 1971 by Mitsui Trading in Anchorage, Alaska, to cut logs and export semifinished lumber to Japan. After running up losses of $68 million, Kodiak Lumber filed for bankruptcy in 1984. Swollen infrastructure costs, low housing starts in Japan and the increased use of recycled paper by Japanese paper mills were blamed for this outcome.

(Appendix A continued)

(Appendix A continued)

A.17. Marcrest Pacific

Marcrest Pacific was established in 1970 as a greenfield joint venture between Marubeni and a US steel firm to manufacture welded steel beams in Carson, California. The plant was closed in 1989 when the steel service center that shared the same location was relocated to Riverside. Marcrest's equipment was too old and the future prospects for its products were apparently not sufficiently encouraging to warrant the continuation of operations.

A.18. Matsushita Electric

The tremendous success of Japanese exports of televisions to the US led to significant trade frictions, which in turn persuaded major Japanese TV set assemblers to start manufacturing in the US. In 1974, Matsushita bought the Franklin Park, Illinois TV assembly plant of Motorola's Quasar television unit. The plant was not unionized but was operated along "Fordist" lines (Kenney, 1999). Quality was dismally low. It improved substantially when Matsushita brought in new equipment and higher quality parts from Japan. However, Matsushita did not succeed in introducing Japanese "lean management" practices such as broad job descriptions, worker job rotation and quality circles (Abo, 1994). The company took advantage of the passage of NAFTA in 1995 to move Franklin Park's TV assembly operations to Mexico. The plant was totally closed in 1997 when its remaining production of microwave ovens was shut down and moved to Matsushita's Appliance Corp. in Danville, Kentucky.

A.19. Micro Power Systems

Seiko put funds in 1972 into Micro Power Systems, a maker of personal computers, terminal printers and liquid crystal displays. It used the firm as a source of technology and as a training ground for its engineers. Micro Power Systems never seemed to have established a strong marketing position because of Seiko's halfhearted approach to marketing and manufacturing. Micro Power's management decided to take the firm over in 1992 in a leveraged buy-out because they felt that Seiko did not understand the business.

A.20. Mitsubishi Aircraft

Mitsubishi Heavy Industry entered the US in 1967 to sell its MU-2 turboprop business jet and then followed up with a jet-engine plane, the Diamond One. Part of the plane was to be built in Japan and part at a manufacturing plant Mitsubishi bought in Texas (Kujawa, 1983). As the Diamond One was going through FAA certification, a door fell off a DC 10 at the Paris Air Show, leading to a tightening of regulations. This forced Mitsubishi to redesign the plane and delayed its launch. In the meantime, the yen had appreciated so much that making part of the plane in Japan was no longer competitive. Mitsubishi ended up selling the plans and technology for the Diamond One to Beech Aircraft, which had excess manufacturing capacity in the US. The Texas plant was liquidated. While it is clear that the direct cause of

(Appendix A continued)

(Appendix A continued)

liquidation was an unexpected change in exchange rates, an additional reason were delays due to Mitsubishi's inexperience with FAA procedures.

A.21. Mount Pleasant Chemical

In 1975, Sumitomo Chemicals entered the US with the hope to sell its Sumithion brand of forest insecticide, which was selling well in Japan. A joint venture, Mount Pleasant Chemical, was established with Stauffer Chemical, an American firm. Sumitomo had, however, apparently underestimated the competitive strength of similar brands of organic phosphate insecticides sold by American Cyanamid and Union Carbide. The joint venture never made money and was liquidated in 1984.

A.22. Nachi Bearing

In 1974, Nachi Fujikoshi, a bearing manufacturer, together with the Japanese general trading firms of Kanematsu-Gosho, Nissho-Iwai and Shima Trading, jointly purchased a bearing plant in South Portland, Maine. In 1987, the plant was closed down when Nachi moved into a new facility in Greenwood, Indiana, closer to Japanese car assembly plants.

A.23. Neptune Packing

Mitsui Trading acquired this Mayaguez, Puerto Rico, tuna packing plant in 1973. Tuna packing is a very labor-intensive activity. At that time, low wages made Puerto Rico attractive. The rise in labor costs in the 1980s and 1990s made such plants uncompetitive. Of the five tuna packing plants established in Puerto Rico, four had closed by the early 1990s, including Neptune Packing, which was closed in 1991 and liquidated in 1993.

A.24. New England Drawn Steel

New England Drawn Steel, a plant making cold drawn steel bars, was acquired in 1973 by a consortium made up of Azuma Steel, Oshima Seisen and Nippon Steel Trading. The Japanese firms' competitive strategy for this rather standard product was based on high quality and low cost. New England Drawn Steel was unionized prior to its acquisition by the Japanese and the new Japanese owners made very few changes to its labor relations (Kujawa, 1983). According to its former president, the business was sold to a Canadian firm in 1981 because of labor problems.

A.25. Oki Electronics

Oki Electronics was set up in 1973, a greenfield wholly owned plant in Oakland Park, Florida, to manufacture and sell private branch exchanges (PBX) to US customers. However, sales never took off and the plant was closed in the mid-1980s.

(Appendix A continued)

(Appendix A continued)

A.26. Olga

In 1978, Wacoal, a women's underwear manufacturer, took a 29% stake in Olga, the fifth ranked US women's underwear manufacturer. One of the motivating factors for securing a manufacturing base in the US was a high US tariff. The agreement was that the remaining 71% of Olga would be transferred to Wacoal in 7 years "if business relations between them had matured sufficiently". However, in the Fall of 1982, Olga asked Wacoal to sell back its whole stake in Olga because of a significant improvement in business performance. The proposed buyback was completed in February 1983. After the repurchase of Wacoal's share, Olga sold itself to Warnaco, which kept the two founders, Jan and Olga Ertesek, as Chairman of the Board and Vice President Design. Wacoal, which had been in discussion with Teenform, another US lingerie manufacturer, finally acquired it in 1983. Two years later, Wacoal built its own plant in Puerto Rico.

A.27. Rosewood Knitting Mills

Toyobo, a textile-spinning firm, bought 40% of Rosewood Knitting Mills in 1973. Rosewood fabrics was making knitwear, which was dyed by Transco textiles. However, demand for synthetic knitwear fell. After an attempt to switch to fabrics, both Rosewood and Transco were sold to Guilford Mills, a US firm, in 1985.

A.28. Sakura Noodle

The plant was set up by Yoahan department store as part of its many diversifications. Yoahan went bankrupt on September 18, 1997 and the subsidiary was sold to Shoachi Suzuki.

A.29. Southern Metal Service

Kanematsu Gosho, a Japanese general trading company, took a 20% stake in 1973 in this Gulfport, Mississippi steel service center that was set up for hot bands and related products using hot-rolled steel imported from Mexico, Brazil, South Africa and other sources. In 1986, the US imposed so-called voluntary restraint agreements on these countries, thus cutting Southern Metal Service's source of steel. Kanematsu decided to close its (by then fully owned) subsidiary. It seems that Southern Metal's supply sources and location made it particularly vulnerable to the imposition of these voluntary restraint agreements. Other Japanese steel service centers seem to have been better able to replace imported steel with US steel or with that produced by Japanese–US joint ventures in the US.

A.30. Topri

Topri was set up in Peachtree City (Georgia) in 1979 by Tokyo Print Industry as a semicaptive supplier of printed wiring board to General Electric's Delco Electronics

(Appendix A continued)

(Appendix A continued)

Division. Although the plant was established with its encouragement, Delco later opened its own facility, drastically reducing Topri's volume. The plant was sold in 1982 to Kollmorgen.

A.31. Transco Textile Industries

In 1975, Toyobo, a Japanese spinning firm, set up a greenfield joint venture with Rosewood Knitting Mills, an American firm it partly owned, to print, dye and finish synthetic knitwear produced by Rosewood. However, the business of Transco fell along with US demand for synthetic knitwear. After an attempt to switch to fabrics, both Rosewood and Transco were sold to Guilford Mills, a US firm, in 1985.

A.32. West Virginia Flat Glass

In 1979, Asahi Glass purchased from Hordis Glass 80% of West Virginia Flat Glass in Clarksburg, West Virginia, a plant making thick glass sheets, which had just been shut down by its owner. Asahi's attempt to convert the plant's production lines from thick to thin glass was unsuccessful. The plant was shut down in 1981 for repairs and refurbishment, reopened but was finally sold in 1986 due to poor productivity.

Notes

1. In some cases, however, foreign investors may face positive discrimination from consumers who have more confidence on imported than on locally made products.
2. As the authors write, establishing a trading room "requires a Reuter monitor, a couple of phone lines and some back-office support to confirm and account for deals. All that a trading room needs to do to become a market-maker is to establish credit lines with a reasonably larger number of banks, start the practice of quoting bid and offer prices with reasonably narrow spreads and publicize the fact that it is ready to receive incoming requests for bid-offer quotes both by word of mouth and by requesting an entry in an established directory of market-makers such as the Foreign Exchange and Bullion Dealers directory published by Hambros bank in London" (p. 443).
3. This was the case whether cultural distance was measured by the Kogut and Singh (1988) index or by Ronen and Shenkar's (1985) cultural clusters.
4. For example, sell-offs make up 67% of all dissolved links in our sample versus 64% for our population.

References

Abo, T., 1994. *Hybrid Factory*. Oxford Univ. Press, New York.

Barkema, H., Bell, J., Pennings, J., 1996. Foreign entry, cultural barriers, and learning. *Strategic Manage. J.* 17, 151–166.

Barkema, H., Shenkar, O., Vermeulen, F., Bell, J., 1997. Working abroad, working with others: how firms learn to operate international joint ventures. *Acad. Manage. J.* 40, 436–442.

Benito, G.R.G., 1997. Why are foreign subsidiaries divested? A conceptual framework. In: Bjorkman, I., Forsgren, M. (Eds.), *The Nature of the International Firm: Nordic Contributions to International Business Research*. Copenhagen Business School Press, Copenhagen, pp. 309–334.

Chang, S.-J., 1996. An evolutionary perspective on diversification and corporate restructuring: entry, exit, and economic performance during 1981–89. *Strategic Manage. J.* 17, 587–611.

Duhaime, I., Grant, J., 1984. Factors influencing divestment decision-making: evidence from a field study. *Strategic Manage. J.* 5, 301–318.

Gomes-Casseres, B., 1987. Joint venture instability: is it a problem? *Columbia J. World Bus.*, 97–102 (Summer).

Hamilton, R.T., Chow, Y.K., 1993. Why managers divest: evidence from New Zealand's largest companies. *Strategic Manage. J.* 14, 479–484.

Hennart, J.-F., 1982. *A Theory of Multinational Enterprise*. University of Michigan Press, Ann Arbor.

Hennart, J.-F., Barkema, H., Bell, J., Benito, G., Larimo, J., Pedersen, T., Zeng, M., 1997. The impact of national origin on the survival of foreign affiliates: a comparative study of North European and Japanese investors in the United States. CIBER Working Paper no. 103, University of Illinois at Urbana-Champaign.

Hennart, J.-F., Kim, D.-J., Zeng, M., 1998. The impact of joint venture status on the longevity of Japanese stakes in U.S. manufacturing affiliates. *Organ. Sci.* 9, 382–395.

Hymer, S., 1960. The international operations of domestic firms: a study of foreign direct investment. PhD dissertation, MIT.

Johanson, J., Vahlne, J.E., 1977. The internationalization process of the firm. *J. Int. Bus. Stud.* 8, 23–32.

Kaplan, S., Welsbach, M., 1992. The success of acquisitions: evidence from divestitures. *J. Finance* 47, 107–138.

Kenney, M., 1999. Transplantation? In: Liker, J., Fruin, M., Adler, P. (Eds.), *Remade in America*. Oxford Univ. Press, New York, pp. 256–293.

Kogut, B., Singh, H., 1988. The effect of national culture on the choice of entry mode. *J. Int. Bus. Stud.* 19, 411–432.

Kujawa, D., 1983. Technology strategy and industrial relations: case studies of Japanese multinationals in the United States. *J. Int. Bus. Stud.*, 22 (Winter).

Lanier, A., 1992. *The rising sun on main street: working with the Japanese*, 2nd ed. Irwin, Glendale, IL.

Larimo, J., 2000. Divestment of foreign production operations by Nordic firms: similar or different determinants? Paper presented at the Academy of International Business annual meetings, Phoenix, Arizona, November.

Li, J., 1995. Foreign entry and survival: effects of strategic choices on performance in international markets. *Strategic Manage. J.* 16, 333–351.

Mata, J., Portugal, P., 2000. Closure and divestiture by foreign entrants: the impact of entry and post-entry strategies. *Strategic Manage. J.* 21, 549–562.

Mata, J., Portugal, P., 2002. Survival of new domestic and foreign-owned firms. *Strategic Manage. J.* 23, 323–343.

McCloughan, P., Stone, I., 1998. Life duration of foreign multinational subsidiaries: evidence from UK Northern Manufacturing Industry, 1970–93. *Int. J. Ind. Organ.* 16, 719–747.

Mezias, J., 2002. Identifying liabilities of foreignness and strategies to minimize their effects: the case of labor lawsuit judgments in the United States. *Strategic Manage. J.* 23, 229–244.

Nanda, A., Williamson, P., 1995. Use joint ventures to ease the pain of restructuring. *Harv. Bus. Rev.*, 119–132 (November/December).

Park, Y.R., Park, S.W., 2000. Determinants of FDI survival: the case of Korean manufacturing firms. Paper presented at the Academy of International Business annual meetings, Phoenix, Arizona, November.

Pennings, J., Barkema, H., Douma, S., 1994. Organizational learning and diversification. *Acad. Manage. J.* 37, 608–640.

Ronen, S., Shenkar, O., 1985. Clustering countries on attitudinal dimensions: a review and synthesis. *Acad. Manage. Rev.* 10, 435–454.

Sharma, A., Kesner, I., 1996. Diversifying entry: some ex-ante explanations for postentry survival and growth. *Acad. Manage. J.* 39, 635–677.

Tsurumi, Y., 1976. *The Japanese are Coming*. Ballinger, Boston.

Tyebjee, T., 1988. A typology of joint ventures: Japanese strategies in the United States. *Calif. Manage. Rev.*, 75–86.

Wilkins, M., 1990. Japanese multinationals in the United States: continuity and change. *Bus. Hist. Rev.* 64, 585–620.

Zaheer, S., Mosakowski, E., 1997. The dynamics of the liability of foreignness: a global study of survival in financial services. *Strategic Manage. J.* 18 (6), 439–464.

40

Divestment and International Business Strategy

Gabriel R.G. Benito

1. Introduction

An impressive number of studies have been conducted since the 1960s regarding the internationalization of firms, especially with a focus on multinational corporations (MNCs), i.e., firms that own and operate units in foreign locations (Dunning, 2001). The interest in MNCs is understandable given the economic clout of such corporations, which, as put by Peter Dicken (2003, p. 198) 'has come to be regarded as the primary shaper of the contemporary global economy'. The term globalization is often used to describe a process of increasing integration of national and regional economies (Whitley, 2001), which works towards a worldwide convergence of institutions, norms, and behaviors. The actions of multinational corporations promote increased economic interdependence among nations and regions thereby making them 'key actors in the globalization process' (Rugman and Verbeke, 2004, p. 3), although the idea that their increased significance necessarily leads to convergence between nations, consumer preferences, or even business behaviors is contested (see e.g., Gertler, 2001; Morgan et al., 2001). It has been noted that MNCs vary considerably, partly reflecting the institutional and contextual particularities of their respective home bases, but partly also as a result of their different internationalization strategies (Morgan et al., 2001). Such variation notwithstanding, Dicken (2003, p. 198) accurately summarizes the general characteristics of MNCs as companies (i) that coordinate and control various stages of value-added activities within and between countries, (ii) are able to take advantage of national differences in resources and policies, and (iii) have considerable potential for location flexibility, i.e., the ability to switch and re-switch their resources and operations between locations at an international, or even global, scale.

Source: *Journal of Economic Geography*, Vol. 5, 2005, pp. 235–251.

It is nonetheless clear that the two first characteristics have received most of the attention so far, with few studies actually looking at the relocation and divestment aspects of MNC activity. In spite of data indicating that divestments are quite common,[1] as pointed out by Benito and Welch (1997, p. 8): '... most of the literature on the international operations of firms has focused on the growth – or positive development – of international business operations.' It is suggestive that terms such as divestment, divestiture, closure, and exit do not even appear as entries in the otherwise comprehensive index included in Rugman and Brewer's authoritative anthology on the state-of-the-art in international business research (Rugman and Brewer, 2001). Likewise, a recent review of research on global strategy does not explicitly touch on the subject at all (Chng and Pangarkar, 2000). Studies on divestment (e.g., Shapiro, 1983; Li, 1995; Benito, 1997a) closure of foreign units (e.g., Mata and Portugal, 2000), relocation (Pennings and Sleuwaegen, 2000), and market exit (Welch and Wiedersheim-Paul, 1980; Matthyssens and Pauwels, 2000; Wrigley and Currah, 2003) are still relatively scarce, despite the apparent significance that continuing MNC operations have for a wide array of actors – ranging from national governments to individual workers – and the repeated calls for more knowledge about the magnitude of foreign divestment, the drivers of divestment, and the ensuing effects (Boddewyn, 1979; Caves, 1995; Benito, 1997b; Burt et al., 2003).

This article looks at divestment through the lens of international business strategy: that is, it deals with the closure or sell-off of units in foreign locations, or conversely units owned by foreign firms, and will examine such actions from the perspective of the firms making such decisions. Specifically, it draws on contemporary analysis of international business strategy to probe into why and when foreign divestment is likely to be a course of action taken by MNCs.

The remainder of the paper proceeds as follows. The next section gives a brief overview of the divestment literature based on economics and business perspectives. The basics of international business strategy are then sketched out, with an emphasis on the core factors in the so-called 'integration-responsiveness' model, which has become a standard framework for analysis of firms' international strategies both in economic geography (Dicken, 1994, 2003) and in the business field (Bartlett and Ghoshal, 1989).[2] The central part of the paper presents an analysis of how the core factors in the integration-responsiveness framework may lead to relocation, divestment, and market exits as the effects of corporate re-structuring and adjustment processes, and not just as failures in foreign markets. Some final remarks conclude the paper.

2. Perspectives on Divestment

Divestment has been studied from a variety of perspectives. The wide ranging and multi-layered characters of the phenomenon imply that appropriate levels of analysis range from nations and regions, via industries, to specific firms, and even individuals. Also, it is one of those phenomena whose significance and complexity both attract and request a diversity of approaches: one should not presume that the insights provided by geography, economics, and business research can make greater claims of fruitfulness and understanding than those provided by sociological and political approaches. Nevertheless, since my point of view is that of firms' behavior, it is the former literatures that are of particular relevance. In an overview of the literature on divestment, Chow and Hamilton (1993) identify three main streams – industrial organization (IO), finance, and corporate strategy – that are also covered in Clark and Wrigley's (1997) seminal treatment of the corporate geography of divestment. Since the majority of empirical studies in the area are confined to domestic settings, it is pertinent also to look specifically to those that have studied foreign divestments.

2.1. The Industrial Organization Approach

The industrial organization literature has been concerned with incentives to exit as well as impediments to exit (Siegfried and Evans, 1994). The most apparent incentive to exit is low profits, or outright losses, which in turn are due to high costs, permanent decreases in demand, or the entry into an industry by aggressive, more efficient new competitors (Siegfried and Evans, 1994). Conversely, the existence of specific assets, i.e., assets which do not have valuable alternative uses (Williamson, 1985), constitutes an essential impediment to exit (Caves and Porter, 1976; Clark and Wrigley, 1997).[3] Inter-relatedness between units can also act as a barrier to exit. For example, joint production and distribution facilities may prevent an, in a strict sense, unprofitable unit from being divested because it may contribute positively to the company's overall activities.

The IO literature also proposes that divestment depends on diversification (Haynes, et al., 2003). Caves and Porter (1976) argue that owners of independent plants have a lower opportunity cost and are therefore willing to accept a lower rate of return than operations belonging to a multi-plant/multi-industry company would be expected to achieve. Markides (1995) argues that 'over-diversified' companies typically divest non-core units in order to recuperate performance. Moreover, divestment is facilitated in diversified companies since decisions are likely to be made by top-managers which are geographically and/or emotionally remote from the units under consideration for divestiture (Wright and Thompson, 1987).

2.2. Financial Studies

Financial studies of divestment have been paying special attention to the impact of divestment on company performance. While a few studies have looked at profitability measures (e.g., Haynes et al., 2002), financial studies have typically looked at the effects on share prices of divestment decisions. The available evidence suggests that divestments usually increase the market value of a company (Markides, 1995), not just for domestic divestiture but also foreign ones (Padmanabhan, 1993). Divestment decisions may hence reflect demands imposed by financial markets.

One obvious reason is that the divested units simply were poor performers, but Weston (1989) points out that operations might be divested for other reasons than poor performance per se. Misguided acquisition policies and, as already noted, corporate diversification strategies appear to be particularly likely to foster divestiture as time passes by (Markides, 1995). The synergistic value of units that were originally acquired in order to achieve synergies with a company's core business may have been illusive, and, if there, weaken, or even disappear, over time. In a similar vein, highly diversified companies may reach a point where a greater degree of relatedness between units is needed. In such cases, both the original acquisition and the subsequent divestment may have a positive impact on the market value of a company.

2.3. Corporate Strategy Perspectives

Early contributions in strategic management tended to look at divestment from the viewpoint of a product life-cycle approach, and argue that divestment is one of several strategic options for 'declining' industries (Davis, 1974; Harrigan, 1980). Divestment was advocated as an appropriate route in 'end game' situations characterized by high volatility and uncertainty regarding future returns. Divestment has also been viewed from a corporate portfolio perspective: a company can be regarded as a portfolio of assets, products, and activities, which should be continuously under review from both financial and strategic points of view (Chow and Hamilton, 1993). The contention that poorly performing units are likely candidates for divestment, is supported in a number of studies (Duhaime and Grant, 1984; Hamilton and Chow, 1993). Studies also indicate that corporate financial performance influences divestment. For example, in their study of 208 divestments made by large New Zealand companies during 1985–90, Hamilton and Chow (1993) report that the necessity of meeting corporate liquidity requirements was among the most important objectives motivating divestment.

In addition to the narrow financial considerations, which are undoubtedly important, strategic considerations also play an important role in the decision to divest. Following Rumelt's (1974) study on the relationship between strategy and performance, a number of empirical studies have found that corporate expansion into related industries leads to better performance and superior survival rates than expansion into unrelated industries (Bane and Neubauer, 1981; Lecraw, 1984; Morck et al., 1990; Pennings et al., 1994). Similarly, interview based studies report that low interdependency between units (Duhaime and Grant, 1984), and the need to focus on core activities (Hamilton and Chow, 1993), strongly motivate the decision to divest. Despite the occasional case of a successful conglomerate, as a whole studies suggest that firms are inclined to, and probably better off by, staying close to their specific competencies.

2.4. Empirical Studies of Foreign Divestment

The number of studies dealing specifically with foreign divestment remains limited. In the 1970s, a high number of nationalization actions in developing countries led to several studies on forced divestment (see for example Kobrin, 1980), but voluntary divestment was largely overlooked. In the 1980s, although concerns were raised about the instability of the then increasingly popular cooperative ventures (Kogut, 1988; Blodgett, 1992), and about the integration problems posed by international acquisitions (Nahavandi and Malekzadeh, 1988; Olie, 1990), hardly any studies of foreign divestments were actually undertaken at the time. It is only quite recently that research on foreign divestment has begun to appear. Some studies have looked at the issue from the viewpoint of relocation of manufacturing capacity inter alia as a response to the increasing cost disadvantages of advanced economies like Belgium (Pennings and Sleuwaegen, 2000) and Japan (Yamamura et al., 2003), and a few have studied the effects of political and institutional transformation in transition economies such as Poland (e.g., Roberts and Thompson, 2003). The divestment of retailing operations has also attracted attention in recent times (Alexander and Quinn, 2002; Burt et al., 2003; Wrigley and Currah, 2003), especially as a result of the much-publicized international failures of companies like Marks and Spencer (Burt et al., 2002; Mellahi et al., 2002) and Royal Ahold (Wrigley and Currah, 2003).

A number of studies of international divestment have taken a firm-level perspective, focusing on the relationship between cultural and experiential aspects of foreign expansion and divestitures (Li, 1995; Barkema et al., 1996; Shaver et al., 1997; Hennart et al., 1998). A basic contention in these studies is that while internationalization exposes companies to an array of difficulties regardless of the actual mode of entry used or the location of the foreign unit, problems are likely to increase when foreign entries are made in culturally distant locations, when there are few other foreign firms operating in the same country,[4] and/or they are made by acquisition or joint venture. Acquisitions and joint ventures involve 'double layered acculturation' in which both another corporate culture and a foreign national culture have to be dealt with. Such processes are difficult, which in turn may lead to inferior performance, and the studies by Li (1995) and Barkema et al. (1996) report that the probability of divestment is higher for joint ventures and acquisitions. However, while Benito (1997a) also finds that acquisitions did indeed increase exit rates, joint ventures did not. Mata and Portugal (2000) take this line of investigation a step further by pointing out that divestments can be made through closure as well as through sell-offs.[5] Finally, in line with several studies of domestic exits, the results from Li's and Benito's studies also indicate that international diversification entails a higher risk of subsequent exit than foreign ventures within the parent company's main line of business.

Taken together, the studies that have been done so far on international divestment have pointed to some relatively consistent patterns regarding how certain characteristics of the modes of entry into a country may have an effect on the fate of the foreign subsidiaries established there. It is noteworthy that the level of analysis has predominantly been the foreign unit or subsidiary. Despite the considerable interest on and discussion of companies' internationalization strategies, especially with regard to so-called global strategies, to this point the potential role of corporate level internationalization strategies has yet to be analysed in the context of foreign divestment.

3. International Business Strategies

3.1. A Typology of International Business Strategies

A central tenet in current international business thinking is that there is no single international strategy (Harzing, 2000). Appropriate strategies are those that match companies' resources and capabilities to given market conditions in various locations. The decisive determinants are the extent to which there are, on one hand, significant competitive advantages to be gained by integrating activities on a world-wide basis – especially economies of scale and scope – and on the other hand, market and resource conditions in specific locations demand local adaptation and responsiveness; hence, the label 'integration-responsiveness' model. In Bartlett and Ghoshal's (1989) typology, international business strategies can be divided into four basic categories: multinational strategy (also called multi-domestic strategy), international strategy, global strategy, and transnational strategy.

Firms following a multi-domestic strategy focus on national differences to achieve their strategic objectives, usually by differentiating their product offer in response to national differences in customer preferences, industry characteristics, and government regulation. Under this strategy, the individual national subsidiaries typically enjoy considerable decision-making autonomy and are largely self-sufficient in terms of the resources needed to implement the strategy.

Firms following an international strategy focus on creating innovations at home and then exploiting them on foreign markets, and occasionally on a world-wide basis. This is perhaps the standard type of firm internationalization as portrayed in for example Vernon's product life cycle model (Vernon, 1966). Their internationalization processes relies heavily on transferring new products, processes, and/or business systems developed from the home-country to markets elsewhere. International strategies tend to treat foreign markets in a one-by-one fashion, and typically make use of exports as a way of serving them, especially in the earlier phases of companies' internationalization (Welch and Luostarinen, 1988). Foreign subsidiaries are normally used relatively late in the internationalization process, and then mostly when entering important markets where the scale of operations justify their use (see e.g., Dicken, 2003, pp. 206–207).

Firms pursuing a global strategy focus on achieving world-wide efficiency, e.g., attaining the lowest cost position or the highest brand recognition for their products. Such companies typically centralize production as well as those other value-generating activities that exhibit high economies of scale. A characteristic of such companies is that they manufacture fairly standardized products for sale around the world. Segal-Horn and Faulkner (1999) mention Gillette razors as a representative example: razors need little local adaptation, the technological production function is well-established, and the marketing message is simple and works acceptably well in most markets, and therefore only distribution and sales need to be handled locally. As put by Segal-Horne and Faulkner (1999, p. 122): '... the global corporation treats overseas operations as delivery pipelines to a unified global market.' Some scholars are unconvinced about the viability of truly global strategies, and doubt that more than a handful of firms actually have implemented them (see, e.g., Rugman, 2000). Instead, it is argued that most MNCs are regional with the largest part of their value activities located in their home region of the triad, i.e., in either North America, the EU, or Japan.

The transnational strategy is an attempt to move beyond the global integration versus local responsiveness trade-off. Hedlund (1986) and later Bartlett and Ghoshal (1989, 1993) have argued that to succeed MNCs will increasingly have to be locally responsive – with learning as a key requirement for success – whilst also achieving global scale and scope efficiencies. While such a double-edged approach to internationalization may look appealing in principle, designing and implementing a transnational strategy involves the daunting task of reconciling the seemingly conflicting objectives of simultaneously achieving global efficiency, being locally responsive and exploiting and leveraging the learning potential in different national operations (Dicken, 2003). Not surprisingly, the occurrence of transnational strategies appears to be low (Leong and Tan, 1993), and only a handful of companies have gained the transnational label.

3.2. The Core Factors in the Integration–Responsiveness Framework

As noted above, the basic drivers of integration benefits across national borders are economies of scale and scope. Scale economies arise through various technological factors that make it cheaper in terms of unit costs to produce a large quantity rather than a small one. Important sources of scale advantages are that high levels of production allow (i) investments in specialized manufacturing machines and tools, (ii) building larger manufacturing operations, e.g., factories, (iii) higher levels of employee specialization, and (iv) spreading overhead costs (Barney, 1996). Scale economies can also be achieved in areas other than production, especially purchasing, advertising, and R&D (Besanko et al., 2000). Scope economies exist because of the cost savings or revenue enhancements that a firm may achieve through the particular mix of activities and products that it is involved in, such as: (a) savings due to sharing distribution networks for different product lines or conducting common research and development, (b) increasing revenue by offering product bundles that provide more value to customers, and (c) mutual forbearance benefits in the context of multipoint competition (Barney, 1996).

Whereas integration drivers promote standardization across borders, splitting-up the range of value activities, and finding the optimal locations worldwide for setting-up large scale operations for specific value activities, drivers of responsiveness work in the opposite direction by requiring local presence and adaptation to local conditions (Yip, 1989). In turn, these forces lead to treating various locations more or less independently of each other. Issues of responsiveness hinge on three main conditions. First, certain resources are immobile or lose considerably in value if exploited elsewhere, as is the case for production processes that are co-located with sources of natural resources and/or utilities; e.g., the processing of metal and alloys, which are extremely power-consuming activities, tend to be located close to energy generating facilities. Another instance of immobility is the co-located as well as co-specialized configuration of supplier-manufacturer relations often found in industrial clusters (Markusen, 1996; Porter, 1998; Pinch et al., 2003). Looking at the spatial stickiness of knowledge and technology, scholars like Gertler (2003), Maskell and Malmberg (1999), and Narula (2003) assert that despite the alleged globalization of technology the distinctiveness and idiosyncrasy of locations has far from vanished: innovation systems remain largely nationally bound, and due to considerable inertia in knowledge creation (and development and usage) it remains concentrated in certain locations, institutions, and firms. Second, local responsiveness is conducive in addressing the needs of customers in various locations, thereby increasing demand for a firm's goods or services. Local adaptation is often necessary in order to compete (see e.g., Solberg, 2000; Yip, 1992); especially in consumer goods markets where demand is a function of local tastes and customs, and where linguistic and cultural differences must be taken into account when marketing the product offer. Third, despite concerted global and regional efforts at reducing barriers towards cross-border flows of products and resources, especially regarding tariffs and quotas, many still exist in the form of technical requirements, preferential treatment practices, and government regulations.

4. An Analysis of Divestment Based on the Integration–Responsiveness Framework

How do the core factors behind choice of international business strategy influence divestment? It is useful to start by distinguishing between different basic types of divestment. Drawing on the work of Benito and Welch (1997) and Clark and Wrigley (1997), divestments can be seen (i) as adjustments, (ii) as failures, and (iii) as a result of re-structuring (see Table 1). They can also (iv) be externally imposed, e.g., expropriation and nationalization (Kobrin, 1980), but here I focus on divestment actions that are brought about the companies themselves, i.e., voluntary divestment, and disregard divestment that has been imposed on the companies by, e.g., adverse governmental action.

Adjustment driven divestments tend to be small and gradual; for example, selling-off a certain entity within a larger subsidiary, outsourcing some activity, or closing down a particular unit – sometimes relocating the unit to a lower cost country (Dicken, 2003). Failure driven divestments involves closing down a particular unit, but normally without repercussions (for the corporation) beyond the actual case.[6] In contrast, divestments due to re-structuring tend to entail orchestrated strategic manoeuvres with seemingly dramatic consequences for the corporate network. They can involve many corporate units performing different activities in a variety of locations, and it is difficult for any given unit to get insulated from such processes at the corporate level.[7] Nevertheless, due to the sheer magnitude and depth of re-structuring processes, they seldom occur. They are necessarily the exception of corporate life; otherwise companies would most likely implode into an unproductive state of chaos and confusion.

4.1. Integration Factors

The quest for scale advantages, fueled by an increased ability to standardize products and processes, is perhaps regarded as the prototypical globalization driver (Yip, 1989). Achieving scale effects entails setting-up large units in manufacturing, distribution, and/or other value activities, which in turn often involves a degree of rationalization amongst the set of foreign subsidiaries operated by the MNC. Activities become concentrated in larger, but necessarily fewer, units worldwide, from which successive stages in the value chain of the corporation, or perhaps even final customers, are then supplied. Hence, as shown in Table 1, the scale economies factor operates as a driver of divestment of the restructuring kind. However, while high levels of divestment should be expected at the initial stages of implementing a global strategy, when the required restructuring has taken place divestment rates are likely to decrease. There are three main reasons. First, the remaining units are large and likely to operate at lower units costs: this is the efficiency effect. Second, since there is a smaller number of remaining units, companies simply have fewer additional re-location alternatives left: this is the scarcity effect. Third, because the division-of-labor amongst the remaining units is likely to be higher, with each unit specializing on only one or at most a small set of activities, the worldwide corporate network becomes much dependent on the various individual units that it consists of: this is the dependence effect. It should be noted that there are, obviously, also diseconomies of scale, principally: managerial diseconomies, increasing distance to suppliers and markets (which in turn leads to higher transportation costs), and greater network complexity which in turn amplifies the burden on the logistics involved.

Table 1
The Effects on Divestment of Integration–Responsiveness Factors

Strategy Drivers	Typical Divestment Motives	Likely Effects on Divestment
Integration factors		
Scale	Re-structuring	Large units less likely to be divested
	Failure	Few units less likely to be divested
		Specialized units less likely to be divested
Scope	Adjustment	Inter-dependent units less likely to be divested
	Failure	Co-specialized units less likely to be divested
Responsiveness factors		
Adaptation	Adjustment	Lower divestment likelihood due to increased performance through local responsiveness
	Failure	Lower divestment likelihood due to local ties
		Increased divestment likelihood due to inferior (worldwide) corporate flexibility and transferability
Immobility	Adjustment	Lower divestment likelihood due to access to unique local resources
	Failure	Increased divestment likelihood due to a (gradual) weakening of resource rents

Whereas scale economies are based on a division-of-labor logic, scope economies arise from the co-specialization between activities and/or organizational entities. In order to achieve such economies, units (or activities) have to work in tandem and accept their interdependencies; e.g., when distribution networks are shared in the marketing of different product lines. From the viewpoint of scope economies, divestment is to occur primarily as a result of adjustments in the level and types of activities undertaken throughout the corporate network of subsidiaries, albeit outright failures must occasionally be expected. It is difficult to design with any great accuracy how scope advantages can be achieved. Surely, certain organizational setups (or architectures, if one will) may be more conducive to than others in achieving scope benefits, but such advantages are foremost developed over time as various combinations are tried out, or some times stumbled into. The quest for scope economies should therefore predictably produce some amount of divestment, simply as the by-product of the learning and adjustments processes involved. Nevertheless, as indicated in Table 1, due to the high degree of interdependence between units required to achieve scope advantages, the likelihood of divestment should be fairly low for individual units: risk is diversified away because they cannot just be treated as stand-alone entities.

4.2. Responsiveness Factors

Multi-domestic and transnational strategies are based on responsiveness factors (Harzing, 2000). The essential idea behind such factors, be they adaptation of products and their marketing to suit local demand patterns, cultivating connections to local authorities, or the use of localized resources, is that they should improve the performance of a unit – either by enhancing its revenue from the market, or by reducing its costs – which in turn ought to increase its survivability. A carefully crafted adaptation to local conditions, which may entail developing rather unique organizational competences and routines, and the privileged access to valuable resources, could be seen as important components of a subsidiary's competitive advantage. Being path-dependent and tied to the specific circumstances of time and place, such advantages are usually hard to imitate: as put by Clark and Wrigley (1997, p. 353), firms 'are held hostage by their history and geography'. That is not to say, of course, that firms' advantages are forever sustainable; they may erode over time, or even made obsolete by developments elsewhere such as the introduction of new technologies or the spill-over of profound changes in consumption and demand patterns. Local responsiveness is a two-edged sword; if the rewards to local adaptation for some reason decline considerably, being tied to a given locality drastically decreases the options open for action. Due to the unique and path-dependent character of their operations and competencies, such units are both less likely to be flexible and less likely to be of vital use to units elsewhere in the corporate network, thereby most possibly raising the divestment rates of subsidiaries based on a locally-oriented strategy.

4.3. The Likelihood of Divestment

The foregoing discussion is summarized in Table 1. Unsatisfactory performance defines the most basic divestment motive (Duhaime and Grant, 1984; Clark and Wrigley, 1997): any subsidiary performing below expectations runs the risk of being divested, especially if under-performance persists. The risk of under-performing, or outright failure, can be related to the type of strategy pursued by companies – in particular, a transnational strategy may due to its complexity be more difficult to pull off successfully, and any given subsidiary of a company pursuing such a strategy may hence carry a higher baseline divestment likelihood – but failure will happen regardless of MNCs' strategies. Divestment propensities may well vary depending on type of strategy, but it is inconceivable that failures can be eliminated altogether. Taking the discussion beyond cases of failure, the distinct effect of scale considerations on divestment is through their call for re-structuring of a corporate network. Such actions are unlikely to take place very often. They can rightly be regarded as major strategic decisions that require thoughtful planning and implementation. When they actually are carried out, they may necessitate drastic changes – for good or for bad – in a company's competitive posture and in the configuration of its units spread around the world. For example, increasing the scale of a given manufacturing operation usually requires very real investments in, say, factory buildings and machinery. Likewise, re-configuring a corporate network by concentrating previously dispersed manufacturing operations into a smaller set of larger facilities, involves closing down a number of hitherto active manufacturing units. Conversely, scope considerations as well as local responsiveness concerns are more liable to require frequent adjustments, of which some will involve divestment through closing down particular units or selling them off, but where many only involve divestments of a more partial kind, such as changing the activity composition of given foreign subsidiaries.

5. International Business Strategies and Divestment of Foreign Subsidiaries

From the viewpoint of a given foreign subsidiary (S_i), what is the likelihood that it will be divested depending on the type of strategy that its parent follows regarding international business? Or put differently, does it matter whether a subsidiary caters to a local market within the scope of a multi-domestic strategy (a S_{MS} subsidiary), or whether the subsidiary is a constituent part of a worldwide production network operated by a global company (a S_{GS} subsidiary)? Does it matter whether it basically is an extension of the parent MNC's domestic operations into foreign markets (a S_{IS} subsidiary), or whether it is a node (a S_{TS} subsidiary) in a MNC's worldwide matrix? Propositions concerning a typology of subsidiaries based on characterization of parent corporations' international strategies must necessarily be broad, and one cannot expect a high degree of predictive power for individual cases. However, the preceding discussion points out to some general tendencies. First, in terms of some initial, or baseline, divestment likelihood one would expect subsidiaries established and operated within the frameworks of international and multi-domestic strategies to be the least likely to be divested. A hallmark of such strategies is that they are country-focused, either on the home country (IS) or the host country (MS). They do not require extensive coordination across borders. S_{IS} subsidiaries typically carry out a limited number of value activities – such as sales – in a foreign market, whereas a S_{MS} subsidiary usually takes on a greater range of activities (hence sometimes earning the label 'miniature replica'), but in both circumstances their management is greatly simplified by the relative lack of crossnational coordination burdens, increased complexity, and, as a consequence, a greater risk of failing that typifies global and transnational strategies. S_{TS} subsidiaries in particular, being parts of really ambitious attempts at reconciling the seemingly divergent demands of global integration versus local responsiveness, must be expected to have relatively high failure rates as they as well as their parent corporations try out workable solutions.

Figure 1
Divestment Likelihood of Different Types of
Foreign Subsidiaries as a Function of Time

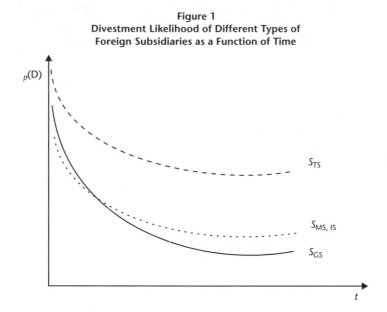

Ranking subsidiaries with regard to divestment probability $p(D)$, the following baseline order should be expected: $p(D)S_{TS} > p(D)S_{GS} > p(D)_{MS} \approx p(D)_{IS}$. Nevertheless, taking a more dynamic view, i.e., bringing a time dimension into the picture, may change that order.[8] In agreement with the literature on the 'liability of newness' (Hannan and Freeman, 1984), the slope of $p(D)$ is generally expected to be negative, as depicted in figure 1, but the rates of decrease vary across the various strategies. Even though subsidiaries in transnational strategies may produce the occasional high pay-off, they persistently face a high risk of failure. As pointed out earlier, while high levels of divestment should also be expected at the initial stages of implementing a global strategy, when companies have done the necessary re-structuring of operations and shake-out of subsidiaries, divestment rates are likely to decrease sharply; partly as a result of the enhanced efficiency of the re-configured worldwide operational networks of the companies, partly due to higher interdependencies among units, and partly as a result of fewer remaining units that can be divested. Over time, it is hence probable that subsidiaries of global operators, $S_{GS,}$ are those that actually reach the lowest divestment propensities of the different types of foreign subsidiaries.

6. Concluding Remarks

Divestments are an integral part of business. They can be seen as the results of ever-evolving processes of change that keep companies and whole economies rejuvenated and in shape.[9] Divestment is a serious issue. It frequently has wide-ranging, and sometimes severe, consequences for those involved; especially individuals that lose their jobs (Storrie, 1993), and towns and regions that lose much-needed employment opportunities (Hudson, 1997; Tomaney et al., 1999).

Public opinion tends to be more negative whenever divestments are made by foreign companies instead of domestic ones. Despite lack of strong evidence sustaining such a claim (see, e.g., Mata and Portugal, 2002), it is commonly believed that the decisions to close down a factory or sell a subsidiary would sometimes not have been taken had the company been run by presumably more considerate national owners.[10]

To the extent that foreign investors are at all welcomed, global players are increasingly seen as the least desirable: the imagery of ruthless and allegedly footloose global companies convey almost exclusively negative connotations. Foreign companies should preferably melt so completely into the local contexts they operate in that they become indistinguishable from indigenous ones: that in fact is the underlying logic of multi-domestic strategies.

Alternatively, foreign companies should foster subsidiaries that take on strategic roles within the worldwide corporate network, as would be the case with so-called 'centers-of-excellence' (Holm and Pedersen, 2000; Benito et al., 2003; Holm et al., 2003). Transnational strategies in particular seemingly cultivate such initiatives. However, an important point from the analysis presented here is that such attitudes may be misguided, at least as regards likelihood of divestment. Subsidiaries in transnational strategies run high risks. Albeit the pay-off may potentially be great, there are actually few success stories to be told. Pay-off is linked to risk, but from the perspective of individuals – and perhaps even locations/regions – that ought to be risk-averse, a low divestment risk is apparently preferable.

Locally-bound subsidiaries may likewise seem desirable, but if presence in a country is based on traditional factors like cost advantages, local tastes, and trade barriers, the location forces holding them there will in many cases be too weak to sustain their survival over time. Once that happens, they will most probably be lost forever. In an increasingly global business landscape, there is in a sense 'no place to hide'. However, if one survives the initial shake-out often produced by the implementation of global strategies, becoming part of global corporate networks is potentially the best place to be.

Acknowledgements

I thank Neil Wrigley and two anonymous reviewers for their helpful comments. This article is based on a Keynote Lecture given at the International Conference on Divestment: Corporate Strategies, The Regions and Policy Responses, Lisbon, September 22–23, 2003. The comments by conference participants, Christian Geisler Asmussen, Sara McGaughey, and Rajneesh Narula on earlier versions of the manuscript are gratefully acknowledged. Research funding was provided by the Research Council of Norway (project 139982/510, 'Globalization and internationalization of the Norwegian Economy').

Notes

1. Barkema et al. (1996) report that of 225 FDIs made by large Dutch MNCs in the period 1966 to 1988 only half were still in existence in 1988. Benito's (1997a) study of Norwegian MNCs shows that more than half of their FDIs in 1982 were divested within a period of ten years. Mata and Portugal (2000) report yearly exit rates of more than 10% for a sample of foreign subsidiaries in Portugal.
2. Important contributions include Doz (1986), Porter (1986), Bartlett and Ghoshal (1989, 1993), Yip (1992), Prahalad and Doz (1997), and Harzing (2000).
3. Specific assets can be either tangible or intangible. In general, the empirical evidence suggests that durable tangible specific assets such as high sunk cost in machinery, and/or property (Guy, 1999), discourage exit (Siegfried and Evans, 1994). Similarly, intangible assets such as goodwill, advertising and R&D intensity, firm-specific human capital, and even emotional attachment to the firm and/or industry, can also operate as exit barriers by raising the perceived cost of leaving the arena (Caves and Porter, 1976).
4. Shaver et al. (1997) argue that knowledge and information about local conditions generated by foreign firms already present in a country create spill-over effects from which new entrants may benefit.
5. In a study of foreign investment in Portugal they report that acquisitions have higher sell-off rates than greenfield investments. The converse is true for geenfields, which turn out to have significantly higher probabilities of being closed down. Similarly, minority joint ventures show higher sell-off rates than majority ventures and wholly owned subsidiaries, but the ownership arrangement had no effect on closures.
6. However, the case of Marks & Spencer's internationalization failures in the late 1990s that led to a corporate crisis from which the company is still recovering from, is a well-known example of the contrary (Burt et al., 2002).
7. Many re-structuring processes of companies have been reported in the international business and corporate strategy literatures. For example, Savary (1996) gives a detailed account of the transformation of the Thompson Consumer Electronics due to evolution of the consumer electronics industry towards globalization.
8. It is obviously difficult to make well-grounded generalizations about long-term developments. Much depends on the overall risk profile of a particular venture. As pointed out earlier, that hinges on a range of factors besides the type of international business strategy; including the host country of the subsidiary (e.g., political risk), the type of industry (e.g., emergent versus sunset industries), the type of activities performed by the subsidiary (e.g., R&D versus manufacturing versus distribution and sales), and the modes of establishment (e.g., greenfield versus acquisitions, and/or joint venture versus wholly-owned subsidiary). Also, the degree of flexibility available to the corporation – e.g., due to operating production sites with spare capacity in different currency areas – has implications for the ease of which activities can be shifted around (Rangan, 1998), and/or ultimately divested.

9. While necessary elements of any well-functioning economic system such processes are not infallible: economic actors (owners, managers, creditors) base their decisions on imperfect information and subjective beliefs; they make mistakes, as do regulators and political institutions.
10. Analysing FDI in Portugal over the period 1982–1989, Mata and Portugal (2002) conclude that foreign and domestic firms display identical exit rates over time. Thomsen (2000) studied company survival in Denmark over the period 1895–1995 and finds that although foreign-owned firms are divested relatively more often than Danish-owned firms, the difference between the two groups is not statistically significant when factors such as size, industry, and capital structure are controlled for.

References

Alexander, N., Quinn, B. (2002) International retail divestment. *International Journal of Retail & Distribution Management*, 30 (2): 112–125.

Bane, W. T., Neubauer, F.-F. (1981) Diversification and the failure of new activities. *Strategic Management Journal*, 2: 219–233.

Barkema, H. G., Bell, J., Pennings, J. M. (1996) Foreign entry, cultural barriers, and learning. *Strategic Management Journal*, 17: 151–166.

Barney, J. B. (1996) *Gaining and Sustaining Competitive Advantage*. Reading, MA: Addison-Wesley Publishing.

Bartlett, C. A., Ghoshal, S. (1989) *Managing Across Borders: The Transnational Solution*. Boston, MA: Harvard Business School Press.

Bartlett, C. A., Ghoshal, S. (1993) Beyond the M-form: toward a managerial theory of the firm. *Strategic Management Journal*, 14 (Winter Special Issue): 23–46.

Benito, G. R. G. (1997a) Divestment of foreign production operations. *Applied Economics*, 29 (10): 1365–1377.

Benito, G. R. G. (1997b) Why are foreign subsidiaries divested? A conceptual framework. In I. Björkman and M. Forsgren (eds) *The Nature of the International Firm*. Copenhagen: Copenhagen Business School Press, 309–334.

Benito, G. R. G., Grøgaard, B., Narula, R. (2003) Environmental influences on MNE subsidiary roles: economic integration and the Nordic countries, *Journal of International Business Studies*, 34 (5): 443–456.

Benito, G. R. G., Welch, L. S. (1997) De-internationalization. *Management International Review*, 37 (Special Issue 2): 7–25.

Besanko, D., Dranove, D., Shanley, M. (2000) *Economics of Strategy*. 2nd edition. New York: John Wiley & Sons.

Blodgett, L. L. (1992) Factors in the instability of international joint ventures: an event history analysis. *Strategic Management Journal*, 13: 475–481.

Boddewyn, J. J. (1979) Foreign divestment: magnitude and factors. *Journal of International Business Studies*, 10 (1): 21–27.

Burt, S., Dawson, J., Sparks, L. (2003) Failure in international retailing: research propositions. *International Review of Retail, Distribution & Consumer Research*, 13(4): 355–373.

Burt, S. L., Mellahi, K., Jackson, T. P., Sparks, L. (2002) Retail internationalization and retail failure: issues from the case of Marks and Spencer. *International Review of Retail, Distribution & Consumer Research*, 12(2): 191–219.

Caves, R. E. (1995) Growth and decline in multinational enterprises: from equilibrium models to turnover processes. In K. Y. Chen and P. Drysdale (eds) *Corporate Links and Foreign Direct Investment in Asia and the Pacific*. Pymble, Australia: Harper Educational, 9–28.

Caves, R. E., Porter, M. E. (1976) Barriers to exit. In R. Masson and P. D. Qualls (eds) *Essays in Industrial Organization in Honor of Joe S. Bain*. Cambridge: Ballinger, 36–69.

Chow, Y. K., Hamilton, R. T. (1993) Corporate divestment: an overview. *Journal of Managerial Psychology*, 8: 9–13

Chng, P.-L., Pangankar, N. (2000) Research on global strategy. *International Journal of Management Reviews*, 2 (1): 91–110.

Clark, G. L., Wrigley, N. (1977) Exit, the firm and sunk costs: reconceptualizing the corporate geography of disinvestment and plant closure. *Progress in Human Geography*, 21 (3): 338–358.

Davis, J. V. (1974) The strategic divestment decision. *Long Range Planning*, 7 (1): 15–18.

Dicken, P.(1994) Global-local tensions: firms and states in the global space-economy. *Economic Geography*, 70 (2): 101–128.

Dicken, P.(2003) *Global Shift: Reshaping the Global Economic Map in the 21st Century*. 4th edition. London: Sage Publications.

Doz, Y. (1986) *Strategic Management in Multinational Companies*. Oxford: Pergamon Press.

Duhaime, I. M., Grant, J. H. (1984) Factors influencing the divestment decision-making: evidence from a field study. *Strategic Management Journal*, 5: 301–318.

Dunning, J. H. (2001) The key literature on IB activities 1960–2000. In A. M. Rugman and T. L. Brewer (eds) *The Oxford Handbook of International Business*. Oxford: Oxford University Press, 36–68.

Gertler, M. S. (2001) Best practice? Geography, learning and the institutional limits to strong convergence. *Journal of Economic Geography*, 1: 5–26.

Gertler, M. S. (2003) Tacit knowledge and the economic geography of context, or the undefinable tacitness of being (there). *Journal of Economic Geography*, 3: 75 99.

Guy, C. (1999) Exit strategies and sunk costs: the implications for multiple retailers. *International Journal of Retail & Distribution Management*, 27(6): 237–245.

Hamilton, R. T., Chow, Y. K. (1993) Why managers divest – evidence from New Zealand's largest companies. *Strategic Management Journal*, 14: 479–484.

Hannan, M. T., Freeman, J. (1984) Structural inertia and organizational change. *American Sociological Review*, 49: 149–164.

Harrigan, K. R. (1980). *Strategies for Declining Business*. Lexington, VA: Lexington Books.

Harzing, A. W. (2000) An empirical analysis and extension of the Bartlett and Ghoshal typology of multinational companies. *Journal of International Business Studies*, 31 (1): 101–120.

Haynes, M., Thompson, S., Wright, M. (2002) The impact of divestment on firm performance: empirical evidence from a panel of UK companies. *Journal of Industrial Economics*, 50 (2): 173–196.

Haynes, M., Thompson, S., Wright, M. (2003) The determinants of corporate divestment: evidence from a panel of UK firms. *Journal of Economic Behavior and Organization*, 52: 147–166.

Hedlund, G. (1986) The hypermodern MNE – a heterarchy? *Human Resource Management*, 25: 9–25.

Hennart, J. F., Kim, D. J., Zeng, M. (1998) The impact of joint ventures status on the longevity of Japanese stakes in US manufacturing affiliates. *Organization Science*, 9(3): 382–395.

Holm, U., Malmberg, A., Sölvell, Ö. (2003) Subsidiary impact on host-country economies: the case of foreign-owned subsidiaries attracting investment into Sweden. *Journal of Economic Geography*, 3: 389–408.

Holm, U., Pedersen, T. (eds) (2000) *The Emergence and Impact of MNC Centres of Excellence: A Subsidiary Perspective*. London: Macmillan.

Hudson, R. (1997) Regional futures: industrial restructuring, new high volume production concepts and spatial development. *Regional Studies*, 31 (5): 467–478.

Kobrin, S. J. (1980) Foreign enterprise and forced divestment in LDCs. *International Organizations*, 34: 65–88.

Kogut, B. (1988) Joint ventures: theoretical and empirical perspectives. *Strategic Management Journal*, 9: 319–332.

Lecraw, D. J. (1984) Diversification strategy and performance. *Journal of Industrial Economics*, 33: 179–198.

Leong, S. M., Tan, C. T. (1993) Managing across borders: an empirical test of the Bartlett and Ghoshal [1989] organizational typology. *Journal of International Business Studies*, 24 (3): 449–464.

Li, J. (1995) Foreign entry and survival: effects of strategic choices on performance in international markets. *Strategic Management Journal*, 16 (5): 333–251.

Markides, C. (1995) *Diversification, Refocusing and Economic Performance*. Cambridge, MA: MIT Press.

Markusen, A. (1996) Sticky places in a slippery space: a typology of industrial districts. *Economic Geography*, 72: 293–313.

Maskell, P., Malmberg, A. (1999) Localised learning and industrial competitiveness. *Cambridge Journal of Economics*, 23: 167–185.

Mata, J., Portugal, P. (2000) Closure and divestiture by foreign entrants: the impact of entry and post-entry strategies. *Strategic Management Journal*, 21 (5): 549–562.

Mata, J., Portugal, P. (2002) The survival of new domestic and foreign-owned firms. *Strategic Management Journal*, 23: 323–343.

Matthyssens, P., Pauwels, P. (2000) Uncovering international market-exit processes: a comparative case study. *Psychology & Marketing*, 17 (8): 697–719.

Mellahi, K., Jackson, P., Sparks, L. (2002) An exploratory study into failure in successful organizations: the case of Marks & Spencer. *British Journal of Management*, 13: 15–29.

Morck, R., Shleifer, A., Vishny, R. N. (1990) Do managerial objectives drive bad acquisitions? *Journal of Finance*, 45: 31–48.

Morgan, G., Kristensen, P.H., Whitley, R. (eds) (2001) *The Multinational Firm: Organizing across Institutional and National Divides*. Oxford: Oxford University Press.

Nahavandi, A., Malekzadeh, A. R. (1988) Acculturation in mergers and acquisitions. *Academy of Management Review*, 13: 79–90.

Narula, R. (2003) *Globalization and Technology: Interdependence, Innovation Systems and Industrial Policy*. Cambridge: Polity Press.

Olie, R. (1990) Culture and integration problems in international mergers and acquisitions. *European Management Journal*, 8: 206–215.

Padmanabhan, P. (1993) The impact of European divestment announcement on shareholder wealth: evidence from the UK. *Journal of Multinational Financial Management*, 2: 185–208.

Pennings, E., Sleuwaegen, L. (2000) International relocation: firm and industry determinants. *Economics Letters*, 67 (2): 179–186.

Pennings, J., Barkema, H., Douma, S. (1994) Organizational learning and diversification. *Academy of Management Journal*, 37: 608–640.

Pinch, S., Henry, N., Jenkins, M., Tallman, S. (2003) From 'industrial districts' to 'knowledge clusters': a model of knowledge dissemination and competitive advantage in industrial agglomerations. *Journal of Economic Geography*, 3: 373–388.

Porter, M. E. (1986) Competition in global industries: a conceptual framework. In M. E. Porter (ed) *Competition in Global Industries*. Cambridge, MA: Harvard University Press, 15–60.

Porter, M.E. (1998) *On Competition*. Boston, MA: Harvard Business School Press.

Prahalad, C.K., Doz, Y. (1987) *The Multinational Mission: Balancing Local Demands and Global Vision*. New York: Free Press.

Rangan, S. (1998) Do multinationals operate flexibly? Theory and evidence. *Journal of International Business Studies*, 29 (2): 217–237.

Roberts, B., Thompson, S. (2003) Entry and exit in a transition economy: the case of Poland. *Review of Industrial Organization*, 22: 225–243.

Rugman, A. M. (2000) *The End of Globalization*. London: Random House.

Rugman, A. M., Brewer, T. L. (eds) (2001) *The Oxford Handbook of International Business*. Oxford: Oxford University Press.

Rugman, A. M., Verbeke, A. (2004) A perspective on regional and global strategies of multinational enterprises. *Journal of International Business Studies*, 35 (1): 3–18.

Rumelt, R. (1974). *Strategy, Structure and Economic Performance*. Cambridge, MA: Harvard University Press.

Savary, J. (1996) Thomson Consumer Electronics: from national champion to global contender. In J. -E. Nilsson, P. Dicken, and J. Peck (eds) *The Internationalization Process: European Firms in Global Competition*. London: Paul Chapman Publishing, 90–108.

Segal-Horne, S., Faulkner, D. (1999) *The Dynamics of International Strategy*. London: Thomson Learning.

Shapiro, D. (1983) Entry, exit, and the theory of the multinational corporation. In C. P. Kindleberger and D. B. Audretsch (eds) *The Multinational Corporation in the 1980s*. Cambridge, MA: MIT Press, 103–122.

Shaver, J., Mitchell, W., Yeung, B. (1997) The effect of own-firm and other-firm experience on foreign entrant survival in the United States. *Strategic Management Journal*, 18 (10): 811–824.

Siegfried, J. J., Evans, L. B. (1994) Empirical studies of entry and exit: a survey of the evidence. *Review of Industrial Organization*, 9: 121–155.

Solberg, C.A. (2000) Standardization or adaptation of the international marketing mix: the role of the local subsidiary/representative. *Journal of International Marketing*, 8 (1): 78–98.

Storrie, D. (1993) *The Anatomy of a Large Swedish Plant Closure*. PhD thesis, Department of Economics, University of Gothenburg, Sweden.

Thomsen, S. (2000) The survival of foreign subsidiaries and domestically-owned companies in Denmark, 1895–1995. *Scandinavian Economic History Review*, 48 (2): 72–86.

Tomaney, J., Pike, A., Cornford, J. (1999) Plant closure and the local economy: the case of Swan Hunter on Tyneside. *Regional Studies*, 33 (5): 401–411.

Vernon, R. (1966) International investment and international trade in the product cycle. *Quarterly Journal of Economics*, 80: 190–207.

Welch, L. S., Luostarinen, R. K. (1988) Internationalization: evolution of a concept. *Journal of General Management*, 14, 34–55.

Welch, L. S., Wiedersheim-Paul, F. (1980) Initial exports – a marketing failure? *Journal of Management Studies*, 17 (3): 333–344.

Weston, J. F. (1989) Divestitures: mistakes or learning? *Journal of Applied Corporate Finance*, 2: 68–76.

Whitley, R. (2001) How and why are international firms different? The consequences of cross-border managerial coordination for firm characteristics and behaviour. In G. Morgan, P. H. Kristensen, and R. Whitley (eds) *The Multinational Firm: Organizing across Institutional and National Divides*. Oxford: Oxford University Press, 27–68.

Williamson, O. E. (1985) *The Economic Institutions of Capitalism*. New York: Free Press.

Wright, W., Thompson, S. (1987) Divestment and the control of divisionalised firms. *Accounting and Business Research*, 17: 259–267.

Wrigley, N., Currah, A. (2003) The stresses of retail internationalization: lessons from Royal Ahold's experience in Latin America. *International Review of Retail, Distribution & Consumer Research*, 13 (3): 221–243.

Yamamura, E., Sonobe, T., Otsuka, K. (2003) Human capital, cluster formation, and international relocation: the case of the garment industry in Japan, 1968–98. *Journal of Economic Geography*, 3: 37–56.

Yip, G. S. (1989) Global strategy ... in a world of nations? *Sloan Management Review*, 30: 29–41.

Yip, G. S. (1992) *Total Global Strategy*. Englewood Cliffs, NJ: Prentice-Hall.

41

Shutting Up Shop: Understanding the International Exit Process in Retailing

Paul Jackson, Kamel Mellahi and Leigh Sparks

The increasing internationalisation of business has made research into the subject an important topic. Research on internationalisation has been a growth industry, both generally and in specific sectors. For example in retailing there are recent texts and edited works by Kacker [1985], Brown and Burt [1992], Kacker and Sternquist [1994], McGoldrick and Davies [1995], Akehurst and Alexander [1996], Alexander [1997], Sternquist [1998] and Alexander and Doherty [2000]. Recent critiques of retail internationalisation research have focused on its lack of engagement with the *process* of internationalisation [Wrigley, 2000; Dawson, 2001a], the *impacts* of internationalisation [Dawson, 2001b] and the issue of internationalisation *failure* [Burt et al., 2002, Burt, Dawson and Sparks, 2003]. A common theme in this criticism is that research has tended to view internationalisation as a static event rather than as a dynamic process.

Away from the retail sector, the internationalisation literature also emphasises market entry and development aspects of the subject. Market failure and exit have been studied far less, although there has been some interest in divestment and exit decisions [e.g. Duhaime and Grant, 1984; Chow and Hamilton, 1993; Hamilton and Chow, 1993; Siegfried and Evans, 1994; Hadjikani and Johanson, 1996; Wright and Ferris, 1996; Benito, 1997a; Benito and Welch, 1997; Matthyssens and Pauwels, 2000; Karakaya, 2000]. Overall, however, comparatively less is known about the extent, motives or processes of exit from international activities than is known about entry and development.

Research on this subject is important for a number of management and business, as well as academic, reasons. 'De-internationalisation' has been viewed as a 'significant phenomenon' in international business [Boddewyn, 1979: 22], and as being more complicated than the internationalisation entry process [Nees, 1978–79]. It involves numerous variables, both internal and external

Source: *The Service Industries Journal*, Vol. 25, No. 3, 2004, pp. 355–371.

to the business and at multiple levels of analysis [Boddewyn, 1983; Ghertman, 1987; Benito, 1997b]. Choosing the wrong divestment strategy, or implementing the correct strategy poorly, can increase the cost of exit or jeopardise any benefits of the whole strategy [Nees, 1978–79; Boddewyn 1983; Ghertman 1987; Chow and Hamilton, 1993; Padmanabhan, 1993]. An improved understanding of the exit *process* could not only make a theoretical contribution towards a more complete theory of the internationalisation of the firm, but could also have considerable managerial implications for firms involved in decisions about international market exits.

From even the brief discussion above, it should be clear that there are academic issues to be resolved over basic definitions [see Burt, Dawson and Sparks, 2003]. Several terms have been used in the literature: for example international divestment and closure [Boddewyn, 1983; Ghertman, 1987], exit [Karakaya, 2000], failure [Burt et al., 2002] and de-internationalisation [Benito and Welch, 1997]. Alexander and Quinn [2002] in their study on retail 'divestment' use the terms divestment, de-internationalisation, failure, withdrawal, reduction in store holdings, exit, disengagement, liquidation, partial or total sales, spin-offs and sell-offs, management buyouts and equity carve-outs to describe aspects of the phenomena. Benito and Welch [1997: 8] note that 'de-internationalisation refers to any voluntary or forced actions that reduce a company's engagement in or exposure to current cross-border activities'. A shortcoming of this definition is that it focuses specifically on the decision-making stage and does not take into account the origins and context of the decision nor the implementation process after the decision has been taken. As a result, it neglects the influence of the institutional actors and the environment on the process. We have therefore followed Burt, Dawson and Sparks [2003] and defined international exit as the 'total withdrawal of a firm from an operational presence in a foreign market. Exit may be accomplished through sale of assets, international store-swaps, bankruptcy or other processes.'

The aim of this article is to explore the *process* of international exit. Retail internationalisation has been much described in recent years and there have been a number of high profile market entries and exits. Little is known about exit beyond initial work on decision making. In particular the process of exit, despite its importance and significance to businesses and its comparative frequency is under-researched. This article explores the exit process, allowing issues to be raised as steps on the way to a general framework. The article is in four main sections. First, we provide a brief literature review on international exit. Second, the research method is described. The main part of the article is an examination of the exit of Marks and Spencer (M&S) from France. Finally some conclusions are drawn.

Literature Review: International Exit

An examination of the literature on international market exit suggests that it has four particular characteristics that relate to this study with its focus on process. First, much of the research adopts a rational economic perspective, to model, predict and explain the occurrence of a firm's exit from international markets [Shapiro, 1993]. Economic factors, and more particularly, financial factors, dominate the reasons given for divestment [Boddewyn, 1979; Boddewyn, 1985; Business International, 1976]. This is particularly the case in research attempting to link modes of entry and post entry strategies with the likelihood of survival and/or exit [Li, 1995; Benito, 1997b; Chang and Singh, 1999; Mata and Portugal, 2000]. The focus is firmly on seeking rational economic explanations for particular discrete events. This focus occurs also in post-divestment concerns e.g. Padmanabhan [1993].

Second, many of the attempts that have sought to investigate the international exit process [Business International, 1976; Marois and Jourde, 1977; Nees, 1978–79; Grunberg, 1981; Boddewyn, 1983; Ghertman, 1987], are dated. Whilst not necessarily reducing their importance, one could argue that international activity is more widespread and involves different forms and firms and more countries and contexts than before. During the last 20 years international managers and consultants have also probably learned a great deal more about the international entry and exit processes.

Third, the comparatively small number of recent studies that have examined international exit focus on issues to do with decision taking. These include the causes and motives behind the exit [Benito and Welsh, 1997; Benito, 1997a; Richbell and Watts, 2000; Burt et al., 2002], de-internationalisation barriers [Karakaya, 2000], forced withdrawal from international markets [Akhter and Choudhry, 1993], exit due to turbulence in the home market [Hadjikhani and Johanson, 1996] and the psychological phenomena of international market-exit [Matthyssens and Pauwels, 2000]. The importance of the 'new man' (sic) in initiating the process of exit has also been emphasised [Gilmour, 1973; Torneden, 1975], as has the locus of any foreign divestment review [Boddewyn, 1979], raising issues of power and dependency relationships. Much of this research stresses the importance of studying the exit process, despite its focus on the aspects of decision making. The exit process itself and its impacts are described only occasionally. Therefore there is little evidence from which to develop an understanding of these aspects of the subject.

Finally, the contextual factors influencing international divestment and exit have relevance to this study. While the process of within country divestment and exit has been explored in some depth [e.g. Porter, 1976; Nargundkar et al., 1996], international exit research is far from mature. We know little about the dynamics and effects of different and complex contexts, including varying business sectors and different national cultures, nor about the interactions of these elements. By ignoring the spatial and cultural contexts within which firms operate, generalisations of findings from the 'within country' exit and divestment literatures are hard to uphold across international, institutional, sectoral and cultural borders. For instance, Boddewyn [1983] argues that foreign barriers to exit are lower than national barriers and that there is a 'distance of psychological detachment' when executing a divestment decision abroad. However it is unclear if these are generalisable 'truths' or whether there are differences due to the contexts of the businesses, sectors, countries and cultures involved or to the type of decision being made. There are many possible reasons for market exit [see Karakaya, 2000; Mellahi et al., 2002] and thus it is likely that there are many components to the processes involved. These contexts will affect issues about the content, presentation, timing and effect of announcements of closure and exit. This may impact attempts at resistance by employees and other interest groups, and affect the market perceptions of the company [McDermott, 1989].

Overall therefore whilst there is research on international divestment decisions, there is less research into the *process* of international exit. Research has suggested the primacy of economic reasons for exit and has focused on the antecedents of the decision to exit. There has been less concern over the impact and operationalisation of the decision, despite its key managerial dimensions. Research has tended to be fragmentary and to be more interested in documenting the event and in particular in trying to explain its origins, rather than considering its implications or outcomes. This is perhaps understandable, but is also regrettable. Research into failure is hard enough [Mellahi et al., 2002]. When failure involves market exit, then there may be few people or little evidence to study or investigate.

It is also notable that much of the previous research has involved manufacturing rather than service sector businesses. It is reasonable to ask whether processes from one sector can or should be applied in other sectors [Dawson, 1994]. The limited research cited above is considerable however when compared to research on retail internationalisation failure and exit. It is only very recently that the issue of exit has been specifically addressed in retail research [Alexander and Quinn, 2002; Burt et al., 2002, Wrigley and Currah, 2003], despite the mounting evidence in the field that exit in retail internationalisation is a common occurrence.

Methodology

This study therefore seeks to build on this literature base, such as it is. Given the paucity of conceptualisation in the subject, particularly if confined to the retail sector, this study explores a particular high profile instance of international market exit. A similar approach focusing on Ahold in Latin America and exploring financial aspects of internationalisation has been attempted by Wrigley and Currah [2003]. It is not the intention to produce generalisable results from such a study, but instead to explore the subject 'from the ground up' and thus to gain insight into the process of exit and suggest areas for future research. It is hoped that others will build on this start.

Marks and Spencer (M&S) is one of Britain's leading businesses. Recently however the company has faced something of a crisis [Bevan, 2001; Mellahi et al., 2002]. As part of its crisis response, the M&S strategic review of its business announced on 29 March 2001 that it was to sell its US retail businesses, turn its Hong Kong stores into franchises and close most of its company-owned stores in continental Europe (see below). The Glasgow Herald [30 March 2001: 23] reported this as being 'the most revolutionary move in (M&S) history'. Whilst the exit announcement had a number of components, the most contentious issues and vociferous complaints arose over the exit from France (see below). This study therefore focuses on France, with only brief considerations of the market exits elsewhere (see Jackson and Sparks [2003] on Hong Kong).

A number of data collection techniques and sources have been used in developing this study. First, the media and stock market analyst coverage of M&S has been enormous, because of their high profile, previous success and the depth of their unfolding crisis. Secondary material is thus extensive and has been analysed to uncover themes. The ongoing crisis itself generated much coverage, including a book [Bevan, 2001], but the market exit announcement expanded this considerably. The announcement produced a torrent of national and trade press commentary, both in the UK and elsewhere. Secondary data on the exit also includes coverage of interviews and announcements by non-M&S management sources such as union representatives, government officials and employees. In addition court cases in France arising from the announcement (see later) have been widely reported.

Second, M&S publications such as annual reports and other statements and documents have covered the company's actions. These have been considered together with public statements by M&S managers and directors available through the press or made, for example, at the Annual General Meeting (which has been attended regularly by one of the research team).

Third, since 1998, one of the authors, a former executive at M&S, has been conducting formal and informal interviews and discussions with M&S management about M&S, utilising his past contacts and colleagues. Formal interviews pre-date the market exit announcement, but provide a background [Mellahi et al., 2002]. Informal discussions have been by telephone and have sought to crosscheck information as it emerged from the research.

Marks and Spencer's Exit from France

Marks and Spencer is a legendary British retailer, whose success has been much studied by academics. There is no need or scope to cover this literature in detail here [see Bevan, 2001; Mellahi et al., 2002; Burt et al., 2002 for recent reviews]. This study is presented as two stages. First, a brief context of M&S's development in France and the post-1997 crisis in the UK is given. The second stage involves the implementation of the exit strategy. The implementation stage is itself developed in two phases. The analysis of the exit process was carried out using a temporal bracketing strategy. This strategy involved decomposing the chronological data into phases. Phases are defined so that there is continuity in the context and actions being pursued within them, but discontinuities at their frontiers. In this case, the boundaries of the chosen periods were defined either by changes in the key people involved, or by a major change in the company's or other interest groupings' policy towards the announced exit strategy. It is important to note that these phases do not represent a predictable sequential process. Yet they are more than just a descriptive convenience. They permit analysis that encourages exploration and replication of ideas generated in this research.

The Context and Planning Stage

In 1998 M&S faced a crisis that threatened its very survival. Prior to the crisis, M&S had been one of the most successful British retailing companies. By 1998 the business had retail sales of almost £8bn, traded from almost 500 M&S stores around the world and owned Brooks Brothers and Kings Supermarkets in the United States. The details of M&S's internationalisation activities have been presented elsewhere [Burt et al., 2002]. They comprised a long-established product export business, the purchase of overseas chains in Canada and the United States, franchise agreements in over 25 countries and the development of company-owned stores, particularly in continental Europe. Excluding the product export business, M&S has been involved in international stores since 1972, with the first continental European store opening in Paris in 1975. As Table 1 shows, growth has never been rapid or smooth in Europe and in 1999 two stores in France and four in Germany were closed. Nonetheless, M&S had a high profile European presence particularly in France. These French stores were smaller than the standard UK stores and sold a more restricted range of goods, but included the classic St Michael clothes and food (41 per cent of sales) ranges. Despite long-run problems resulting in the closure of the Canadian retail operations, in 2000 M&S's international activities represented 25 per cent of the company's retail floorspace and 17 per cent of its retail turnover. It yielded, however, only 1.25 per cent of the pre-tax profits. Even in M&S's best financial year (1997), this international percentage of pre-tax profits was only 8.3 per cent.

By 1998 M&S was in crisis. The long-run growth of the company had stopped, and then reversed. Between 1998 and 2001, there was a massive decline in pre-tax profits (after exceptional items) from £1.15 bn to £0.14 bn. Mellahi et al.'s [2002] study of the origins of and reactions to the M&S crisis

Table 1
Company-owned Marks and Spencer Stores in Europe

Country	Year of Entry	No. of Stores					Exit Outcome (2001/2)
		1980	1985	1990	1995	2001	
France	1975	3	6	8	16	18	Sold to Galeries Lafayette
Belgium	1975	1	2	2	3	4	Closed
Ireland	1979	1	1	3	3	4	Integrated into UK
Spain[a]	1990	–	–	1	5	9	Sold to El Corte Ingles
Netherlands	1991	–	–	–	2	2	Closed
Germany	1996	–	–	–	–	2	Closed
Luxembourg	N/a	–	–	–	–	1	Closed
Portugal[b]	2000	–	–	–	–	2	Sold to Inditex
Total		5	9	14	29	42	

[a]The Spanish operation appears to have begun as a franchise, but was then converted into a joint venture with Cortefiel (80% M&S), who were themselves bought out by M&S in April 1999 for £6.2 m.
[b]Portugal began in 1988 as a franchise operation, achieving 6 stores by 1997, but this agreement was terminated in 1999, with a smaller number of company owned stores opening in 2000.
Source: Annual Reports and Accounts.

reported that during the early stage of the crisis, the internal culture, personalities, values and characteristics of the decision makers left a strong imprint on strategic behaviour. The company's history and its embedded management culture encouraged denial and restricted management capacity to respond and enact strategic change [Bevan, 2001]. Mellahi et al. [2002] argue that because top management helped design the strategies that caused the crisis, it made them reluctant to openly admit their failure. Additionally, M&S stuck to its previous routine procedures and commitment, including to international expansion, as evidenced by large-scale modernisation of some of its European stores in the late 1990s, including extensions to its flagship Paris store.

In an attempt to turn around the company, in February 2000, Luc Vandevelde (a Belgian national) was appointed as chairman. He joined M&S from Promodès, a French multinational retailer (6,000 stores in 16 countries), where he was president and chief operating officer for four years. Following the August 1999 announcement of the merger between Carrefour and Promodès he had been named as the executive vice-chairman designate of the merged group (the world's second largest retailer). During early 2000, top management at M&S therefore comprised both new 'outsiders' focusing on internal processes and promoting radical change and willing to question the company's practices and activities and 'old insiders' promoting continuity and commitment to long-standing policies.

Differences between the new 'external' management and the longer-tenured 'internal' management resulted in divergent perceptions of the causes of organisational decline and therefore the best way to deal with them [Bevan, 2001]. In particular, 'old' managers attributed failure to external, uncontrollable and temporary causes, whereas 'new' managers saw the causes of decline as operational and systemic, but controllable. A focus on coalition hampered management from initiating large-scale change in the firm's strategic orientation. The continued poor performance of the company signalled to the shareholders that the alignment with the external environment was not occurring at a desirable speed. The 'coalition' did not have the characteristics necessary to initiate and manage a radical strategic change [Bevan, 2001]. This triggered a legitimacy crisis, when the 'new outside' managers withdrew support and loyalty to old key figures and replaced them with those who were prepared to consider radical change. The new chairman described the recovery plan that had emerged during this 'coalition' period as 'not good enough to address the real problems of the company . . . the plan was like feeding a tree that was already overgrown and unhealthy. What it really needed was serious pruning back. Having reached this conclusion, my next step was to appoint a new team.' This new management team was now able to openly criticise old strategy and initiate radical change without the embarrassment of being associated with the failure. Changes in leadership at the top created an opportunity for the redirection of the historical course of M&S' ambition to be the first true international British retailing company.

On 18 September 2000, the chairman ousted three executive directors. It was the fifth management shake-up in two years and by far the biggest in M&S's 116-year history [Business Week, 2000]. In October 2000, M&S started a process of a strategic review of its business activities. On 29 March 2001, M&S

announced a fundamental overhaul of its business, described by (now) Chief Executive and Chairman Luc Vandevelde as an 'urgent' plan for recovery, totally focused on the UK business. The measures announced included the closure (by 31 December 2001) of all its company-owned stores in Continental Europe except for those in Ireland, the franchising of the company-owned stores in Hong Kong and the sale of American chains Brooks Brothers and Kings Supermarkets. There were also changes to UK operations and approach and a reconstruction of the balance sheet through property value release. £2 bn was to be returned to shareholders. Bevan [2001: 236] described the decision as one 'that only an outsider free of the emotional baggage of the past could make'. The company reported that it was losing £34 million a year in continental Europe. M&S budgeted £250–300 m as the cost of withdrawal and by the end of December 2001 M&S had mostly completed its exit from continental Europe, though the process was far from smooth (see below).

The M&S crisis was essentially a crisis of trading in the UK, as this dominated the financial heart of the business. The financial survival of the company depended therefore on improving business and financial performance. Initially, management decisions were driven by attempts to optimise performance from the assets. This gave way to a view that directly managed international activities were often 'distractions' both to the business generally and to the turnaround strategy. The international activities were both complicated [Burt et al., 2002] and viewed as under-performing. Economic rationality therefore dictated that steps had to be taken to improve the return. Whilst many in the business expected therefore some restructuring in continental Europe and Hong Kong and the sale of the American chains had long been mooted, no-one expected the wholesale closure that was announced. This was particularly true in France, the largest component (Table 1) of M&S in Europe (18 stores, c. 1,700 employees).

The Implementation Stage

As identified earlier, we have divided the implementation stage into two phases. The first considers the announcement itself and its initial impact. The second covers the appointment of a new president for M&S France and a change in the method of exit from the market. Table 2 provides some milestones in the timeline, with the boundary between the phases marked at the 2 May 2001.

First Phase: The Announcement and the Initial Impact

On 29 March 2001, M&S sent a message by e-mail to its management in European branches informing them of the plan to close its operations in Europe and to place 'total focus on the recovery of the UK business'. Shortly after receiving the information, the company's closure plan was presented to the central Works Council of the French subsidiary at an extraordinary meeting. These communications took place a few minutes before the London Stock Exchange opened and the formal announcement was made through the Stock Exchange. M&S share prices rose by 7 per cent on the day of the announcement. Following the announcement, workers organised demonstrations outside M&S stores in France against the closure plan and the way it was announced. Some stores closed for the day. The demonstrations marked the start of a series of unanticipated and undesirable consequences for M&S.

Table 2
M&S Exits France – The Timeline from Announcement to Sale

29 March 2001	The announcement of closure
30 March 2001	Condemnation of the announcement by french trade unions, politicians and the media in France begins
9 April 2001	M&S loses in a court case brought by french trade unions and is obliged to undergo a new round of consultation
April/May 2001	Demonstrations and strikes in France and demonstration in London
2 May 2001	Alain Juillet appointed as president of M&S France to oversee withdrawal
May/July 2001	Discussions about the closure and 'social' plans with workers representatives, with little progress
22 June 2001	Strikes over pay in France, just ahead of major sale season
25 July 2001	M&S France stores put up for sale rather than closure
19 September 2001	M&S European Council accepted as legally established by court
16 October 2001	Galeries Lafayette agree to purchase M&S stores, subject to negotiations over the 'social plan'
30 November 2001	Final agreement by unions to M&S closure plan, after long negotiations – formally signed off 11 days later
17 January 2002	85 per cent of M&S workers have chosen to accept redundancy not alternative employment
26 March 2003	Galeries Lafayette sue M&S for £40 m compensation over terms of the redundancy package offered to staff

Source: Various Press, Le Monde, 18 October 2001: 20.

M&S management misjudged the extent to which France's unions, media and political class would unite in condemning both the closure and the way the company handled the closure announcement. While the decision to close the branches in France made economic sense (Table 3) to M&S management (particularly in the UK), interest groups in France looked beyond business measures to question the rationality and *process* of the decision. They were concerned about job losses, social responsibilities and the legality of the M&S approach to the decision.

Table 3
Economic Performance of the M&S French Stores

Year	Turnover (Million €)	Profit/Loss (Million €)
1997	296.73	2
1998	303.82	0.21
1999	282.66	–25.99
2000	258.42	–44.53

Source: Libre Service Actualite (LSA), 5 April 2001: 37.

Three days after the announcement, French trade unions launched a legal action against M&S to forestall the planned closure. They challenged the technicality of the closure procedures, claiming that M&S failed to undertake appropriate consultation or provide due warning to employees' representatives, before it made its announcement to close its French branches. Under French and European law, local and multinational firms must hold annual meetings with employee-elected Works Councils. Further, the Works Council must be informed and consulted about business relocation or closure proposals as they arise. The unions believed that M&S had not consulted at all and had simply announced a closure plan. This impression was reinforced in the M&S media conference in London where the plan was described as 'final'. M&S argued that the announcement in its press release made it clear that the plan was subject to consultation ('intends to divest or close non-core businesses and assets, subject to consultation with its employees'). The issue was thus one of timing and the perceived sincerity of any consultation process.

The announcement itself and the unions' immediate concerns over consultation and the method of communication provoked a negative spiral of intensifying hostility. The media in France condemned the M&S action, deriding them as 'stock market sackings'. The closure dominated national news for several weeks. Four topics were seen as controversial [c.f. *L'Humanite*, 26 July 2001, 5 April 2001; *Le Monde*, 9 April 2001: 18; 14 April 2001: 18]. First, the strategic reasons for the closure were seen as being to satisfy UK shareholders and the City of London, a view supported by the positive reaction of the stock market to the announcement. Second, the e-mail process of information dissemination was viewed as shocking. Third, the French condemned what they saw as the export of brutal Anglo-Saxon management practices to France. Finally, the closure was contrasted with the chairman's expected annual bonus of £650,000.

Furthermore, the political class had immediately united against M&S. The French Prime Minister Lionel Jospin commented:

> The case of M&S is particularly unacceptable. It appears that employees and even, seemingly, the managers of outlets in France were advised by the British management at the same time as the press and the Stock Exchange, by e-mail . . . The employees who enriched M&S shareholders should be treated better. Such behaviour (by the company) should be punished. [*Agence France Presse*, 31 March 2001].

The French Finance Minister Laurent Fabius argued that 'we are in the twenty-first century and you can't really treat staff in that way, without any consideration'. The French Labour Minister Elisabeth Guigou called upon the state prosecutor to launch an investigation under penal law that could impose a prison sentence of up to one year on M&S's senior French management, as well as a FF25,000 fine. At the European level the European Commissioner for Social Affairs branded the act of the announcement 'shameful'. A French judge quickly (9 April 2001) found that, in failing to consult its workforce about the proposed closures, M&S breached French and EU law. The judge fined the company for 'manifestly illegal troublemaking', ordered M&S to suspend its closure plans, undertake a proper consultation process and develop a new 'social plan' (i.e. the redundancy and/or re-employment package). Elsewhere in Europe, and particularly in Belgium and Germany, similar concerns against M&S were raised. However, outside France, there was no basis for legal intervention.

Complying with different local laws and regulations when announcing closure is not a straightforward decision. Laws governing closure differ from one country to another. Host country laws and regulations may sometimes clash with that of the home country. For instance, M&S argued that they tried to balance the need to report the announcement to the London Stock Market, according to stock exchange regulations, with the French legal requirement for consultation and information. As Bevan [2001: 238] notes: 'Pulling out of Europe was price-sensitive information that needed to be reported to the Stock Exchange first – failure to do so would have been a breach of the Financial Exchange Act'.

In addition to the arguably crass errors of process, the unfortunate timing of the announcement exacerbated the reaction. The closure was announced during a heated political debate over workers rights and work conditions in France [*The Economist*, 16 June 2001: 52] and in an election campaign, where M&S could become an easy 'political football'. A 'social modernisation' bill was passed by the French parliament on 11 January 2001. The core of the legislation aimed to strengthen the right to work, improve redundancy prevention and tackle 'precarious' (i.e. casual and temporary) employment. Further, on the same day that M&S announced its plan to exit from France, Danone, the French-based food multinational and the world's second largest food processing group, also announced a re-organisation of its biscuits division. Their plan involved the re-organisation of five plants in Europe and the closure of six others, with a net loss of around 1,800 jobs (approximately the same as M&S France). Their closure was planned to start in early 2002 and would last until mid-2004. Danone announced wide-ranging measures to minimise the effect on employees and communities, including redeployment, outplacement assistance, retraining and advice. Whilst several demonstrations called for the boycott of Danone products, and strikes took place at the affected plants, the response of the trade unions was somewhat less aggressive than towards M&S. The media and unions contrasted the two-to-three year timetable closure for the Danone closure with the M&S's announcement of virtually immediate closure.

On 3 April 2001, M&S had initiated a consultation process with its European Works Council (EWC). The legality of this process was also challenged in court by three French unions. According to the French unions, the M&S European Council is not a genuine EWC but a unilateral management initiative aimed at avoiding the requirements of the EWCs. The unions claimed that, although on 3 April 2001, the company informed and consulted the M&S European Council about the closures, this did not constitute information and consultation as required by the European Directive. They alleged that the M&S EWC was established by M&S management in violation of the French legislation. The court eventually dismissed this claim in September 2001.

Second Phase: A New President and a New Approach to Closure

Because so much anti-M&S momentum was built immediately after the announcement, unions sought to broaden the protest. The closure plans in France continued to be a focus of demonstrations and strikes at the stores. The Union Network International (UNI), which represents retail workers from around the world, together with the UK Trades Union Congress (TUC), organised a demonstration in London on 17 May 2001. Around 2,000 protesters, including M&S employees from France, Belgium, Spain and Ireland, attended the protest rally. The British TUC primarily focused on the need to ensure European legislation was enacted in the UK rather than the specifics of the M&S France case. In any event, by this time, M&S had moved to better manage the dispute.

The French dispute was costing significant time, energy, frustration and money. Conflict of this magnitude and publicity was damaging to the organisation's reputation. Whilst taken from a union viewpoint, the French view of M&S was generally negative:

> On Thursday 29 March, Marks & Spencer displayed the true face of capitalism, one that Baron Seilliere campaigned for, a capitalism which does not get embarrassed by dishonesty (twisting and turning), one that in the past threw children down mines to work, one that buys shoes from third world countries for 4FF and sell them for 400FF, one that shuts the door in the face of its employees to inform them that they should leave. [*Le Monde*, 5 April 2001: 18]

As a result of this pressure, the strategic decision-making process, which had been initially and predominately based on an economic rationale, began to view the closure decision through a wider lens. This change in management perception was, perhaps, developed through a reconsideration of institutionally advocated modes and standards of behaviour. The company needed a new strategy, encompassing containment and a revised exit process.

On 2 May 2001, M&S France appointed a new president, Alain Juillet, to lead the closure operation in France. He had extensive experience in restructuring companies in France, and added new perspectives to the M&S closure strategy. Though the objective remained the same, to manage market exit by the end of 2001, Juillet's aim was to carry out the process in a 'socially responsible' manner. From the outset, Juillet changed the tone. For example he stated that '*Un salarié ne se jette pas comme un Kleenex* – employees should not be disposed of like a Kleenex (tissue)' [*Nouvelle Observateur*, 17 May 2001]. He repeatedly stressed that M&S would apply the legal requirements and particularly the 'code du travail'. He noted that Marks & Spencer never wanted to break the French law. A new 'social' scheme was proposed. There would be no dismissals. All employees would be offered another job. The transfer of any stores would be accompanied by the best possible protection of the employees, by offering current employees the chance to continue in their job [*Nouvelle Observateur*, 2001]. This represented a fundamental rethinking of the approach. This does not mean that the relationships eased. Negotiations about the closure and the 'social plan' stuttered onwards. Employees occupied the company's French headquarters in June and went on strike over pay rates. They felt they had nothing to lose.

In July 2001 however, M&S decided to 'sell' rather than 'close' its French stores and began the process of looking for a purchaser. A number of chains were said to be interested, but it was Galeries Lafayette (a leading French retailer) which made an offer to buy the French M&S stores. The deal was approved by M&S management but subject to an agreement with the unions. Protracted negotiations about the 'social plan' and the exact offer to the M&S employees took place. On 30 November 2001 the workers' council at the French division announced that it would not contest the M&S plans to sell its stores to Galeries Lafayette. Galeries Lafayette required this consent for the deal as a condition for its offer to take over the 18 shops and their 1,500 employees from M&S. Galeries Lafayette, however, only wanted six of the stores for themselves, with the others being operated by H&M (eight stores), Virgin, Fnac and Surcouf. On 11 December 2001, the employees' committee of M&S France approved the takeover plan. M&S had made it clear that it was to close its operations in France by 31 December regardless of the outcome of the negotiations. The M&S employees in France had three options. They could accept the offer by the new employer and keep their job. They could obtain another job with the new employer at another site. In both these cases, their pay rates and other conditions were likely to be lower. Alternatively they could accept redundancy with compensation payment. *Le Monde* [17 January 2002: 21] reports that 85 per cent of the M&S workers preferred this final option.

As can be imagined, the negotiations over the 'social plan' and the offer were complex, involving a number of companies. Moreover, the original high wages and good conditions offered by M&S complicated the situation. There was also the question of employee 'fit' with the new businesses. The unions pointed out that despite the national labour market situation, M&S workers, sometimes of very long service, did not have the 'heart' to work for someone else and might in any case not be suitable for a youth-oriented fashion business with a very different culture (e.g. H&M). Alain Juillet, perhaps giving voice to some of the tensions the dispute had engendered, commented: 'They (the workers) have behaved like spoilt children by preferring to take a redundancy pay-off and become unemployed at the public expense' [*Financial Times*, 6 February 2002: 6].

In a rather delayed postscript to this saga, Galeries Lafayette announced in March 2003 [*Times*, 26 March 2003: 25] that they were to sue M&S for £40 m over the redundancy terms agreed by M&S. Galeries Lafayette claim that it cost them more than they anticipated at the time of the agreement to buy the stores from M&S and that in addition the lack of workers transferring to them (which caused them operational problems) was due to the over-generous financial redundancy package agreed by M&S. Whatever the outcome of this, it demonstrates that the *process* of exit has many dimensions, and can last a long time. Managers need to think through the implications of their decisions very carefully.

It is appropriate to consider briefly the outcomes elsewhere in Europe (see Table 1). This article has focused on France, where exit was concluded via a sale of the business. Belgium also saw considerable disruption and protest, but this fell away as legal challenges failed to materialise. With no company willing to take on all the stores and safeguard employees' jobs, the stores were closed and the leases sold for re-letting. Similar closures took place in Germany, Netherlands and Luxembourg. In Spain and Portugal the stores were sold to other retailers after guarantees about employment. In some of these countries, a 'social plan' was agreed with workers' representatives. As Labour Research [2001] point out, the worst-off were staff in the UK where the lack of union recognition and the absence of legislation saw redundant workers receive much smaller redundancy packages than elsewhere.

Conclusions

This study has been set within the context of research on exit processes from international markets. As such, two levels of conclusions may be drawn, relating first to M&S and second to the overall issues for research on the process of international market exit.

M&S was a company in crisis by 1998. Two years later and after seemingly interminable board-level wrangling, progress on turning around the company was slow. But by late 2000 the new management team was in total control, and could devise a radical strategy. They had to be seen to be addressing the issues. Closure of the continental stores should be viewed in the context of their 'distractive' potential for the UK chain. Whether actually much effort was involved in Europe, or any losses would been reversed by the same enhanced operations being introduced in the UK, will never be known. To a great extent, the external financial market forced the radical decision to close, and celebrated the closure with a rise in the share price. A purely economic reading of the exit decision is possible.

However, the decision itself is not the end of the matter, and the process of closure was handled extraordinarily badly. Whilst M&S may have had good intentions towards its staff, the announcement and the process of closure was a disaster for the company. Why this should occur under a Belgian chief executive, who had previously managed one of France's leading retailers, remains a mystery. One could argue that management attention was elsewhere, but this hardly sits with the continental stores being a 'distraction'. It shows however that implementation remains fundamental to managerial decision taking. Whilst there was some recovery from the nadir of April/May 2001, real damage to M&S's international reputation was sustained. An economic decision sets in motion a process that has social as well as economic consequences. These wider social (and contextual) issues may be missed by solely economically fixated management. Such processes, impacts and implications tend to be underestimated in the academic literature as well.

M&S had operated a range of stores across Europe. In some countries there was no problem with the closure plan, as there was neither strong employee nor European-wide legislation at the time, reflecting different cultural and legal contexts. These differences in culture and approach are contextually important to an international business, on entry and exit. M&S had a mix of freehold and leasehold shops, which made closure or sale very different options in different countries. It was also revealed that whilst France was loss making, the stores in Spain were profitable. Contexts are therefore important. Was there a systemic problem in M&S's retailing that could be put right given the historical legacy, or did the business simply not want to be persuaded that it was possible? The business model in place in Europe was a mixture of historical decisions and accidents. As such management may not have really wanted to 'start from here'. The exit process may be more context-specific than the literature assumes.

More widely, this article emphasises three overall points in terms of the academic consideration of exit and internationalisation. First, it is important that the terminology in this area is clarified [see Burt, Dawson and Sparks, 2003].

We have used the concept of exit. We have argued that the exit seen here was a result of failure and was operationalised through closure of stores and the sale of stores and businesses. It would be helpful if future research could relate to, or amend, such concepts and develop such definitions and approaches.

Second, many of the previous research themes in market exit appear relevant today. An economic and financial rationale (both internal to the company and external from the stock market) was present. A new management team was necessary to take the decision to exit. The decision was taken in the home market with little or no regard for the foreign markets. Presentation issues were important. However, whilst these components are present, it is clear that more needs to be done to understand them as a process. The literature tends to focus on the antecedents of the decision to exit. Future research needs to be undertaken to investigate the managerial and operational consequences of the decisions that have been taken. Such consequences are critical for the ongoing form and its stakeholders, as well as those directly affected by the decision itself.

Third, the context and/or environment are fundamentally important to our understanding of exit. Retail exit may be easier than exit involving other sectors, though this is not certain. Certainly the options available seem greater for retailing and the consequences of decisions may be easier to manage, e.g. lack of environmental legacy. Barriers to exit may vary by sector and definitely vary by country. Such barriers may also become barriers to entry as much as they are barriers or inhibitors to exit. The cultural context is also important in allowing certain activities to occur or prohibiting others. The approach to social issues, state intervention and the employee–employer balance are as much cultural as legal issues, as is well illustrated in France. It is however notable that there is now pressure for both stricter and more standard legislation in this area at the European level. The pressure on a business may also affect the decision making. Publicly quoted companies feel greater external pressure to justify actions and operations. Research is thus needed in a range of sectors and contexts to gather data on different and similar situations and thus to begin to draw out managerial implications of such decisions and their contexts.

We argue that it is vital to investigate and understand the *processes* and contexts involved in internationalisation and international exit. There are dynamic, contextually different and inter-related issues. Much has made in the press for example of the withdrawal of M&S from international markets. However whilst some markets have been exited, M&S are still pursuing international activities and have subsequently opened franchises in India and Saudi Arabia. Exit and entry are thus related ongoing processes. As Luc Vandevelde stated at the time of the closure announcement, 'We are sitting on a potential gold mine in Europe, but the retail solution we applied to that gold mine was clearly not adequate' [*Financial Times*, 30 March 2001: 24]. This clearly hinted at a future European presence for M&S, probably through franchising, which it uses in over 25 countries. However, the mismanagement of the subsequent exit process in France will make re-entry to that market, even via a franchise, more difficult. The exit process may well have permanently damaged the M&S brand in France (and possibly elsewhere). Understanding such relationships and implications is critical to management and academics alike.

References

Agence France Press (2001) Le gouvernement lance une procedure judiciaire contre le groupe Marks and Spencer. 31 March.

Akehurst, G. and Alexander, N. (eds) (1996) *The Internationalisation of Retailing*, London: Frank Cass.

Akhtar, S.H. and Choudhry, Y.A. (1993) Forced withdrawal from a country market: managing political risk, *Business Horizons*, 36(3), pp. 47–55.

Alexander, N. (1997) *International Retailing*, Oxford: Blackwell.

Alexander, N. and Doherty, A.M. (eds) (2000) The internationalisation of retailing, *International Marketing Review*, 17(4/5), pp. 307–475.

Alexander, N. and Quinn, B. (2002) International retail divestment, *International Journal of Retail and Distribution Management*, 30(2), pp. 112–25.

Benito, G.R.G. (1997a) Divestment of foreign production operations, *Applied Economics*, 29(10), pp. 1365–77.

Benito, G.R.G. (1997b) Why are foreign subsidiaries divested? A conceptual framework. In I. Björkman and M. Forsgen (eds), *The Nature of the International Firm*, Copenhagen: Handelshøjskolens Forlag.

Benito, G.R.G. and Welch, L. (1997) De-internationalisation, *Management International Review*, 37(2), pp. 7–25.

Bevan, J. (2001) *The Rise and Fall of Marks and Spencer*, London: Profile Books.

Boddewyn, J.J. (1979) Foreign divestment: magnitude and factors, *Journal of International Business Studies*, 10, pp. 21–6.

Boddewyn, J.J. (1983) Foreign and domestic divestment and investment decisions: like or unlike? *Journal of International Business Studies*, 11, pp. 23–35.

Boddewyn, J.J. (1985) Theories of foreign direct investment and divestment: a classificatory note, *Management International Review*, 25(1), pp. 57–65.

Brown, S. and Burt, S.L. (eds) (1992) Retail internationalization, *European Journal of Marketing* Special Issue, 26(8/9).

Burt, S.L., Dawson, J.A. and Sparks, L. (2003) Failure in international retailing: research propositions, *International Review of Retail, Distribution and Consumer Research*, 13, pp. 355–73.

Burt, S.L., Mellahi, K., Jackson, T.P. and Sparks, L. (2002) Retail internationalisation and retail failure: issues from the case of Marks and Spencer, *International Review of Retail, Distribution and Consumer Research*, 12, pp. 191–219.

Business International (1976) *International Divestment: A Survey of Corporate Experience*, Geneva and New York: Business International.

Business Week On line (2000) Lighting a fire under Marks & Sparks: can a management shake-up revive the troubled retailer? October.

Chang, S. and Singh, H. (1999) The impact of modes of entry and resources fit on modes of exit by multinational firms, *Strategic Management Journal*, 20, pp. 1019–35.

Chow, Y.K. and Hamilton, R.T. (1993) Corporate divestment: an overview, *Journal of Managerial Psychology*, 8, pp. 9–13.

Dawson, J.A. (1994) Internationalisation of retail operations, *Journal of Marketing Management*, 10, pp. 267–82.

Dawson, J.A. (2001a) Strategy and opportunism in European retail internationalisation, *British Journal of Management*, 12, pp. 253–66.

Dawson, J.A. (2001b) Towards a model of the impacts of retail internationalisation. Paper presented at the Asian Retail and Distribution Workshop, University of Marketing and Distribution Sciences, Kobe, November.

Duhaime, I.M. and Grant, J.H. (1984) Factors influencing divestment decision-making: evidence from a field study, *Strategic Management Journal*, 5, pp. 301–18.

Ghertman, M. (1987) Foreign subsidiary and parent roles during strategic investment and divestment decisions, *Journal of International Business Studies*, 15, pp. 47–67.

Gilmour, S.C. (1973) *The Divestment Decision Process*. Unpublished DBA dissertation, Harvard University, Graduate School of Business Administration.

Grunberg, L. (1981) *Failed Multinationals Ventures: The Political Economy of International Divest-ments*, Lexington, MA: Lexington Books.

Hadjikhani, H. and Johanson, J. (1996) Facing foreign market turbulence: three Swedish multinationals in Iran, *Journal of International Marketing*, 4(4), pp. 53–74.

Hamilton, R.T. and Chow, Y.K. (1983) Why managers divest – evidence from New Zealand's largest companies, *Strategic Management Journal*, 14, pp. 479–84.

Jackson, T.P. and Sparks, L. (2003) Ma Za and the End of Empire: Marks and Spencer in Hong Kong. Paper presented at the SARD Conference, Kobe, April.

Kacker, M. (1985) *Transatlantic Trends in Retailing*, Westport, CT: Greenwood Press.

Kacker, M. and Sternquist, B. (1994) *European Retailing's Vanishing Borders*, Westport, CT: Quorum.

Karakaya, F. (2000) Market exit and barriers to exit: theory and practice, *Psychology and Marketing*, 17(8), pp. 651–68.

Labour Research (2001) M&S staff keep fingers crossed, *Labour Research*, 1 October.

Li, J. (1995) Foreign entry and survival: effects of strategic choices on performance in international markets, *Strategic Management Journal*, 16(5), pp. 333–51.

Libre Service Actualite (2001) *Marks & Spencer: Une restructuration qui ne resout rien*, Libre Service Actualite, 5 April, 1717, pp. 34–7.

Marois, B. and Jourde, J.E. (1977) Le desinvestissement des firms francaises a l'etranger, *Banque*, April, pp. 405–11.

Mata, J. and Portugal, P. (2000) Closure and divestiture by foreign entrants: the impact of entry and post-entry strategies, *Strategic Management Journal*, 21, pp. 549–62.

Matthyssens, P. and Pauwels, P. (2000) Uncovering international market-exit processes: a comparative case study, *Psychology and Marketing*, Vol.17(8), pp. 697–719.

McDermott, C.M. (1989) *Multinationals: Foreign Divestment and Disclosure*, London: McGraw-Hill.

McGoldrick, P. and Davies, G. (eds) (1995) *International Retailing: Trends and Strategies*, London: Pitman.

Mellahi, K., Jackson, T.P. and Sparks, L. (2002) An exploratory study into failure in successful organizations: the case of Marks and Spencer, *British Journal of Management*, 13, pp. 15–29.

Nargundkar, S.V., Karakaya, F. and Stahl, M.J. (1996) Barriers to market exit, *Journal of Managerial Issues*, 8(2), pp. 239–59.

Nees, D.B. (1978–79) The divestment decision process in large and medium-sized diversified companies: a descriptive model based on clinical studies, *International Studies of Management and Organisation*, Winter, pp. 67–95.

Nouvelle Observateur (2001) Marks & Spencer: Il n'y aura pas de licenciements, *Nouvelle Observateur*, 17 May, p. 1908.

Padmanabhan, P. (1993) The impact of European divestment announcements on shareholder wealth: evidence from the UK, *Journal of Multinational Financial Management*, 2, pp. 185–208.

Porter, M.E. (1976) Please note location of nearest exit – exit barriers and planning, *California Management Review*, Vol.19(2), pp. 21–33.

Richbell, S.M. and Watts, H.D. (2000) Plant closures in multiplant manufacturing firms: adding an international perspective, *Management Decision*, 38(2), pp. 80–88.

Siegfried, J.J. and Evans, L.B. (1994) Empirical studies of entry and exit: a survey of the evidence, *Review of Industrial Organization*, 9, pp. 121–55.

Shapiro, D.M. (1993) Entry, exit, and the theory of the multinational corporation. In C.P. Kindleberger and D.B. Audretsch (eds), *The Multinational Corporation in the 1980s*, Boston, MA: MIT Press.

Sternquist, B. (1998) *International Retailing*, New York: Fairchild.

Torneden, R.L. (1975) *Foreign Disinvestment by U.S. Multinational Corporations: With Eight Case Studies*, New York: Praeger.

Wright, P. and Ferris, S.P. (1997) Agency conflict and corporate strategy: the effect of divestment on corporate value, *Strategic Management Journal*, 18, pp. 77–83.

Wrigley, N. (2000) Strategic market behaviour in the internationalisation of food retailing: interpreting the third wave of Sainsbury's US diversification, *European Journal of Marketing*, 34, pp. 891–918.

Wrigley, N. and Currah, A. (2003) The 'stresses' of retail internationalisation: lessons from Royal Ahold's experience in Latin America, *International Review of Retail, Distribution and Consumer Research*, 13, pp. 221–43.

SECTION 3
Global Strategy

1. Competitive Strategy

42

Competition in Global Industries:
A Conceptual Framework

Michael E. Porter

Conceptual Development

International competition ranks high on the list of issues confronting firms today. The growing importance of international competition is well recognized both in the business and academic communities, for reasons that are clear when one examines just about any data set that exists on international trade or investment. Figure 1, for example, compares world trade and world GNP. Something interesting started happening around the mid-1950s, when the growth in world trade began to exceed significantly the growth in world GNP.[1] A few years later, by 1963, foreign direct investment by firms in developing countries began to grow rapidly.[2] The 1950s marked the beginning of a fundamental change in the international competitive environment. The change has been accelerated by the emergence across a wide range of industries of potent new international competitors, from countries such as Japan, Korea, and Taiwan, calling into question theories of international competition that placed advanced nations in the driver's seat. It is a trend that continues to cause sleepless nights for many business managers.

The subject of international competition is far from new. A large body of literature rooted in the principle of comparative advantage has investigated the many implications of the various theoretical models of international trade.[3] Considerable research on the multinational firm exists, reflecting the growing importance of the multinational since the turn of the century. I think it is fair to characterize this work as resting heavily on the multinational's ability to exploit know-how and expertise gained in one country's market in other countries at low costs, thereby offsetting the unavoidable extra costs of doing business in a foreign country.[4] A related body of knowledge also exists in companies and in writing on the problems of entry into foreign markets and the life cycle of how a firm should compete abroad, beginning with export or licensing and ultimately

Source: Michael E. Porter, *Competition in Global Industries: A Conceptual Framework*, Cambridge, MA: Harvard Business School Press, 1986, pp. 15–60.

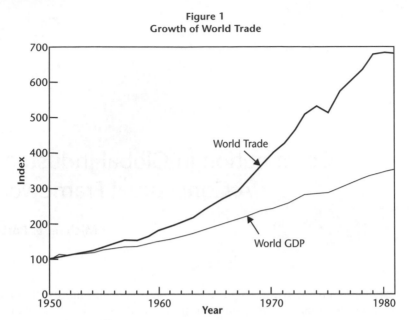

Figure 1
Growth of World Trade

Source: United Nations, *Statistical Yearbooks*, various years.

moving to the establishment of foreign subsidiaries.[5] Finally, many of the functional fields in management have their branch of thinking about international issues, for example, international marketing, international finance. Most attention is concentrated, by and large, on the problems of doing business in a foreign country.

As rich as it is, however, our knowledge of international competition does not address some pressing questions facing today's international firms. Though research and practice have provided some guidance for considering incremental investment decisions to enter new countries, at best we have an incomplete view of how to conceive of a firm's overall international strategy and how such a strategy should be selected. Put another way, we know more about the problems of becoming a multinational than about strategies for managing an established multinational.[6]

This chapter and those that follow seek to explore the implications of international competition for competitive strategy. In particular, what are the distinctive questions for competitive strategy that are raised by international, as opposed to domestic, competition? Many of the strategy issues for a company competing internationally are very much the same as for one competing domestically: a firm must still analyze its industry structure and competitors, understand its buyer and the sources of buyer value, diagnose its relative cost position, and seek to establish a sustainable competitive advantage within some competitive scope, whether it be across the board or in an industry segment. These are subjects I have written about extensively.[7] But there are some questions for strategy that are peculiar to international competition, and that add to rather than replace those examined by other authors. These questions all revolve, in one way or another, around how what a firm does in one country affects or is affected by what is going on in other countries – the degree of connection among country competition. It is this connection that is the focus of this book.

Patterns of International Competition

The appropriate unit of analysis in setting international strategy is the industry, because the industry is the arena in which competitive advantage is won or lost. The pattern of international competition differs markedly from industry to industry. Industries vary along a spectrum from *multidomestic* to *global* in their competitive scope.

In multidomestic industries, competition in each country (or small group of countries) is essentially independent of competition in other countries. A multidomestic industry is one that is present in many countries (e.g., there is a consumer banking industry in Sri Lanka, one in France, and one in the United States), but one in which competition occurs on a country-by-country basis. In a multidomestic industry, a multinational firm may enjoy a competitive advantage from the one-time transfer of know-how from its home base to foreign countries. However, the firm modifies and adapts its intangible assets in order to employ them in each country, and the competitive outcome over time is then determined by conditions in each country. The competitive advantages of the firm, then, are largely specific to the country. The international industry becomes a collection of essentially domestic industries – hence the term multidomestic. Industries where competition has traditionally exhibited this pattern include retailing, consumer packaged goods, distribution, insurance, consumer finance, and caustic chemicals.

At the other end of the spectrum are what I term global industries. The term global – like the word "strategy" – has become overused and perhaps misunderstood. The definition of a global industry employed here is an industry in which a firm's competitive position in one country is significantly affected by its position in other countries or vice versa.[8] Therefore, the international industry is not merely a collection of domestic industries but a series of linked domestic industries in which the rivals compete against each other on a truly worldwide basis. Industries exhibiting or evolving toward the global pattern today include commercial aircraft, TV sets, semiconductors, copiers, automobiles, and watches.

The implications for international strategy of this distinction between multidomestic and global are quite profound. In a multidomestic industry, a firm can and should manage its international activities like a portfolio. Its subsidiaries or other operations around the world should each control all the important activities necessary to do business in the industry and should enjoy a high degree of autonomy. The firm's strategy in a country should be determined largely by the competitive conditions in that country; the firm's international strategy should be what I term a country-centered strategy.

In a multidomestic industry, competing internationally is discretionary. A firm can choose to remain domestic or can expand internationally, if it has some advantage that allows it to overcome the extra costs of entering and competing in foreign markets. The important competitors in multidomestic industries will either be domestic companies or multinationals with stand-alone operations abroad. Such is the situation in each of the multidomestic industries listed earlier. In a multidomestic industry, then, international strategy collapses to a series of domestic strategies. The issues that are uniquely international revolve around how to do business abroad, how to select good countries in which to compete (or assess country risk), and how to achieve the one-time transfer of know-how or expertise. These are questions that are relatively well developed in the literature.

In a global industry, managing international activities like a portfolio will undermine the possibility of achieving competitive advantage. In a global industry, a firm must in some way integrate its activities on a worldwide basis to capture the linkages among countries. This integration will require more than transferring intangible assets among countries, though it will include such transfer. A firm may choose to compete with a country-centered strategy, focusing on specific market segments or countries where it can carve out a niche by responding to whatever local country differences are present. However, it does so at some considerable peril from competitors with global strategies. All the important competitors in the global industries listed above compete worldwide with increasingly coordinated strategies.

In international competition, a firm has to perform some functions in each of the countries in which it competes. Even though a global competitor must view its international activities as an overall system, it still has to maintain some country perspective. It is the balancing of these two perspectives that becomes one of the essential questions in global strategy.[9]

Causes of Globalization

If we accept the distinction between multidomestic and global industries as an important taxonomy of patterns of international competition, a number of questions arise. When does an industry globalize? What exactly do we mean by a global strategy, and is there more than one kind? What determines the type of international strategy best suited to a particular industry?

An industry can be defined as global if there is some competitive advantage to integrating activities on a worldwide basis. To make this statement operational, however, we must be very precise about what we mean by activities and also what we mean by integrating. To diagnose the sources of competitive advantage in any context, whether it be domestic or international, it is necessary to adopt a disaggregated view of the firm, which I call the value chain.[10] Every firm is a collection of discrete activities performed to do business in its industry – I call them value activities. The activities performed by a firm include such things as salespeople selling the product, service technicians performing repairs, scientists in the laboratory designing products or processes, and accountants keeping the books. Such activities are technologically and, in most cases, physically distinct. It is only at the level of these discrete activities, rather than the firm as a whole, that competitive advantage can be truly understood.

A firm may possess two types of competitive advantage: (1) *low cost*, or (2) *differentiation*. These grow out of the firm's ability to perform the activities in the value chain either more cheaply or in a unique way relative to its competitors. The ultimate value a firm creates is what buyers are willing to pay for what the firm provides, which includes its physical product in addition to any ancillary services or benefits, such as design assistance, repair or more timely delivery than competitors. Profit results if the value created through performing the required activities exceeds the collective cost of performing them. Competitive advantage is a function of either providing comparable buyer value more efficiently than competitors (low cost), or performing activities at comparable cost but in unique ways that create more buyer value than competitors and, hence, command a premium price (differentiation).

The value chain, shown in Figure 2, provides a systematic means of displaying and categorizing activities. The activities performed by a firm in any industry can be grouped into the nine generic categories shown. The labels may differ based on industry convention, but every firm performs these basic categories of activities in some way or another. Within each category, a firm typically performs a number of discrete activities that are particular to the industry and to the firm's strategy. In service, for example, firms typically perform such discrete activities as installation, repair, parts distribution, and upgrading.

The generic categories of activities can be grouped into two broad types. Along the bottom are what I call *primary activities,* which are those involved in the physical creation of the product or service, its delivery and marketing to the buyer, and its support after sale. Across the top are what I call *support* activities, which provide inputs or infrastructure that allow the primary activities to take place on an ongoing basis.

Procurement is the obtaining of purchased inputs, such as raw materials, purchased services, machinery, and so on. Procurement stretches across the entire value chain because it supports every activity, that is, every activity uses purchased inputs of some kind. There are typically many different discrete procurement activities within a firm, often performed by different people. Technology development encompasses the activities involved in designing the product as well as in creating and improving the way the various activities in the value chain are performed. We tend to think of technology in terms of the product or manufacturing process. In fact, every activity involves a technology or technologies, which may be simple or sophisticated, and a firm has a stock of know-how about how to perform each activity. Technology development typically involves a variety of different discrete activities, some performed outside the R & D department.

Human resource management is the recruiting, training, and development of personnel. Every activity involves human resources, and thus human resource management activities span the entire chain. Finally, firm infrastructure includes activities such as general management, accounting, legal, finance, strategic planning, and all the other activities outside of specific primary or support activities but essential to enable the entire chain's operation. Each category of activities is of differing relative importance to competitive advantage in different industries, although they are present in all industries.

Activities in a firm's value chain are not independent, but are connected through what I call linkages. The way one activity is performed frequently affects the cost or effectiveness of other activities. If more is spent on the purchase

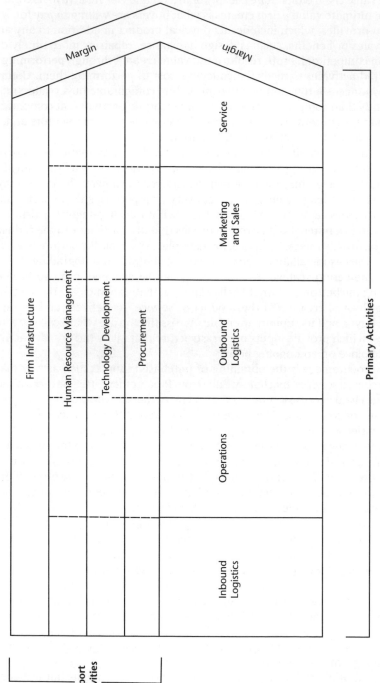

**Figure 2
The Value Chain**

of a raw material, for example, a firm may lower its cost of fabrication or assembly. There are many linkages that connect activities, not only within the firm but also with the activities of its suppliers, channels, and ultimately its buyers. The firm's value chain resides in a larger stream of activities that I term the value system. Suppliers have value chains that provide the purchased inputs to the firm's chain; channels have value chains through which the firm's product or service passes; buyers have value chains in which the firm's product or service is employed. The connections among activities in this system also become essential to competitive advantage. For example, the way suppliers perform particular activities can affect the cost or effectiveness of activities within the firm.

A final important building block in value chain theory, necessary for our purposes here, is the notion of *competitive scope*. Competitive scope is the breadth of activities the firm performs in competing in an industry. There are four basic dimensions of competitive scope: segment scope, or the range of segments the firm serves (e.g., product varieties, customer types); industry scope, or the range of related industries the firm competes in with a coordinated strategy; vertical scope, or what activities are performed by the firm versus suppliers and channels; and geographic scope, or the geographic regions in which the firm operates with a coordinated strategy. Competitive scope is vital to competitive advantage because it shapes the configuration of the value chain, how activities are performed and whether activities are shared among units.

International strategy is an issue of geographic scope. Its analysis is quite similar to that of whether and how a firm should compete locally, regionally, or nationally within a country. In the international context, government tends to have a greater involvement in competition and there are more significant variations among geographic regions in buyer needs. Nevertheless, these differences are matters of degree and the framework here can be readily applied to the choice of strategy by firms who compete in large countries consisting of several regions or cities.

International Configuration and Coordination of Activities

A firm that competes internationally must decide how to spread the activities in the value chain among countries. A distinction immediately arises between the activities labeled downstream on Figure 3, and those labeled upstream activities and support activities. The location of downstream activities, those more related to the buyer, is usually tied to where the buyer is located. If a firm is going to sell in Japan, for example, it usually must provide service in Japan and it must have salespeople stationed in Japan. In some industries it is possible to have a single sales force that travels to the buyer's country and back again; some other specific downstream activities such as the production of advertising copy can sometimes also be performed centrally. More typically, however, the firm must locate the capability to perform downstream activities in each of the countries in which it operates. Upstream activities and support activities, conversely, could conceptually be decoupled from where the buyer is located in most industries.

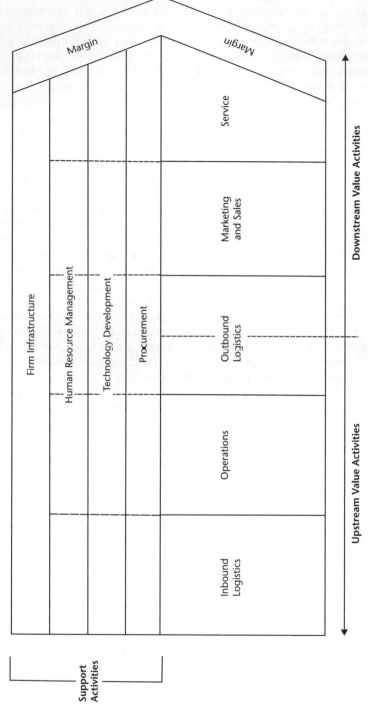

Figure 3
Upstream and Downstream Activities

This distinction carries some interesting implications. First, downstream activities create competitive advantages that are largely country specific: a firm's reputation, brand name, and service network in a country grow largely out of a firm's activities in that country and create entry/mobility barriers largely in that country alone. Competitive advantage in upstream and support activities often grows more out of the entire system of countries in which a firm competes than from its position in any one country.

Second, in industries where downstream activities or other buyer-tied activities are vital to competitive advantage, there tends to be a more multidomestic pattern of international competition. In many service industries, for example, not only downstream activities but frequently upstream activities are tied to buyer location, and global strategies are comparatively less common.[11] In industries where upstream and support activities such as technology development and operations are crucial to competitive advantage, global competition is more common. In global competition, the location and scale of these potentially footloose activities is optimized from a worldwide perspective.[12]

The distinctive issues in international, as contrasted to domestic, strategy can be summarized in two key dimensions of how a firm competes internationally. The first I call the *configuration* of a firm's activities worldwide, or the location in the world where each activity in the value chain is performed, including in how many places. The second dimension I call *coordination*, which refers to how like or linked activities performed in different countries are coordinated with each other. If, for example, there are three plants – one in Germany, one in Japan, and one in the United States – how do the activities in those plants relate to each other?

A firm faces an array of options in both configuration and coordination for each activity in the value chain. Configuration options range from *concentrated* – performing an activity in one location and serving the world from it, for example, one R & D lab, one large plant – to *dispersed*, that is, performing the activity in every country. In the extreme case, each country would have a complete value chain. Table 1 illustrates an example of configuration of worldwide activities in an industry.[13] A firm need not concentrate all its activities in the same country. Today, in fact, it has become common to concentrate activities in different countries.

Coordination options range from none to many. For example, a firm producing in three plants could at one extreme allow each plant to operate with full autonomy, including different production steps and/or different part numbers. At the other extreme, the plants could be tightly coordinated by employing the same information system, the same production process, the same parts, specifications, and so forth. Options for coordination in an activity are typically more numerous than the configuration options, because there are many possible types of coordination and many different facets of an activity on which to coordinate.

Table 2, lists some of the configuration issues and coordination issues for several categories of value activities. In technology development, for example, the configuration issue is where R & D is performed: at one location or two or more locations and in what countries? The coordination issues have to do with such things as the allocation of tasks among R & D centers, the extent of interchange among them, and the location and sequence of product introduction

Table 1
Illustrative Configuration of Activities Globally for a U.S. Company

Activities	U.S.	Canada	U.K.	France	Germany	Japan
Inbound logistics	X		X		X	X
Operations						
Components	X		X			
Assembly	X				X	X
Testing	X				X	X
Outbound logistics						
Order processing	X					
Physical distribution	X	X	X	X	X	X
Marketing and sales						
Advertising	X	X	X	X	X	X
Sales force	X	X	X	X	X	X
Promotional materials	X					
Service	X	X	X	X	X	X
Procurement	X					X
Technology development	X					X
Human resource management	X	X	X	X	X	X
Firm infrastructure	X					

Table 2
Configuration and Coordination Issues by Category of Activity

Value Activity	Configuration Issues	Coordination Issues
Operations	Location of production facilities for components and end products	Allocation of production tasks among dispersed facilities Networking of international plants Transferring process technology and production know-how among plants
Marketing and Sales	Product line selection Country (market) selection Location of preparation of advertising and promotional materials	Commonality of brand name worldwide Coordination of sales to multinational accounts Similarity of channels and product positioning worldwide Coordination of pricing in different countries
Service	Location of the service organization	Similarity of service standards and procedures worldwide
Technology Development	Number and location of R & D centers	Allocation of research tasks among dispersed R & D centers Interchange among R & D centers Developing products responsive to market needs in many countries Sequence of product introductions around the world
Procurement	Location of the purchasing function	Locating and managing suppliers in different countries Transferring knowledge about input markets Coordinating purchases of common items

around the world. There are configuration issues and coordination issues for every activity.[14]

Figure 4 is a way of summarizing these basic choices in international strategy geographically on a single diagram, with coordination of activities on the vertical axis and configuration of activities on the horizontal axis. The firm has to make a set of choices for each activity. If a firm employs a very dispersed configuration, placing an entire value chain in every country (or small group of contiguous countries) in which it operates and coordinating little or not at all among them, then the firm is competing with a country-centered strategy.[15] The domestic firm, operating in only one country, is the extreme case of a firm with a country-centered strategy. As we move from the lower left-hand corner of the diagram up or to the right, we have strategies that are increasingly global. Figure 4 can be employed to map strategic groups in an international industry because its axes capture the most important sources of competitive advantage from an international strategy.[16]

Figure 4
The Dimensions of International Strategy

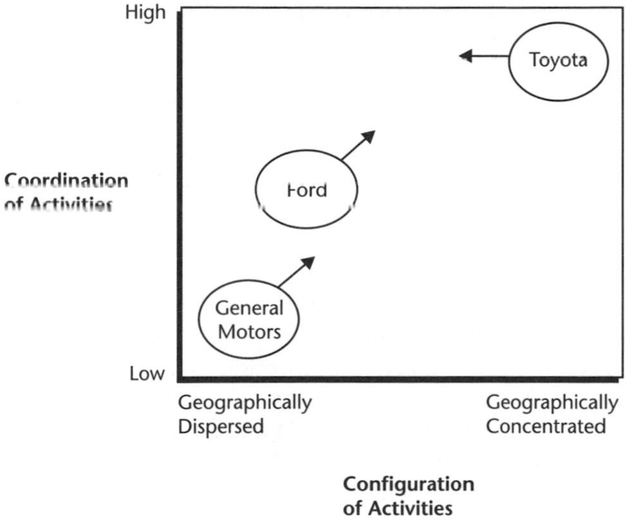

Figure 5 illustrates some of the possible variations in international strategy. The simplest global strategy is to concentrate as many activities as possible in one country, serve the world from this home base, and tightly coordinate through standardization those activities that must inherently be performed near the buyer. This is the pattern adopted by many Japanese firms in the 1960s and 1970s, such as Toyota. The position of Toyota is plotted on Figure 4 along with key competitors. However, the options apparent in Figures 5 and 6 make it clear that there is no such thing as one global strategy.

There are many different kinds of global strategies, depending on a firm's choices about configuration and coordination throughout the value chain. In copiers, for example, Xerox has until recently concentrated R & D in the United States,

Figure 5
Types of International Strategy

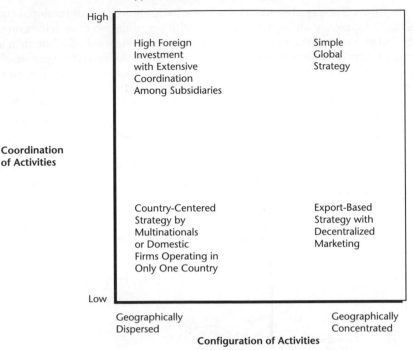

High

High Foreign
Investment
with Extensive
Coordination
Among Subsidiaries

Simple
Global
Strategy

**Coordination
of Activities**

Country-Centered
Strategy by
Multinationals
or Domestic
Firms Operating in
Only One Country

Export-Based
Strategy with
Decentralized
Marketing

Low

Geographically
Dispersed

Geographically
Concentrated

Configuration of Activities

but dispersed other activities, in some cases using joint-venture partners to perform them. On dispersed activities, however, coordination has been quite high. The Xerox brand, marketing approach, and servicing procedures have been quite standardized worldwide. Canon, on the other hand, has had a much more concentrated configuration of activities through somewhat less coordination of the dispersed activities. The vast majority of Canon's support activities plus most manufacturing have been performed in Japan. Aside from the requirement to use the Canon brand, however, local marketing subsidiaries have been given quite a bit of latitude in each region of the world.

Competitors with country-centered and global strategies can coexist in an industry, but global strategies by some competitors frequently force other firms to follow suit. In automobiles, for example, Toyota has employed a relatively simple global strategy to achieve the position of low-cost producer. General Motors has historically competed with a country-centered international strategy, with separate manufacturing facilities and even separate brand names in different regions, while Ford has practiced only regional coordination. As the arrows indicate, all three companies are modifying their international strategies today – the U.S. firms toward more global strategies and Toyota toward becoming more dispersed as its international position grows.

A global strategy can now be defined more precisely as one in which a firm seeks to *gain competitive advantage from its international presence through either a concentrated configuration, coordinating among dispersed activities, or both.*

The one-time transfer of intangible assets, emphasized in the literature, is just one of many ways. Measuring the presence of a global industry empirically must reflect both dimensions and not just one. Market presence of firms in many countries and some export and import of components and end products are characteristic of most global industries. Hence, intra-industry trade is a good sign of the presence of global competition, and its growth is one indication that the incidence of global industries has increased. High levels of foreign investment or the mere presence of multinational firms are not reliable measures, however, because firms may be managing foreign units like a portfolio.

Configuration/Coordination and Competitive Advantage

Understanding the competitive advantages of a global strategy and, in turn, the causes of industry globalization, requires that we specify the conditions under which concentrating activities globally and/or coordinating dispersed activities leads to either lower cost or differentiation. In each case, there are structural characteristics of an industry that work for and against globalization.

The factors that favor concentrating an activity in one or a few locations to serve the world are as follows:

- economies of scale in the activity;
- a proprietary learning curve in the activity;
- comparative advantage of one or a few locations for performing the activity;
- coordination advantages of co-locating linked activities such as R & D and production.

The first two factors relate to *how many* sites an activity is performed at, while the last two relate to *where* these sites are. Comparative advantage can apply to any activity, not just production. There may be some locations in the world that are better places than others to perform other activities such as research or creation of advertising materials. India has become a center for software writing, for example. Government can promote the concentration of activities by providing subsidies or other incentives to employ a particular country as an export base – in effect altering comparative advantage – a role many governments are attempting to play today.

There are also structural characteristics that favor dispersion of an activity to many countries, because they create concentration costs. Local product needs may differ, nullifying the advantages of scale or learning from one-site operation of an activity. Dispersing a range of activities in a country may facilitate marketing in that country by signaling commitment to local buyers and/or providing greater local responsiveness. Dispersing an activity may facilitate learning or gaining know-how in the activity, as a number of sites increases information flow and managers get closer to more markets. Transport, communication, and storage costs can make it inefficient to concentrate the activity in one location.

Government is also frequently a powerful force for dispersing activities, through tariffs, nontariff barriers, and nationalistic purchasing (nationalistic purchasing can exist without a direct government role as well). Governments typically want firms to locate the entire value chain in their country, because this creates benefits and spillovers to the country that often go beyond local content.[17] Dispersing some activities may sometimes allow the concentration of others, through placating governments or through linkages among activities that will be described below. Dispersion is also encouraged by the risks of performing an activity at one place: exchange rate risk, political risk, risk of interruption, and so on. The balance between the advantages of concentrating and dispersing an activity normally differ for each activity (and industry). The best configuration for R & D is different from that for component fabrication, and this is different from that for assembly, installation, advertising, and procurement.[18]

The desirability of coordinating like or linked activities that are dispersed involves a similar balance of structural factors. Coordination potentially allows the sharing and accumulation of know-how and expertise among dispersed activities. If a firm learns how to operate the production process better in Germany, transferring that learning may make the process run better in U.S. and Japanese plants. Differing countries, with their inevitably differing conditions, provide a fertile basis for comparison as well as opportunities for arbitrating knowledge, obtained in different places about different aspects of the business. Knowledge may accumulate not only in product or process technology but also about buyer needs and marketing techniques. A firm coordinating internationally may also receive early warning of industry changes by spotting them in one or two leading countries before they become broadly apparent and transferring the knowledge to other guide activities elsewhere. The initial transfer of knowledge in establishing a foreign subsidiary is recognizable as one case of coordination among dispersed activities. However, it is clear that knowledge is continually created and can flow among all subsidiaries. The ability to accumulate and transfer this knowledge among units is a potent advantage of the global competitor over domestic or country-centered competitors.[19]

Coordination among dispersed activities also potentially improves the ability to reap economies of scale in activities if subtasks are allocated among locations to allow some specialization, for example, each R & D center has a different area of focus. This illustrates how the way a network of foreign locations is managed can have a great influence on the ability to reap the benefits of any given configuration of activities. Viewed another way, close coordination is frequently a partial offset to dispersing an activity.

Closely related to this is the relationship between international coordination in one activity and the configuration of another. For example, coordination in the marketing activity involving information exchange about buyer needs in many countries may allow a central R & D facility to design a standard or easy-to-modify product for sale worldwide, unlocking the scale economies of a concentrated configuration in R & D and production. Such a linkage among separate activities has been exploited by Canon in the design of its personal copier. Similarly, dispersing procurement may allow concentrating manufacturing, since sourcing from many countries can open up the opportunity to export to them.

Coordination may also allow a firm to respond to *shifting* comparative advantage, where movements in exchange rates and factor costs are significant and hard to forecast. For example, incrementally increasing production at the location currently enjoying favorable exchange rates can lower costs. Coordination can also reinforce a firm's brand reputation with buyers through ensuring a consistent image and approach to doing business on a worldwide basis. This is particularly valuable if buyers are mobile or information about the industry flows freely around the world. Coordination may also differentiate the firm with multinational buyers if it allows the firm to serve them anywhere and in a consistent way. Coordination (and a global approach to configuration) enhances leverage with local governments if the firm is able to grow or shrink activities in one country at the expense of others. Finally, coordination yields flexibility in responding to competitors, by allowing the firm to respond to them differently in different countries and to retaliate in one country to a challenge in another. A firm may choose, for example, to compete aggressively in the country from which a challenger draws its most important volume or cash flow in order to reduce the competitors' strength in other countries. IBM and Caterpillar have practiced this sort of defensive behavior in their Japanese operations.

Coordination of dispersed activities usually involves costs that differ by form of coordination and by industry. Local conditions in countries may vary in ways that may make a common approach across countries suboptimal. For example, if every plant in the world is required to use the same raw material, the firm pays a penalty in countries where that raw material is expensive relative to satisfactory substitutes. Business practices, marketing systems, raw material sources, local infrastructures, and a variety of other factors may differ across countries as well, in ways that may mitigate the advantages of a common approach or of the sharing of learning. Governments may restrain the flow of information required for coordination, or impose other barriers to it. Transaction costs of coordination among countries can also be high. International coordination involves long distances, language problems, and cultural barriers to communication. Such problems may mean in some industries that coordination is not optimal. They also suggest that forms of coordination that involve relatively infrequent decisions, such as adopting common service standards or employing the same raw materials, will enjoy advantages over forms of coordination involving ongoing interchange such as transshipping components and end products among facilities.

There are also substantial organizational challenges involved in achieving cooperation among subsidiaries, because of difficulties in aligning subsidiary managers' interests with those of the firm as a whole. The German branch does not necessarily want to tell the U.S. branch about their latest breakthroughs on the production line because it may make it harder for them to outdo the Americans in the annual comparison of operating efficiency among plants. These vexing organizational problems mean that country subsidiaries often view each other more as competitors than collaborators.[20] As with configuration, a firm must make an activity-by-activity choice about where there is net competitive advantage to coordinating in various ways.

Some factors favoring dispersion of activities also impede coordination, while others do not. Transport costs raise few barriers to coordination, for example, while product heterogeneity creates substantial ones. Product heterogeneity and the actions of government often have the special characteristics of impeding *both* concentration and oordination, giving them a particularly strategic role in affecting the pattern of international competition.

Coordination in some activities may be necessary to reap the advantages of configuration in others as noted earlier. The use of common raw materials in each plant, for example, allows worldwide purchasing. Moreover, tailoring some activities to countries (not coordinating) may allow concentration and standard-ization of others. For example, tailored marketing in each country may allow the same product to be positioned differently and hence sold successfully in many countries, unlocking possibilities for reaping economies of scale in production and R & D. Thus, coordination and configuration interact.

Diversification into related industries can also shape the best global config-uration/coordination in a single industry. For example, a diversified firm may be able to produce a number of related products in dispersed plants, instead of concentrating production of one product in a single plant, and still achieve economies of scale. This reflects the fact that sharing activities among units competing in related industries may serve the same strategic purpose as sharing them in competing in many countries – namely, scale or learning economies.[21]

Diversification can also create new options for bargaining with governments. For example, exports in one business unit can be traded for the ability to import in another. IBM follows this approach, seeking a balance of trade in each country in which it operates. Diversification in a variety of industries may also facilitate bartering. Conversely, diversification may raise a firm's overall commitment to a country, increasing the host government's leverage. For all these reasons, the extent of a firm's diversification should be a consideration in its choice of international strategy.

Configuration/Coordination and the Pattern of International Competition

Industries globalize when the benefits of configuring and/or coordinating globally exceed the costs of doing so. The way in which an industry globalizes reflects the specific benefits and costs of global configuration and/or coordin-ation of each value activity. The activities in which global competitors gain competitive advantage will differ correspondingly. Configuration/coordination determines the ongoing competitive advantages of a global strategy, growing out of a firm's overall international position. These are additive to competitive advantages a firm derives/possesses from its domestic market positions. An initial transfer of knowledge from the home base to subsidiaries, is thus one, but by no means the most important, advantage of a global competitor.[22]

In some industries, the competitive advantage from a global strategy comes in technology development, and firms gain little advantage from concentrating primary activities which means that they are dispersed around the world. A good example is the manufacture of glass and plastic containers, where transport cost leads to a dispersion of plants but opportunities to perform R & D centrally and to transfer production know-how among plants yield significant advantages to global firms. In other industries, such as cameras or videocassette recorders, firms gain advantages from concentrating production to achieve economies of scale and learning, but give subsidiaries much local autonomy in sales and marketing. Finally, in some industries there is no net advantage to a global strategy and country-centered strategies dominate; the industry is multidomestic.

An industry such as commercial aircraft represents an extreme case of a global industry (e.g., placement in the upper right-hand corner of Figure 4). Three competitors, Boeing, McDonnell Douglas, and Airbus, all have global strategies. In value activities important to cost and differentiation in the industry, there are compelling net advantages to concentrating most activities to serve worldwide markets and coordinating the dispersed activities extensively. Yet, host governments have a particular interest in the commercial aircraft industry because of its large trade potential, defense implications, and R & D spillovers. The competitive advantages of a global strategy are so great that all the successful aircraft producers have sought to achieve and preserve them. In addition, the power of government to intervene has been mitigated by the paucity of viable worldwide competitors and the enormous barriers to entry created, in part, by the advantages of a global strategy. The result has been that firms have been able to assuage government through procurement. Boeing, for example, is very careful about where it buys components. Boeing seeks to develop suppliers in countries that are large potential customers. This requires a great deal of extra effort by Boeing to transfer technology and to work with suppliers to ensure that they meet its standards. Boeing realizes that this is preferable to compromising the competitive advantage of its strongly integrated worldwide strategy. It is willing to employ one value activity (procurement), where the advantages of concentration are modest, to help preserve the benefits of concentration in other activities. Recently, commercial aircraft competitors have entered into joint ventures and other coalition arrangements with foreign suppliers to achieve the same effect, as well as to spread the risk of huge development costs.

Segments and vertical stages of an industry frequently vary in their pattern of globalization. In aluminum, the upstream (alumina and ingot) stages are global industries. The downstream stage, semifabrication, is a group of multidomestic businesses, because product needs vary by country, transport costs are high, and intensive local customer service is required. Scale economies in the value chain are modest. In lubricants, automotive motor oil tends to be a multidomestic industry, while marine engine lubricants is a global industry. In automotive oil, countries have varying driving standards, weather conditions, and local laws. Production involves blending various kinds of base oils and additives, and is subject to few economies of scale but high shipping costs. Distribution channels are important to competitive success and vary markedly from country to country. Country-centered competitors, such as Castrol and Quaker State, are leaders in most countries. In the marine segment, conversely, ships move freely around the world and require the same oil everywhere. Successful competitors are global. A third and different industry is lodging, where most segments are multidomestic because the majority of activities in the value chain are tied to buyer location and country differences lead to few benefits from coordination. In high-priced business-oriented hotels, however, competition is more global. Global competitors such as Hilton, Marriott, and Sheraton have dispersed value chains, but employ common brand names, common service standards, and worldwide reservation systems to gain advantages in serving highly mobile busi-ness travelers.[23]

Just as the pattern of globalization may differ by segment or industry stage, so may the pattern differ by groups of countries. There are often *subsystems* of countries within which the advantages of configuration/coordination are greater than with other countries. For example, configuration/coordination possibilities may be high in competing in countries with similar climatic conditions (such as the Nordic countries) because they have similar product needs. Subsystems can be based on geographic regions, climatic conditions, language, state of economic development, extent of government intervention in competition, and historical or current political ties. In the record industry, for example, possibilities for co-ordination are great among the Spanish-speaking countries and countries with a large Spanish-speaking population such as the United States. Where there is extreme government intervention, geographic isolation, or very unusual product needs, countries can be effectively outside the global system or any subsystem.

International strategy has often been characterized as a choice between worldwide standardization and local tailoring, or as the tension between the economic imperative (large-scale efficient facilities) and the political imperative (local content, local production). It should be clear from the discussion so far that neither characterization captures the complexity of a firm's international strategy choices. A firm's choice of international strategy involves the search for competitive advantage from global configuration/coordination throughout the value chain. A firm may standardize (concentrate) some activities and tailor (disperse) others. It may also be able to standardize and tailor at the same time through the coordination of dispersed activities, or use local tailoring of some activities (e.g., different product positioning in each country) to allow standard-ization of others (e.g., production). Similarly, the economic imperative is not always for a global strategy – in some industries a country-centered strategy is the economic imperative. Conversely, the political imperative in some industries may be to concentrate activities where governments provide strong export incentives and locational subsidies.

The essence of international strategy is not to resolve tradeoffs between concentration and dispersion, but to eliminate or mitigate them. This implies concentrating and dispersing different value activities depending on industry structure, dispersing some activities to allow concentration of others, and minim-izing the tradeoff between concentration and dispersion by coordinating dispersed activities.[24]

The Process of Industry Globalization

Industries globalize because the net competitive advantage of a global approach to configuration/coordination becomes significant. Sometimes this is due to exogenous environmental changes, such as shifts in technology, buyer needs, government policy, or country infrastructure. In automotive supply, for example, the industry is globalizing as buyers (the auto producers) become increasingly global competitors. In other industries, strategic innovations by a competitor can unlock the potential for globalization. For example, a firm may perceive a means of providing local content without dispersing scale-sensitive value activities, such as local installation and testing. Other tools to unlock globalization include: reducing the cost of modifying a centrally designed and produced product to meet local needs, such as modularizing the power supply in an otherwise standard product; increasing product homogeneity by designing a product that incorporates the features demanded by every significant country; or homogenizing worldwide demand through product repositioning. In electronic products such as communications switching equipment, for example, Northern Telecom, NEC Corporation, and Ericsson have benefited from product architectures which permit modularization of software and relatively low-cost modification to fit different country needs. Environmental changes and strategic insights frequently go hand in hand in changing the pattern of international competition.

There may be problems in the transition from multidomestic to global competition in industries where domestic or country-centered competitors have already established entry or mobility barriers that are market-specific. The possession by country-centered or domestic competitors of strong brand names, strong distribution channel relationships, or long-standing buyer relationships, will retard the penetration of global firms. Firms also face difficulties in shifting from country-centered to global strategies if they have a legacy of dispersed worldwide activities and organizational norms that place great authority at the country level. Domestic firms can sometimes be more successful than established multinationals in becoming global competitors, because they start with a cleaner slate than do firms who must rationalize and reorient their international activities.

The ultimate leaders in global industries are often first movers: the first firms to perceive the possibilities for a global strategy and move to implement one. For example, Boeing was the first global competitor in aircraft, as was Honda in motorcycles, IBM in computers, Kodak in film, and Becton Dickinson in disposable syringes. First movers gain scale and learning advantages that make competing with them difficult. First-mover effects are particularly important in global industries, because of the association between globalization and economies of scale, learning, and flexibility achieved through worldwide configuration/coordination. Global leadership can shift if industry structural change provides the opportunity for leapfrogging to new products or new technologies that nullify past leaders' scale and learning; again, the first mover to the new generation/technology often wins.

Global leaders often begin with some advantage at home, whether it be low labor cost or a product design or marketing advantage. They use this as a lever to enter foreign markets. Once there, however, the global competitor converts the initial home advantage into competitive advantages that grow out of its overall worldwide system, such as production scale economies or the ability to amortize R & D costs. While the initial advantage may have been hard to sustain, the global strategy creates *new* advantages that can be much more durable.

A good example is automobiles, where Toyota and Nissan initially competed in simple, small cars on the basis of low labor costs. As these companies achieved worldwide penetration, however, they gained economies of scale and accelerated down the learning curve. World scale allowed aggressive investments in new equipment and R & D. Today, the Korean competitor Hyundai competes in small, simple cars based on low labor costs. Toyota and Nissan have long since graduated to broad lines of increasingly differentiated cars, drawing on the advantages of their worldwide positions.

Global Strategy and Comparative Advantage

It is useful to pause and reflect on the relationship between the framework I have presented and the notion of comparative advantage. Is there a difference? The traditional concept of comparative advantage is that factor-cost or factor-quality differences among countries lead to production in countries with advantages in a particular industry which export the product elsewhere in the world. Competitive advantage, in this view, grows out of *where* firms perform activities.

The location of activities is clearly one source of potential advantage in a global firm. The global competitor can locate activities wherever comparative advantage lies, decoupling comparative advantage from the firm's home base or country of ownership. Indeed, the framework presented here suggests that the comparative advantage story is richer than typically told, because it not only involves production activities (the usual focus of discussions) but also applies to other activities in the value chain, such as R & D, processing orders, or designing advertisements. Comparative advantage is specific to the *activity* and not the location of the value chain as a whole.[25] One of the potent advantages of the global firm is that it can spread activities to reflect different preferred locations, something a domestic or country-centered competitor does not do. Thus, components can be made in Taiwan, software written in India, and basic R & D performed in Silicon Valley, for example. This international specialization and arbitrage of activities within the firm is made possible by the growing ability to coordinate and configure globally, and can be difficult to accomplish through arm's-length or quasi-arm's-length transactions because of risks of contracting with independent parties as well as high transaction costs.

While my framework suggests a more complex view of comparative advantage, it also suggests, however, that many forms of competitive advantage for the global firm derive less from *where* it performs activities than from *how* it performs them on a worldwide basis; economies of scale, proprietary learning, and differentiation with multinational buyers are not tied to countries but to the configuration and coordination of the firm's worldwide system. While these advantages are frequently quite sustainable, traditional sources of comparative advantage can be very elusive sources of competitive advantage for an international competitor today, because comparative advantage frequently shifts. A country with the lowest labor cost is overtaken within a few years by some other country; as has happened repeatedly in shipbuilding as Japan has replaced Europe only to be replaced by Korea. Moreover, falling direct labor cost as a percentage of total costs, increasingly global markets for raw materials and other inputs, and freer flowing technology have diminished the role of traditional sources of comparative advantage.

My research on a broad cross-section of industries suggests that the achievement of sustainable world leadership follows a more complex pattern than the exploitation of comparative advantage per se. A competitor may start with a comparative-advantage-related edge that provides the basis for penetrating foreign markets, but this edge is rapidly translated into a broader array of advantages that arise from the global approach to configuraiton and coordination described earlier. Japanese firms, for example, have done a masterful job in many industries of converting fleeting labor-cost advantages into durable systemwide advantages because of scale and proprietary know-how. Over time, these systemwide advantages are further reinforced with country-specific advantages such as brand identity in many countries as well as distribution channel access.

Many Japanese firms were fortunate enough to make their transitions from country-based comparative advantage to global competitive advantage in a buoyant world economy while nobody paid much attention to them. European and U.S. competitors were willing to cede market share in "less desirable" segments such as the low end of the product line, or so they thought. The Japanese translated these beachheads into world leadership by broadening their lines and reaping advantages in scale and proprietary learning. The Koreans and Taiwanese, the latest entrants in consumer electronics and other industries with low-price strategies, may have a hard time replicating Japan's success. Products have standardized and growth is slow, while Japanese and U.S. competitors are alert to the threat. Japanese firms enjoyed first-mover advantages in pursuing their strategies that the Koreans and Taiwanese do not.

Global Platforms

The interaction of the home country conditions and competitive advantages from a global strategy that transcend the country suggest a more complex role of the country in firm success than implied by the theory of comparative advantage. To understand this more complex role of the country, I define the concept of a "global platform." A country is a desirable global platform in an industry if it provides an environment yielding firms domiciled in that country an advantage in competing globally in that particular industry. The firm need not necessarily be owned by investors in the country, but the country is its home base for competing in a particular industry. An essential element of this definition is that it hinges on success *outside* the country, and not merely country conditions that allow firms to successfully master domestic competition. In global competition, a country must be viewed as a platform and not as the place where all a firm's activities are performed.

There are two broad determinants of a good global platform in an industry, which I have explored in more detail elsewhere.[26] The first is comparative advantage, or the factor endowment of the country as a site to perform particular important activities in the industry. Today, *simple factors* such as low-cost unskilled labor and natural resources are increasingly less important to global competition than *complex factors* such as skilled scientific and technical personnel as well as advanced infrastructure. Direct labor is a minor proportion of cost in many manufactured goods and automation of nonproduction activities is shrinking it further, while markets for resources are increasingly global and technology has widened the number of sources of many resources. A country's factor endowment is partly exogenous but partly endogenous, the result of attention and investment in the country.

The second determinant of the attractiveness of a country as a global platform in an industry are the characteristics of a country's demand and local operating environment. A country's demand conditions include the size and timing of its demand in an industry, factors recognized as important by authors such as Linder and Vernon.[27] They also include, however, the sophistication and power of local buyers and channels, and the particular product features and attributes demanded. These latter factors are frequently more important today than size and timing of demand, because income differences among many developed countries are relatively small and industries develop simultaneously in many countries. Local operating conditions relevant to investment success include the customs and conditions for doing business in a particular industry as well as the intensity of local competition. Strong local competition frequently benefits a country's success in international competition rather than impedes it, a view sometimes used to advocate the creation of "national champions." Japanese machine tool and electronic firms, Italian ski boot manufacturers, German high performance automakers, and American minicomputer companies all illustrate the spur of local competition to success abroad.

Local demand and operating conditions provide a number of potentially powerful sources of competitive advantage to a global competitor based in that country. The first is first-mover advantages in perceiving and implementing the appropriate global strategy. Pressing local needs, particularly peculiar ones, lead firms to embark early to solve local problems and gain proprietary know-how. This is then translated into scale and learning advantages as firms move early to compete globally. The second benefit is motivation. Sophisticated, powerful customers, tough operating problems, and a formidable local rival or two promote rapid progress down the learning curve and conceiving of new ways of competing. The final potential benefit of local demand conditions is a baseload of demand for product varieties that will be sought after in international markets. The role of the country in the success of a firm internationally, then, is in the interaction between conditions of local supply, the composition and timing of country demand, and the nature of the local operating environment with economies of scale and learning.

The two determinants of country competitiveness in an industry interact in important and sometimes counterintuitive ways. Local demand and needs frequently influence private and social investment in endogenous factors of production. A nation with oceans as borders and dependence on sea trade, for example, is more prone to have universities and scientific centers dedicated to oceanographic education and research. Similarly, factor endowment seems to influence local demand. The per capita consumption of wine is highest in wine-growing regions, for example.

"Comparative disadvantage" in some factors of production can be an advantage in global competition when combined with pressing local demand. Poor growing conditions have led Israeli farmers to innovate in irrigation and cultivation techniques, for example. The shrinking role of simple factors of production relative to complex factors such as technical personnel seem to be enhancing the frequency and importance of such circumstances. What is important today in international success is unleashing innovation in the proper direction, instead of passive exploitation of a country's static cost advantages, which shift rapidly and can be overcome. International success today is a dynamic process resulting from continued development of products and processes. The forces that guide firms to undertake such activity are central to the success of a country's firms in international competition.

A good example of the interplay among these factors is the television set industry. In the United States, early demand was in large screen console sets because TV sets were initially luxury items kept in the living room. As buyers began to purchase second and third sets, sets became smaller and more portable. They were used increasingly in the bedroom, the kitchen, the car, and elsewhere. As the TV set industry matured, table model and portable sets became the universal product variety. Japanese firms, because of the small size of Japanese homes, gained early experience in small sets. They dedicated most of their R & D to developing small picture tubes and compact sets. The Japanese also faced a compelling need to reduce power consumption of sets because of the existing energy crisis, which led them to rapid introduction of solid-state technology. This, in turn, facilitated reducing the number of components and automating manufacturing. The whole process was accelerated by the more rapid saturation of the Japanese home market than the American market and a large number of Japanese competitors who were competing fiercely for the same pie.

In the process of naturally serving the needs of their home market and dealing with local problems, then, Japanese firms gained early experience and scale in segments of the industry that came to dominate world demand. U.S. firms, conversely, pioneered large-screen console sets with fine furniture cabinets. As the industry matured, the experience base of U.S. firms centered on a segment that was small and isolated to a few countries, notably the United States. Aided by intense competitive pressure, Japanese firms were able to penetrate world markets in a segment that was not only uninteresting to foreign firms but also one in which the Japanese had initial-scale learning- and labor-cost advantages. Ultimately the low-cost advantage disappeared as production was automated, but global scale and learning economies rapidly took over as the Japanese advanced product and process technology at a rapid pace. This example illustrates how early demand for TV sets in the United States proved to be a disadvantage rather than the advantage that some views of international competition paint it to be. Moreover, Japan's comparative disadvantage in energy proved to be an advantage in TV sets (and a number of other industries).

The two broad determinants of a good global platform rest on the interaction between country characteristics and firms' strategies. The literature on comparative advantage, through focusing on country factor endowments, minimizing the demand side, and suppressing the individual firm, is most appropriate in industries where there are few economies of scale, little proprietary technology or technological change, or few possibilities for product differentiation.[28] While these industry characteristics are those of many traditionally traded goods, they describe few of today's important global industries.

The Historical Evolution of International Competition

Having established a framework for understanding the globalization of industries, I am now in a position to view the phenomenon in historical perspective. This discussion provides a way of validating the framework and isolating important issues for global competitors today. If one goes back far enough, relatively few industries were global. Around 1880, most industries were local or regional in scope. The reasons are rather self-evident in the context of my framework. There were few economies of scale in production until fuel-powered machines and assembly-line techniques emerged. There were heterogeneous product needs among regions within countries, much less among countries. There were few if any national media; the *Saturday Evening Post* was the first important national magazine in the United States and developed in the teens and twenties. Communication between regions was difficult before the telegraph, telephone, and railroad systems became well developed.

These structural conditions created little impetus for the widespread globalization of industry. Those industries that were global reflected classic comparative-advantage considerations. Goods were simply unavailable in some countries who imported them from others, or differences in the availability of land, resources, or skilled labor made some countries desirable suppliers to others. Export of goods produced locally was the predominant form of global strategy adapted. There was little need for widespread government barriers to international trade during this period, although trade barriers were quite high in some countries for some commodities.

Developments around the 1880s, however, marked the beginnings of what today has blossomed into the globalization of many industries. The first wave of modern global competitors grew up in the late 1800s and early 1900s. Many industries went from local (or regional) to national in scope, and some began globalizing. Firms such as Ford, Singer, Gillette, National Cash Register, Otis, and Western Electric had commanding world market shares by the teens, and operated with integrated worldwide strategies. Early global competitors were principally U.S. and European companies.

Driving this first wave of modern globalization were rising production scale economies, because of the advancements in technology that outpaced the growth of the world economy. Product needs also became more homogenized in different countries as knowledge and industrialization diffused. Transport improved, first through the railroad and steamships and later in trucking. Communication became more efficient with the telegraph, telephone, and efficient mail service. At the same time, trade barriers were either modest or overwhelmed by the strong competitive advantages of the new large-scale firms.

The burst of globalization soon slowed, however. Most of the few industries that were global moved increasingly toward a multidomestic pattern. Multinationals remained, but between the 1920s and 1950 many evolved toward becoming federations of autonomous subsidiaries. The principal reason was a strong wave of nationalism and resulting high-tariff barriers, partly caused by the world economic crisis and world wars. Another barrier to global strategies, chronicled by Chandler, was a growing web of cartels and other interfirm contractual agreements. These limited the geographic spread of firms.

The early global competitors began rapidly dispersing their value chains. The situation of Ford Motor Company is no exception. While in 1925 Ford had almost no production outside the United States, by World War II its overseas production had risen sharply. Firms that first became multinationals during the interwar period tended to adopt country-centered strategies. European multinationals, operating in a setting where there were many sovereign countries within a relatively small geographical area, were very early to establish self-contained and quite autonomous subsidiaries in many countries. A more tolerant regulatory environment also encouraged European firms to form cartels and other cooperative agreements among themselves, which limited their foreign market entry.

Between the 1950s and the late 1970s there was a strong reversal of the interwar trends. As the outcome in Figure 1 implied, there have been very strong underlying forces driving the globalization of industries. The important reasons can be understood using the configuration/coordination framework. The competitive advantage of competing worldwide from concentrated activities rose sharply, while concentration costs fell. There was a renewed rise in scale economies in many activities because of advancing technology. The minimum efficient scale of an auto assembly plant more than tripled between 1960 and 1975, for example, while the average real cost of developing a new drug more than quadrupled. The pace of technological change has increased, creating more incentive to amortize R & D costs over worldwide sales.

Product needs have continued to homogenize among countries, as income differences have narrowed, information and communication has flowed more freely around the world, and travel has increased.[29] Growing similarities in business practices and marketing systems (e.g., chain stores) in different countries have also been a facilitating factor in homogenizing needs. Within countries there has been a parallel trend toward greater market segmentation, which some observers see as contradictory to the view that product needs in different countries are becoming more similar. However, segments today seem based less on country differences and more on buyer differences that transcend country boundaries, differences such as demographic, user-industry, or income groups. Many firms successfully employ global segmentation strategies in which they serve a narrow segment of an industry worldwide, as do Daimler-Benz and Rolex.

Another driver of post-World War II globalization has been a sharp reduction in the real costs of transportation. This has occurred through innovations in transportation technology including increasingly large bulk carriers, container ships, and larger more efficient aircraft. At the same time, government impediments to global configuration have been falling in the postwar period. Tariff barriers have gone down, international cartels and patent-sharing agreements have disappeared, while regional economic pacts such as the European Community have emerged to facilitate trade and investment, albeit imperfectly.

The ability to coordinate globally has also risen markedly in the postwar period. Perhaps the most striking reason is falling communication costs, in voice, data, and travel time for individuals. The ability to coordinate activities in different countries has also been facilitated by growing similarities among countries in marketing systems, business practices, and infrastructure; country after country has developed supermarkets and mass distributors, TV advertising, and so on. Greater international mobility of buyers and information has raised the payoff to coordinating how a firm does business around the world. Increasing numbers of firms who are themselves multinational have created growing possibilities for differentiation by suppliers who were global. Growing volatility of exchange rates has raised the advantage of coordinating production in an international plant network.

The forces underlying globalization have been self-reinforcing. The globalization of firms' strategies has contributed to the homogenization of buyer needs and business practices. Early global competitors must frequently stimulate the demand for uniform global varieties, for example, as Becton Dickinson has done with disposable syringes and Honda did with motorcycles. Globalization of industries begets globalization of supplier industries. The increasing globalization of semiconductor manufacturers is a good example. Pioneering global competitors also stimulate the development and growth of international telecommunication infrastructure as well as the creation of global advertising media, for example, *The Economist* and *The Wall Street Journal*.

Japan has clearly been the winner in the postwar globalization of competition. Japan's firms not only had an initial labor cost advantage but the orientation and skills to translate this into more durable competitive advantages such as scale and proprietary technology. The Japanese context also offered an excellent platform for globalization in many industries, given postwar environmental and technological trends. With home market-demand conditions favoring compactness, a compelling need to cope with high energy costs, and a national conviction to raise quality, Japan has proved a fertile incubator of global leaders.

Japanese multinationals had the advantage of embarking on international strategies in the 1950s and 1960s when the imperatives for a global approach to strategy were beginning to accelerate, but without the legacy of past international investments and modes of behavior.[30] Japanese firms also had an orientation toward highly concentrated activities that fit the strategic imperative of the time. Most European and many U.S. multinationals, conversely, were well established internationally before the war. They had legacies of local subsidiary autonomy that reflected the interwar environment. As Japanese firms spread internationally, they dispersed activities only grudgingly and engaged in extensive global coordination. European and country-centered U.S. companies struggled to rationalize overly dispersed configurations of activities and to boost the level of global coordination among foreign units. They found the decentralized organization structures so fashionable in the 1960s and 1970s to be a hindrance.

Strategic Implications of Globalization

When the pattern of international competition shifts from multidomestic to global in an industry, there are many implications for the strategy of an international firm. At the broadest level, globalization casts new light on many issues that have long been of interest to students of international business. In areas such as international finance, marketing, and business-government relations, the emphasis in the literature has been on the unique problems of adapting to local conditions and ways of doing business in a foreign country.

In a global industry these concerns must be supplemented with an overriding focus on the ways and means of international configuration and coordination. In government relations, for example, the focus must shift from stand-alone negotiations with host countries (appropriate in multidomestic competition) to a recognition that negotiations in one country will both affect other countries and be shaped by possibilities for performing activities in other countries. In finance, measuring the performance of subsidiaries must be modified to reflect the contribution of one subsidiary to another's cost position or differentiation in a global strategy, instead of viewing each subsidiary as a stand-alone unit. In battling with global competitors, it may be appropriate in some countries to accept low profits indefinitely – in multidomestic competition this would be unjustified.[31] In global industries, the overall system matters as much or more than the country.

Overall International Strategy

The most basic question raised by the globalization of an industry is what overall international strategy a firm should adopt. In a global industry, a global strategy that captures the particular advantages of configuration/coordination present in that industry is necessary to attain a leading position. The firm must examine each activity in the value chain to see if there is a competitive advantage to concentrating and/or to coordinating the activity globally in various ways. However, many firms may not have the resources or initial position to pursue a global strategy, particularly domestic competitors. It is important, as a result, to explore strategic options short of a full-blown global strategy that may be present in global industries.

Abstracting from the particular configuration/coordination a firm adopts for competing internationally, there are four broad types of possible strategies in a global industry, illustrated schematically in Figure 6. Any strategy involves a choice of the type of competitive advantage sought (low cost or differentiation) and the competitive scope within which the advantage is to be achieved.[32] In global industries, competitive scope involves both the industry segments in which a firm competes and whether it seeks the benefits of configuration/coordination across countries or chooses instead a country-centered approach to competing. These dimensions lead to four broad strategies, illustrated in Figure 6.

Global Cost Leadership or Differentiation: Seeking the cost or differentiation advantages of global configuration/coordination through selling a wide line of products to buyers in all or most significant country markets. Global cost leaders (e.g., Toyota, Komatsu) tend to sell standardized products and reap scale advantages in technology development, procurement, and production. Global differentiators (e.g., IBM, Caterpillar) often use their scale and learning advantages to lower the cost of differentiating (e.g., offering many models and frequent model changes) and exploit their worldwide position to reinforce their brand reputation and/or product differentiation with multi-national buyers.

Figure 6
Strategic Alternatives in a Global Industry

Geographic Scope

		Global Strategy	Country-Centered Strategy
Many Segments		Global Cost Leadership or Differentiation	Protected Markets
Few Segments		Global Segmentation	National Responsiveness

Segment Scope

Global Segmentation: Serving a particular industry segment worldwide, such as Toyota in lift trucks and Mercedes in automobiles. A variant of this strategy is competing in a subset of countries where the advantages of concentration/coordination are particularly great. In some industries, global segmentation is the only feasible global strategy because the advantages of a global configuration/coordination exist only in particular segments (e.g., high-priced business hotels). A global strategy can make entirely new segmentations of an industry possible, because serving a segment worldwide overcomes scale thresholds that make serving the segment in one country impractical.

Global segmentation, which captures the advantages of a global strategy but marshalls resources by focusing on a narrow segment, is frequently a viable option for a smaller multinational or domestic competitor. The strategy has been quite common among multinationals from smaller countries such as Finland and Switzerland. It is also frequently the first step in a sequenced strategy to move from a domestic to a global strategy. In industries such as motorcycles, farm tractors, and TV sets, for example, initial beachheads were established by Japanese firms following global segmentation strategies focused on the smaller-sized end of the product line, later expanded into full-line positions.

Protected Markets: Seeking out countries where market positions are protected by host governments. The protected markets strategy rests on government impediments to global competition such as high tariffs, stringent import quotas, and high local content requirements, which effectively isolate a country from the global industry. Protected markets strategies usually imply the need for *early* foreign direct investment in a country and can encompass only a subset of countries, because if government impediments were pervasive the industry would be multidomestic. They are generally most feasible in developing countries with protectionist industrial policies such as India, Mexico, and Argentina, though developed countries such as France and Canada offer havens for protected markets strategies in selected industries.

National Responsiveness: Focus on those industry segments most affected by local country differences though the industry as a whole is global. The firm aims to meet unusual local needs in products, channels, and marketing practices in each country, foregoing the competitive advantages of a global strategy. The national responsiveness strategy may imply that a firm compete only in those countries where segments with unusual needs are significant in size. The national responsiveness strategy is based on *economic* impediments to global configuration/coordination, while the protected markets strategy rests on government impediments. National responsiveness and protected markets can be pursued simultaneously if government protection only covers certain segments.

Protected markets or national responsiveness strategies rest on the costs of global configuration/coordination that remain even in industries that globalize. They rely on careful focus on certain segments/countries to hold off global competitors, and represent natural options for domestic firms without the resources to become international as well as multinationals who lack the resources or skills to concentrate/coordinate their activities worldwide. The sustainability of a national responsiveness strategy depends on continued national differences in some segments as well as the price differential between locally tailored and global varieties. If the extra cost to buy a better performing global variety is small or the price premium to buy a tailored local variety is too great, global competitors may overtake country-centered ones. Moreover, there is a tendency for global competitors to widen their product lines over time as they overcome market-specific barriers to entry in a country, even into segments that appear subject to local differences. In motorcycles, for example, global Japanese competitors eventually entered the large bike segment even though it is insignificant in size in Japan and many other countries. They employed shared dealer networks, brand names, and production facilities built up through competing in the global small bike segment.[33]

The sustainability of the protected markets strategy rests on continued government impediments to global competitors as well as the sanctity of a firm's favored status. Governments often invite additional competitors into their markets as the markets grow, however, and also escalate their demands on a firm once it has sunk investments in a country. Because protected markets strategies lack a competitive advantage in economic terms, their choice depends on a sophisticated prediction about future government behavior.

In many industries, two or more of the strategies can co-exist.[34] Segments with strong national differences and/or countries with high levels of protection lead to situations where there are global competitors, country-centered multinationals, and domestic firms all competing in the industry. Timing plays an important role in the industry structures observed. Early entry by a global competitor often retards the development of country-centered multinationals and domestic firms. Conversely, first-mover advantages garnered by country-centered or domestic firms can erect country-specific entry/mobility barriers that offset the advantages of a global competitor. The importance of timing suggests that multiple outcomes may be possible.

Functional Implications of Global Competition

Competing internationally with global strategy creates unique challenges for each functional area of a firm when compared to country-centered or domestic strategy. I will sketch some of the most important issues here that global strategy raises for each function, including marketing, production, technology development, finance, and government relations. In global industries, government relations take on particular importance for firm success. The chapters that follow in this book examine each functional area in more detail from the perspective of global strategy.

Production and Global Strategy

There are a number of important production issues in a global strategy. One is the configuration of the global production system (including procurement), which itself can be broken into two areas of inquiry. The first is which activities within production to concentrate and which to disperse. A highly concentrated configuration is one extreme, in which all activities occur at one location and finished goods are exported around the world for local distribution, sales, marketing, and service. This approach is characteristic of Japanese companies. A highly dispersed production configuration is the other extreme, characterized by concentrating only a few activities such as the fabrication of key components, with the balance of operations including design modifications, fabrication, and assembly carried out in each major country. The considerations that bear on the choice between concentrated and dispersed configurations have been described previously.

The second issue in global production system configuration has to do with the path along which goods flow internationally. Historically, global production has meant a production system in which components and/or end products moved from the home base to foreign countries (in what might be termed a "hub and spoke" configuration). More recently, an alternative configuration is being employed as well, which I term a "networked" configuration. In it, components and/ or end products are transshipped among specialized and dispersed production facilities located in different countries. There are a number of alternative ways of networking. One is to network by stage of the process (e.g., component and assembly plants). A firm locates one or more efficient-scale component plants and one or more efficient-scale assembly facilities in different countries. Components are shipped to assembly plants and finished goods are shipped to markets (including countries with component plants). Another approach is to network based on product varieties. Items in the line are produced in different plants that become worldwide sources for that product variety, with plants often located in countries where the product variety is particularly demanded. A good example of this approach is Stihl's production configuration in chain saws, in which a U.S. plant produces small saws for the world while European plants produce larger saws. A final networking concept, open to diversified firms, is to group products with similar manufacturing technologies in plants located in various countries.

A networked production configuration is a means to reap scale and learning economies while at the same time overcoming high tariff and nontariff barriers. Networking also allows activities in the value chain to be located where there is comparative advantage. For example, labor-intensive assembly might be located in low-wage countries, while skill- and scale-sensitive component fabrication or testing is located where appropriate skilled labor and infrastructure are present. Finally, networking allows local content *as well as* export potential in many countries. The networked configuration implies that many countries have both imports and exports depending on how they fit into the overall system, and the exports may be used to offset import restrictions. IBM, for example, seeks to configure its worldwide production activities so as to achieve a balance of imports and exports in each country.

The appropriateness of the networked configuration depends on low to moderate transport costs in components or finished goods and on the willingness of local governments to credit exports against imports. Networking also requires extensive coordination and increases risks of supply. Frequently, supply risk is mitigated by establishing two production sites for each component/product variety. Modern telecommunications and information systems along with lighter, more compact products are making networked configurations more feasible.

Configuration is only the first and in some ways the easiest issue in global production management. The second issue is the need for ongoing coordination of the global production system, involving such areas as scheduling, technical, and process coordination. Coordination is necessary to reap the advantages of worldwide production, but is made difficult by geographic distance, language differences, cultural differences, and so on. Another issue for production in a global strategy is the improvement and diffusion of the production process to multiple locations, an issue that also relates closely to the R & D function.

Marketing and Global Strategy

Many marketing activities are inherently tied to buyer location. However, there are opportunities in many industries for global coordination in marketing, in areas such as brand name, sales force, service network, and pricing. The product development function in global industries is particularly complex, because it requires the collection and coordination of information from around the world. This makes an already difficult coordination task between marketing and R & D even more difficult in global strategies.

These unique marketing issues in a global industry do not replace marketing's normal functions, but overlay them. Marketing must still understand local buyer needs, marketing systems, media, and so on, in not just one country but in many countries. As a result, marketing has perhaps the most acute need to both contribute to global coordination *and* respond to local market conditions.

Technology Development and Global Strategy

There is a technological dimension to competition in most global industries, which places demands on the technology development function. One increasingly complex issue is where R & D should take place. There is a body of literature that suggests broadly that R & D should take place in proximity to large (or potentially large) markets, and in proximity to "advanced" or sophisticated markets representing the cutting edge of industry development.[35] The global competitor has the option of performing technology development anywhere. Increasingly, the best place to do R & D is not necessarily the United States or advanced European countries, and the best place may differ for subtasks within the R & D function and for different products in the line. In copiers, for example, Xerox does research on small copiers in Japan, on medium-volume copiers in Europe, and on high-volume copiers in the United States. While this allocation may reflect the fact that Xerox has coalition partners overseas, it does appear that Japan is the most advanced market for low-volume copiers and the United States is the most advanced market for high-volume copiers. Similarly, a number of Japanese firms do R & D for medical products and semiconductors in the United States. Ronstadt's (1978) work has indicated that there are organizational pressures to enlarge foreign R & D activities once established and to direct them toward indigenous needs. Such pressures are typical of those in other activities and a global firm must organize to minimize them.

There are also many coordination issues involving technology development in global strategy. R & D must play its role in product development for worldwide markets, which requires that the R & D function have an unusual knowledge of technical issues and buyer needs globally. Similarly, process R & D is often crucial in global industries to facilitate the development of global-scale economies and learning to achieve consistent quality. Not only must R & D develop new products and processes, but new process technology must often be transferred to facilities around the world that operate under different economic and cultural circumstances. Sharing "best demonstrated practice" among facilities can be one of the major benefits of global coordination.

Finance and Global Strategy

Competing on a coordinated worldwide basis raises a variety of finance issues. The first is how to exploit a global presence in order to lower the overall cost of capital. Increasingly, global firms are raising capital in many countries. Other important issues in global strategy are the management of foreign exchange position and the related question of minimizing taxes. Tax regimes differ around the world, affecting global system configuration. Another way to affect the cost of capital is to take advantage of government financial incentives, prevalent in many global industries. How should a firm evaluate various types of financial incentives, and determine whether they contribute to global coordination or cause difficulties in doing so?

A global competitor typically has flows of products, components, and raw materials around the world and investments in facilities and working capital in many currencies. This creates more complex foreign exchange issues than for the firm that operates self-contained subsidiaries in many countries. A related question is the measurement of performance of individual plants or country operations in a global strategy. Global strategy implies linked investments rather than stand-alone ones, and the whole evaluation question is complicated by exchange rates. Firms often confuse nominal performance with true performance.

Government Relations and Global Strategy

Because government can be both an obstacle and a benefactor to the global firm, the relationship between a firm and government takes on special importance in global strategy. An international competitor with a country-centered strategy must also deal with government, but the absence of global configuration/coordination simplifies the task. A country-centered competitor can view government relations in each country largely on a stand-alone basis, while a global competitor must respond to government requirements at the least possible compromise to its global strategy and entice government to enhance its global strategy rather than merely act as a force for dispersing more and more activities to the country.

Dealing with governments in a globally coordinated way is a skill just being developed in many companies. A firm must understand the significance of various government policy instruments for its ability to configure/coordinate, and the factors that will shape its long-term bargaining position with government. As governments get more sophisticated, the challenge facing firms becomes greater.

Coalitions and Global Strategy

A coalition is a long-term agreement linking firms but falling short of merger. I use the term coalition to encompass a whole variety of arrangements that include joint ventures, licenses, supply agreements, and other kinds of interfirm relationships. International coalitions, linking firms in the same industry based in different countries, have become an important part of international strategy in the past decade.

International coalitions are a way of configuring activities in the value chain on a worldwide basis jointly with a partner. International coalitions are present in many industries, and are particularly common in automobiles, aircraft, aircraft engines, robotics, consumer electronics, semiconductors, and pharmaceuticals. While international coalitions have long been present, their character has been changing. Historically, firms from developed countries formed coalitions with firms in lesser-developed countries to perform marketing activities there. Today, we observe more and more coalitions in which two firms from developed countries are teaming up to serve the world, as well as coalitions that extend beyond marketing activities to encompass activities throughout the value chain and multiple activities.[36] Production and R & D coalitions are very common, for example.

Organization and Global Strategy

The need to configure and coordinate globally in complex ways creates some obvious organizational challenges. Any organizational structure for competing internationally has to balance two dimensions: a country dimension, because some activities are inherently performed in the country; and a global dimension, because the advantage of global configuration/coordination must be achieved.

In a global industry, the ultimate authority must represent the global dimension if a global strategy is to prevail. However, there are strong pressures within any international firm to disperse more activities once it disperses any. Moreover, forces are unleashed that lead subsidiaries to seek growing autonomy.

The organizational challenges of managing a global strategy and some of the solutions. It stresses the need to go beyond purely structural solutions and modify the systems and management functions that may have become deeply embedded in historical modes of international strategy. Flaherty stresses the importance of information systems and the many dimensions that valuable coordination can take.

The Future of International Competition

Since the late 1970s, there have been some gradual but significant changes in the pattern of international competition that carry important implications for international strategy. Foreign direct investment has been growing more rapidly and flowing in new directions, while growth in trade has slowed. This book's framework provides a template with which I can examine these changes and probe their significance. The factors shaping the global configuration of activities by firms are developing in ways that contrast with the trends of the previous thirty-years.

Homogenization of product needs among countries appears to be continuing, though segmentation within countries is as well. As a result, consumer packaged goods are becoming increasingly prone toward globalization, though they have long been characterized by multidomestic competition. There are also signs of globalization in some service industries as the introduction of information technology creates scale economies in support activities and facilitate coordination in primary activities. Global service firms are reaping advantages in hardware and software development as well as in procurement.

In many industries, however, limits have been reached in this scale economies that have been driving the concentration of activities. These limits grow out of classic diseconomies of scale that arise in very large facilities, as well as new, more flexible technology in manufacturing and other activities that is often not as scale sensitive as previous methods. At the same time, though, flexible manufacturing allows the production of multiple varieties (to serve different countries) in a single plant. This may encourage new movement toward globalization in industries in which product differences among countries have remained significant and have blocked globalization in the past. Another important change is the declining labor content in many industries due to automation of the value chain, which is reducing the incentive to locate activities in low-wage countries such as South Korea and Singapore.

There also appear to be some limits to further decline in transport costs, as innovations such as containerization, bulk ships, and larger aircraft have largely run their course. However, a parallel trend toward smaller, lighter products and components may keep some downward pressure on transport costs. The biggest change in the benefits and costs of concentrated configuration has been the sharp rise in protectionism in recent years and the resulting rise in nontariff barriers akin to the 1920s. As a group, these factors point to less need and less opportunity for highly concentrated configurations of activities and explain why growth in direct investment has been outpacing growth in trade. Falling labor content also suggests that more foreign investment will flow to developed countries (to secure market access) instead of low-wage countries.

When the coordination dimension is examined, the picture looks quite different. Communication and coordination costs are dropping sharply, driven by breathtaking advances in information systems and telecommunication technology. We have just seen the beginning of developments in this area, which are spreading throughout the value chain.[37] Boeing, for example, is employing computer-aided design technology to jointly design components on-line with foreign suppliers. Engineers in different countries are communicating via computer screens. Marketing systems and business practices continue to homogenize, facilitating the coordination of activities in different countries. The mobility of buyers and information is also growing rapidly, greasing the international spread of brand reputations and enhancing the importance of consistency in the way activities are performed worldwide. Increasing numbers of multinational and global firms are begetting globalization by their suppliers. There is also a sharp rise in the computerization of manufacturing as well as other activities throughout the value chain, which greatly facilitates coordination among dispersed sites.

The imperative of global strategy is shifting, then, in ways that will require a rebalancing of configuration and coordination. Concentrating activities is less necessary in economic terms, and less possible as governments force more dispersion. These forces are pushing firms to intermediate positions on the config uration axis as shown in Figure 7. At the same time, the ability to coordinate

Figure 7
Future Trends in International Competition

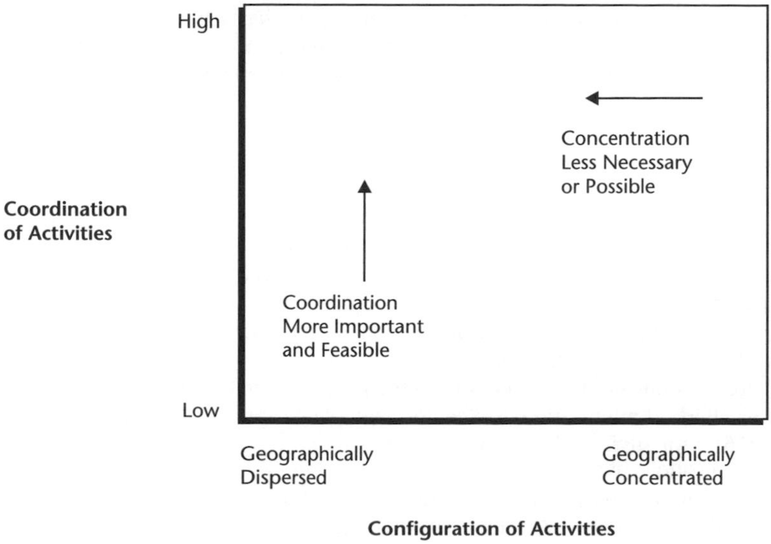

globally throughout the value chain is increasing dramatically through modern technology. The need to coordinate is also rising to offset greater dispersion and to respond to buyer needs. Moreover, intermediate configurations often require greater coordination, and coordination can neutralize some of the costs of dispersion forced on firms by governments. These considerations imply an upward movement in Figure 7. Thus, simpler first generation global strategies (e.g., concentration and export) seem to be giving way to more complex global strategies involving multiple though coordinated R & D activities, sophisticated networking of overseas plants, worldwide procurement, and so on.

Thus, today's game of global strategy seems increasingly to be a game of coordination – getting dispersed production facilities, R & D laboratories, and marketing activities to truly work together. Widespread coordination remains the exception rather than the rule today in many multinationals. Successful international competitors in the future will be those who can seek out competitive advantages from global configuration/coordination anywhere in the value chain, and overcome the organizational barriers to exploiting them.

Notes

This chapter has benefited from comments by Richard A. Rawlinson, M. Therese Flaherty, and Louis T. Wells, Jr.

1. Intra-industry trade, where a country both exports and imports goods in the same industry, has grown markedly as well. The reasons will be made clear by the framework below.
2. United Nations Center on Transnational Corporations (1984).
3. For a survey, see Caves and Jones (1985).
4. See, particularly, the work of Hymer, Kindleberger, and Caves. There are many books on the theory and management of the multinational, which are too numerous to cite here. For an excellent survey of the literature, see Caves (1982). A more recent stream of literature emphasizes how the multinational firm internalizes transactions to circumvent imperfections in various intermediate markets, most importantly the market for knowledge. Prominent examples of this work are Buckley and Casson (1976) and Teece (1981). For a survey and extension, see Teece (1985).
5. Knickerbocker's (1973) work on oligopolistic reaction adds an important dimension to the process of entering foreign markets through illuminating bunching in the timing of entry into a country by firms in an industry and relating this to defensive considerations. Vernon's product cycle of international trade combines a view of how products mature with the evolution in a firm's international activities to predict the patterns of trade and investment in developed and developing countries (Vernon 1966). Vernon himself, among others, has raised questions about how general the product cycle pattern is today.
6. There are some notable exceptions to the general paucity of thinking on the strategy of established multinationals. See, for example, Stopford and Wells (1972), Franko (1976), Stobaugh et al. (1976).
7. Porter (1980, 1985a).
8. The distinction between multidomestic and global competition and some of its strategic implications were first described in Hout, Porter, and Rudden (1982).

9. Perlmutter's (1969) concept of ethnocentric, polycentric, and geocentric multinationals is an interesting but different one. It takes the firm, not the industry, as the unit of analysis and is decoupled from industry structure. It focuses on management attitudes, the nationality of executives, and other aspects of organization. Perlmutter presents ethnocentric, polycentric, and geocentric as stages of an organization's development as a multinational, with geocentric as the goal. A later paper (Wind, Douglas, and Perlmutter 1973) tempers this conclusion based on the fact that some companies may not have the required sophistication in marketing to attempt a geocentric strategy. Products embedded in the lifestyle or culture of a country are also identified as less susceptible to geocentrism. The Perlmutter et al. view does not attempt to link management orientation to industry structure and strategy. International strategy should grow out of the net competitive advantage in a global industry of different types of worldwide coordination. In some industries, a country-centered strategy, roughly analogous to Perlmutter's polycentric idea, may be the best strategy irrespective of company size and international experience. Conversely, a global strategy may be imperative given the competitive advantage that accrues from it. Industry and strategy should define the organization approach, not vice versa.

10. Porter (1985a) describes value chain theory and its use in analyzing competitive advantage.

11. There is a growing globalization of service firm strategies, however, as service firms serve multinational buyers. Developments in information technology raise the importance of R & D, and automation pervades the primary activities of service firms. Service firms tend to draw advantages from a global strategy largely in the support activities in the value chain.

12. Buzzell (1968), Pryor (1965), and Wind, Douglas, and Perlmutter (1973) point out that national differences are in most cases more critical with respect to marketing than with production and finance. This generalization reflects the fact that marketing activities are often inherently country based. However, this generalization is not reliable because in many countries, production and other activities are widely dispersed.

13. In practice, a diagram such as Table 1 would involve each important discrete activity (not broad categories) and include all the countries in which a firm operates.

14. M. Therese Flaherty provided helpful comments that clarified the configuration/coordination distinction.

15. Here, the firm makes only a one-time transfer of knowledge in establishing each subsidiary, which gives it an advantage over local firms. Transaction costs dictate the multinational form rather than market transactions.

16. Strategic groups are described in Porter (1980), *Competitive Strategy*, New York: Free Press, chapter 7.

17. For example, governments may desire national autonomy in decision making and the spillovers from domestic R & D and training of skilled workers.

18. A number of authors have framed the globalization of industries in terms of the balance between imperatives for global integration and imperatives for national responsiveness, a useful distinction. See Prahalad (1975), Doz (1976), and Bartlett (1979). I relate that distinction here to more basic issues of where and how a firm performs the activities in the value chain internationally.

19. Transactional failures make coordination between independent firms or coalition partners even more difficult than the initial transfer of knowledge in establishing a foreign subsidiary, not to mention ongoing coordination among subsidiaries.

20. Bartlett's chapter in this book provides a sophisticated treatment of the organizational issues in geographic coordination. The difficulties in coordinating across

business units competing in different industries within the diversified firm as described in Porter (1985a), chapter 11.

21. For a discussion, see Porter (1985a), *Competitive Advantage*, New York: Free Press, chapter 9.
22. Empirical research has found a strong correlation between R & D and advertising intensity and the extent of foreign direct investment (for a survey, see Caves 1982). Both these factors have a place in our model of the determinants of globalization, but for quite different reasons. R & D intensity suggests scale advantages for the global competitor in developing products or processes that are manufactured abroad either due to low production scale economies or government pressures, or that require investments in service infrastructure. Advertising intensity, however, is much closer to proxying the possibilities for the classic transfer of marketing knowledge to foreign subsidiaries. High advertising industries are also frequently those where local tastes differ and manufacturing scale economies are modest, both reasons to disperse many activities.
23. This description draws on a study of the incidence of multinationals in the hotel industry by Dunnina and McQueen (1981).
24. There is an analogy here between the Lawrence and Lorsch (1967) idea that differentiation of functions within a firm along with providing effective integration improves performance, a point suggested by M. Therese Flaherty.
25. It has been recognized that comparative advantage in different stages in a vertically integrated industry sector such as aluminum can reside in different countries. Bauxite mining will take place in resource-rich countries, for example, while smelting will take place in countries with low electrical power cost (see Caves and Jones 1985, p. 142). The argument here extends this thinking *within* the value chain of any stage, and suggests that the optimal location for performing individual activities may vary as well.
26. See Porter (1985b). The issues in this section are the subject of a major current research project involving nine countries.
27. See Linder (1961), Vernon (1966), and Gruber, Mehta, and Vernon (1967).
28. Where it does recognize scale economies, trade theory views them narrowly as arising from production in one country.
29. Levitt's (1983) article provides a supporting view. Porter (1985), *Competitive Advantage*, New York: Free Press, Chapter 11.
30. Japan's limited prewar international sales were handled largely through trading companies. Levitt's (1983) article provides a supporting view. Trading companies still handled a good portion of Japanese exports in the 1970s but have become less important in newer and high-technology industries.
31. For a discussion, see Hunt, Porter, and Rudden (1982). For a recent treatment, see Hamel and Prahalad (1985).
32. For a discussion, see Porter (1985a), Porter (1985), *Competitive Advantage*, New York: Free Press, chapters 1 and 2.
33. A key consideration in the sustainability of national responsiveness strategies is the ability of broad-line competitors to share activities among segments. See Porter (1985a), see Porter (1985), *Competitive Advantage*, New York: Free Press, chapter 7, for a generic treatment.
34. Mixed strategies are also observed in which a firm employs a global strategy in one group of countries and country-centered strategies in others. In the sewing machine industry, for example, otherwise global competitions product pedal-powered sewing machines that meet local needs in developing countries with high levels of protection.
35. See, for example, Hirsch (1970) and Ronstadt (1978).

36. Hladik's recent study of international joint ventures provides supporting evidence, see Hladik (1984).
37. For a discussion, see Porter and Millar (1985).

References

Bartlett, C. A. "Multinational Structural Evolution: The Changing Decision Environment in the International Division." D.B.A. diss., Harvard Graduate School of Business Administration, 1979.

Buckley, P. J., and M. C. Casson. *The Future of the Multinational Enterprise*. London: Holms and Meier, 1976.

Buzzell, R. D. "Can You Standardize Multinational Marketing?" *Harvard Business Review* (November/December 1968): 102–13.

Casson, M. C. "Transaction Costs and the Theory of the Multinational Enterprise," in A. Rugman, ed., *New Theories of the Multinational Enterprise*. London: Croom Helm, 1982.

Caves, R. E. *Multinational Enterprise and Economic Analysis*. Cambridge, England: Cambridge University Press, 1982.

Caves, R. E., and R. W. Jones. *World Trade and Payments*, fourth edition. Boston: Little, Brown, 1985.

Doz, Y. "National Policies and Multinational Management." D.B.A. diss., Harvard Graduate School of Business Administration, 1976.

Dunning, J., and M. McQueen. "The Eclectic Theory of International Production: A Case Study of the International Hotel Industry." *Managerial and Decision Economics* 2 (December 1981): 197–210.

Franko, L. G. *The European Multinationals: A Renewed Challenge to American and British Big Business*. Stanford, Conn.: Greylock, 1976.

Knickerbocker, F. *Oligopolistic Reaction and Multinational Enterprise*. Cambridge, Mass.: Harvard University Press, 1973.

Gruber, W., D. Mehta, and R. Vernon. "The R & D Factor in International Trade and Investment of United States Industries." *Journal of Political Economy* (February 1967): 20–37.

Hamel, G., and C. K. Prahalad. "Do You Really Have a Global Strategy?" *Harvard Business Review* (July/August 1985): 139–48.

Hirsch, S. "Technological Factors in the Composition and Direction of Israel's Industrial Exports," in Vernon, R., ed., *Technological Factors in International Trade*. New York: National Bureau of Economic Research, 1970, 365–408.

Hladik, K. "International Joint Ventures: An Empirical Investigation into the Characteristics of Recent U.S.-Foreign Joint Venture Partnerships." Ph.D. diss., Business Economics Program, Harvard University, 1984.

Hout, T., M. E. Porter, and E. Rudden. "How Global Companies Win Out." *Harvard Business Review* (September/October 1982): 98–108.

Lawrence, P. R., and J. W. Lorsch. *Organization and Environment*. Boston: Division of Research, Harvard Graduate School of Business Administration, 1967.

Levitt, T. "The Globalization of Markets." *Harvard Business Review* (May/June 1983): 92–102.

Linder, S. *An Essay on Trade and Transformation*. New York: John Wiley, 1961.

Perlmutter, H. V. "The Tortuous Evolution of the Multinational Corporation." *Columbia Journal of World Business* (January/February 1969): 9–18.

Porter, M. E. *Competitive Strategy: Techniques for Analyzing Industries and Competitors.* New York: Free Press, 1980.

———. *Competitive Advantage: Creating and Sustaining Superior Performance.* New York: Free Press, 1985*a*.

———. "Beyond Comparative Advantage." Working Paper, Harvard Graduate School of Business Administration, August 1985*b*.

Porter, M. E., and V. Millar, "How Information Gives You Competitive Advantage." *Harvard Business Review* (July/August 1985): 149–60.

Prahalad, C. K. "The Strategic Process in a Multinational Corporation." D.B.A. diss., Harvard Graduate School of Business Administration, 1975.

Pryor, M. H. "Planning in a World-Wide Business." *Harvard Business Review* 43 (January/ February 1965): 130–9.

Ronstadt, R. C. "International R&D: The Establishment and Evolution of Research and Development Abroad by Seven U.S. Multinationals." *Journal of International Business Studies* (Spring/Summer 1978): 7–23.

Stobaugh, R. B., et al. "Nine Investments Abroad and Their Impact at Home: Case Studies on Multinational Enterprise and the U.S. Economy." Boston: Division of Research, Harvard Business School, 1976.

Stopford, J. J., and L. T. Wells, Jr. *Managing the Multinational Enterprise: Organization of the Firm and Overlap of Subsidiaries.* New York: Basic Books, 1972.

Teece, D. J. "Multinational Enterprise: Market Failure and Market Power Considerations." *Sloan Management Review* 22, no. 3 (September 1981): 3–17.

———. "Transaction Cost Economics and the Multinational Enterprise: An Assessment." Working Paper IB-3, Business School, University of California at Berkeley, January 1985.

United Nations Center on Transnational Corporations, *Salient Features and Trends in Foreign Direct Investment*, United Nations, New York, 1984.

Vernon, R. "International Investment and International Trade in the Product Cycle." *Quarterly Journal of Economics* 80 (May 1966): 190–207.

Williamson, O. *Markets and Hierarchies.* New York: Free Press, 1975.

Wind, Y., S. P. Douglas, and H. B. Perlmutter. "Guidelines for Developing International Marketing Strategies." *Journal of Marketing* 37 (April 1973): 14–23.

43

The Triad World View

Kenichi Ohmae

Only fifteen years ago, Japan had extremely serious pollution problems. Policemen at the busiest intersections in Tokyo wore gauze masks to filter out airborne particles. But Japan didn't care about pollution as much as it cared about increasing industrial production. Japan turned its people into industrious swarms of busy worker bees whose average per capita income was equivalent to only about $3,000 in today's dollars.

Despite the oil crises, per capita GNP rose to $5,000 in 1974. Less than ten years later, in 1982, it topped $10,000, and the next year, it rose to $11,000. (See Exhibit 1.) Other countries with per capita GNPs more than $10,000 include the United States, West Germany, France, Switzerland and Sweden. England's per capita GNP is more than $9,000 and Italy's is more than $6,000.

In the process of this rapid growth, Japan rose from the ranks of the semi-developed nations, catching up and finally aligning itself with the advanced industrial nations, whose economic growth in the meantime was far slower. Japan was the first non-Euro-American country to achieve this.

When a country's per capita GNP is $5,000 or less, Engel's coefficient (the percentage of income spent on food) exceeds 50 percent and very little disposable income remains. However, when per capita GNP rises to about $10,000, Engel's coefficient sinks to 20 or 30 percent and about 70 percent of income is disposable income. At this point, disposable income translates into considerable purchasing power.

This is precisely what happened in the decade 1972–1982; patterns of consumption and lifestyles altered substantially. The first Japanese McDonald's opened on the Ginza in 1971. At the time, the idea of eating while walking was a disturbing innovation. Japanese mothers had always said, "Sit down and finish eating!" But in the 1970s, the Japanese began to see people walking down the street with food in their hands – and their mouths. It was the first of a series of culture shocks, but this particular shock is over today. Young couples stroll down the street arm-in-arm eating ice cream and nobody notices. The generation that would still hesitate to do this is now a small minority.

Source: *The Journal of Business Strategy*, Vol. 7, 1987, pp. 8–19.

Exhibit 1
Japan Entered into the $10,000 Club in the Late 1970s

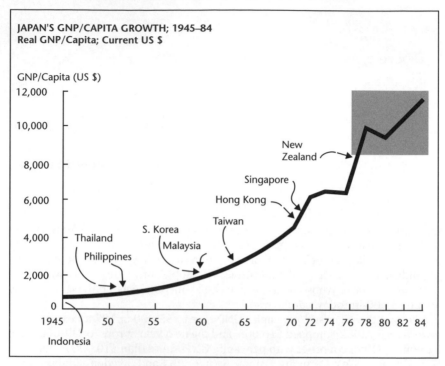

JAPAN'S GNP/CAPITA GROWTH; 1945–84
Real GNP/Capita; Current US $

Source: World Bank Atlas; Ministry of Health and Welfare; MOF; Bank of Japan.

Other things have changed. Ten years ago, sneakers were only worn during gym or recess at school. Adults wore leather shoes, and "exercise shoes," as they were then known, were not acceptable street wear. Today, people of every generation wear whatever shoes they prefer. The degree of tolerance of different expressions of individuality and of diverse styles has grown tremendously.

The simplest description of the ten-year trend in Japanese life-styles is "westernization." Westernization has been in progress in Japan since the 1860s, but few decades have worked such deep and lasting changes in our daily lives as the ten years before Japan's per capita GNP reached the $10,000 level. Even toilet paper has changed. It was not so long ago that the Japanese used single sheets of crinkly rice paper taken from shallow box-shaped baskets hung in toilets. Before that, they used old newspapers cut into squares. Both have been replaced by soft toilet paper on rolls of exactly the same type used in the United States. Toilet paper is just one example of how every facet of modern life, from clothing to food and housing, has undergone such radical change that the Japanese life-style is now fundamentally the same as in any other advanced industrial nation.

Rather than saying that Japan has gone overboard about Western ways, I prefer to believe that when income exceeds a certain level, life-styles change in ways that were first experienced in the West. When people no longer have to work for sustenance and begin working to permit recreation, they spontaneously begin to choose similar and relaxed life-styles. Japan is simply undergoing the same natural process that the West has experienced.

There are No National Boundaries between Life-Styles

The wealthy industrialized nations, of which Japan has recently become a member, share high disposable income levels. With disposable income having reached comparable levels, people's educational levels, academic and cultural backgrounds, life-styles, and access to information in the urban centers begin to be the same. As these cultural elements begin to resemble each other qualitatively, even such extremely subjective factors as demand for material possessions, ways of spending leisure time, and aspirations for the future, become increasingly homogeneous.

Young Japanese in Tokyo's Harajuku, the mecca of the fashionable young set, wear styles and carry goods indistinguishable from those of California: Nike sneakers, L.L. Bean trousers, Fila T-shirts, Prince tennis rackets, and Lancel bags. The same fashions are found in New York City, Copenhagen, and Amsterdam. If roller skating becomes a fad in California, it soon spreads throughout the world. These young people also share musical tastes. They listen to songs on the hit charts in Los Angeles. Japan's Yellow Magic Orchestra and other digital musicians have become popular around the globe.

Businessmen of the traditional stamp in Tokyo, New York, and Dusseldorf wear the same navy blue suits, Bally shoes and Hermes neckties. The Mark Cross wallets in their pockets contain thin Casio calculators. They lunch together at sushi bars in business districts around the world, and choose between Technics or Kenwood stereo systems when they buy audio equipment.

In Japan, Mister Donut is not just a hangout for high school and college students; even families are regular customers, and workers from nearby construction sites come in for a coffee during their rest periods. Cities of modest size throughout Japan display signs for Kentucky Fried Chicken, Wimpy's, Baskin-Robbins, Shakey's Pizza, Denny's, and 7-Eleven. In Tokyo a tourist will also see stands selling David's and Mrs. Fields' cookies. Fast food has hit Japan with a vengeance.

Japanese homes store bottles of Johnson's window cleaner, Pampers disposable diapers, Scottie's and Kleenex tissues, Lux soap, Cheer detergent, and Johnson & Johnson Band-aids. In a Japanese supermarket one will see Knorr, Campbell and Maggi soups, V-8 juices, Nestle coffee, Lipton tea, McCormick spices, Ritz crackers, Kellogg's cornflakes, Granola bars, Dannon yogurt, Borden's ice cream, Kodak film, and scores of familiar products from all over the world. Probably the biggest difference between American and Japanese supermarkets is the pickling paste and the dried fish in Japanese stores.

Japanese drugstores are also full of international brands: Wella shampoos, Nivea skin creams, Max Factor and Revlon cosmetics, Herb candies, Vick's cough drops, Contac cold capsules, Bayer aspirin, and many more. The brands that have managed to gain an especially good reputation for high quality in Japan include Cross, Parker, and Sheaffer pens, Louis Vuitton, Givenchy, and Nina Ricci handbags; Yves Saint-Laurent, Pierre Cardin, and Ungaro fashions; and Estee Lauder, Clinique and Chanel perfumes.

> About 90 percent of all high value-added, high-technology manufactured goods are produced and consumed in North America, Western Europe, and Japan.

Sporting goods stores are filled with racks of products by Adidas, Lacoste, Teng, Fila, Wilson, Prince, and Head. More than 50 percent of the skis used in Japan come from Europe; their presence proves that non-Japanese product concepts are well received by Japanese consumers and have a lasting place in Japanese life.

Today, nationality is not a factor in daily consumption. National borders don't exist in the supermarket. Added to these similarities is the quasi-equality of road, telecommunication, power transmission and sewerage networks, administrative systems, and other infrastructures. The telephone network is especially important, as it provides the basis for the development of high-technology industry. It greatly facilitates use of facsimile and teletext terminals and other digital and data processing equipment. Roads are another important factor. When most roads are paved, a market is opened for such high value-added products as radial tires and sports cars, which put real money into a manufacturer's coffers. They can't be designed or built without advanced technology.

As access to information becomes increasingly important to modern societies, it fragments markets into highly individualized segments at the same time that the overall needs of the world population become increasingly homogeneous. This is an age where *netsuke* and other items of Japanese cuisine or art barely known to the Japanese enjoy booms in New York City.

In advanced industrial countries, consumers' lives, life-styles, and aspirations are becoming increasingly alike as people the world over find the same things interesting or attractive and the same foods tasty. People live in similar residential neighborhoods, learn similar things at school, watch similar programs on television, and buy the same goods at the supermarket or department store.

The Triad Market: 630 Million Buyers with Similar Tastes

In essence, this means that 630 million people – the combined populations of Japan (120 million), the United States (250 million), and Western Europe (260 million) – form a single market with common needs. For the market researcher, their needs can be analyzed more effectively in terms of groups or clusters with similar habits and tastes than in terms of nationalities. Consumer behavior today is more influenced by educational background and disposable income than by ethnic characteristics. Even religion becomes a declining "industry" in economies with over $5,000 per capita income. In the advanced industrial countries, the generation gap is greater than national or cultural disparities. People in their twenties are now interested in different things than people in their thirties, and each generation, including the increasingly powerful senior citizen bracket, has its own tastes which are the same throughout the triad.

A world view based on outmoded concepts of nationality and traditional antagonisms between nations and ethnic groups is not useful in today's trade. In fact, to dismiss it outright and treat the inhabitants of Japan, Europe, and the United States as a single race of consumers with shared needs and aspirations is the first conceptual leap toward a pragmatic and productive businessperson's world view. This is critical, because how can one be aware of new opportunities if one is unaware of new realities?

Business Opportunities in the Triad Market

The first group of consumers to favor Sony Walkmans were the young people of California. Almost simultaneously, Walkmans became the rage in Japan and Europe. The fad spread like wildfire, as can happen with any attractive product in the triad market. The reason is that the market is homogeneous. As soon as the Walkman came on the market, consumers in the United States, Europe, and Japan simultaneously felt the need to listen to recorded music while strolling.

Canon's AE1 became instantly popular worldwide within six months of its launching. The Minolta a-7000, an automatic focus single lens reflex camera, also won instant global popularity. People's needs are the same, wherever they live in the industrialized world. When they take pictures, they want to take good ones, in sharp focus. It's not their goal to use a camera made in their own country.

Five or six years ago, I used a calculator with a sound generator that permitted the user to play games when he or she wasn't calculating. I had picked up this item at an airport shop on my way to the United States and it aroused such interest that people asked me to get them one on my next trip. Recently, however, when I was showing off my very thin Casio calculator, which fits inside my visiting card case, a Dutchman smiled and pulled out his own, and pointed out that it was even thinner. The latest Casio had been launched simultaneously in all regions of the triad, so that it reached certain parts of the Netherlands faster than a local shop in Japan.

Today, new products circle the globe with the speed of a satellite. It no longer holds that innovations trickle down like a cascade from the most to the least technologically advanced countries. (See Exhibit 2.) This was true in the past; for example, it took decades for the custom of carpeting floors and watching television to reach Japan from the United States.

For a manufacturer to assume that the need for its new product will spread slowly is equivalent to giving its competitors a head start on the global market. In the past, firms first attacked and conquered the domestic market before moving into overseas markets because they were certain that they could monopolize their proprietary technology and know-how for a considerable period. They also assumed that they could extend their networks throughout the world, provided that they spent the necessary time.

Over the past few years, with the spread of technology, the increasing speed of its development, and the convergence of capabilities of high-technology firms,

Exhibit 2
MNC: Waterfall Model

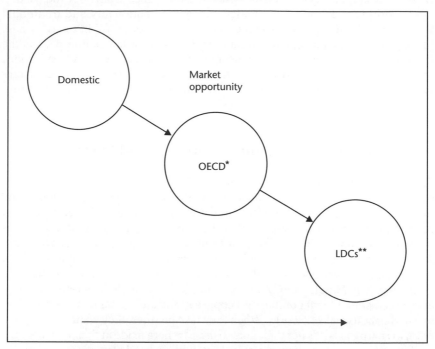

*Organization for Economic Cooperation and Development
**Less developed countries

it has become impossible to be certain that one will have sole access to a new technology and know-how for more than a year. Moreover, the tremendous cost of research and development of high-technology products that appeal to consumers makes it impossible to recover the investment solely from sales in the domestic market. From the very start, firms simply must target the entire triad market. They must launch products in all sales territories virtually simultaneously and have the capacity to promote sales on a global scale if they are to have any chance of success.

The British firm EMI developed the first computer tomographic (CT) scanner, a machine that made marvelous imaging applications possible to modern medicine. The triad's medical electronics sales networks were controlled by Toshiba in Japan, General Electric in the United States, Siemens in Germany, and Philips elsewhere in the European Economic Community. Moving alone, first into the United States, EMI tried to establish its own networks, but failed. While EMI was building up its sales organization, Toshiba, General Electric, Siemens, and Philips were developing their own CT scanners. They soon pushed EMI out of the market. Since market and sales force development takes longer than a decade, even the most proprietary product will thus be outdated by the time a corporation can establish its global sales readiness.

The point, from the other side of the coin, is that product and service strategies targeted only for the domestic population are less and less likely to be successful. When planning takes the much larger triad population into consideration, one's strategy holds together under a variety of circumstances. Universally applicable strategies and the resulting product and service concepts are more competitive and stand a much greater chance of success. This does not mean that companies don't have to tailor their overall strategies to local situations, but that is what companies do anyway when they segment their markets, even in their home countries. Now, however, supranational segments exist in the triad, and paying attention to commonalities across national boundaries is often much more profitable than debating the differences of customers based on nationalities. Some Japanese youngsters can be clustered together with the Californians.

Consortia for Survival

For a firm with a good grasp of the shared needs of 630 million people and the courage to launch a product in the triad market, it is essential to have networks that can deliver a newly developed product almost simultaneously to scores of different points on the globe.

IBM and Nestle began to extend their networks, region by region, during an age when they enjoyed relatively little competition; at that time, the "cascade" model still worked. However, this is an age that no longer permits the leisure of waiting for a product to trickle down from the most to the least sophisticated consumers. The "sprinkler" model of product diffusion better meets the needs of today's markets. Manufactured goods must be deliverable at high speed from a central point as soon as the production "faucet" is turned on.[1] To do this, companies have tried various methods of market penetration, including joint ventures, acquisitions, and mergers, but few of these attempts have succeeded. American or European joint ventures, acquisitions, or merged firms have often failed to penetrate the Japanese market, and the same applies to Japanese firms in American or European markets. The fusion of two corporate cultures is a difficult feat, and the contracts and other legal constraints binding joint ventures tend to hinder rather than boost their operations.

Presently the most pragmatic and productive method of expanding a product's market is the formation of a consortium alliance. Consortia usually involve the swapping of new products and models premised on the mutual inviolability of the partners' home markets. In this way, products resulting from expensive development programs can be backed quickly by strong sales capacity in the entire triad market to ensure that investments are recouped.

When one looks at the leading-edge companies around the world, it is striking to notice how much fixed cost they have accumulated over the past ten years. (See Exhibit 3.) Increasingly expensive R&D cannot be considered a variable through licenses, for example, unless a company has its own strong products and also crosslicenses with others. The manufacturing process has also acquired many expensive robots and flexible manufacturing cells during this time. The sales force is a fixed cost a company has to keep regardless of how good a portfolio

Exhibit 3
"Fixed Cost Game" Requires a Corporation to become "World Class" to Survive

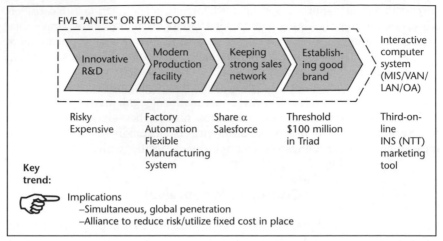

FIVE "ANTES" OR FIXED COSTS

Innovative R&D   Modern Production facility   Keeping strong sales network   Establishing good brand   Interactive computer system (MIS/VAN/LAN/OA)

| Risky Expensive | Factory Automation Flexible Manufacturing System | Share α Salesforce | Threshold $100 million in Triad | Third-on-line INS (NTT) marketing tool |

Key trend:

Implications
–Simultaneous, global penetration
–Alliance to reduce risk/utilize fixed cost in place

of products it has. In order to establish a brand recognition in the triad that will actually affect customers, the minimum ante in consumer and office product areas is certainly $100 million. On top of all this, the information network of a company – its value-added network (VAN), local area network (LAN) and the like – are all fixed costs. There is no such thing as a half-baked computer. It either works or does not work.

> In advanced industrial countries, consumers' lives, life-styles and aspirations are becoming increasingly alike.

All these key elements of a company's business system have become fixed costs. They will add significantly to unit costs unless a company finds a way to amortize them with larger volume throughput. Even the Japanese market of 120 million people is too small if a competitor is a triadian depreciating its fixed costs over 630 million people. If a company can afford to establish its own global network, that is certainly an option. IBM, Coca-Cola and Nestle have all done so. Another option is to find partners who will help to maximize the contribution margin to the fixed cost. That is a basic principle in international corporate economics today, and triad consortium alliances which form global businesses are one result of its application. If a Japanese company has an unusually good product being developed in its laboratory, but not a strong network in Europe, it might want to find a strong European partner. It is hoped that the partner also will have a good product, so that the Japanese partner can distribute it in Japan. It has rarely made sense to distribute a strong product through a weak sales channel, but in today's global business it is close to economic suicide.

Similarly, if its production facility has extra capacity, a company might produce another company's product under its name, an arrangement known as OEM (original equipment manufacturing). If a sales force is capable of selling more than its product division can pump out, then a company might distribute its ally's products either under its own brand or under the partner's.

The old Western model for international business was more or less imperial: a company invested in a joint venture and for a precisely projected return. For a number of reasons, this model is not working well. Partners in a consortium alliance do not expect returns on investment, but they do expect returns on sales (ROS). What they are doing is maximizing contribution to their fixed costs, in effect getting more margins by joining with allied companies that "replace" part of their business system. So long as the blood flows through the system, and they feel the warmth of their partners, the relationship will be fine, but it will have to be mutual. Instead of the old imperialistic model, which was aimed at conquest, one now sees the triad alliance model appearing, because it is much more pragmatic and it enhances global interdependence.

Today, trilateral consortia are being formed in nearly every area of leading-edge industry, including biotechnology, computers, robots, semiconductors, jet engines, nuclear power, carbon fibers, and other new materials. And one also sees them developing in mature industries such as steel and chemicals.

Originally, few Japanese firms showed any interest in consortia. They tended to keep to themselves whatever relatively advanced in-house technology they possessed, trusting in their own capacity to expand their markets even when they lacked adequate sales networks. Ironically, some academics are now attacking alliances as another MITI-inspired plan to dominate the West. According to their argument, Japanese firms use alliances to sap their partners' strengths and then abandon them. American and European partners try to do the same thing, they say, but fail.

Part of this is merely a new form of Japan-bashing. Japan's JVC is criticized, for example, for innovating too fast for its partners Thorne-EMI and Thompson.

> JVC has constantly accelerated the pace of new product development, of improved product manufacturability, of transitions to new product generations (that is to "slim line" VCRs), so its partners constantly have to catch up, retool, gear up for new types, reinvest in manufacturing, and – given the smaller volume they make jointly for Europe, compared with JVC's own Far East production – incur permanently higher unit costs than JVC despite formidable efforts at cost reduction.

All this has thwarted Thompson's plan to "learn from JVC's product engineering and manufacturing skills, in order then to re-assert its independence."[2]

Partnerships are what partners make of them. They provide contributions to fixed costs but they don't create fixed strengths. "Therein the patient must minister unto himself." Moreover, partnerships don't necessarily last forever. They're somewhere between a marriage and a weekend affair. In a world where currency fluctuations, technology and partnering itself make strategies more slippery and uncertain than sustainable, partnerships – like competitive advantage – need to be reinvigorated often by *each* party or they will collapse, having made a brief but not enduring contribution to each partner's bottom line.

All this notwithstanding, companies are learning how to make both short- and long-term partnerships work. Technology consortia recently formed to produce videotape, for example, have registered noticeable successes. Sony and the

Matsushita group (Panasonic, Quasar, Japan Victor (JVC) and Technics) developed competitive products, the Beta and VHS formats, respectively. These were put simultaneously on the market in Japan, the United States, and Europe, through both direct and joint sales channels. The Matsushita group gained a 15 percent share of the American market through its own sales channels. Then it conquered a further 45 percent share through OEM (original equipment manufacturer) agreements which allowed other companies to put their brand names on its products. In Europe, its partner, Victor Company of Japan, won a spectacular 77 percent share for VHS-format products.

In comparison with Matsushita's successes through the strategy of sales consortia, the Dutch Philips managed their video bid in their traditional fashion. Philips, confident in its own V2000 format video technology, planned first to develop the European market, to let American Philips conquer the U.S. market, and then to move into Japan at a later stage. While Philips was unhurriedly proceeding with its plan, however, the Beta and VHS camps formed consortia in the triad almost simultaneously. Before Philips could react, shops around the world were unwilling to put V2000 products and their tapes on their shelves.

Many established European companies have misjudged the accelerating pace of technological diffusion. Philips's strategy would have worked very well back in the days of black-and-white television, or even in the beginning of the color television era. But today, companies have to be able simultaneously to meet the demands of the combined triad population; the step-by-step approach no longer works. When incompatible products compete, as in the case of the VCR, it is particularly vital to arrive in advance of one's competitors. The speed with which a new product is delivered is a decisive factor for victory or defeat, and the pace of the race is still increasing day by day. Philips today has learned the lesson, and it took the lead in reaching an agreement on the compact disc player format as well as its video version called CDV.

> One of the emerging strategies is teaming up with foreigners to meet domestic threats.

Perhaps because one so frequently uses the terms "international competition" and "trade war," the Japanese tend to overact when foreign companies "threaten" to "invade" their markets. However, the real competitors, the ones that can pose a very serious challenge to the best firms in any country, are the second- and third-ranking firms of that same country. General Motors's biggest rival is Ford, not Japanese auto companies, and the same holds true in electronics and many other markets.

Early in the 1970s, Japanese color television sets were the most powerful contenders on the world television market because Japan's makers had made intensive efforts to upgrade production methods and counter the effects of the oil crises. They switched to integrated circuits, halved the number of parts, and automated assembly lines. The changes were very effective and enabled them to manufacture high-quality televisions at half their European and American competitors' prices. Today, however, the industry is in the midst of a structural recession. Makers all over the world are finding it easy to make sets, but hard to make profits. Color televisions have become an engineered commodity. Both in technology as well as costs, there is not much difference between televisions of different makes because manufacturers all buy their key components and parts from the same global suppliers.

During the 1970s, Japan's color television makers were making profits and inroads into foreign markets. The United States and Europe consequently moved to protect domestic makers with import quotas and high tariff barriers, and Japanese makers responded by increasing local production. Sony built plants in San Diego, Matsushita in Chicago, Sanyo in Arkansas, and Toshiba in Tennessee. However, efforts to penetrate overseas markets did not allow Japan to capture the massive market shares that the United States and Europe feared they would lose. Sony has a 19 percent share in Japan, but holds only 8 percent of the American market and 5 percent of the European Community market. Matsushita has an average 30 percent domestic share, but Panasonic and Quasar together account for less than 10 percent of the American market and 5 percent of the European market. Together, Japanese makers have a share amounting to 20 percent of both the American and European color television markets. In the United States, Zenith and RCA each has 20 percent shares, and no competitor has a larger slice of the pie. In short, color televisions promised big profits in overseas markets a decade ago, but protectionism closed the doors to outsiders.

> Now the tide of the times worldwide is again turning toward protectionism.

Now the tide of the times worldwide is again turning toward protectionism. When "invaders" from overseas gain a modest market share, protectionistic mechanisms go into action to impede further penetration, in effect slamming the door in the intruder's face. Again it will be very difficult for companies to gain large shares offshore.

Many companies have been overly cautious about foreign competitors and have not paid enough attention to *domestic* rivals who might be a bigger threat to market share. Ironically, one of the emerging strategies of international "competition" is teaming up with foreigners to meet a more dangerous domestic threat. This has often been done in the United States. General Electric joined with Japanese and European firms in order to strengthen its position against Westinghouse. AT&T allied itself with Olivetti and Philips in Europe and Toshiba in Japan. Despite the uproar over the "U.S.-Japan automobile war," it was General Motors that joined with Toyota, Isuzu, and Suzuki; Ford that took over Mazda; and Chrysler that went to Mitsubishi Motors for a hedge against its American rivals.

A Local Presence

This idea can be carried one step further, for in order for firms to gain in strength and grow with stability, they will be forced, in the end, to go global. Today and in the twenty-first century, management's ability to transform the organization and its people into a global company is a prerequisite for survival, because both its customers and competitors have become cosmopolitan.

Often this may mean establishing a presence and influence in the countries in which the company has major sales. Firms that are perceived as invaders fall prey to protectionism and import restrictions and find the doors to markets closed. If a firm succeeds in becoming a true insider, however, markets will remain open to it, even when other firms nominally of the same nationality are excluded. This was the case with Sony, for example: when the outcry against Japanese television brought other makers to court to avoid the imposition of import quotas and levies, Sony was expressly exempted from these proceedings because it had a large assembly plant in San Diego. When a firm makes its products locally, providing jobs and paying local taxes on its profits, it can usually avoid being branded an outsider. Nestle, with a 70 percent share of the Japanese instant coffee market, will be considered an honorary citizen, should something drastic happen to shut the foreign contenders out of the market. Both IBM and NCR are also good examples of insiders in the Japanese computer market.

Many economic experts recommend focusing on one's own national markets. Nevertheless, a Japanese firm seeking world-scale status needs to do just the opposite – it must make itself independent of Japan. Heads of Japanese companies come to my office and say, "We're too dependent on exports. We want to establish a firmer base in Japan." When I inquire just how much of what they produce is exported, they reply, "60 or 70 percent." Assume that they are producing for the triad market of 630 million consumers. Since Japan accounts for only 120 million, only about one-fifth of their production should normally be consumed domestically. That leaves 80 percent for export. If a company feels insecure with a domestic base of only 20 percent, it's not independent enough to succeed in the world market. The notion that Japan is a special island apart from the rest of the world is one that needs to be discarded.

Switzerland has a population of about 6 million – definitely a minuscule home market. Nevertheless, it is the home of some of the world's argest firms. Sulzer is an interesting example because it is the largest builder of ship's engines, with a world market share of over 70 percent. But the only ship engines used domestically are on the tourist boats that ply Switzerland's lakes.

To be sure, some Japanese firms have been daring in seeking to excel in overseas markets. Sony was one, of course, but there are many lesser known examples. A small supermarket chain based in Shizuoka Prefecture, Yaohan, challenged the vastly greater Daiei and Ito-Yokado chains but failed in its attempt to establish a nationwide presence in Japan. In 1974, however, it opened its first overseas store in Singapore. Now it owns six large supermarkets there and is Singapore's largest food retailer. It's on its way to becoming a major factor in other Asian markets as well.

Fujitec, the elevator manufacturer, is smaller than any of its major competitors in Japan – Mitsubishi, Hitachi, Toshiba, and Toyo Otis, but this has not prevented it from finding many customers in the United States and all over Asia. As a result, Fujitec moved its headquarters from Tokyo to New York in 1983.

There is no need for a company to keep its headquarters in Japan just because it began as a Japanese firm. In fact, the ideal place to locate a world-scale firm is Anchorage, Alaska, because it is equidistant from Japan, Europe, and the rest of the United States. Whether one actually moves to Anchorage or not, it is important at least to locate oneself mentally in a neutral position and not to overstress one's roots.

Triadic Thinking

The triad is the advanced world. Eighty-five to 90 percent of all high value-added high-technology manufactured goods are produced and consumed in North America. Western Europe, and Japan. Of the roughly 10,000 patents registered in the world, 85 percent were filed in five countries: Japan, the United States, West Germany, France, and Great Britain. What this means is that it is wrong to think of the world's countries as flat spots on a map; one must create a threedimensional view. Even today, the majority of multinational firms tend to take pride in the number of countries where they are present but treat these countries as mere names, numbers, or red pins on a map. This flat approach will not guarantee survival in the face of tomorrow's global competition.

> In order for firms to gain in strength and grow with stability, they will be forced, in the end, to go global.

Ideally, a firm should be equidistant figuratively from the three strategic regions at the points of the triad. When the firm stands above the map, so to speak, it forms a perfect tetrahedron or trigonal pyramid with itself at the apex. The third leg is the key developing countries. (See Exhibit 4.)

A firm seeking to globalize should base its thinking on such a tetrahedral world view and not on a flat-map model, because it illustrates how the three points of the base can be most efficiently reached from the center (i.e., the firm). Seeking to globalize by expanding into countries of little or no strategic import-ance is simply unproductive dissipation of corporate energy. That means that companies should be far more selective with their investments in developing countries. In order to hedge against exchange rate uncertainties, a Japanese cor-poration might choose to have three locations for production in the triad: Japan, European Community/USA, and Asian Newly Developed Countries (NICs). This is a rather new but important phenomenon. As a consequence of the extreme volatility in the exchange rate between the U.S. dollar and Japanese yen (and other major European currencies), global competitors are now finding NICs as their preferred production sites. For all practical purposes, one can treat the NICs as America's home market since their currencies are normally pegged against the dollar.[3]

This notwithstanding, however, it is vital for a firm to become an insider in each of the triad regions. Failure in any one would be like losing one leg of a tripod, with a consequent loss of stability. Transforming branches of the enterprise into insiders at overseas locations through one's own effort, or indirectly through effective tie-ups with local firms, is now a matter of corporate life or death. Today's triad market simply has no place for intruders.

Exhibit 4
The Jue Tetrahedron

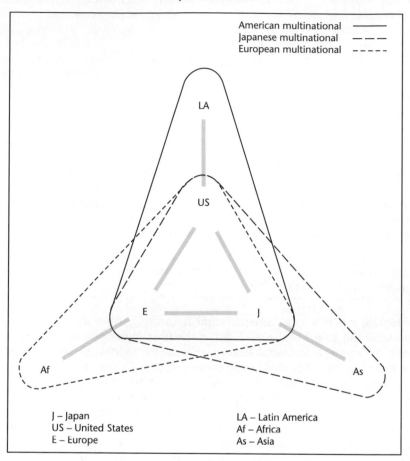

J – Japan   LA – Latin America
US – United States   Af – Africa
E – Europe   As – Asia

Fine-Tuning Product Concepts

The reality of shared tastes does not mean that a product will necessarily succeed worldwide without adjustments for different countries. Furthermore, the degree of adjustment necessary will vary greatly depending on the type of product.[4]

The same product concept without any variation will serve very well the world over, in the case of cameras, watches, radio-cassette tape recorders, Walkmans, and so on, but it is always necessary to adjust concepts applied to stereo systems and televisions. Japanese and European audiophiles generally prefer compact component stereos, which do not sell well in the United States. Americans like big, solid speakers and amplifiers, which, to them, continue to be the mark of high quality. Germans like to see functional symbols on their equipment, such as double arrows to indicate fast rewind.

In televisions, also, Americans prefer big screens in big cabinets that sit directly on the floor. Japanese houses are generally small, however, and the Japanese view their sets from an average distance of less than six feet. Big screens look fuzzy from up close (although the advent of high-definition televisions may change the picture).

Rice cookers are subject to very strong regional preferences. Most are sold in Japan, China, and Taiwan, but in these countries, they are expected to cook rice in different ways. The Japanese like a moist, sticky rice, the Chinese prefer an almost dry rice, and Arabs demand that their rice have a scorched crust.

How well a company can respond to these variations is an extremely important factor in ensuring the product's success. Most companies, however, find it difficult to balance between localization and globalization needs, and they tend to think on either extreme of the scale. Neither is reality, and companies have to develop a feel for the optimum balance point by moving their people around as well as by using sound analyses.

Playing Chinese Telephone Won't Work in Product Design

This ability to fine-tune products is dependent, of course, on accurate knowledge of life-styles and tastes in different regions. Such knowledge cannot be obtained from market research data alone. Designers must pack their bags and go to the target area for hands-on experience in other cultures.

In Japan, it's hard to find a piano that's not black. Pianos were used in Japanese schools long before they became common in homes, and this firmly established the image of the black piano. In other countries, however, not everybody likes his or her piano black. Americans and Europeans think of a piano as a piece of furniture and order ones made of various woods, such as mahogany or rosewood, to match the interiors of their homes. Furthermore, they expect the wood to be well-finished. Japanese piano makers would not have succeeded in exporting to the rest of the world if they had stuck to a local product concept. They realized this after they sent people abroad to find from first-hand experience what people expected.

One cannot design something for an American living room if one has never been in one. What applies to pianos also applies to stereo equipment. A Japanese audio designer can have no idea of the space that his machine will occupy or how it will be used unless he visits other countries. Speakers will be dwarfed when placed beside the kind of big cabinets that Americans like. Globally, producers of conceived products must take these factors into account.

Also, one cannot design for young people without spending a lot of time in California. Many Japanese manufacturers, however, are still unaware that they must send their designers abroad if they want universally applicable designs. An audio maker had a product planning process that was reminiscent of "Chinese telephone," the game where children get in a circle of ten to twenty and whisper a message to the person next to them, saying, "Pass it on." The message is inadvertently altered each time it is repeated so that the last person to hear it gets a very different message from the original one. In the case of the audio maker, local dealers compiled lists of desiderata, and foreign offices collected these lists and sent them to people in the manufacturing division at international headquarters, who passed the information on to the planning section in the sales division. The planning section drafted a plan based on this information and sent it to the chief designer at the tail of the chain. Each person in the chain summarized the information in his own fashion, and the message that eventually reached designers was often incomprehensible. It would have been a miracle if designers by this process created anything that managed to satisfy local consumers.

It's logical to seek global concepts and products from globe-trotters. Designers must be sent out to see the world with their own eyes. Regardless of criticism from their fellows that they spend half the year on vacation, they must have hands-on experience if they are to adapt products to real needs. The cost of this is a negligible fraction of what is spent on advertising and other steps in product development. My ex-McKinsey colleagues, Tom Peters and Bob Waterman, wrote that one of the keys for becoming an excellent company is managing by walking around (MBWA).[5] The key to becoming a triad power is to MBWA around the world.

Notes

This article is taken from his book, *Beyond National Borders* (Dow Jones-Irwin, 1987). Excerpted with permission.

1. explore the argument in greater detail in my book. *Triad Power*, which was published in five languages (Chinese, English, French, German, and Japanese) simultaneously. I wanted to show firms to which I recommend a "simultaneous world attack" or sprinkler approach that it's possible in publishing to do what I preach in my consulting.
2. *Financial Times*, Oct. 17, 1986.
3. See Ohmae, "Rethinking Global Strategy," *Wall Street Journal*, April 29, 1985.
4. See K. Ohmae, *Triad Power* (1985), pp. 118–193.
5. *In Search of Excellence: Lessons From America's Best-Run Companies* (1982).

44

Global Strategy ...
in a World of Nations?

George S. Yip

Whether to globalize, and how to globalize, have become two of the most burning strategy issues for managers around the world. Many forces are driving companies around the world to globalize by expanding their participation in foreign markets. Almost every product market in the major world economies – computers, fast food, nuts and bolts – has foreign competitors. Trade barriers are also falling; the recent United States/Canada trade agreement and the impending 1992 harmonization in the European Community are the two most dramatic examples. Japan is gradually opening up its long barricaded markets. Maturity in domestic markets is also driving companies to seek international expansion. This is particularly true of U.S. companies that, nourished by the huge domestic market, have typically lagged behind their European and Japanese rivals in internationalization.

Companies are also seeking to globalize by integrating their worldwide strategy. Such global integration contrasts with the multinational approach whereby companies set up country subsidiaries that design, produce, and market products or services tailored to local needs. This multinational model (also described as a "multidomestic strategy") is now in question.[1] Several changes seem to increase the likelihood that, in some industries, a global strategy will be more successful than a multidomestic one. One of these changes, as argued forcefully and controversially by Levitt, is the growing similarity of what citizens of different countries want to buy.[2] Other changes include the reduction of tariff and nontariff barriers, technology investments that are becoming too expensive to amortize in one market only, and competitors that are globalizing the rules of the game.

Companies want to know how to globalize – in other words, expand market participation – and how to develop an integrated worldwide strategy. As

Source: *Sloan Management Review*, Vol. 30, 1989, pp. 29–41.

depicted in Figure 1, three steps are essential in developing a total worldwide strategy:

- Developing the core strategy – the basis of sustainable competitive advantage. It is usually developed for the home country first.
- Internationalizing the core strategy through international expansion of activities and through adaptation.
- Globalizing the international strategy by integrating the strategy across countries.

Figure 1
Total Global Strategy

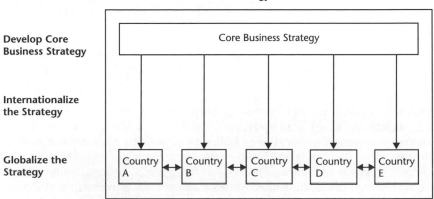

Multinational companies know the first two steps well. They know the third step less well since globalization runs counter to the accepted wisdom of tailoring for national markets.[3]

This article makes a case for how a global strategy might work and directs managers toward opportunities to exploit globalization. It also presents the drawbacks and costs of globalization. Figure 2 lays out a framework for thinking through globalization issues.[4]

Industry globalization drivers (underlying market, cost, and other industry conditions) are externally determined, while global strategy levers are choices available to the worldwide business. Drivers create the potential for a multinational business to achieve the benefits of global strategy. To achieve these benefits, a multinational business needs to set its *global strategy levers* (e.g., use of product standardization) appropriately to industry drivers, and to the position and resources of the business and its parent company.[5] The organization's ability to implement the strategy affects how well the benefits can be achieved.

What is Global Strategy?

Setting strategy for a worldwide business requires making choices along a number of strategic dimensions. Table 1 lists five such dimensions or "global

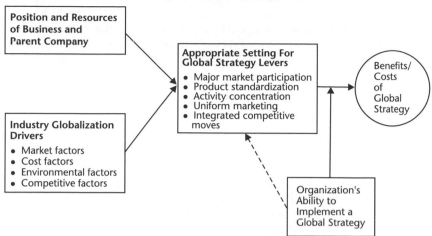

Figure 2
Framework of Global Strategy Forces

Table 1
Globalization Dimensions/Global Strategy Levers

Dimension	Setting for Pure Multidomestic Strategy	Setting for Pure Global Strategy
Market Participation	No particular pattern	Significant share in major markets
Product Offering	Fully customized in each country	Fully standardized worldwide
Location of Value-Added Activities	All activities in each country	Concentrated – one activity in each (different) country
Marketing Approach	Local	Uniform worldwide
Competitive Moves	Stand-alone by country	Integrated across countries

strategy levers" and their respective positions under a pure multidomestic strategy and a pure global strategy. Intermediate positions are, of course, feasible. For each dimension, a multidomestic strategy seeks to maximize worldwide performance by maximizing local competitive advantage, revenues, or profits; a global strategy seeks to maximize worldwide performance through sharing and integration.

Market Participation

In a multidomestic strategy, countries are selected on the basis of their stand-alone potential for revenues and profits. In a global strategy, countries need to be selected for their potential contribution to globalization benefits. This may mean entering a market that is unattractive in its own right, but has global strategic significance, such as the home market of a global competitor. Or it may mean building share in a limited number of key markets rather than undertaking more widespread coverage. A pattern of major share in major markets is advocated in Ohmae's USA-Europe-Japan "triad" concept.[6] In contrast, under a multidomestic strategy, no particular pattern of participation is required – rather, the pattern accrues from the pursuit of local advantage. The Electrolux

Group, the Swedish appliance giant, is pursuing a strategy of building significant share in major world markets. The company aims to be the first global appliance maker. In 1986, Electrolux took over Zanussi Industries to become the top producer of appliances in Western Europe. Later that year, Electrolux acquired White Consolidated Industries, the third largest American appliance manufacturer.

Product Offering

In a multidomestic strategy, the products offered in each country are tailored to local needs. In a global strategy, the ideal is a standardized core product that requires minimal local adaptation. Cost reduction is usually the most important benefit of product standardization. Levitt has made the most extreme case for product standardization. Others stress the need for flexibility, or the need for a broad product portfolio, with many product varieties in order to share technologies and distribution channels.[7] In practice, some multinationals have pursued product standardization to a greater or lesser extent.[8] Differing worldwide needs can be met by adapting a standardized core product. In the early 1970s, sales of the Boeing 737 began to level off. Boeing turned to developing countries as an attractive new market, but found initially that its product did not fit the new environments. Because of the shortness of runways, their greater softness, and the lower technical expertise of their pilots, the planes tended to bounce a great deal. When the planes bounced on landing, the brakes failed. To fix this problem, Boeing modified the design by adding thrust to the engines, redesigning the wings and landing gear, and installing tires with lower pressure. These adaptations to a standardized core product enabled the 737 to become the best selling plane in history.

Location of Value-Added Activities

In a multidomestic strategy, all or most of the value chain is reproduced in every country. In another type of international strategy – exporting – most of the value chain is kept in one country. In a global strategy, costs are reduced by breaking up the value chain so each activity may be conducted in a different country. One value chain strategy is partial concentration and partial duplication. The key feature of a global position on this dimension is the strategic placement of the value chain around the globe.

Many electronics companies now locate part or all of their manufacturing operations in Southeast Asia because of that region's low-cost, skilled labor. In addition, a key component (the semiconductor chip) is very cheap there. Under the United States-Japan Semiconductor Agreement, the Japanese agreed not to sell chips in the United States below cost. But in an industry plagued by overcapacity, the chips had to go somewhere. The agreement resulted in Japanese chips being sold below cost in Southeast Asia. The lower cost of chips combined with the lower labor cost has attracted many manufacturers of computers and other electronic equipment to Southeast Asia.

Marketing Approach

In a multidomestic strategy, marketing is fully tailored for each country, being developed locally. In a global strategy, a uniform marketing approach is applied around the world, although not all elements of the marketing mix need be uniform.[9] Unilever achieved great success with a fabric softener that used a globally common positioning, advertising theme, and symbol (a teddy bear), but a brand name that varied by country. Similarly, a product that serves a common need can be geographically expanded with a uniform marketing program, despite differences in marketing environments.

Competitive Moves

In a multidomestic strategy, the managers in each country make competitive moves without regard for what happens in other countries. In a global strategy, competitive moves are integrated across countries. The same type of move is made in different countries at the same time or in a systematic sequence: a competitor is attacked in one country in order to drain its resources for another country, or a competitive attack in one country is countered in a different country. Perhaps the best example is the counterattack in a competitor's home market as a parry to an attack on one's own home market. Integration of competitive strategy is rarely practised, except perhaps by some Japanese companies.[10]

Bridgestone Corporation, the Japanese tire manufacturer, tried to integrate its competitive moves in response to global consolidation by its major competitors – Continental AG's acquisition of Gencorp's General Tire and Rubber Company, General Tire's joint venture with two Japanese tire makers, and Sumitomo's acquisition of an interest in Dunlop Tire. These competitive actions forced Bridgestone to establish a presence in the major U.S. market in order to maintain its position in the world tire market. To this end, Bridgestone formed a joint venture to own and manage Firestone Corporation's worldwide tire business. This joint venture also allowed Bridgestone to gain access to Firestone's European plants.

Benefits of a Global Strategy

Companies that use global strategy levers can achieve one or more of these benefits (see Figure 3):[11]

- cost reductions;
- improved quality of products and programs;
- enhanced customer preference; and
- increased competitive leverage.

Figure 3
How Global Strategy Levers Achieve Globalization Benefits

Global Strategy Levers	Benefits				Major Drawbacks
	Cost Reduction	Improved Quality of Products and Programs	Enhanced Customer Preference	Increased Competitive Leverage	All Levers Incur Coordination Costs, Plus
Major Market Participation	Increases volume for economies of scale		Via global availability, global serviceability, and global recognition	Advantage of earlier entry; Provides more sites for attack and counter-attack, hostage for good behavior	Earlier or greater commitment to a market than warranted on own merits
Product Standardization	Reduces duplication of development efforts; Allows concentration of production to exploit economies of scale	Focuses development and management resources	Allows consumers to use familiar product while abroad; Allows organizations to use same product across country units	Basis for low-cost invasion of markets	Less responsive to local needs
Activity Concentration	Reduces duplication of activities; Helps exploit economies of scale; Exploits difference in country factor costs; Partial concentration allows flexibility vs. currency changes, and vs. bargaining parties	Focuses effort; Allows more consistent quality control		Allows maintenance of cost advantage independent of local conditions	Distances activities from the customer; Increases currency risk
Uniform Marketing	Reduces design and production costs of marketing programs	Focuses talent and resources; Leverages scarce, good ideas	Reinforces marketing messages by exposing customer to same mix in different countries		Reduces adaptation to local customer behavior and marketing environment
Integrated Competitive Moves				Provides more options and leverage in attack and defense	Local competitiveness may be sacrificed

Cost Reductions

An integrated global strategy can reduce worldwide costs in several ways. A company can increase the benefits from economies of scale by *pooling production or other activities* for two or more countries. Understanding the potential benefit of these economies of scale, Sony Corporation has concentrated its compact disc production in Terre Haute, Indiana, and Salzburg, Austria.

A second way to cut costs is by *exploiting lower factor costs* by moving manufacturing or other activities to low-cost countries. This approach has, of course, motivated the recent surge of offshore manufacturing, particularly by U.S. firms. For example, the Mexican side of the U.S.-Mexico border is now crowded with "maquiladoras" – manufacturing plants set up and run by U.S. companies using Mexican labor.

Global strategy can also cut costs by *exploiting flexibility*. A company with manufacturing locations in several countries can move production from location to location on short notice to take advantage of the lowest costs at a given time. Dow Chemical takes this approach to minimize the cost of producing chemicals. Dow uses a linear programming model that takes account of international differences in exchange rates, tax rates, and transportation and labor costs. The model comes up with the best mix of production volume by location for each planning period.

An integrated global strategy can also reduce costs by *enhancing bargaining power*. A company whose strategy allows for switching production among different countries greatly increases its bargaining power with suppliers, workers, and host governments. Labor unions in European countries are very concerned that the creation of the single European market after 1992 will allow companies to switch production from country to country at will. This integrated production strategy would greatly enhance companies' bargaining power at the expense of unions.

Improved Quality of Products and Programs

Under a global strategy, companies focus on a smaller number of products and programs than under a multidomestic strategy. This concentration can improve both product and program quality. Global focus is one reason for Japanese success in automobiles. Toyota markets a far smaller number of models around the world than does General Motors, even allowing for its unit sales being half that of General Motors's. Toyota has concentrated on improving its few models while General Motors has fragmented its development funds. For example, the Toyota Camry is the U.S. version of a basic worldwide model and is the successor to a long line of development efforts. The Camry is consistently rated as the best in its class of medium-sized cars. In contrast, General Motors's Pontiac Fiero started out as one of the most successful small sports cars, but was recently withdrawn. Industry observers blamed this on a failure to invest development money to overcome minor problems.

Enhanced Customer Preference

Global availability, serviceability, and recognition can enhance customer preference through reinforcement. Soft drink and fast food companies are, of course, leading exponents of this strategy. Many suppliers of financial services, such as credit cards, must have a global presence because their service is travel-related. Manufacturers of industrial products can also exploit this benefit. A supplier that can provide a multinational customer with a standard product around the world gains from worldwide familiarity. Computer manufacturers have long pursued this strategy.

Increased Competitive Leverage

A global strategy provides more points from which to attack and counterattack competitors. In an effort to prevent the Japanese from becoming a competitive nuisance in disposable syringes, Becton Dickinson, a major U.S. medical products company, decided to enter three markets in Japan's backyard. Becton entered the Hong Kong, Singapore, and Philippine markets to prevent further Japanese expansion.[12]

Drawbacks of Global Strategy

Globalization can incur significant management costs through increased coordination, reporting requirements, and even added staff. It can also reduce the firm's effectiveness in individual countries if overcentralization hurts local motivation and morale. In addition, each global strategy lever has particular drawbacks.

A global strategy approach to *market participation* can incur an earlier or greater commitment to a market than is warranted on its own merits. Many American companies, such as Motorola, are struggling to penetrate Japanese markets, more in order to enhance their global competitive position than to make money in Japan for its own sake.

Product standardization can result in a product that does not entirely satisfy *any* customers. When companies first internationalize, they often offer their standard domestic product without adapting it for other countries, and suffer the consequences. For example, Procter & Gamble stumbled recently when it introduced Cheer laundry detergent in Japan without changing the U.S. product or marketing message (that the detergent was effective in all temperatures). After experiencing serious losses, P&G discovered two instances of insufficient adaptation. First, the detergent did not suds up as it should because the Japanese use a great deal of fabric softener. Second, the Japanese usually wash clothes in either cold tap water or bath water, so the claim of working in all temperatures was irrelevant. Cheer became successful in Japan only after the product was reformulated and the marketing message was changed.

A globally standardized product is designed for the global market but can seldom satisfy all needs in all countries. For instance, Canon, a Japanese company, sacrificed the ability to copy certain Japanese paper sizes when it first designed a photocopier for the global market.

Activity concentration distances customers and can result in lower responsiveness and flexibility. It also increases currency risk by incurring costs and revenues in different countries. Recently volatile exchange rates have required companies that concentrate their production to hedge their currency exposure.

Uniform marketing can reduce adaptation to local customer behavior. For example, the head office of British Airways mandated that every country use the "Manhattan Landing" television commercial developed by advertising agency Saatchi and Saatchi. While the commercial did win many awards, it has been criticized for using a visual image (New York City) that was not widely recognized in many countries.

Integrated competitive moves can mean sacrificing revenues, profits, or competitive position in individual countries, particularly when the subsidiary in one country is asked to attack a global competitor in order to send a signal or to divert that competitor's resources from another country.

Finding the Balance

The most successful worldwide strategies find a balance between overglobalizing and underglobalizing. The ideal strategy matches the level of strategy globalizaton to the globalization potential of the industry. In Figure 4 both

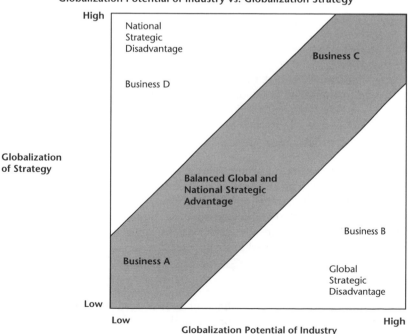

Figure 4
Globalization Potential of Industry vs. Globalization Strategy

Business A and Business C achieve balanced global and national strategic advantage. Business A does so with a low level of strategy globalization to match the low globalization potential of its industry (e.g., frozen food products). Business C uses a high level of strategy globalization to match the high globalization potential of its industry (e.g., computer equipment). Business B is at a global disadvantage because it uses a strategy that is less globalized than the potential offered by its industry. The business is failing to exploit potential global benefits such as cost savings via product standardization. Business D is at a national disadvantage because it is too globalized relative to the potential offered by its industry. The business is not tailoring its products and programs as much as it should. While there is no systematic evidence, executives' comments suggest that far more businesses suffer from insufficient globalization than from excessive globalization. Figure 4 is oversimplified in that it shows only one overall dimension for both strategy and industry potential. As argued earlier, a global strategy has five major dimensions and many subdimensions. Similarly, the potential of industry globalization is multidimensional.

Industry Globalization Drivers

To achieve the benefits of globalization, the managers of a worldwide business need to recognize when industry globalization drivers (industry conditions) provide the opportunity to use global strategy levers. These drivers can be grouped in four categories: market, cost, governmental, and competitive. Each industry globalization driver affects the potential use of global strategy levers (see Figure 5).

Market Drivers

Market globalization drivers depend on customer behavior and the structure of distribution channels. These drivers affect the use of all five global strategy levers.

Homogeneous Customer Needs

When customers in different countries want essentially the same type of product or service (or can be so persuaded), opportunities arise to market a standardized product. Understanding which aspects of the product can be standardized and which should be customized is key. In addition, homogeneous needs make participation in a large number of markets easier because fewer different product offerings need to be developed and supported.

Global Customers

Global customers buy on a centralized or coordinated basis for decentralized use. The existence of global customers both allows and requires a uniform

Figure 5
Effects of Industry Globalization Drivers or the Potential Use of Global Strategy Levers

Industry Drivers	Strategy Levers				
	Major Market Participation	Product Standardization	Activity Concentration	Uniform Marketing	Integrated Competitive Moves
Market					
Homogeneous needs	Fewer varieties needed to serve many markets	Standardized product is more acceptable			Allows sequenced invasion of markets
Global customers			Marketing process has to be coordinated	Marketing content needs to be uniform	
Global channels			Marketing process has to be coordinated	Marketing content needs to be uniform	
Transferable marketing	Easier to expand internationally			Allows use of global brands/advertising, etc.	
Cost					
Economies of scale and scope	Multiple markets needed to reach economic scale	Standardization needed to reach economic scale	Concentration helps reach economic scale	Uniform marketing cuts program development and production costs	Country interdependence affects overall scale economies
Learning and experience	Multiple markets accelerate learning	Standardization accelerates learning	Concentration accelerates learning		
Sourcing efficiencies			Centralized purchasing exploits efficiencies		
Favorable logistics	Easier to expand internationally		Allows concentrated production		Allows export competition
Differences in country costs & skills			Exploited by activity concentration		Increase vulnerability of high-cost countries
Product development costs	Multiple markets needed to payback investment	Standardization reduces development needs	Concentration cuts cost of development		

(Figure 5 continued)

(Figure 5 continued)

Industry Drivers	Strategy Levers				
	Major Market Participation	Product Standardization	Activity Concentration	Uniform Marketing	Integrated Competitive Moves
Government					
Favorable trade policies	Affects nature/extent of participation	May require or prevent product features	Local content rules affect extent of concentration possible		Integration needed to deal with competitive effects of tariffs/subsidies
Compatible technical standards	Affects markets that can be entered	Affects standardization possible			
Common marketing regulations				Affects approaches possible	
Competitive					
Interdependence of countries	More participation leverages benefits	Accept tradeoffs to get best global product	Locate key activities in lead countries	Use lead country to develop programs	Integration needed to exploit benefits
Competitors globalized or might globalize	Expand to match or preempt	Match or preempt	Match or preempt	Match or preempt	Integration needed to exploit benefits

marketing program. There are two types of global customers: national and multinational. A national global customer searches the world for suppliers but uses the purchased product or service in one country. National defense agencies are a good example. A multinational global customer also searches the world for suppliers, but uses the purchased product or service in many countries. The World Health Organization's purchase of medical products is an example. Multinational global customers are particularly challenging to serve and often require a global account management program. Companies that implement such programs have to beware of global customers using the unified account management to extract lower global prices. Having a single global account manager makes it easier for a global customer to negotiate a single global price. Typically, the global customer pushes for the lowest country price to become the global price. But a good global account manager should be able to justify differences in prices across countries.

Global Channels

Analogous to global customers, channels of distribution may buy on a global or at least a regional basis. Global channels or middlemen are also important in exploiting differences in prices by buying at a lower price in one country and selling at a higher price in another country. Their presence makes it more necessary for a business to rationalize its worldwide pricing. Global channels are rare, but regionwide channels are increasing in number, particularly in European grocery distribution and retailing.

Transferable Marketing

The buying decision may be such that marketing elements, such as brand names and advertising, require little local adaptation. Such transferability enables firms to use uniform marketing strategies and facilitates expanded participation in markets. A worldwide business can also adapt its brand names and advertising campaigns to make them more transferable, or, even better, design global ones to start with. Offsetting risks include the blandness of uniformly acceptable brand names or advertising, and the vulnerability of relying on a single brand franchise.

Cost Drivers

Cost drivers depend on the economics of the business; they particularly affect activity concentration.

Economies of Scale and Scope

A single-country market may not be large enough for the local business to achieve all possible economies of scale or scope. Scale at a given location can be increased through participation in multiple markets combined with product standardization or concentration of selected value activities. Corresponding risks include rigidity and vulnerability to disruption.

In the past few years, the economics of the electronics industry have shifted. As the cost of circuits has decreased, the economic advantage has gone to companies that can produce the lowest-cost components. Size has become a major asset. Thomson, the French electronics firm, understands the need to have a worldwide presence in an industry characterized by economies of scale. In 1987, Thomson greatly increased both its operating scale and its global coverage by acquiring the RCA television business from General Electric.

Learning and Experience

Even if economies of scope and scale are exhausted, expanded market participation and activity concentration can accelerate the accumulation of learning and experience. The steeper the learning and experience curves, the greater the potential benefit will be. Managers should beware, though, of the usual danger in pursuing experience curve strategies – overaggressive pricing that destroys not just the competition but the market as well. Prices get so low that profit is insufficient to sustain any competitor.

Sourcing Efficiencies

Centralized purchasing of new materials can significantly lower costs. Himont began as a joint venture between Hercules Inc. of the United States and Montedison Petrolchimica SpA of Italy, and is the leader in the global polypropylene market. Central to Himont's strategy is global coordination among manufacturing facilities in the purchase of raw materials, particularly monomer, the key ingredient in polypropylene production. Rationalization of raw material orders significantly strengthens the venture's low-cost production advantage.

Favorable Logistics

A favorable ratio of sales value to transportation cost enhances the company's ability to concentrate production. Other logistical factors include nonperishability, the absence of time urgency, and little need for location close to customer facilities. Even the shape of the product can make a crucial difference. Cardboard tubes, such as those used as cores for textiles, cannot be shipped economically because they are mostly air. In contrast, cardboard cones are transportable because many units can be stacked in the same space.

Differences in Country Costs and Skills

Factor costs generally vary across countries; this is particularly true in certain industries. The availability of particular skills also varies. Concentration of activities in low-cost or high-skill countries can increase productivity and reduce costs, but managers need to anticipate the danger of training future offshore competitors.[13]

Under attack from lower-priced cars, Volkswagen has needed to reduce its costs. It is doing so by concentrating its production to take advantage of the differences in various country costs. In Spain, hourly labor costs are below DM 20 per hour, while those in West Germany are over DM 40 per hour. To take advantage of this cost differential, the company moved production of Polos from Wolfsburg to Spain, freeing up the high-wage German labor to produce the higher-priced Golf cars. Another example of this concentration occurred when Volkswagen shut down its New Stanton, Pennsylvania, plant that manufactured Golfs and Jettas. The lower end of the U.S. market would be served by its low-wage Brazilian facility that produced the Fox. The higher end of the product line (Jetta and Golf) would be exported from Europe. This concentration and coordination of production has enabled the company to lower costs substantially.

Product Development Costs

Product development costs can be reduced by developing a few global or regional products rather than many national products. The automobile industry is characterized by long product development periods and high product development costs. One reason for the high costs is duplication of effort across countries. The Ford Motor Company's "Centers of Excellence" program aims to reduce these duplicating efforts and to exploit the differing expertise of Ford specialists worldwide. As part of the concentrated effort, Ford of Europe is designing a common platform for all compacts, while Ford of North America is developing platforms for the replacement of the midsized Taurus and Sable. This concentration of design is estimated to save "hundreds of millions of dollars per model by eliminating duplicative efforts and saving on retooling factories."[14]

Governmental Drivers

Government globalization drivers depend on the rules set by national governments and affect the use of all global strategy levers.

Favorable Trade Policies

Host governments affect globalization potential through import tariffs and quotas, nontariff barriers, export subsidies, local content requirements, currency and capital flow restrictions, and requirements on technology transfer.[15] Host government policies can make it difficult to use the global levers of major market participation, product standardization, activity concentration, and uniform marketing; they also affect the integrated-competitive-moves lever.

National trade policies constrain companies' concentration of manufacturing activities. Aggressive U.S. government actions including threats on tariffs, quotas, and protectionist measures have helped convince Japanese automakers and other manufacturers to give up their concentration of manufacturing in Japan. Reluctantly, Japanese companies are opening plants in the United States.

Honda has even made a public relations virtue out of necessity. It recently gave great publicity to the first shipment of a U.S.-made Honda car to Japan.

The easing of government restrictions can set off a rush for expanded market participation. European Community regulations for banking and financial services will be among those harmonized in 1992. The European Community decision to permit the free flow of capital among member countries has led European financial institutions to jockey for position. Until recently, the Deutsche Bank had only fifteen offices outside of Germany, but it has recently established a major presence in the French market. In 1987, Deutsche Bank also moved into the Italian market by acquiring Bank of America's one hundred branches there. Other financial organizations, such as J.P. Morgan of the United States, Swiss Bank Corporation, and the S.P. Warburg Group in Britain have increased their participation in major European markets through acquisitions.

Compatible Technical Standards

Differences in technical standards, especially government-imposed standards, limit the extent to which products can be standardized. Often, standards are set with protectionism in mind. Motorola found that many of their electronics products were excluded from the Japanese market because these products operated at a higher frequency than was permitted in Japan.

Common Marketing Regulations

The marketing environment of individual countries affects the extent to which uniform global marketing approaches can be used. Certain types of media may be prohibited or restricted. For example, the United States is far more liberal than Europe about the kinds of advertising claims that can be made on television. The British authorities even veto the depiction of socially undesirable behavior. For example, British television authorities do not allow scenes of children pestering their parents to buy a product. And, of course, the use of sex is different. As one extreme, France is far more liberal than the United States about sex in advertising. Various promotional devices, such as lotteries, may also be restricted.

Competitive Drivers

Market, cost, and governmental globalization drivers are essentially fixed for an industry at any given time. Competitors can play only a limited role in affecting these factors (although a sustained effort can bring about change, particularly in the case of consumer preferences). In contrast, competitive drivers are entirely in the realm of competitor choice. Competitors can raise the globalization potential of their industry and spur the need for a response on the global strategy levers.

Interdependence of Countries

A competitor may create competitive interdependence among countries by pursuing a global strategy. The basic mechanism is through sharing of activities. When activities such as production are shared among countries, a competitor's market share in one country affects its scale and overall cost position in the shared activities. Changes in that scale and cost will affect its competitive position in all countries dependent on the shared activities. Less directly, customers may view market position in a lead country as an indicator of overall quality. Companies frequently promote a product as, for example, "the leading brand in the United States." Other competitors then need to respond via increased market participation, uniform marketing, or integrated competitive strategy to avoid a downward spiral of sequentially weakened positions in individual countries.

In the automobile industry, where economies of scale are significant and where sharing activities can lower costs, markets have significant competitive interdependence. As companies like Ford and Volkswagen concentrate production and become more cost competitive with the Japanese manufacturers, the Japanese are pressured to enter more markets so that increased production volume will lower costs. Whether conscious of this or not, Toyota has begun a concerted effort to penetrate the German market: between 1984 and 1987, Toyota doubled the number of cars produced for the German market.

Globalized Competitors

More specifically, matching or preempting individual competitor moves may be necessary. These moves include expanding into or within major markets, being the first to introduce a standardized product, or being the first to use a uniform marketing program.

The need to preempt a global competitor can spur increased market participation. In 1986, Unilever, the European consumer products company, sought to increase its participation in the U.S. market by launching a hostile takeover bid for Richardson-Vicks Inc. Unilever's global archrival, Procter & Gamble, saw the threat to its home turf and outbid Unilever to capture Richardson-Vicks. With Richardson-Vicks's European system, P&G was able to greatly strengthen its European positioning. So Unilever's attempt to expand participation in a rival's home market backfired to allow the rival to expand participation in Unilever's home markets.

In summary, industry globalization drivers provide opportunities to use global strategy levers in many ways. Some industries, such as civil aircraft, can score high on most dimensions of globalization.[16] Others, such as the cement industry, seem to be inherently local. But more and more industries are developing globalization potential. Even the food industry in Europe, renowned for its diversity of taste, is now a globalization target for major food multinationals.

Changes over Time

Finally, industry evolution plays a role. As each of the industry globalization drivers changes over time, so too will the appropriate global strategy change. For example, in the European major appliance industry, globalization forces seem to have reversed. In the late 1960s and early 1970s, a regional standardization strategy was successful for some key competitors.[17] But in the 1980s the situation appears to have turned around, and the most successful strategies seem to be national.[18]

In some cases, the actions of individual competitors can affect the direction and pace of change; competitors positioned to take advantage of globalization forces will want to hasten them. For example, a competitor with strong central manufacturing capabilities may want to accelerate the worldwide acceptance of a standardized product.

More than One Strategy is Viable

Although they are powerful, industry globalization drivers do not dictate one formula for success. More than one type of international strategy can be viable in a given industry.

Industries vary across drivers. No industry is high on every one of the many globalization drivers. A particular competitor may be in a strong position to exploit a driver that scores low on globalization. For example, the dominance of national government customers offsets the globalization potential from other industry drivers, because government customers typically prefer to do business with their own nationals. In such an industry a competitor with a global strategy can use its other advantages, such as low cost from centralization of global production, to offset this drawback. At the same time, another multinational competitor with good government contacts can pursue a multidomestic strategy and succeed without globalization advantages, and single-country local competitors can succeed on the basis of their very particular local assets. The hotel industry provides examples both of successful global and of successful local competitors.

Global effects are incremental. Globalization drivers are not deterministic for a second reason: the appropriate use of strategy levers adds competitive advantage to existing sources. These other sources may allow individual competitors to thrive with international strategies that are mismatched with industry globalization drivers. For example, superior technology is a major source of competitive advantage in most industries, but can be quite independent of globalization drivers. A competitor with sufficiently superior technology can use it to offset globalization disadvantages.

Business and parent company position and resources are crucial. The third reason that drivers are not deterministic is related to resources. A worldwide business may face industry drivers that strongly favor a global strategy. But global strategies are typically expensive to implement initially even though great cost savings and revenue gains should follow. High initial investments may be needed to expand within or into major markets, to develop standardized products, to relocate value activities, to create global brands, to create new organization units or coordination processes, and to implement other aspects of a global strategy. The strategic position of the business is also relevant. Even though a global strategy may improve the business's long-term strategic position, its immediate position may be so weak that resources should be devoted to short-term, country-by-country improvements. Despite the automobile industry's very strong globalization drivers, Chrysler Corporation had to deglobalize by selling off most of its international automotive businesses to avoid bankruptcy. Lastly, investing in nonglobal sources of competitive advantage, such as superior technology, may yield greater returns than global ones, such as centralized manufacturing.

Organizations have limitations. Finally, factors such as organization structure, management processes, people, and culture affect how well a desired global strategy can be implemented. Organizational differences among companies in the same industry can, or should, constrain the companies' pursuit of the same global strategy. Organization issues in globalization are a major topic, and cannot be covered in the space here.[19]

References

1. See: T. Hout, M.E. Porter, and E. Rudden, "How Global Companies Win Out," *Harvard Business Review*, September–October 1982, pp. 98–108.

   My framework, developed in this article, is based in part on M.E. Porter's pioneering work on global strategy. His ideas are further developed in: M.E. Porter, "Competition in Global Industries: A Conceptual Framework," in *Competition in Global Industries*, ed. M.E. Porter (Boston: Harvard Business School Press, 1986). Bartlett and Ghoshal define a "transnational industry" that is somewhat similar to Porter's "global industry." See: C.A. Bartlett and S. Ghoshal, "Managing across Borders: New Strategic Requirements," *Sloan Management Review*, Summer 1987, pp. 7–17.

2. T. Levitt, "The Globalization of Markets," *Harvard Business Review*, May–June 1983, pp. 92–102.

3. These obstacles are laid out in one of the rejoinders provoked by Levitt's article. See: S.P. Douglas and Y. Wind, "The Myth of Globalization," *Columbia Journal of World Business*, Winter 1987, pp. 19–29.

4. For a more theoretical exposition of this framework see: G.S. Yip, "An Integrated Approach to Global Competitive Strategy," in *Frontiers of Management*, ed. R. Mansfield (London: Routledge, forthcoming).

5. The concept of the global strategy lever was first presented in: G.S. Yip, P.M. Loewe, and M.Y. Yoshino, "How to Take Your Company to the Global Market," *Columbia Journal of World Business*, Winter 1988, pp. 37–48.

6. K. Ohmae, *Triad Power: The Coming Shape of Global Competition* (New York: The Free Press, 1985).

7. G. Hamel and C.K. Prahalad, "Do You Really Have a Global Strategy?" *Harvard Business Review*, July-August 1985, pp. 139–148; B. Kogut, "Designing Global Strategies: Profiting from Operational Flexibility," *Sloan Management Review*, Fall 1985, pp. 27–38.

8. P.G.P. Walters, "International Marketing Policy: A Discussion of the Standardization Construct and Its Relevance for Corporate Policy," *Journal of International Business Studies*, Summer 1986, pp. 55–69.

9. For a discussion of the possibilities and merits of uniform marketing see: R.D. Buzzell, "Can You Standardize Multinational Marketing?" *Harvard Business Review*, November–December 1968, pp. 102–113; and J.A. Quelch and E.J. Hoff, "Customizing Global Marketing," *Harvard Business Review*, May–June 1986, pp. 59–68.

10. P. Kotler et al., *The New Competition* (Englewood Cliffs, NJ: Prentice-Hall, 1985), p. 174.

11. Figure 3 is also presented in Yip (forthcoming).

12. M.R. Cvar, "Case Studies in Global Competition," in Porter (1986).

13. See: C.C. Markides and N. Berg, "Manufacturing Offshore Is Bad Business," *Harvard Business Review*, September-October 1988, pp. 113–120.

14. "Can Ford Stay on Top?" *Business Week*, 28 September 1987, pp. 78–86.

15. Three public sector activities that can protect domestic competitors are blocking access to the domestic market, providing subsidies, and creating spillovers in research and development. See: M.A. Spence, "Industrial Organization and Competitive Advantage in Multinational Industries," *American Economic Review* 74 (May 1984): 356–360.

16. M.Y. Yoshino, "Global Competition in a Salient Industry: The Case of Civil Aircraft," in Porter (1986).

17. Levitt (May–June 1983).

18. C. Baden Fuller et al., "National or Global? The Study of Company Strategies and the European Market for Major Appliances" (London: London Business School Centre for Business Strategy, working paper series, No. 28, June 1987).

19. See: Yip et al. (1988); and C.K. Prahalad and Y.L. Doz, *The Multinational Mission: Balancing Local Demands and Global Vision* (New York: The Free Press, 1987).

45

Mapping the Characteristics of a Business

C.K. Prahalad and Yves L. Doz

As the emerging patterns of competition in a wide variety of businesses become of increasing concern, especially the intense competition brought about by overseas competitors, the words "global business" and "global competition" have entered the lexicon of most managers. However, the distinction between the intrinsic characteristics of a business[1] – its cost structure, technology, and customers, for example, at a given point in time – and the characteristics of competition in that business is not always well understood. Further, labeling businesses as "global" or "multidomestic" may hide broad variations in the underlying managerial tasks. In this chapter, we shall develop a methodology for capturing, in a managerially meaningful scheme, the characteristics of a wide range of businesses or for understanding the "existing rules of the game" in a business.

The Building Blocks

The building blocks of the methodology for mapping the characteristics of a business start with the managerial demands that it imposes on senior management.

Global Integration of Activities

Integration refers to the centralized management of geographically dispersed activities on an ongoing basis. Managing shipments of parts and subassemblies

Source: *The Multinational Mission: Balancing Local Demands and Global Vision*, New York: Free Press, 1987, pp. 13–37.

across a network of manufacturing facilities in various countries is an example of integration of activities.

The need for integration arises in response to pressures to reduce costs and optimize investment. Pressures to reduce cost may force location of plants in countries with low labor costs, such as South Korea, Taiwan, and Malaysia. Products are then shipped from those plants to the established markets of the United States and Europe. The same pressures may also lead to building large-scale, highly specialized plants, to realize economies of scale. Ford's European operations and IBM's worldwide manufacturing operations are examples of the phenomenon. In either case, the goal is leveraging the advantages of low manufacturing cost. Managerially, that translates into a need for ongoing management of logistics that cut across multiple national boundaries.

Global Strategic Coordination

Strategic coordination refers to the central management of resource commitments across national boundaries in the pursuit of a strategy. It is distinct from the integration of ongoing activities across national borders. Typical examples would involve coordinating R&D priorities across several laboratories, coordinating pricing to global customers, and facilitating transfers of technology from headquarters to subsidiaries and across subsidiaries. Unlike activity integration, strategic coordination can be selective and nonroutine.

Strategic coordination is often essential to provide competitive and strategic coherence to resource commitments made over time by headquarters and various subsidiaries in multiple countries. The goal of strategic coordination is to recognize, build, and defend long-term competitive advantages. For example, headquarters may assign highly differentiated goals to various subsidiaries in the same business in order to develop a coherent response to competition.

Strategic coordination, like integration of activities, often involves headquarters and one or several subsidiaries. Coordination decisions transcend a single subsidiary.

Local Responsiveness

Local responsiveness refers to resource commitment decisions taken autonomously by a subsidiary in response to primarily local competitive or customer demands. In a wide variety of businesses, there may be no competitive advantage to be gained by coordinating actions across subsidiaries; in fact, that may prove to be detrimental.

Typically, businesses where there are no meaningful economies of scale or proprietary technology (e.g. processed foods) fall into this category. The need for significant local adaptation of products or differences in distribution across national markets may also indicate a need for local responsiveness.

Characteristics of a Business and Managerial Demands

The three building blocks described above – global integration of activities, global strategic coordination, and local responsiveness – refer to the nature of relationships between headquarters and subsidiaries, as well as among subsidiaries in a multinational setting. However, those relationships are *dependent* on the nature of the businesses in the DMNC. The economic, technological, and competitive characteristics of a business enable us to define the pressures for global integration of activities and local responsiveness. The need for strategic coordination is harder to focus on. Typically, businesses that need significant global integration of activities also require strategic coordination. However, given active global competition, locally responsive businesses may demand strategic coordination as well. We shall identify situations where businesses that would require integration and coordination in conditions of free competition are forced to be locally responsive, at least in part. At this stage it is useful to recognize two essential demands – global integration and local responsiveness – and assume that the extent of strategic coordination is related to the need for integration. We shall identify those linkages by examining one DMNC in detail.

Mapping the Characteristics of a Business

Let us take the case of Corning Glass.[2] As of 1975 it operated internationally in six business categories with more than 60,000 line items. The businesses were:

- *Television products*, which included supplying TV bulbs to original equipment manufacturers (OEM) like RCA, Philips, and Sylvania. The technology was mature, and competition was based on costs, delivery, product development, and ability to meet bulb specifications, which differed according to transmission standards in different countries. Corning had few competitors around the world in this business and had an identifiable, small set of relatively large OEM customers.
- *Electronic products*, which consisted of components like resistors and capacitors used by computer, communication, and military equipment manufacturers. Most of the products were mature, and the business was extremely price sensitive. Customers shopped around worldwide for the best prices and technical specifications.
- *Consumer products*, chiefly Corningware, the leading cookware product in the United States. The mass market for cookware was reached through retailers. Distribution channels varied by country. While some large, global competitors like Noritake of Japan existed, most competitors were regional and local.
- *Medical products*, consisting of scientific instruments such as blood gas analyzers and diagnostic reagents. The instruments were high-value-added products, manufactured in small quantities, using a highly technical process. Product development was a key task in this business, and

product life cycles were short. A direct sales force was used. Differences existed between various country markets, which made product development difficult.

- *Science products*, specifically laboratory glassware, an old, mature product line. Competition was primarily based on price. This business category also included chemical systems like heat exchangers and process piping designed for specific applications.
- *Technical products*, mostly ophthalmic products, which consisted of photochromatic eyeglass blanks, produced in a variety of thicknesses, curvatures, and so forth. Because of the variety of shapes, sizes, colors, and materials in which the product had to be delivered, sourcing decisions were critical. This business group also contained technical materials, which involved supplying specialty subassemblies to governments and OEMs.

Corning's overseas activities comprised fourteen major foreign manufacturing operations and a host of licensees. Its products were produced abroad, and the overseas sales volume was significant. Its overseas manufacturing and sales involvement in the six broad business categories is shown in Table 1.

Table 1
Corning's Overseas Involvement, 1974

Business Group	Overseas Manufacturing Plants in	Approximate Overseas Sales as a % of Total Sales for that Business
Television products	France, Brazil, Mexico, Taiwan, and Canada; licensees in Europe and Japan	30%
Electronics products	France, U.K.	35%
Consumer products	France, U.K., Argentina, Australia, Holland	35%
Medical products	U.K.	25%
Science products; lab ware	France, U.K., Argentina, Mexico, Brazil, Japan, India, Australia	40%
Chemical systems	France, U.K.	65%
Technical products; ophthalmic products	France, Brazil	33%
Technical products	–	15%

With such a spread of overseas activities in both manufacturing and marketing, should Corning treat all its businesses as global? Are there differences among those businesses that transcend the location of plants and the distribution of markets around the world?

It is a great temptation to categorize businesses as diverse as Corningware and electronic products as either global (meaning their activities can and should be integrated across borders) or multidomestic (meaning that they are local businesses in multiple countries). However, each business is subject to varying degrees of economic, competitive, and technological pressures that push it toward becoming global or toward remaining locally responsive. Some of the Corning businesses have to accommodate both pressures simultaneously.

The Integration–Responsiveness Grid

The Integration–Responsiveness (IR) grid provides us with a way of capturing the pressures on a given business – pressures that make *strategic coordination* and *global integration of activities* critical, as well as the pressures that make being sensitive to the diverse demands of various national markets and achieving *local responsiveness* critical.

We can use the following criteria for evaluating the pressures for global co-ordination and integration, as well as local responsiveness.

Pressures for Global Strategic Coordination

Importance of Multinational Customers
The dependence of a business on multinational OEM customers imposes a need for global strategic coordination. For example, in the TV bulbs business, a significant portion of the total sales went to multinational OEM customers like Philips and Sylvania. Multinational customers can, and often do, compare prices charged them by their suppliers around the world, demand the same level of service and product support, and have centralized vendor certification. The product is often sold at the center, say to the OEM's product division, and delivered around the world – wherever the multinational customer may need it. The percentage of sales to multinational OEM customers and their importance to the business can thus dictate the need for global coordination. In the case of Corning-ware, the opposite was true. Its customers were mostly local, and it was primarily a mass-marketed item.

Presence of Multinational Competitors
The presence of competitors who operate in multiple markets indicates the potential for global competition. Consequently, it is crucial to gather intelligence on competitors across national markets, to understand their strategic intent, and to be ready to respond to their actions wherever most appropriate. The presence of multinational competitors calls for global strategic coordination. Competitors for Corning's various businesses ranged from global competitors in electronic products, to regional competitors in TV products, to local competitors in lab ware and Corning cookware.

Investment Intensity
If an aspect of the business is investment-intensive (e.g. R&D, manufacturing), the need to leverage that investment increases the need for global coordination. Worldwide product strategies have to be developed and implemented quickly to make the large initial investments profitable.

At Corning, the intensity of the R&D effort in the medical products business and the intensity of investment in manufacturing and product development in the electronics business indicated that a high level of global coordination and integration was required in those two businesses. In the lab ware business, the pressure for international strategic coordination was not felt.

Technology Intensity

Technology intensity and the extent of proprietary technology often encourage firms to manufacture in only a few selected locations. Having fewer manufacturing sites allows easier control over quality, cost, and new product introduction. Centralized product development and manufacturing operations in a few locations result in global integration, particularly when the markets are widely dispersed.

Again, at Corning the technological intensity differed from business to business. For example, the lab ware required a very low technology as compared to the medical products business. Medical products had short life cycles, with constantly renewed markets, whereas lab ware had stable products and applications.

Pressure for Cost Reduction

Global integration is often a response to pressure for cost reduction. Cost reduction requires sourcing the product from low-factor-cost locations (global sourcing), or exploiting economies of scale and experience by building large plants that serve multiple national markets. Either approach to lowering costs imposes a need for global integration.

Some of Corning's businesses, such as electronic products, were subject to severe cost pressures, while others, like Corningware, were less so.

Universal Needs

If the product meets a universal need and requires little adaptation across national markets, global integration is obviously facilitated.

Electronic products – capacitors, resistors – are good examples of universal products. They do not vary by country. On the other hand, Corningware is not universal. It must be adapted to suit various market needs. For example, the "oven-to-freezer" feature may be a big hit in the United States but may not be appropriate in France; a soufflé dish popular in France may not have a big market in the Midwest.

Access to Raw Materials and Energy

Access to raw materials and a cheap and plentiful supply of energy can force manufacturing to be located in a specific area. Aluminum smelters, paper mills, and, increasingly, petrochemicals tend to be located where the raw materials are available. That tendency in some businesses suggests global coordination and integration. None of Corning's businesses had to contend with this issue.

Pressures for Local Responsiveness

Differences in Customer Needs

Businesses that thrive on satisfying a diverse set of customer needs, most of which is nation- or region-specific, require a locally responsive strategy.

Several businesses within Corning have satisfied country-specific needs. Corningware, technical materials, and to some extent chemical systems were designed with specific customers of individual countries in mind. On the other hand, electronic products met a universal need.

Differences in Distribution Channels

Differences in distribution channels in various countries and the differences in pricing, product positioning, promotion, and advertising that those differences entail indicate the need for local responsiveness.

In the lab ware business at Corning, the distribution system used to access the school systems in various countries varied; comparable differences in distribution channels characterized Corningware. On the other hand, in the electronic and TV products businesses, which were primarily serving OEM customers, the differences among national markets were only marginal.

Availability of Substitutes and the Need to Adapt

If a product function is being met by local substitutes, with differing price–performance relationships in a given national market, or if the product must be significantly adapted to be locally competitive, then a locally responsive strategy is indicated.

Corningware had a significant number of substitutes – cooking ware made from other materials, as well as cooking ware promoted differently. It also needed to be adapted to suit local conditions. In the case of electronic products, neither condition was important: Products were universal and faced no differentiated local substitutes.

Market Structure

Market structure includes the importance of local competitors as compared to multinational ones, as well as the extent of their concentration. If local competitors tend to control a significant portion of the market and/or if the industry is not concentrated, then a locally responsive posture is most usually indicated (unless there are merits to competing globally to make the industry structure evolve in your favor). A fragmented industry with local competitors indicates that there may be no inherent advantages to size and scale, unless product and process technology can be changed.

Again, among Corning's businesses, lab ware had to compete in each national market with a large number of local competitors in a fragmented industry, while TV products had to cope with only a handful of large competitors in a globally concentrated industry.

Host Government Demands

Demands imposed by host governments for local self-sufficiency for a variety of reasons – from concerns of national development to concerns of national security – can force a business to become locally responsive.

Mapping Corning's Businesses in the Integration–Responsiveness Grid

It is obvious that Corning does not operate in any one type of business – either global or multidomestic. Each of its businesses is subject to a different combination of pressures toward global coordination and integration and toward local responsiveness – pressures that elude a simple "either-or" classification. We can identify the differences using the criteria we have developed, as shown in Table 2.

Table 2
Comparison of Three Businesses within Corning

Criteria	Electronics	TV Products	Corningware
Pressures for Global Strategic Coordination			
Importance of multinational customers	high	high	low
Importance of multinational competitors	high	medium/high	low
Investment intensity	high	high	low/medium
Pressures for Global Operational Integration			
Technology intensity	medium	medium	low
Pressure for cost reduction	high	high	low
Universal needs	high	medium	low
Access to raw materials and energy	NA	NA	NA
Need for Global Integration	*high*	*medium*	*low*
Pressures for Local Responsiveness			
Differences in customer needs	low	medium?	high
Differences in distribution	low	low	high
Need for substitutes and product adaptation	low	low	high
Market structure	Concentrated	Concentrated	Fragmented
Host government demands	NA	NA	NA
Need for Local Responsiveness	*low*	*medium*	*high*

The characteristics of the three businesses can now be captured in an Integration–Responsiveness Grid, as shown in Figure 1. From the foregoing analysis, the following generalizations can be drawn:

1. The mapping of the characteristics of the various businesses illustrates the differences among them, even though all six businesses share the same corporate logo and all evolved out of the same broad glass technology. Because of those differences, managers must examine each business individually to develop strategies rather than treat them all alike.

2. Classifying businesses broadly as either global or local can be misleading. There are few businesses that are totally local. If there were no advantages to be gained in that business by an MNC, then it is likely to be very fragmented with no scope for leveraging knowledge, products, financial muscle, or brands across markets. On the other hand, few businesses are totally global. A variety of factors, including the need for a responsive and differentiated local presence in various countries, make it difficult to ignore totally the demands of various national markets.

3. The purpose of the IR framework is to assess the *relative importance* of the two sets of conflicting demands on a business and to determine which of the two provides strategic leverage at a given point in time.

4. In the case of Corning, some businesses tend toward global integration (e.g. electronics, medical products). In those businesses, strategic advantage

Figure 1
Integration–Responsiveness Grid: Characteristics of Corning's Business

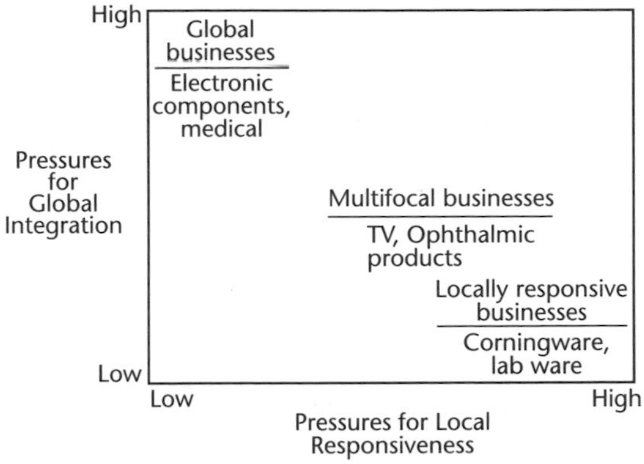

will accrue to the competitor who is organized to exploit the benefits of strategic coordination in investments, product policy, product development, pricing, monitoring competitors, and so forth. In businesses that tend toward local responsiveness (e.g. Corningware, lab ware), strategic advantage accrues to the firm that is sensitive to the need for decentralized pricing, promotion, and product policy. There may be little benefit in strategic coordination.

5. In Corning's case the real challenge to management is not in managing the extremes; it is in managing multifocal businesses, which demand sensitivity to both dimensions *at the same time*, as is the case with the TV products business. This implies that in such businesses it is unwise to make a one-time tradeoff in favor of either global integration or local responsiveness. Both demands have to be managed simultaneously.

Some Implications

Several managerial conclusions can be derived from mapping the characteristics of a business on the IR grid.

1. Corning's electronic components, which is high on the need for global integration and low on the need for local responsiveness, suggests that managers developing strategies for that business must pay considerably more attention to leveraging aspects like economies of scale, product development, global customers, and global competitors than to issues of local responsiveness. This also implies that resource allocation decisions with respect to key elements of strategy for that business (such as plant location and investment, pricing, product development, and key account management) may have to be centralized. In other words, for the electronic components business, the locus of strategic management is the central worldwide business management group. On the other hand, for Corningware or lab ware, the key strategic choices (pricing, promotion, choice of channels) have to be managed in a decentralized mode.

The center for strategy making is the regional or the national subsidiary managers, as contrasted with the center for the electronic components business, as shown in Figure 2.

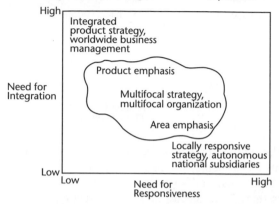

Figure 2
Integration–Responsiveness Grid:
Strategic Focus and Organizational Adaptation

2. In both those businesses representing the extremes – electronic components and Corningware – managers can make "clear one-time choices" of what aspects of the business to leverage. Therefore, a clear and simple organizational form – worldwide business management in the case of electronic components and area management in the case of Corningware – is possible. In other words, the relative simplicity of the strategic priorities enables a clearcut choice of simple organization.

3. In the case of the TV business the strategic choice is not all that clearcut. Some elements of strategy, like plant size and technology, may have to be managed centrally. On the other hand, deliveries, competitors, and some key customers may have to be managed both regionally and locally. That implies that managers cannot make a "one-time choice" on which of the two dimensions to leverage. They must *simultaneously focus their attention* on aspects of the business that require global integration and aspects that demand local responsiveness, and on varying degrees of strategic coordination. This need for *multiple focal points for managing* suggests that managers must reflect the need for multiple points of view – the need to integrate and be responsive at the same time – in the way that business is organized. That requires the organization to be *multifocal* or matrix.

In general, many businesses that have the characteristics of Corning's TV business will need a multifocal or matrix organization, despite all the problems of managing such an organization.

The IR grid is not just a tool for discovering the essential orientation of a business for strategy making. It also enables managers to decide on the appropriate form of organization to manage the strategic orientation desired.

Mapping the Dynamics of a Business on the IR Grid

While taking Corning to illustrate the basic approach to mapping the characteristics on the IR grid, we have assumed our data and have assessed the characteristics of a business at a given point in time, rather than the way it might change over time. For the strategist, the direction of possible change in the characteristics of a business is even more interesting than the situation at a given point in time. Now we shall identify the factors that can change the location of a business in the IR grid over time as well as suggest the type of data that might be useful in understanding such trends early.

Changes in Underlying Industry Economics

Shifts in the location of a business on the IR grid are often a result of shifts in the underlying economics of the industry. Let us take the example of ethylene oxide. During the early 1970s, most chemical firms operated plants of an annual capacity of 50 million to 75 million pounds. In most markets of the world, especially in the United States and Europe, that meant firms could dedicate a plant (or more) to each important national market. As each market could afford its own manufacturing and marketing facilities, and as ethylene oxide was a commodity product, managers could be very sensitive to local needs. In the early 1970s most firms operated with considerable local responsiveness and a low level of global integration. However, over the period 1972–75, several chemical firms, especially ICI in the United Kingdom, started building plants with a capacity as large as 250 million to 400 million pounds. The cost advantage arising from the economies of scale was around 12 to 15 percent over traditional, smaller plants. Because a single national market could not absorb the output of the large-scale plants, the firm had to coordinate prices, product specifications, logistics, and, most importantly, investments across several, so far autonomous national markets. In a very short time, the center of gravity for strategy making in the ethylene oxide business for several chemical firms had shifted toward high need for integration and low need for responsiveness. Given a 12 to 15 percent cost advantage in a commodity chemical, few competitors could resist the pressure to build large plants in order to remain competitive. On the IR grid, the ethylene oxide business would be depicted as locally responsive until 1972. It moved toward international integration because of changes in industry economics during 1972–75.

Could that have been predicted? Clearly, the technology breakthrough that was required to build large plants was no secret, nor were the cost advantages that would accrue as a result. The nature of the shift in industry economics that would result from a dramatic increase in plant size was obvious. The implications of the trend for the business could have been predicted.

Impact of Governments

During the same period drug companies also faced a shift in their business. The proprietary drug business, involving significant investment in R&D and requiring strict quality controls in manufacturing, is best managed centrally, from a few locations. However, the politics of health care in many countries around the world force drug firms to manufacture in multiple locations. They are also subject to local clinical testing, registration procedures, and pricing restrictions. As governments and quasi-government agencies control a significant portion of the health care budget in most countries, they are in a position to demand a high level of local responsiveness. That has forced most drug firms into simultaneously facing a high need for global integration and a high need for local responsiveness.

Shifts in the Competitive Focus of Customers

Supplier industries tend to follow the shifts in the industries they serve. For example, the automobile industry has become global in terms of its sourcing and design, as well as manufacturing. In firms like General Motors, design teams out of the United States, Germany, and Great Britain may be working on a series of "world cars." That trend has had impact on suppliers to the auto industry. For example, paint manufacturers, who manufacture paints for household use as well as car finishes, have typically operated on a locally responsive basis. The trend in the auto industry has forced one segment of their operations, car finishes, to become globally integrated. Product planners and purchasing agents in the auto industry would like to contract with a set of suppliers who can supply the same quality of car finish around the world. Yet the home paint segment is still locally responsive. Paint manufacturers who saw their business as essentially locally responsive had to contend with the realization that the auto industry internationalization was changing the nature of customer relations in a segment of their business; they had to recognize that they could no longer treat both segments of their business – car finishes and home paints – alike.

Resegmenting a Business

Often resegmenting a business provides an opportunity for reexamining the appropriate location of a business in the IR grid. While we have assumed the business as a unit of analysis, a reexamination of "what constitutes a business" may provide useful insights. For example, if the business is defined as health care products, based on the criteria we have developed, it might occupy a certain location in the IR grid. On the other hand, if we segment the business into its constituent parts – proprietary drugs, ethical drugs, and health care supplies – we may see three distinct trends. Each one of those segments is subject to a distinctly different set of economic and competitive forces. The dynamics of change in a business in the IR grid is shown in Figure 3.

Firms Learn

The way a business is perceived in the IR grid may shift as firms learn about their businesses and see new opportunities and problems. For example, when a processed food firm, Nabisco, went overseas, its management assumed the businesses could be managed centrally and that the benefits of coordinating in advertising and product development outweighed the benefits of local responsiveness. It soon became apparent that the habits of consumers were harder to change in some of the businesses than originally thought; a locally responsive strategy made more sense.

Figure 3
Mapping Mobility of Businesses in the IR Grid

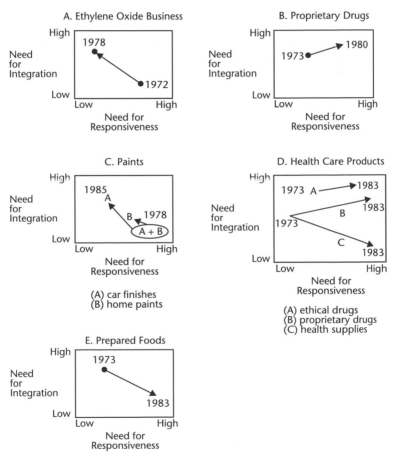

Changing the "Rules of the Game"

Other firms saw opportunities to do exactly the opposite. Otis elevator saw an opportunity in the late 1960s to integrate its operations in the elevator market in Europe. At that time the market was dominated by local firms; most MNCs also operated on a locally responsive mode. Through a process of acquisitions and consolidations, by standardizing elevator design, and by cutting costs, Otis changed the rules of the game. It changed the economics of the industry to a point where regional integration, if not global integration, became the dominant mode. The first company to initiate and exploit that change can gain a considerable advantage over its competitors, who are slower to move toward international integration.

The success of Japanese competitors in a variety of industries can be attributed to their ability to pick primarily locally responsive industries, even those populated by MNCs, and change them to globally integrated businesses. Examples abound. Traditional competitors who were multinational prior to the Japanese competitive thrust in the auto industry (e.g. General Motors), ball bearings (e.g. SKF), and television sets (e.g. Philips) operated on a locally responsive basis. They were caught off guard. Once a determined competitor changes the rules of the game, the degrees of freedom available to others may be limited, as in the case of ethylene oxide or in the auto and elevator industries.

Mapping Mobility of Businesses in the IR Grid

In Figure 3, the shifts discussed above are illustrated. It is important to note the mobility of businesses within the IR grid. That mobility requires that managers not only recognize the balance of the forces of global integration and local responsiveness to which a business is subject to at a given point in time, but also assess the pattern of change in that posture over time. A careful analysis of the underlying cost structure of the industry (e.g. ethylene oxide), the political pressures on it (e.g. ethical drugs, computers), shifts in the competitive focus of customers (e.g. paints for the auto industry), opportunities for resegmentation (e.g. health care), and an ability to change the rules of the game (e.g. elevators) are crucial for assessing the opportunities and threats in the industry. In addition to data on the behavior of costs, changes in technology, and shifts in the policies of host governments, managers have to make judgments on how fast those factors will have an impact on the industry. In many cases, managers *can and do change the rules of the game*, proactively, as in the case of elevators or ball bearings. In other words, an analysis and understanding of "objective data" tell us only part of the story. The movement of a business within the IR grid is very much influenced by the perceptions, judgments, and ambitions of managers on how it can be resegmented or changed. Significant shifts in the location of a business in the IR grid imply that the key success factors in that business have changed dramatically, leading to shifts in strategy. Strategy development is therefore not just an exercise in assessing the "rules of the game" in a given business, at a given point in time (i.e., the location of a business in the IR grid); it is as much developing viable "new rules of the game" (i.e., identifying opportunities for mobility within the IR grid). That calls for marrying analysis of objective data and current industry patterns and managerial perceptions together with judgments on how the business can be changed.

Capturing Perceptions of Managers

In order to capture the perceptions and judgments of managers regarding the potential for change in a business, we suggest the use of questionnaires similar to the ones in Figure 4 (for assessing the extent of local responsiveness) and Figure 5 (for assessing the extent of global integration). Each questionnaire captures aspects of a business, like the nature of competiton, evolution of technology, scope for manufacturing economies, and so forth, on a seven-point scale. Managers are asked to:

1. Identify the relative importance of each factor to the business by ranking, the most important being 1 and the least important 6, in the questionnaire on local responsiveness.

2. Identify where the business was three years ago, where it is now, and where it is likely to be, in his or her judgment, in the next three years, on the seven-point scale for each dimension. This provides a method for capturing his or her perception of the changes that have taken place in that business, in each dimension, (the difference between now and three years ago), as well as the extent of change that he or she expects in that dimension in the near future (the difference between the score now and three years from now). By consolidating the weighted scores for the dimensions representing the forces of local responsiveness and global integration, we can represent the extent of change in that business as well as the expectation for change in the perception of each manager. We can also develop a score for the management group as a whole.

Figure 6 shows the managerial perceptions of change in, for example, the polypropylene business for the period 1971 (three years ago), to 1974 (now) and 1977 (three years hence). The data were collected using a questionnaire similar to the one shown in Figures 4 and 5, in one large U.S.-based chemical firm. The overall managerial perceptions of change correspond well with the trends in the industry at that time. The benefits of using the questionnaire to identify managerial perceptions are several. For example:

1. If managers' perceptions, as identified by their responses to the questionnaire, do not match the industry trends, as identified by an independent analysis of the changes in technology, cost structures, and competitor behavior, then the managers' perceptions can be challenged.

2. The perceptions of change by different groups of managers can be compared. For example, in Figure 7, we show the perceptions of managers from three distinct groups – from head office representing the product division, area managers representing the perceptions of the national organization (and subsidiaries), and joint venture partners. It is interesting to note that while joint venture partners perceive a need for greater global integration, they also perceive a greater need for local responsive-ness. A similar analysis of data

Figure 4
Sample Questionnaire for Assessing the Required Extent of Local Responsiveness

O = Three years ago
X = At present
✓ = Three years from now

MARKET
Heterogeneous. Customers and customer needs are not clearly identified. Customer motivations tend to be complex. The perceived value of the product is unclear. The trends in the market are not easily foreseen.

1 2 3 4 5 6 7
+—+—+—+—+—+—+

MARKET
Homogeneous. Customer segments are clearly identified. The customers' decision process and perception of value of the products are clear. Market trends are clear.

COMPETITIVE SITUATION
Competition is diffuse, with a large number of competitors. Competitors' strategies are unclear. There are no typical characteristics of the firm in the industry.

1 2 3 4 5 6 7
+—+—+—+—+—+—+

COMPETITIVE SITUATION
Competition is easily identified. There are only few competitors, and their strategies can be identified and interpreted.

TECHNOLOGY
Technology is evolving. A variety of unknowns in process and product specifications and cost structure exist. Rates of change in products and production processes are both rapid and unpredictable.

Product
1 2 3 4 5 6 7
+—+—+—+—+—+—+
+—+—+—+—+—+—+
1 2 3 4 5 6 7
Process

TECHNOLOGY
Relatively stable technology and a high level of manufacturing sophistication. Products are relatively mature. Production technology improvements and cost minimization are seen as important.

ECONOMICS OF MANUFACTURE
The key determinant of manufacturing cost is still unclear. Costs are not affected by size or location of plant. Raw materials are easily available.

1 2 3 4 5 6 7
+—+—+—+—+—+—+

ECONOMICS OF MANUFACTURE
The key determinants of manufacturing cost are size of plant and capacity utilization. Locational advantages exist. Availability of raw materials poses a problem.

EXECUTIVE GROUP
Executives do not have any shared experiences – educational, cultural, or professional. They do not share a feeling of belonging to the organization.

1 2 3 4 5 6 7
+—+—+—+—+—+—+

EXECUTIVE GROUP
Executives share substantial experience together – educational, professional, and cultural. They share a sense of belonging to the organization.

from functional groups – technical, marketing, and general management, shows the same diversity of perceptions. While all three groups agree on where the business is headed, they disagree on where they are coming from and how much they have to change.

3. The charting of the differences in the perceptions of the various managerial groups suggests that the same "objective evidence" may be interpreted differently by various groups. They may perceive the changes required as significant (e.g. marketing) or relatively slight (general management), and even quarrel with the direction of change (joint venture partners). If the various groups perceive the *need for change*, the *extent of change*, and *the urgency for change* differently, internal tensions can develop. The questionnaire becomes

Figure 5
Sample Questionnaire for Assessing the Required Extent of Global Integration

O = Three years ago
X = At present
✓ = Three years from now

STRATEGIC
Capacity and manufacturing
technology decisions are made
with a view to provide multiplant
linkages and multiplant sourcing
potenetial.

1 2 3 4 5 6 7
+—+—+—+—+—+—+

STRATEGIC
Capacity and process decisions are
made on a project-by-project basis
with a view to serving specific
market areas.

MARKETING
Product and quality specifications
are developed and coordinated to
serve multiple geographically
defined markets.

1 2 3 4 5 6 7
+—+—+—+—+—+—+

MARKETING
Product and quality specifications
are developed with a single, specific
geographical market in view.

Pricing strategy, support to
various market segments,
assessment of the importance
of various market priorities for
allocation of capacity and other
such market-related decisions
are made with the total worldwide
corporate interest in focus.

1 2 3 4 5 6 7
+—+—+—+—+—+—+

Pricing, support to various market
segments, perceived importance of
the segments to the corporation,
allocation of capacity and other
such market-related decisions are
made with the needs of the local
market in view.

The various subsidiaries do not
serve multinational customers.

The subsidiaries sell a substantial
part of their output to the same
multinational customers worldwide.

1 2 3 4 5 6 7
+—+—+—+—+—+—+

The customers are very dissimilar
worldwide.

The customers have the same level of
income, education, and motivtions
worldwie.

1 2 3 4 5 6 7
+—+—+—+—+—+—+

TECHNOLOGY
Development effort is carried out
in multiple locations, each location
specializing in a specific technical
area and/or a product line. This
output is shared by all subsidiaries

Product
1 2 3 4 5 6 7
+—+—+—+—+—+—+

+—+—+—+—+—+—+
1 2 3 4 5 6 7
Process

TECHNOLOGY
Development effort is carried out in
a single central location, and the
results are passed on to all locations
needing the technology.

MANUFACTURING
Substantial movements of semifinished and finished products
exists between local subsidiaries.
This movement is governed by
formal agreements. Problems in
one plant (e.g., quality of product
or strike) can affect other plants
and markets adversely.

1 2 3 4 5 6 7
+—+—+—+—+—+—+

MANUFACTURING
Local subsidiaries are basically
independent of each other in terms
of product flows.

CONTROL
Production planning, inventory
and quality control, and cost
control are managed centrally.

1 2 3 4 5 6 7
+—+—+—+—+—+—+

CONTROL
Production planning, inventory and
quality control, and cost control
remain the responsibility of local
subsidiaries. Corporate groups
provide only broad guidelines or no
guidelines.

Figure 6
Managerial Perceptions of Change – Polypropelene Business, 1971–1977

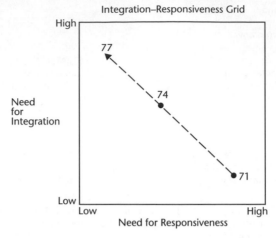

Integration–Responsiveness Grid

Figure 7
The Perception of Change of Functional Groups in the Polypropelene Business

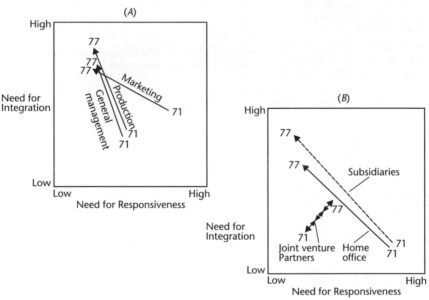

an aid in identifying the differences in perceptions and making those explicit. That allows for a debate and facilitates narrowing of differences.

IR Pressures May Affect Functions within a Business Differently

We have assumed, so far, in identifying the pressures for global integration and local responsiveness that the unit of analysis is a discrete business. In some cases, however, functions within a business may respond differently to those pressures. For example, in the computer industry, integrated R&D is common. Manufacturing may be somewhat decentralized, and marketing fairly locally responsive, as shown in Figure 8. An integrated R&D function allows the firm to conserve scarce human resources, protect proprietary knowhow, and reduce the investment required in R&D. It also allows R&D to be centrally managed. On the other hand, the need for sensitivity to diverse national customers' requirements may suggest a locally responsive marketing function.

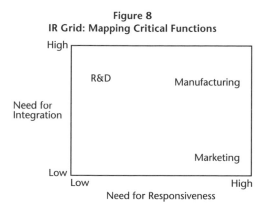

Figure 8
IR Grid: Mapping Critical Functions

Functions such as R&D, manufacturing, marketing, and service may be used to identify pressures for global integration and local responsiveness, when each function represents a significant commitment of distinct types of resources and different underlying cost structures (significant economies of scale in R&D and the need for differentiated marketing tasks by country), and when internal mechanisms exist or can be developed to coordinate the functions that are managed differently.

Global Business versus Global Competition

We have so far examined the characteristics of a business using the IR grid and have identified factors that cause mobility of a business within that framework. However, the location of a business in the IR framework does not always identify the pattern of competition in a business. It is likely that if a business is high on global integration and low on local responsiveness, (e.g. semiconductors), it will be run, by most firms participating in that business, on a worldwide basis. On the other hand, a business high on local responsiveness and low on global integration (e.g. processed foods), is likely to be run with significant local autonomy. Businesses that are high on both dimensions (e.g. telecommunications, ethical drugs), may require a complex structure that accommodates the pressures of both integration and responsiveness. But those patterns do not identify the nature of competition that may exist in a given business.

Notes

1. In this chapter, the word "business" refers to a set of related product markets and tasks, not to a company. Our use of the word "business" thus covers more than a product line but typically less than a whole industry.
2. The Corning Glass Works example relies on data made public in the case series from Michael Y. Yoshino and Christopher A. Bartlett, "Corning Glass Works International (BI)," Case 9-381-161. Boston: Harvard Business School, 1981. Reprinted by permission.

46

Global Strategy Implementation at the Business Unit Level: Operational Capabilities and Administrative Mechanisms

Kendall Roth, David M. Schweiger and Allen J. Morrison

A critical issue in the study of businesses competing in global industries is the relationship between international strategy and implementation requirements. To date there have been numerous empirical studies that have examined the relationship between strategy and organizational design in multinational corporations [Daniels, Pitts & Tretter 1984, 1985; Egelhoff 1982, 1988a; Fouraker & Stopford 1968; Stopford & Wells 1972]. These studies have found that as the strategy of a multinational corporation (MNC) changed, it was important that the organizational design be realigned in order to implement the new strategy successfully [Egelhoff 1988b]. The organization design dimensions examined have focused on macro-organizational structures, such as worldwide product divisions, international divisions, and matrix structures. Similarly, international strategy has been broadly defined as "foreign product diversity" or the extent to which the organization is international in scope. However, there appears to be an emerging consensus that additional design dimensions of the MNC such as management systems, communication processes, and managerial philosophies rather than only formal macro-organizational structures should be studied [Bartlett 1983; Doz & Prahalad 1986; Galbraith & Nathanson 1978; Hedlund & Rolander 1990]. Recent advances in the conceptualization of international strategy emphasize the need to examine the pattern of resource deployments and resource configuration across country locations to distinguish among alternate strategy types [Ghoshal 1987; Kogut 1985a, b; Porter 1986]. Thus while previous research has been useful in improving our understanding of the relationship between international strategy and macro-organizational structure, the use of

Source: *Journal of International Business Studies*, Vol. 22, No. 3, 1991, pp. 369–402.

restricted conceptualizations of both strategy and organization design (i.e., implementation requirements) have limited these studies. This study represents an attempt to address these limitations by examining an implementation framework based on matching the organizational design to the selected international strategy. In general, it is argued that alternate international strategies – global versus multidomestic – create different implementation requirements and therefore the administrative systems and capabilities of the organization must be designed to fit these requirements. Moreover, it is also argued that the fit achieved between strategy and the subsequent organizational design will affect business unit performance.

Framework for Understanding International Strategy

Our theoretical framework for understanding international strategy implementation is based on the following premises: (1) The choice of international strategy influences the extent to which the activities of an international business must be linked or integrated across countries. (2) International operational capabilities – defined by the level of coordination, managerial philosophy, and geographic configuration – determine an organization's ability to manage these intraorganizational linkages. (3) The international operational capabilities are created and controlled through three administrative mechanisms: centralization, formalization, and integrating mechanisms. It is then posited that the match or fit achieved among international strategy, operational capabilities, and administrative mechanisms will be associated positively with business unit performance. This framework is depicted in Figure 1 and an overview of the framework follows.

Porter [1986] argued that within an international context businesses make a fundamental strategic choice of competing on a global or country-by-country basis. Businesses competing with a country-by-country or multidomestic strategy

Figure 1
International Strategy Implementation Framework

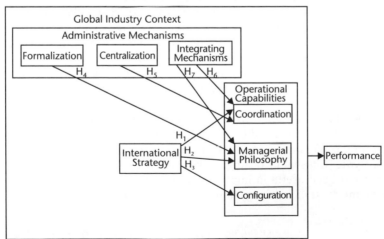

attempt to isolate themselves from global competitive forces through protected market positions or by competing in industry segments that are most affected by local differences [Porter 1986: 48]. The competitive advantage of a multi-domestic strategy is therefore based on developing nonimitable responsiveness within each country context. In contrast, a global strategy is defined through a pattern of goal-directed decisions based on an industry position in which the competitive forces are perceived to span national boundaries. Because the industry is linked across countries, the business pursuing a global strategy considers that its "competitive position in one national market is affected by its competitive position in other national markets" [Ghoshal 1987: 425]. This linking of competitive positions across country locations implies that the international activities of the organization must be integrated in a manner that develops and sustains advantage in response to the cross-national competitive forces [Prahalad & Doz 1987].

The integration necessary to develop cross-national competitive responses may be further understood by defining the primary sources of sustained advantage of a global strategy. Sources of advantage are: (1) *competitive advantages* developed through international scale and scope economies, and (2) *location-specific advantages* exploited through arbitrage opportunities resulting from differences that exist in the factor costs across country locations [Ghoshal 1987; Kogut 1985a, b; Porter 1980]. International scale economies are derived from cost reductions achieved through the accumulation of volume across country locations and international aggregation of market segments [Kogut 1990]. International scope economies arise when existing international operations benefit from the introduction of additional activities or products, since the cost of an incremental addition may be less than the sum of the individual costs. The essential operational implication of both these sources of competitive advantage is the transfer of organizational resources within the firm. International economies of scale necessitate actual product or technology flows across national markets as product or product components are produced in single locations from which global markets are served. Furthermore, transfers of market information are required for the identification and development of similar product/market segments across geographic locations. Similarly, international scope economies require cross-national linkages in order to know which activities are most susceptible to such economies (i.e., global brand labelling, global product-line broadening, cross-national introduction of existing products, etc.) as well as support their implementation.

Location-specific advantage opportunities exist through arbitrage of cost differences in factors of production, product pricing, or government policies [Kogut 1990]. Organizational activities may be physically located or production and sourcing shifted among different countries in order to exploit favorable exchange rate movements, tax minimization, capital costs, or raw material cost or availability. Capturing these arbitrage-based gains necessitates that the organization both recognizes and responds to the variance across countries. Intra-firm linkages, in the form of raw materials and product components, capital, and information flows will therefore be necessary for the business to exploit these arbitrage opportunities.

In summary, the fundamental advantages of a global strategy are developed by integrating an MNC's position across national markets. The implementation requirement for accomplishing such integration is the management of various forms of resource flows throughout the multinational network [Casson 1987; Herbert 1984; Kogut 1989, 1990]. This view of global strategy is supported in Cvar's [1984] study which found that a significant level of cross-border asset flows (i.e., semifinished and finished goods) accompanies integrated worldwide competitive responses. Developing operational capabilities to manage the inter-dependencies resulting from international resource flows is consequently, the primary task in implementing a global strategy. As depicted in Figure 1, three capabilities within the multinational corporation have been suggested as determining the ability to manage these interdependencies: the *coordination* of functional activities [Bartlett & Ghoshal 1989; Porter 1985, 1986], the *managerial philosophy* [Bartlett 1983; Bartlett & Ghoshal 1989; Doz & Prahalad 1988], and the *configuration* of functional activities within the organization [Porter 1986; Yip 1989].

The first operational capability – coordination – establishes concerted action among functional activities or organizational subunits [Cyert & March 1963; Thompson 1967] and is therefore important in managing interdependencies. Studies identify two important administrative mechanisms for achieving coordination within the international organization. These are *centralization* [Bartlett & Ghoshal 1989; Ghoshal 1989] and *integrating mechanisms* [Galbraith 1973; Galbraith & Nathanson 1978]. Although important, coordination is insufficient in and of itself in fully managing interdependencies [Bartlett 1983; Prahalad & Doz 1987]. It does not necessarily result in the internalization of norms or beliefs by managers [Edström & Galbraith 1977]. Consequently, a second operational capability – a shared managerial philosophy for decisionmaking within the organization – is also critical for controlling interdependencies within an international organization [Ghoshal & Nohria 1989]. *Integrating mechanisms* and *formalization* play important roles in affecting managers acceptance and commitment to the organization's managerial philosophy.

The third operational capability – configuration – defines the geographic location of the organization's functional activities. To implement a global strategy, Porter [1986] and Yip [1989] argue that the most effective configuration of activities is geographic concentration; each functional activity (i.e., manufacturing, purchasing, marketing, etc.) should be located in a single country with the selection of the country based on cost differentials of factor inputs. In contrast, a multidomestic strategy is best implemented by locating all functional activities (i.e., the complete value chain) of the business within each country to maximize the responsiveness of each activity to the local context.

Thus, the international strategy framework proposed in this study suggests that business units utilize three administrative mechanisms – formalization, integrating mechanisms, and centralization – to create operational capabilities of configuration, coordination, and managerial philosophy – to support the international strategy choice. The following section will detail the specific relationships among elements in the framework.

Hypotheses

The hypotheses will be presented in three groups examining (1) the relationship between international strategy and operational capabilities, (2) the relationship between administrative mechanisms and operational capabilities, and (3) the contingency relationship among international strategy, operational capabilities, and administrative mechanisms.

Relationship between International Strategy and Operational Capabilities

Implementing an international strategy requires that the dimensions of coordination, managerial philosophy, and configuration are made consistent with the choice of strategy. The design of each dimension is discussed in the following section.

Coordination

Recognizing that global competitive advantage is achieved through international resource flows provides a basis for identifying the particular organizational capabilities that must accompany a global strategy. Resource flows between subunits lead to increased interdependencies within the organization; i.e., the activities of one subunit are controlled by or are contingent upon the activities of another subunit(s) [Grant 1988; Victor & Blackburn 1987]. This reciprocal interdependency among subunits necessitates greater coordination [Thompson 1967; Van de Ven, Delbecq & Koenig 1976], a theme carried forward in the global strategy literature [Bartlett & Ghoshal 1989; Ghoshal 1987; Kogut 1989; Prahalad & Doz 1987]. Coordination is considered in Porter's [1986] international framework as one of two dimensions necessary for implementing alternate international strategies. He suggests that the essential form of coordination is how "like" activities of the value chain are related throughout an entire business irrespective of country location [1986: 23–26]. This form of coordination is illustrated by how Procter and Gamble manages its worldwide research and development. Increased worldwide coordination of its R&D centers in U.S., Japan, and Europe allowed P&G to develop "world" liquid detergents that incorporated the best innovations from each location. Thus, given the increased interdependencies accompanying a global strategy, extensive coordination of functional activities within the business unit are necessary to implement the strategy.

To compete with a multidomestic strategy the business seeks to "meet unusual local needs in products, channels, and marketing practices in each country" [Porter 1986: 48]. Operationally, this requires that the activities of the business remain largely independent across country locations since the competence to recognize and create local adaptation and responsiveness will reside predominantly within each country location [Doz 1986]. Furthermore, there is evidence to suggest that the costs or benefits of coordination are contingent on the business

strategy [Grant 1988]. Gupta and Govindarajan [1986] found that intraorganizational resources flows are more beneficial for an "efficiency-based" strategy
as opposed to a "differentiation-based" strategy. Considering the importance of
local responsiveness to a multidomestic strategy as well as the costs of coordination in this context – increased response time in responding to competitors'
moves or market changes because of geographic and cultural separation, and
reduced managerial flexibility – the final argument forwarded is that implementing a multidomestic strategy will not require extensive coordination within the
business unit.

> Hypothesis 1: Emphasizing a global strategy will be positively associated with
> the coordination of functional activities.

Managerial Philosophy

The managerial philosophy of an organization is a potential distinctive competence; a special activity or capability that an organization is able to develop at
a level that exceeds that of its competitors [Barney 1986; Selznick 1957]. The
findings of Miles and Snow [1978] suggest that different distinctive competencies are developed to implement the organization's selected strategy. Subsequent
investigations have quite consistently supported this contention as patterns of
distinctive competencies (i.e., functional activities) vary depending on the strategy being pursued [Gupta & Govindarajan 1984; Hitt & Ireland 1985; Hitt,
Ireland & Palia 1982; Hitt, Ircland & Stadler 1982; Snow & Hrebiniak 1980].

The activities of top management have been advanced as one distinctive
competence important to the success of a business [Das 1981; Miles 1982]. Top
management develops a managerial philosophy or a "dominant general management logic" that influences the way in which the business is managed [Donaldson
& Lorsch 1983]. According to Prahalad and Bettis [1986] the dominant logic of
the organization is "a mind set or world view or a conceptualization of the business" [1986: 491]. It is embedded in schemas (i.e., values, theories, and propositions) that managers have developed over time as they interpret and experience
organizational situations. As schemas develop they allow managers "to categorize an event, assess its consequences, and consider appropriate actions"
[Prahalad & Bettis 1986: 489]. This provides for certain efficiencies and consist-
encies in the ways in which managers respond to discontinuities or changes.
As related specifically to business strategy, Prahalad and Bettis assert that the
effectiveness of schemas is a function of the *strategic variety* of the business.
That is, subunits within a business that are interrelated or are strategically
similar should be managed using a *single* dominant general managerial logic
whereas subunits that have considerable strategic variety should be managed
using *multiple* dominant logics.

As argued previously, global strategy consists of a common strategy across
country locations. A single or "shared" managerial philosophy within the entire
business unit would therefore support a global strategy, particularly since a shared
managerial philosophy provides consistency of decisions in the context of
geographical and cultural separation. Recent prescriptions in the international literature which call for the development of a "common world view"

[Prahalad & Doz 1987], shared "organizational philosophy" [Bartlett & Ghoshal 1989], or "organizational pivots" such as common principles of management [Doz & Prahalad 1988] to effectively implement a global strategy are consistent with this theme. Consequently, as suggested by Bartlett and Ghoshal [1989: 66] unification through a shared organizational philosophy is a critical organizational capability to be developed and managed by organizations intending to pursue a global strategy; multiple philosophies appear to undermine the development of a global orientation [Hofstede 1976; Leontiades 1986]. In contrast, the multi-domestic strategy requires considerable strategic variety as each country-based subunit is predominantly self-contained and pursues its own strategy. Thus, the strategic variety within the business unit (across locations) suggests that multiple dominant logics should accompany the multidomestic strategy.

Hypothesis 2: Emphasizing a global strategy will be positively associated with a shared managerial philosophy.

Configuration

Configuration specifies the country location(s) of each functional activity of the business [Porter 1986]. Configuration however, goes beyond a strict foreign direct investment decision. While explanations of foreign direct investment recognize MNC advantages such as the internalization of factor markets [Buckley & Casson 1976] or the exploitation of market imperfections [Hymer 1976], configuration shifts the focus to the *strategic value* of operating assets in multiple locations accessed by both location specific and competitive advantages [Kogut 1985a]. Essentially, the location of functional activities becomes a source of competitive advantage (for the firm pursuing a global strategy) developed through "superior exploitation of comparative advantages among countries" [Kogut 1985a: 15]. Such exploitation is developed by locating each functional activity in the country "which has the least cost for the factor that the activity uses most intensely" [Ghoshal 1987: 432]. For example, labor-intensive activities are located where labor is inexpensive and capital-intensive activities are located where capital is inexpensive. However, achieving the advantage cannot be simply reduced to a static "where to locate" decision since relative factor endowments are susceptible to change. Wages, materials, capital charges, foreign exchange rates, and taxation structures are subject to considerable fluctuation. The configuration of the business determines the strategic flexibility that the firm has in translating change into competitive advantage since configuration establishes the international network within which shifts, transfers, and adjustments may be made to optimize the total system.

Configuration may take a variety of patterns. The location of activities may reflect not only the international strategy but also the evolutionary expansion and distinctive competencies of the firm. Thus, the configuration of activities may range considerably for a given global strategy orientation. While it may be difficult to specify configuration at a functional level, considering the complete value chain (i.e., all functional activities) Porter [1986] suggests that configuration ranges from *dispersed* – with an entire value chain being replicated within each country – to *concentrated*, where individual activities of the value chain are disaggregated and placed in single-country locations. It is asserted that a global strategy is implemented most effectively through a concentrated configuration [Porter 1986; Yip 1989]. The efficiency of resources flows is thereby enhanced because the selected locations are able to exploit location-specific advantages through the country choice. Furthermore, the total organization is served by a minimized number of locations, thereby securing increased scale economies. For example, manufacturing may be performed in a single country location supported by an international distribution system. In contrast, the most effective configuration to implement a multidomestic strategy is a dispersed configuration. A dispersed configuration allows the entire value chain of the business to reside within each country location, thereby providing for the responsiveness of all functional activities to the local context.

Hypothesis 3: Emphasizing a global strategy will be positively associated with geographic concentration of the value chain.

Relating Administrative Mechanisms to Organizational Capabilities

Considering the task of global strategy implementation, management must utilize various administrative mechanisms to facilitate the development of the desired organizational capabilities. Since the Aston studies, two mechanisms, formalization and centralization, have been central in studying the management of resource flow exchange within complex organizations. In the international literature, socialization (i.e., normative integration) has also been proposed as being a particularly critical mechanism [Edström & Galbraith 1977; Ouchi 1980]. Support for all three administrative mechanisms may be found in both the domestic [Miller & Dröge 1986] and international [Ghoshal & Nohria 1989] literatures.

Formalization

Formalization is the degree to which organizational norms are defined explicitly [Hall 1982]. Through the use of rules and procedures, formalization prescribes allowable and nonallowable behaviors [Pfeffer 1978]. Therefore, formalization directly affects organization members by defining the nature of acceptable task performance and criteria for decisionmaking [Fredrickson 1986]. Two arguments support the relationship between formalization and a shared dominant logic or managerial philosophy. First, formalization has been found to be associated with rationality in decisionmaking and interactive decisionmaking [Miller 1987]. Rationality in decisionmaking implies the use of professional staffs – technocrats and specialists – to pursue systematic analyses [Mintzberg, Raisinghani & Theoret 1976]. This results in *many* managers being involved in interactive decisionmaking processes; such a process is more likely to yield "consensus-building" or shared values among managers [Miller 1987]. Formalization further creates consensus and shared values since it reduces role ambiguity and enhances predictability of outcomes in interdependency relationships [Aiken & Hage 1968].

Second, Ouchi's research [1977] suggests that formalization provides for organizational control through modifying behavior rather than through controlling outputs resulting from behavior. Through prescribing the bounds of behavior, formalization limits decisionmaking discretion and restricts professional autonomy, thus reducing goal incongruencies among members [Fredrickson 1986; Ouchi 1978]. This is because the enhanced specificity of organizational goals ultimately affects behavior through the behavior becoming an end in itself [Fredrickson 1986]. In fact, prescribed behavior may become so institutionalized that it dominates the managerial values of the organization with new decisions yielding only "marginal" departures from current decisions [Quinn 1980]. Thus formalization restricts the latitude of behavior within the organization as planned responses become institutionalized within managers' value system. These findings also suggest that formalization may serve to socialize managers to prescribed approaches to decisionmaking and behavior.

In the international context, formalization has been suggested as decreasing the discretion of managers in both headquarters and subsidiary locations [Bartlett & Ghoshal 1989]. Specifically, formalization reduces headquarter's direct involvement in subsidiaries by replacing central control with rules and procedures and thus organizational norms that indirectly regulate organization outcomes. By developing a dominant logic the actions of managers in different geographic locations will tend to be similar.

> Hypothesis 1: For business units competing in a global industry, formalization
> will be positively associated with a shared managerial philosophy.

Centralization

Centralization of decisionmaking authority is considered a primary means of establishing coordination within the multinational corporation (see Egelhoff [1988b] for an extensive review of this research). It has been argued previously that compared to the multidomestic strategy a global strategy leads to increased interdependencies within the business thereby requiring increased coordination among functional activities. Additional coordination results in increased bureaucratic costs therefore a net benefit will be realized only when the gains from coordination exceed the costs [Jones & Hill 1988]. McCann and Galbraith [1981: 66] note that this potential benefit is "situational and subject to considerable influence" with administrative mechanisms – such as shared appreciations and the location of decisionmaking authority – being critical determinants.

Considering the specific role of decisionmaking authority, organizational control from the "corporate center" is thought to be necessary for achieving coordination in the context of reciprocal interdependencies [Jones & Hill 1988]. When interdependencies exist among subunit activities, decisionmaking is not easily decentralized without system suboptimization. This is because with the separation of activities the organization becomes subject to "divisive tendencies" with each subunit becoming specialized in the performance of its own complex tasks, pursuing its own functional goals, and confronting different demands from the environment [Cray 1984; Pfeffer 1978]. Furthermore, individual subunits are unlikely to have the information necessary to make the ensuing trade-offs among subunits. Edström and Galbraith [1977] found that when managers were imbedded in a highly interdependent network, they were not able to make choices beneficial for the entire organization. This was due to a lack of information to assess the overall impact of their decision. Bureaucratic costs would likely exceed the benefits gained by each subunit gathering and processing the necessary information to make these trade-off decisions. Consequently, given that a global strategy requires that decisionmaking must appropriate resources among subunits and functional activities, decisionmaking must be pushed up the hierarchy where there is a more complete understanding of the various subunits or activities. Centralized decisionmaking in this context establishes "effective coordination and joint problem solving" [Govindarajan 1986: 846], "facilitates coordination among subunits, and prevents suboptimization" [Egelhoff 1988b: 131].

Hypothesis 5: For business units competing in a global industry, centralization will be positively associated with coordination of functional activities.

Integrating Mechanisms

Another important determinant of coordination are integrating mechanisms [Galbraith 1973; Galbraith & Nathanson 1978; Thompson 1967; Van de Ven, Delbecq & Koenig 1976]. Integrating mechanisms, such as task forces and committees, are used to develop collaborative efforts among organizational subunits [Galbraith 1973; Lawrence & Lorsch 1967]. These mechanisms develop within the organization coordinated "informal" structures that supplement the formal structure of the business [Galbraith & Edström 1977]. Such informal structures have been noted by numerous authors as being critical to managing the international firm [Bartlett 1983; Egelhoff 1984; Franko 1974; Prahalad & Doz 1987].

Integrating mechanisms affect coordination through either impersonal procedures of prescribed action or by mutual adjustments through personal interaction. Focusing on personal interactions, Galbraith [1973] suggests a hierarchy of integrating mechanisms: direct contact between managers, liaison roles between departments, temporary task forces or permanent teams, and integrating roles; the mechanisms are ordered based on being increasingly complicated and expensive. The choice of the "appropriate" integrating mechanisms for an organization depends largely on its information processing needs [Galbraith 1973]. As task interdependency increases, the organization must develop additional capacity to process information to support decisionmaking. This is necessary because as task interdependency increases, the mutual adjustments that must be made between subunits or activities increases the volume and frequency of communication and decisionmaking that occurs between units [Victor & Blackburn 1987]. The information to support mutual adjustments is not easily embedded in impersonal rules or procedures given task complexity and uncertainty, particularly in the cross-national context. However, the personal and more complex forms of integrating mechanisms – such as interdepartmental transfers – result in increased communication among managers, increased use of informal communication patterns and reciprocal relations, all of which contribute to the managers' ability to gather and process information [Galbraith 1973]. This view is supported by Van de Ven, Delbecq and Koenig [1976] who found that in situations of high task interdependence personal integrating mechanisms resulted in increased coordination. Therefore, given the interdependency arising from a global strategy, integrating mechanisms may be used to develop coordination within the business unit.

Hypothesis 6: For business units competing in a global industry, the use of integrating mechanisms will be positively associated with coordination of functional activities.

Integrating mechanisms are also instrumental in creating a single managerial philosophy within the organization. As discussed previously, the specific content of the managerial philosophy is established by top management The process by which the managerial philosophy is communicated and becomes accepted by managers occurs primarily through the use of integrating mechanisms. For example, movement of personnel gives rise to the transmission of information to other organization members "for just as members of a society are carriers of the culture which they transmit consciously and unconsciously to the next generation, so members of an organization are carriers of its subculture..." [Baty, Evan & Rothermel 1971: 430].

Through the use of personal integrating mechanisms, shared values and domain consensus may be developed [Ghoshal & Nohria 1987; Van Maanen & Schein 1979]. McCann and Galbraith [1981] argue that these shared appreciations determine the extent to which interdependencies within the firm are beneficial or dysfunctional. Consequently, it is presumed that the role of integrating mechanisms in implementing global strategy is quite important. It can be expected that integrating mechanisms lead to the development of a shared managerial philosophy for two reasons. First, a highly selective process regarding the choice of managers involved in integrating roles is thought to occur. Typically, managers in integrative roles are influential and highly competent [Lawrence & Lorsch 1967]. They are likely to be selected, in part, due to their commitment to and understanding of the organization. Thus, these managers have internalized organizational values to the extent that they have become "trusted" managers. Within the MNC this selection process may be further reinforced as managers are placed repeatedly in international integrative roles. Attachments to other value systems diminishes as the only constant social system for the manager is the organization [Kaufman 1960]. Furthermore, managers may be making considerable personal sacrifices in taking international transfers. Galbraith and Edström suggest that such sacrifices produce increased commitment to the organization. Consequently "not only are socialized individuals selected, but the process of transfer itself is hypothesized to produce socialization effects which reinforce the selected attitudes" [1977: 257]. Integrating managers therefore ascribe to the management philosophy and become a mechanism for transmitting that philosophy to other organizational units through their integrating role and their visibility within the organization.

Second, integrating mechanisms induce interactions among managers. Task forces, committees, teams, and integrating departments provide a forum for managerial interaction. Such interactions provide the opportunity for managers to generate, scrutinize, and reconcile divergent perspectives and to build consensus [Miller 1987; Miller, Dröge & Toulouse 1988]. In fact, social involvement with colleagues is considered to be an important component in developing a shared commitment to the organization [Sheldon 1971]. Thus, it is hypothesized that the use of integrating mechanisms plays an important role in the development of shared values and norms within the organization.

> Hypothesis 7: For business units competing in a global industry, the use of integrating mechanisms will be positively associated with a shared managerial philosophy.

Contingency Hypothesis

The specification of the framework to this point consists of a set of hypotheses suggesting simple relationships among variables in the framework. This "congruence approach" was used initially to establish the framework, given the lack of prior research linking the design variables in the framework to the international strategy of a business. A congruence perspective is limited, however, in that it is essentially a reductionistic perspective that fails to capture adequately the normative implication of the total system of variables in a model [Venkatraman & Prescott 1990]. Theorists increasingly assert that it is the "coalignment" or simultaneous fit between strategy and its context that has a significant impact on organizational performance [Fry & Smith 1987; Galbraith & Nathanson 1978; Venkatraman & Prescott 1990]. A "systems approach" is viewed as being superior to other approaches as it takes into account the contingencies among multiple interrelated dimensions in organizational design [Drazin & Van de Ven 1985]. From the systems perspective, the real test of the framework is in examining the "simultaneous and holistic pattern of interlinkages" between international strategy, operational capabilities, and administrative mechanisms and their collective affect on organizational performance [Venkatraman & Prescott 1990: 5].

The first seven hypotheses forwarded relationships among global strategy, organizational capabilities, and administrative mechanisms. Given the theoretical arguments supporting these hypotheses, it follows that if business units pursuing a global strategy are properly matched to their organizational capabilities and administrative mechanisms they will sustain higher levels of performance than business units that are "mismatched." Similarly, if business units pursuing a multidomestic strategy are properly matched to their required organizational capabilities and administrative mechanisms they too should outperform business units that are mismatched. Table 1 summarizes the fit hypothesis tested in this study.

> Hypothesis 8: A fit between global strategy, organizational capabilities, and administrative mechanisms will be positively associated with business unit performance.

Table I
Ideal Profiles of Implementation Variables for the
Global and Multidomestic Strategy Types[a]

Implementation Variable	Global Strategy	Multidomestic Strategy
Coordination	High	Moderate-low
Managerial philosophy	Shared	Diverse/county specific
Configuration	Concentrated	Dispersed
Formalization	High	Moderate-low
Centralization	High	Low
Integrating mechanisms	High	Low

[a]It should be noted that the specification of the three administrative mechanisms is based on the prescribed state of the operational capabilities.

Research Method and Data

Sample and Data Collection

Data were collected from the President or CEO of business units competing in global industries. Porter has suggested that, "intra-industry trade is a good sign of the presence of global competition, and its growth is one indication that the incidence of global industries has increased" [1986: 29]. Studies by Cvar [1984] and Prescott [1983] are consistent with Porter's contention, as a very high level of exports and imports were found in their research to be a key discriminating variable in classifying industries as "global" or "highly international." Thus, consistent with Cvar and exceeding Prescott's criterion, a necessary condition for an industry to be considered global was a minimum 50% trade level (trade as a percentage of total consumption]. Examining trade flow levels obtained through both industry sources and the United States International Trade Commission, *Summary of Trade and Tariff Information*, USITC Publications, 225 manufacturing industries (at the 4-digit SIC code level) were examined. Twelve industries met or exceeded the trade level criterion.[1]

To evaluate the validity of the identified industries a review of the international management literature indicated that each industry had been identified previously as being a "global" industry [Cvar 1984; Hout, Porter & Rudden 1982; Porter 1980; 1986; Prahalad & Doz 1987]. Furthermore, as a final validation of the industry selection and consistent with researchers' suggestions that a competitor in the industry must be competing globally for the industry to actually become global [Hout, et al. 1982; Hamel & Prahalad 1985; Porter 1986], the existence of industry participants competing globally was verified. A review of secondary data sources including industry reports, published case studies, and annual reports, confirmed the existence of at least one global competitor in each industry. While it is not asserted that this three-stage procedure resulted in the identification of an exhaustive set of global industries, we were generally confident that the industries identified were indeed global in nature.

A mail survey was the primary means of data collection. The questionnaire was developed through a four-stage process. The process involved: (1) conducting field interviews with general managers of business units competing in global industries, (2) reviewing research to identify existing measures for the constructs being examined, (3) pretesting an initial questionnaire with six academicians in order to assess content validity, and (4) pretesting the questionnaire with six executives to assess clarity and comprehensiveness. The instrument was then administered to seventeen executives from six businesses to establish consensus among multiple respondents. This helped insure that the responses represented business unit-level data and not the idiosyncratic perspectives of one individual. A convenience sample was used with three businesses representing each of the basic strategy types of the study. The responses within each business unit were found to be consistent for each construct in the study, based on the coefficient of concordance (Kendall's *tau*) of the responses. It is recognized however, that the limited number of respondents suggests that this is a very tentative assessment of inter-rater reliability.

The data collection procedure consisted of two phases. In the first phase, participation was solicited from 322 business units competing in the selected industries, as listed in Dun and Bradstreet's *America's Corporate Families* and *The Directory of Corporate Affiliations*. The first questionnaire requested industry, goal structure, international strategy, and performance information. The initial mailout and two follow-up mailouts to nonrespondents resulted in general managers of 147 business units responding. Five months later, a second questionnaire requesting information on each business unit's administrative mechanisms and organizational capabilities was sent to these 147 respondents. Gathering information at different points in time was designed to reduce some of the problem of common methods variance in that the organization design responses would be less influenced by the strategy and performance responses. This mailout (sent with summary results of the first survey) was again followed by two additional mailouts to nonrespondents resulting in 82 business units responding to the second questionnaire. To assess non-response bias an analysis of thirty randomly selected nonresponding business units indicated that nonrespondents did not differ significantly from the respondents, with respect to total sales and number of employees. Furthermore, the average sales, average return of sales, and average growth rate for the responding businesses did not differ significantly from their respective industry norms. Thus, given the response rate and the followup analysis, the responding businesses appeared to be representative of their industries.

Measures

The Appendix outlines the measurement scales and response format for each variable. Table 2 provides the summary statistics and correlation coefficients for the variables.

Table 2
Response Structure of Variables

Variable	Mean	S.D.	1	2	3	4	5	6	7	8	9	10
			Zero-Order Correlation Coefficient[a]									
1 International strategy	3.23	0.87										
2 Coordination	5.39	1.12	.22*									
3 Managerial philosophy	5.02	0.60	.21*	.13								
4 Configuration	7.70	4.37	.11	.03	.12							
5 Formalization	33.47	6.73	.04	.41***	.38***	.42***						
6 Centralization	17.86	2.90	.08	.01	.05	.10	.08					
7 Integrating mechanisms	3.87	1.16	.13	.33**	.58***	.29*	.44***	.09				
8 ROI (objective)	4.35	1.89	−.19	.05	−.05	.02	.01	−.01	−.19			
9 Sales growth (objective)	5.00	1.71	.03	−.03	.07	.08	.08	.03	.09	.34**		
10 ROI (relative)	3.78	1.21	.03	.19	−.12	.07	.07	.17	.02	.60***	.09	
11 Sales growth (relative)	3.40	1.26	.09	.16	.16	.23*	.23*	.15	.38**	.13	.40***	.47***

[a]$N=82$
  *$p<.05$
 **$p<.01$
***$p<.001$

International Strategy

No standard instrument was available for measuring international strategy. As discussed in the theory section, global and multidomestic strategy may be distinguished by whether the business unit competes in industry segments characterized by global competitive forces or in industry segments isolated from such forces [Porter 1985]. Thus, an instrument was developed which was designed to capture the strategy of the business unit from the business's structural position within the industry [Porter 1980]. This measurement approach was selected for two reasons. First, global strategy has become a popularized notion and has often been cited as a necessary strategy for businesses to compete internationally. The pretest indicated that if questions regarding the importance of a global strategy were asked directly, a response bias may exist from the perceived social desirability of a global strategy. Second, the measure was consistent with the requirement in this study of distinguishing between the two basic strategic positions rather than attempting to identify the specific content or patterns of emphasis within a particular strategy type.

The construct validity and reliability of this measure was assessed in three ways. First, the internal reliability (Cronbach's coefficient *alpha*) was examined and found acceptable ($\alpha=0.73$). Second, fifteen business units were randomly selected and a content analysis of annual reports, popular press, and industry reports was conducted. Two researchers then independently classified the businesses as pursuing either a multidomestic or global strategy. Agreement was found for the classification of all but one of the businesses for which secondary information was available (13 of 15). Furthermore, the researchers' classifications (12 of the 15) were also consistent with the strategic classification based on the survey instrument. Third, in a separate section of the instrument, a self-typing measure of global and multidomestic strategies was provided. A description of the two strategies was provided and each executive was asked to select the description that best characterized their business. Values for the descriptive classification were correlated significantly with values for the global strategy measure ($r=.30$, $p<.007$).

Coordination

The measure of coordination was designed to operationalize the specific form of coordination considered critical for a global strategy. This form of coordination focuses on the extent to which similar functional activities are coordinated within the entire business unit [Porter 1985]. Fourteen items that comprise Porter's value chain were used. An index of coordination was developed by summing the extent to which each activity was reported as being coordinated and then dividing by the total number of items. A score of 7 would indicate that all the activities of the business were highly coordinated within the business unit, whereas a score of 1 would indicate that none of the activities of the business were coordinated. The reliability estimate for the coordination measure was 0.85.

Managerial Philosophy

Executives were asked to indicate the extent to which managers in their business unit have a shared or common philosophy on how to run their business. Four dimensions of managerial philosophy were assessed using an instrument derived from Weber [1988]. The dimensions – innovation/risk-taking, managerial interdependence, power interrelationships, and personal motivation – were chosen based on empirical research on top management decisionmaking [Donaldson & Lorsch 1983; Dutton & Duncan 1987; Gordon & Cummins 1979]. Previous research has established the construct validity and reliability of an earlier version of this measure [Weber 1988]. Our own assessment indicated that the reliability was acceptable ($\alpha=0.79$). The inter-rater reliability was also assessed by administering the measure to seven executives within a single business unit. The inter-rater reliability was found acceptable, based on the coefficient of concordance (Kendall's *tau*) of the responses among the seven executives.

Configuration

The fourteen functional activities used in operationalizing coordination were also used for the configuration measure. For each of the fourteen activities, the CEO was asked to indicate whether the activity was performed in a single location for their entire business unit (scored 0) or in multiple international locations (scored 1). A configuration index was calculated for each business by summing the responses across all functional activities. A score of 14 indicates that the activities of the business are dispersed geographically whereas a score of zero indicates that the activities are concentrated.

Formalization

Formalization was measured using the control scale of Miller and Dröge [1986: 560] and Khandwalla [1974]. The internal reliability of the measure (0.71) was comparable to the reliability reported by Miller, Dröge and Toulouse [1988]. To assess construct validity, formalization was also measured using the Aston [Inkson, Pugh & Hickson 1970] scale. As expected, the values from the two scales were correlated positively ($r = 0.40$, $p < .001$).

Centralization

Centralization was measured with the Aston scale [Inkson, Pugh & Hickson 1970]. Previous research has reported the validity of this scale [Inkson et al. 1970; Pugh et al. 1968, 1969]. In this study, the reliability (0.82) was consistent with that reported by Miller, Dröge and Toulouse [1988].

Integrating Mechanisms

The use of integrating mechanisms was measured with Miller and Dröge's structural liaison scale. This scale was modified, however, to incorporate a more comprehensive set of integrating mechanisms, as found in Galbraith [1973], and to measure the use of each mechanism specifically in the international context. Particular attention was given to this section of the questionnaire during the pretest, in an attempt to verify the comprehensiveness and interpretation of the integrating mechanisms listed. The internal reliability of this scale was 0.91.

Performance

Two indicators of performance – return on investment and sales growth – were assessed with *self-reported* objective and subjective measurement scales. Our pretest indicated that executives would be hesitant to provide exact levels of objective performance. Consequently, for the objective measures, executives were asked to provide their ROI and sales growth figures within a set of pre-specified ranges. The relative performance measures were adapted from an instrument developed by Dess and Davis [1984].

The performance measures were self-reported because secondary data are not consistently available at the business unit level. Although there is evidence supporting the general reliability of self-reported performance measures (see, for example, Dess and Robinson [1984]; Venkatraman and Ramanujam [1987]), a potential reporting bias does exist. To assess this potential bias, a review was conducted in an attempt to obtain performance data for each business unit through secondary data sources. Sources included Standard and Poor's *Industry Survey, Corporate and Industry Research Reports*, corporate annual reports, and various popular press articles. Performance data (sales growth and return on investment) was found for twenty-six business units (32% of the respondents). The secondary data was then compared to the self-reported objective sales growth and return on investment ranges. Agreement between the secondary and self-reported data was found for 92% of the business units (24 of 26).

Furthermore, the correlation between the two sales growth measures was significant ($r=0.77, p<.001$) as was the correlation between the two profitability measures ($r=0.64, p<.001$). It should be noted that the twenty-six observations were all large business units of public corporations. Consequently, although the analysis suggests that the self-reported data is reliable, such a conclusion may not be generalizable to small or privately held business units.

Additional Variables

Research suggests that centralization and formalization are related to the size of an organization [Child 1973; Miller & Dröge 1986; Pugh, et al. 1969]. Organizational growth necessitates increased decentralization and formalization as the number of decision areas a manager may confront is limited [Gates & Egelhoff 1986]. This is due to the difficulty of controlling geographically dispersed subunits [Garnier 1982]. Support for this proposition has been mixed in research examining the relationship in the international context. While Garnier's research supports the relationship, Egelhoff [1988b] found mixed support with only centralization of marketing being negatively associated with size. Despite the ambiguity surrounding the relationship, it was considered important to control for the potential confounding influence of size, operationalized by the logarithm of the total number of employees of the business unit.

It was also considered important to control for internationalization of the business unit. There is some evidence to suggest that as the size of the foreign activities of a business increases, the opportunities for increased resource flows and coordination also increase [Egelhoff 1988b: 76]. Thus internationalization, operationalized by the percentage of international sales to total sales, was controlled when examining the hypothesized relationships.

Industry Effects

Studies indicate that the industry type has a significant impact on many organizational dimensions [Dess, Ireland & Hitt 1990]. In this study it could be expected that industry may influence the variables in the framework, particularly coordination, configuration, and performance. It was therefore important to examine the impact of industry type prior to aggregating the data for subsequent hypothesis testing. Classifying industry by four-digit SIC codes none of the variables in the study were found to vary significantly ($p<.05$) among the industries sampled. One variable, the relative return of investment measure, was found to vary at the $p<.10$ level, but no differences between individual industries were found (Duncan's multiple range test).

Analysis

Two sets of analyses were performed to test the international strategy implementation framework. Relationships between individual variables comprising the framework (H1 through H7) were evaluated with multiple regression analysis.

The second set of analyses tested the contingency hypothesis (H8) considering the normative implication of the collective set of design variables. This hypothesis was tested using the systems approach advocated by Drazin and Van de Ven [1985], who found that this method was the most appropriate analytical procedure for contingency theories that involved design patterns. The systems approach is considered a direct test of contingency hypotheses as it incorporates deviations from an "ideal" profile for a multivariate specification of fit. Thus the dependent affect of the conditional associations among the independent variables is assessed. The approach assumes that different design patterns are feasible with alternate designs equally effective if they are internally consistent and matched to the contingencies confronting the business [Venkatraman & Prescott 1990]. For this study, the relationship among the independent variables is depicted in Figure 1. The posited alternate design patterns among the variables comprising the contingency hypothesis (H8) are summarized in Table 1. The systems approach provides for examining the performance impacts of co-alignment to these ideal designs.

The systems approach involved four steps. First, scores of the six implementation variables were standardized in order to establish a uniform scale. Second, the ideal profiles of the global and multidomestic strategy types were generated. The top five performers of each strategy type were identified based on overall performance. The means for each implementation variable were then computed for each strategy type to create an empirically derived pattern of design that may be considered ideal.[2] The resulting scores were compared using ANOVA to verify that statistically different patterns had been identified. The third step involved calculating a fit score by measuring the euclidean distance between each business unit's scores and the ideal profile scores. The resulting composite measure, therefore, represents the extent to which the business unit deviates from the ideal design profile. In the final step, the relationship between the fit measure and business unit performance was assessed. A negative and significant correlation between the fit score and performance supports the design hypothesis that the greater the distance from the ideal profile the lower the performance. To avoid the upward bias that would occur through using the same set of observations on which the profile was derived to also test the hypothesis, the high performers (used to develop the profile) were excluded from this step of the analysis.[3]

Results

Hypotheses 1 through 7

Regression analysis was used to examine Hypotheses 1 through 7. Hypotheses 1, 5 and 6 suggest that coordination is a function of pursuing a global strategy, centralization, and use of integrating mechanisms. The estimated equation, after controlling for the internationalization and size of the business unit, is the first equation reported in Table 3. As the first equation indicates coordination was found to be related positively to pursuing a global strategy and using integrating mechanisms while not related to the centralization of decisionmaking authority. Thus, H1 and H6 were supported while H5 was not.

Table 3
Results of Multiple Regression Analysis

Independent Variables	Dependent Variables[a]		
	Coordination	Managerial Philosophy	Configuration
International strategy	0.377*	0.154[†]	0.413
	(.176)	(.090)	(.638)
Centralization	−0.046		
	(.054)		
Integrating mechanisms	−0.307*	0.250***	
	(.128)	(.079)	
Formalization		0.015	
		(.015)	
Size	0.214	−.003	0.110
	(.137)	(.073)	(.363)
Internationalization	0.003	−.037	0.815*
	(.093)	(.033)	(.363)
Constant	2.347	3.108	2.689
R^2	0.33	0.37	0.24
Adjusted R^2	0.26	0.31	0.20
F	4.62**	6.93***	5.79***

[a]$N=82$
[†]$p<.10$
*$p<.05$
**$p<.01$
***$p<.001$

Hypotheses 2, 4 and 7 posited that a shared managerial philosophy is a function of pursuing a global strategy, formalization, and use of integrating mechanisms. The second estimated equation in Table 3 provides the basis for evaluating these hypotheses. A shared managerial philosophy was found to be positively related to pursuing a global strategy and the use of integrating mechanisms. Thus support was found for H2 and H6.[4] Hypothesis 4 was not supported as formalization was not significantly related to a shared managerial philosophy. The final congruence hypothesis, H3, was not supported as the data in the third equation in Table 3 indicates that the geographic configuration of a business unit did not depend on the international strategy choice.

Aggregate Hypothesis

The results of the systems approach used to test the contingency hypothesis are reported in Table 4 and Table 5. The ideal profile for each international strategy type is presented in Table 4. Each design dimension was tested using ANOVA, and as indicated in Table 4, four of the six implementation variables showed significant differences at the 0.10 level. With the exception of configuration, all differences were in the predicted direction.

Table 4
Profile of Implementation Variables for Global and Multidomestic Strategy Types[a]

Implementation Variable	Global Strategy	Multidomestic Strategy	F
Coordination	0.34	−0.27	0.82
Managerial philosophy	0.31	−0.25	0.64
Configuration	0.68	−0.54	4.93[t]
Formalization	0.65	−0.53	4.25[t]
Centralization	0.62	−0.49	3.68[t]
Integrating mechanisms	0.54	−0.72	4.19[t]

[a]Profiles are standardized values
[t]$p<.10$

Table 5
Correlation of Fit Measures with Business Unit Performance

	Objective Performance		Relative Performance		
International Strategy	ROI	Sales Growth	ROI	Sales Growth	N
All units[a]	−0.202	0.263*	−0.300*	0.290[t]	73
Subgroups[b]					
Global	−0.143	−0.464**	−0.316*	−0.334[t]	32
Multidomestic	−0.156	−0.472*	−0.412[t]	−0.367	31

[a]Excludes 9 business units with missing performance data
[b]Excludes the 10 business units used to define the ideal profiles
[t]$p<.10$
*$p<.05$
**$p<.01$

Table 5 details the correlations between the fit index and business unit performance. A negative correlation indicates that business unit performance declines as the distance of the business unit from its ideal profile increases. For global strategy the relationship between fit and performance was significant for objective sales growth ($r=-0.464$, $p<.01$), relative return on investment ($r=-0.361$, $p<.05$), and relative sales growth ($r=-.334$, $p<.10$). For multidomestic strategy, the relationship between fit and performance was significant for objective sales growth ($r=-0.472$, $p<.01$) and relative return on investment ($r=-0.412$, $p<.10$). Thus the results generally support H8, though the support is stronger for business units pursuing a global strategy than for business units pursuing a multidomestic strategy. The results did not find support for the relationship between fit and the objective return on investment measure. The importance of the design fit was further substantiated by additional regression analysis. Regressing business unit performance on international strategy, design variables, and the fit measure, the regression model ($R^2=0.41$, $p<.06$) and the fit coefficient ($t=3.11$, $p<.004$) were significant.

Discussion

While the exploratory nature of the study warrants conclusions of a tentative nature, the findings suggest several organizational design considerations. For the congruence hypotheses the findings may be summarized as follows:

(1) pursuing a global strategy was related to increased coordination and a shared managerial philosophy within the business unit, (2) increased coordination and a shared managerial philosophy were related to the use of integrating mechanism within the business unit, (3) centralization was not found to be related to coordination, and formalization was not found to be related to managerial philosophy, and (4) configuration was not related to the international strategy of the business unit.

The results of the systems approach generally supported the international strategy implementation framework. When there was a proper alignment between the international strategy, organizational capabilities, and administrative mechanisms, superior performance occurred. This systems fit was stronger for the global strategy business units than for the multidomestic units.

There were two major departures from the theoretical predictions of the implementation framework that warrant attention. The first departure concerns the normative implication of the system design. Although support was found for the importance of organizational alignment along three performance measures, the fit or misfit of the organization was not found to be associated with the objective return of investment measure. This result may have been due to measurement error. Although we were generally confident in the ROI measure, testing the framework with secondary rather than self-reported objective data may have yielded more powerful results. A second explanation regarding this result is that if the decision to pursue a global strategy was relatively recent, the organization may be in a period of transition and therefore not yet capturing the return on its international commitments. While sales growth and relative performance may be affected in the short term, the business unit's return on investment may not be realized until years in the future.

It should also be noted that the multidomestic units did not have as strong a relationship between their design and performance. Multidomestic strategies have often been characterized as pursuing "political" strategies in that market interventions are often necessary to develop an industry position protected from global competitive forces. The multidomestic units may therefore, be modifying or reconstructing their context through political or symbolic processes thereby not requiring the redesign of their organizational capabilities and administrative mechanisms.

The second departure concerns our initial theoretical position that a global strategy is associated with a concentrated configuration, whereas a multidomestic strategy is associated with a dispersed configuration. The regression results found no relationship between international strategy and configuration and the empirically derived profiles indicated the exact opposite design. This finding was particularly interesting given the often cited importance of a concentrated configuration in the global strategy literature [Porter 1986; Yip 1989]. Three interpretations may partially explain this result. First, the historical expansion of multinational corporations has generally followed a multidomestic approach in that "mini replicas" (i.e., complete value chains) of the parent have been located abroad. The decision to pursue a global strategy is likely a recent decision as the awareness of needing to compete on a global basis has not been long-standing. Thus the configuration of the business may predate the decision to compete with a global strategy. The business would therefore be constrained by implementing a global strategy in the context of an existing configuration or it may be in the process of moving to a concentrated configuration. This interpretation is partially supported by the configuration results which were found to depend on the internationalization of the business unit (Table 3).

The second explanation relates to the specificity of the configuration measure. Consistent with Porter's definition, the configuration measure considered the composite of the functional activities of the business unit. Even when the measure was disaggregated no significant differences in the configuration of individual functional activities between the global and multidomestic units were found. However, Porter's categorization of functional activities may fail to fully capture the complexities of configuration. For example, manufacturing operations may be decomposed into numerous subprocesses (e.g., component development, assembly) each of which may be performed in different locations. Therefore, it may be that it is these *subprocesses* that are concentrated rather than the more broadly defined functional activities used in this study. A final explanation concerns Porter's conceptualization of the configuration. Bartlett and Ghoshal [1989] and Kogut [1985b] suggest that a key advantage of a global strategy is in developing operational flexibility. This flexibility permits the business to exploit the uncertainty in future changes (i.e., factor costs, competitive moves, or government policy) through shifting activities among its many locations, which is only achieved by decreasing the dependence of the organization on single sourcing locations. Therefore, in contrast to Porter's concentrated configuration, the results are more consistent with the "transnational solution" suggesting that the creation of a global "network" and strategic flexibility are necessary for implementing a global strategy.

However, it may also be that other organizational capabilities are better able to distinguish between the implementation of the two strategies. The results provide strong support for the importance of increased coordination. This may imply that implementing a global strategy may be based fundamentally on the exploitation of interdependencies through coordination irrespective of the particular configuration. That is, to implement a global strategy it may be acceptable to continue to have complete value chains located in multiple countries so long as these subunits are tightly integrated. Recalling that a global strategy is comprised of exploiting location-specific advantage and competitive advantage, location-specific advantage is exploited through the country location of functional activities while competitive advantage is based predominantly on integrating competitive positions among multiple national markets. Consequently, this result – the importance of coordination to a global strategy – has important theoretical implications in that it suggests that a global strategy may be based more on competitive advantages (coordination) as compared to location-specific advantages (configuration decisions), a finding inconsistent with many discussions of global strategy. This result warrants further investigation for additional validation and to more fully understand the competitive basis of a global strategy. But it does suggest that it may be more beneficial to focus on operational linkages rather than operational sites when considering implementing a global strategy.

A final implication of the international strategy framework concerns the role of managerial philosophy and integrating mechanisms. While important to the overall organizational design, centralization and formalization did not contribute directly to either coordination or the shared managerial philosophy of the organization. In contrast, the use of integrating mechanisms was associated with developing both organizational capabilities. These results extend the role of personal control structures or managerial socialization, as advocated by Franko [1974, 1976] and Edström and Galbraith [1977], to global strategy implementation. A need apparently exists to refocus on the people and people movements as the determinants of organizational capabilities, and in particular, developing the coordination and shared managerial philosophy to facilitate pursuing a global strategy. Consistent with the transnational solution [Bartlett & Ghoshal 1989], rather than looking to reorganizations or formal administrative mechanisms, the capability to compete globally is determined through creating a shared philosophy and cooperation among managers and this is achieved through the use of integrative mechanisms such as international transfers and international committees. Thus, pursuing a global strategy is not simply a redistribution of the operations of the organization. Rather, it entails a major investment and commitment on the part of the organization as complex and expensive forms of administrative mechanisms are required.

Several methodological limitations of this study provide areas for future research. First, the present study relied on self-report measures. Although effort was made to ensure the reliability and validity of the measures, future investigations using institutional data could provide more powerful results. Second, the responses were provided by a single respondent. Validity assessments were made to evaluate the appropriateness of this approach however, the possibility of common methods variance remains. Furthermore, gathering information from multiple locations within the business would reduce the reliance on the awareness of a single individual for constructs that reflect characteristics of the entire business unit. Third, the framework was examined in a single country context. Even though the sample included business units from different nationalities, all business units were based in the U.S. thereby limiting the generalizability of the results. Fourth, although the theory supporting the implementation framework suggested clear causal directions, the cross-sectional nature of the data precluded tests for causality. A causal design would allow research to more clearly understand the implementation of a global strategy given the operational capabilities of the business as well as providing additional insights as to why misfits occur or under what conditions misfits are likely to result.

Other areas for future research may be suggested. The results provided evidence that different organizational designs are required to implement alternate international strategies. The strategy classification used, however, did not incorporate the specific content of alternate strategies nor did it allow for alternate patterns of competitive response within each strategy type. Future research is needed to further refine the content of international strategies and how the implementation task must be tailored for each type. Second, as discussed previously, configuration was measured at a single point in time. However, a evolutionary process is likely occurring as firms move towards a global strategy. This study suggests some administrative mechanisms and organizational capabilities that are important to use in this evolutionary process. However, the specific nature of the process, i.e., how a business manages the transitional state as it becomes a global competitor was not examined. There may be transitional organizational designs and strategies as businesses begin pursuing a global strategy. What are the interim global states and what is the final form remains an open research question. Third, there are many other administrative systems and practices that may support the international strategy of the business. Human resource practices, training and development, employee selection processes, compensation systems, are but a few of the administrative characteristics of the business that are likely modified and tailored to support the international strategy choice. Finally, our study focused on the coordination of like activities within the entire business unit. However, other forms of coordination such as coordination across activities should be incorporated into future research. The unit of analysis of coordination should also be expanded to include a more refined view of coordination. This would include coordination within the business unit at a subprocess level as well as coordination among multiple business units within the corporation or other interorganizational relationships and alliances. Research in these areas could provide a more holistic and complete understanding of the complex task of implementing an international strategy.

Appendix

Global Strategy

Executives were provided five variables designed to determine the strategic position of their business. Executives were asked to indicate, on a 5-point scale ranging from "not at all characteristic" to "extremely characteristic," the extent that worldwide standardization of customer needs, worldwide product awareness, worldwide standardization of product technology, competitors existing in all key markets, and competitors marketing standardized products worldwide characterized the industry segment in which their business unit competes. To develop an overall indicator of global strategy, the responses on the five items were summed and the mean calculated to develop an index measure of the business unit's international strategy, with higher values indicating a strategy stronger on global and lower values indicating a strategy stronger on multidomestic. Using descriptions of global and multidomestic strategies offered by Porter [1985] and Prahalad and Doz [1987], each respondent was also asked to select the description that best characterized their business unit strategy: (1) a relatively slow rate of technological change, a high level of responsiveness on a country-by-country basis and products customized to meet local tastes and preferences; (2) a high rate of technological change, exploiting global scale economies, and responsiveness to international standardized product demand.

(Appendix continued)

(Appendix continued)

Coordination

This construct was operationalized based on Porter's [1985] value chain of the activities comprising a business unit. Executives were instructed to "indicate the extent to which coordination has been achieved among similar functional activities within their business unit." The coordination of each functional activity was rated using a 7-point scale ranging from "not currently coordinated at all" to "currently coordinated to a great extent." An index of the total extent of coordination within the business unit was calculated by summing the responses across all activities for each business. The functional activities listed were: manufacturing operations, raw materials and parts procurement, product research and development, process research and development, accounting/legal activities, government and public relations, human resource management, product distribution, customer service, product promotion and advertising, information systems and data processing, sales activities, cash flow management, and raising and managing capital.

Managerial Philosophy

Business unit managers were asked to indicate, on a 7-point scale ranging from "little agreement exists regarding this belief" to "managers share this belief to a very high degree," the extent that beliefs are shared by all managers within their business unit. Eighteen items assessing beliefs of managers were evaluated. Examples of each of the four dimensions are as follows:

1. Innovation/risk-taking
   - Managers should take chances on good ideas.
   - Managers should be innovative rather than conservative in decision-making.
2. Managerial interdependence
   - Managers should maintain/develop relationships with managers of other departments.
   - Various subunit managers should make efforts to understand each other's problems.
3. Power interrelationships
   - Top management should provide support and warmth to those managers below them.
   - Those in power should try to look as powerful as possible.
4. Personal motivation
   - There should be continuous pressure to improve personal and group performance.
   - The emphasis is on individual initiative and achievement.

Configuration

The identical list of functional activities used to operationalize coordination were repeated for the configuration measure. Respondents were instructed to "indicate the extent that the activity is performed at a given [country] location for the entire

(Appendix continued)

(Appendix continued)

business unit." Response categories were that the functional activity was "located in only one domestic or international location" (scored 0) or "located in multiple international locations" (scored 1). Responses across the functional activities were summed to provide an overall index. Thus low scores would indicate a geographically concentrated configuration and high scores would indicate geographic dispersion.

Formalization

Executives were asked to rate the extent to which a set of control devices were used to assess the performance of their business unit. The control devices were: (1) cost centers, (2) comprehensive management information systems, (3) profit centers, (4) quality control procedures, (5) standard cost measures, and (6) formal performance appraisals. A 7-point scale was used where "1" indicated that the device was used rarely or for a small part of the operations and "7" indicated that the device was used frequently or throughout the business. An index of formalization was calculated by summing the responses across the six categories.

Centralization

The centralization measure was based on the Aston scales. Executives were provided a list of ten decision areas: (1) number of production employees required, (2) production employee hiring, (3) internal labor disputes, (4) overtime to be worked at shop level, (5) delivery dates and priority of orders, (6) production scheduling, (7) dismissal of a production employee, (8) methods of personnel selection, (9) machinery or equipment selection, and (10) allocation of work among production employees. Managers were then asked to indicate the level in the business unit that had the authority to make each decision. The decision levels were (1) top-level managers or divisional/subsidiary managers, (2) middle-level managers, and (3) lower-level supervisors.

Integrating Mechanisms

An initial set of integrating mechanisms was developed from Miller and Dröge [1986], Lawrence and Lorsch [1967], and Galbraith [1973]. The set was then modified to address the use of each mechanism to the international context. Executives were asked to rate, on a 7-point scale ranging from "used rarely" to "used very often," the extent to which each integrative mechanism was currently being used to facilitate coordination of the functional activities of the business. The integrative mechanisms listed were: (1) coordination of decisions via a master plan, (2) personal contact between managers at the same domestic location, (3) personal contact between managers from different domestic locations, (4) personal contact between managers from different international locations, (5) interdepartmental transfers of managers at the same domestic location, (6) transfers of managers between different domestic geographic locations, (7) transfers of managers between different international locations, (8) interdepartmental committees that are set up to allow domestic managers to

(Appendix continued)

(Appendix continued)

engage in joint decisionmaking, (9) interdepartmental committees that are set up to allow domestic and international managers to engage in joint decision-making, (10) task forces that are temporary bodies set up to facilitate interdepartmental collaboration on a specific project, (11) liaison personnel whose specific job it is to coordinate the efforts of domestic functional areas, and (12) liaison personnel whose specific job it is to coordinate the efforts of international functional areas. An index was then developed based on the average level of integrating mechanisms used by the business unit.

Performance

Both subjective and objective measures were used to enhance the validity of the performance measures. The pretest indicated that executives would be hesitant to provide objective performance information. Consequently, they were asked to rate their business's average performance during the past three years using a 7-point range:

After-tax return on total investment was (circle number):

7 greater than 25%
6 between 20% and 25%
5 between 15% and 20%
4 between 10% and 15%
3 between 5% and 10%
2 between 0% and 5%
1 negative net return on investment

Annual increase in total sales was (circle number):

7 greater than 25%
6 between 20% and 25%
5 between 15% and 20%
4 between 10% and 15%
3 between 5% and 10%
2 between 0% and 5%
1 negative net drop in sales

The subjective return on investment and sales growth performance was measured using a 5-point scale adapted from Dess and Davis [1984]. Executives were asked to indicate their business's performance over the last three years compared to other businesses in the industry, where 1 = "lowest 20%," 2 = "lower 20%," 3 = "middle 20%," 4 = "next 20%" and 5 = "top 20%."

Acknowledgements

The authors gratefully acknowledge the support of the Center for International Business Education and Research at the University of South Carolina and the Plan for Excellence at the University of Western Ontario.

Notes

1. The following industries were identified for this study: balances, watches and puts, textile machinery, mining machinery, oilfield machinery, certain consumer electronic products, semiconductors, sewing machinery, electro medical and x ray apparatus, synthetic insecticides and fungicides, civil aircraft and parts, and typesetting machinery.
2. Ideal profiles may be either empirically or theoretically derived [Drazin & Van de Ven 1985]. Theoretically based profiles avoid the loss of degrees of freedom and arbitrariness of using observations to define the ideal profile. However, the theoretically based profiles fail to recognize that the design variables may take values other than the end-points of the scale. Furthermore, an empirically derived profile is considered appropriate where the theory is stated in ordinal terms (e.g., high centralization for global strategy, low centralization for multidomestic) [Drazin & Van de Ven 1985; Gresov 1989]. Thus for the implementation framework in this study, the empirically derived profile was considered more appropriate. To examine the superiority of the empirically derived profile, the fit analysis was also conducted with the theoretical endpoints. The theoretical end-points produced only two significant correlations and failed to have a good fit with this data.
3. Venkatraman and Prescott [1990] note that the removal of the top performing business units could bias the subsequent analysis since the mean value of the performance variables will shift lower. They suggest removing a corresponding number of low performing business units to reduce this potential bias. In this study, this procedure was not considered feasible given the limited sample size. However, given that performance was measured with a 7-point scale rather than a ratio scale, it was expected that the influence of this bias would be moderate. Reanalyzing the data, excluding the ten low performers confirmed this expectation as the reported significance levels were consistent for both analytical procedures.
4. As indicated in Table 2, formalization and the use of integrating mechanisms are correlated. The possibility of imprecise parameter estimates in the regression equation was examined through the procedure recommended by Belsley, Kuh and Welsch [1980] and through respecifying the model alternately dropping out each of the variables. The presence of collinearity did not appear to degrade the regression estimates based on these procedures.
5. Additional analyses were conducted to determine if other profiling procedures were more appropriate. First, as suggested by Gresov [1989], observations scoring in the middle quintile of the international strategy measure were omitted in order to create additional demarcation between the two strategy types. This resulted in no additional significance between the design dimensions and the overall fit assessment was reduced. Second, the high performing groups were defined using alternate performance dimensions. Here again, no significant gains were made in either the profile definitions or the overall fit assessment.

References

Aiken, Michael & Jerald Hage. 1968. Organizational interdependence and intraorganizational structure. *American Sociological Review*, 33: 912–30.

Barney, Jay B. 1986. Organization culture: Can it be a source of sustained competitive advantage? *Academy of Management Review*, 11: 656–65.

Bartlett, Christopher A. 1983. MNCs: Get off the reorganization merry-go-round. *Harvard Business Review*, 61(2): 138–47.

Bartlett, Christopher A. & Sumantra Ghoshal. 1989. *Managing across borders: The transnational solution*. Boston, MA: Harvard Business School Press.

Baty, Gordon B., William M. Evan & Terry W. Rothermel. 1971. Personnel flows as interorganizational relations. *Administrative Science Quarterly*, 16: 430–43.

Belsey, D.A., E. Kuh & R.E. Welsch. 1980. *Regression diagnostics*. New York: John Wiley and Sons.

Child, John. 1973. Strategies of control and organizational behavior. *Administrative Science Quarterly*, March: 1–17.

Cray, David. 1984. Control and coordination in multinational corporations. *Journal of International Business Studies*, 15(2): 85–98.

Cvar, Margaret. 1984. Competitive strategies in global industries. Unpublished Ph.D. dissertation, Harvard Business School.

Cyert, Richard M. & James G. March. 1963. *A behavioral theory of the firm*. Englewood Cliffs, NJ: Prentice-Hall.

Daniels, John D., Robert A. Pitts & Marietta J. Tretter. 1984. Strategy and structure of U.S. multinationals: An exploratory study. *Academy of Management Journal*, 27: 292–307.

———. 1985. Organizing for dual strategies of product diversity and international expansion. *Strategic Management Journal*, 6: 223–37.

Das, Rajan. 1981. *Managing diversification: The general management perspective*. New Delhi: Macmillan India.

Dess, Gregory & Peter Davis. 1984. Porter's generic strategies as determinants of strategic group membership and organizational performance. *Academy of Management Journal*, 27: 467–88.

Dess, Gregory & Richard B. Robinson. 1984. Measuring organizational performance in the absence of objective measures: The case of the privately-held firms and conglomerate business unit. *Strategic Management Journal*, 5: 265–73.

Dess, Gregory, Duane Ireland & Michael A. Hitt. 1990. Industry effects and strategic management research. *Journal of Management*, 16: 7–27.

Donaldson, Gordon & Jay W. Lorsch. 1983. *Decision making at the top*. New York: Basic Books.

Doz, Yves. 1986. *Strategic management in multinational corporations*. Oxford: Pergamon Press.

——— & C.K. Prahalad. 1988. Quality of management: An emerging source of global competitive advantage. In N. Hood & J. Vahlne, editors, *Strategies in global competition*, 345–69. London: Croom Helm.

Drazin, Robert & Andrew H. Van de Ven. 1985. Alternative forms of fit in contingency theory. *Administrative Science Quarterly*, 30: 514–59.

Dutton, Jane E. & Robert B. Duncan. 1987. The creation of momentum for change through the process of strategic issue diagnosis. *Strategic Management Journal*, 8: 279–95.

Edström, Anders & Jay R. Galbraith. 1977. Transfer of managers as a coordination and control strategy in multinational organizations. *Administrative Science Quarterly*, 22: 248–63.

Egelhoff, William G. 1982. Strategy and structure in multinational corporations: An information processing approach. *Administrative Science Quarterly*, 27: 435–58.

———. 1984. Patterns of control in U.S., U.K. and European multinational corporations. *Journal of International Business Studies*, 15(2): 73–81.

———. 1988a. Strategy and structure in multinational corporations: A revision of the Stopford and Wells model. *Strategic Management Journal*, 9: 1–14.

———. 1988b. *Organizing the multinational enterprise*. Cambridge, MA: Ballinger.

Fouraker, Lawrence E. & John M. Stopford. 1968. Organizational structure and multi-national strategy. *Administrative Science Quarterly*, 13: 47–64.

Franko, Lawrence. 1974. The move toward a multi-divisional structure in European organizations. *Administrative Science Quarterly*, 19: 473–506.

———. 1976. *The European multinationals*. Greenwich, CT: Greylock Press.

Fredrickson, James W. 1986. The strategic decision process and organization structure. *Academy of Management Review*, 11: 280–97.

Fry, Louis & Deborah A. Smith. 1987. Congruence, contingency, and theory building. *Academy of Management Review*, 12: 117–32.

Galbraith, Jay A. 1973. *Designing complex organizations*. Reading, MA: Addison-Wesley.

——— & Daniel A. Nathanson. 1978. *Strategy implementation: The role of structure and process*. St. Paul, MN: West Publishing.

Garnier, Gerard H. 1982. Context and decision making autonomy in the foreign affiliates of U.S. multinational corporations. *Academy of Management Journal*, 25: 893–908.

Gates, Stephen R. & William G. Egelhoff. 1986. Centralization in headquarters-subsidiary relationships. *Journal of International Business Studies*, 17(2): 71–92.

Ghoshal, Sumantra. 1987. Global strategy: An organizing framework. *Strategic Management Journal*, 8: 425–40.

——— & Nitia Nohria. 1989. International differentiation within multinational corporations. *Strategic Management Journal*, 10: 323–37.

Gordon, George C. & Walter M. Cummins. 1979. *Managing management climate*. Lexington, MA: Lexington Books.

Govindarajan, Vijay. 1986. Decentralization, strategy, and effectiveness of strategic business units in multibusiness organizations. *Academy of Management Review*, 11: 844–56.

Grant, Robert M. 1988. On "dominant logic," relatedness and the link between diversity and performance. *Strategic Management Journal*, 9: 639–42.

Gresov, Christopher. 1989. Exploring fit and misfit with multiple contingencies. *Administrative Science Quarterly*, 34: 431–53.

Gupta, Anil K. & Vijay Govindarajan. 1986. Resource sharing among SBU's: Strategic antecedents and administrative implications. *Academy of Management Journal*, 29: 695–714.

Hall, Richard H. 1982. *Organizations*. Englewood Cliffs, NJ: Prentice-Hall.

Hamel, Gary & C.K. Prahalad. 1985. Do you really have a global strategy? *Harvard Business Review*, 63(4): 139–47.

Hedlund, Gunnar & Dag Rolander. 1990. Action in heterarchies – New approaches to managing the MNC. In C. Bartlett, Y. Doz & G. Hedlund, editors, *Managing the global firm*. London: Routledge.

Herbert, Theodore T. 1984. Strategy and multinational organization structure: An interorganizational relationships perspective. *Academy of Management Review*, 9: 259–71.

Hitt, Michael A. & Duane R. Ireland. 1985. Corporate distinctive competence, strategy, industry and performance. *Strategic Management Journal*, 6: 273–93.

——— & K.A. Palia. 1982. Industrial firms' grand strategy and functional importance: Moderating effects of technology and uncertainty. *Academy of Management Journal*, 25: 315–298.

Hitt, Michael A., Duane R. Ireland & G. Stadler. 1982. Functional importance and company performance: Moderating effects of grand strategy and industry type. *Strategic Management Journal*, 3: 315–30.

Hofstede, Geert. 1976. Nationality and espoused values of managers. *Journal of Applied Psychology*, 61(2): 148–55.

Hout, Thomas, Michael Porter & Eileen Rudden, 1982. How global companies win out. *Harvard Business Review*, 60(5): 98–108.

Hymer, Stephen H. 1976. *The international operations of national firms: A study of direct investment*. Cambridge, MA: MIT Press.

Inkson, John H.K., Derek Pugh & David Hickson. 1970. Organization, context, and structure: An abbreviated replication. *Administrative Science Quarterly*, 15: 41–65.

Jones, Gareth R. & Charles W.C. Hill. 1988. Transaction cost analysis of strategy-structure choice. *Strategic Management Journal*, 9: 159–72.

Kaufman, Herbert. 1960. *The forest ranger*. Baltimore, MD: The Johns Hopkins University Press.

Khandwalla, Pradiz N. 1974. Mass output orientation of operations technology and organizational structure. *Administrative Science Quarterly*, 19: 74–97.

Kogut, Bruce. 1985a. Designing global strategies: Comparative and competitive value-added chains. *Sloan Management Review*, Summer: 15–28.

———. 1985b. Designing global strategies: Profiting from operational flexibility. *Sloan Management Review*, Fall: 27–38.

———. 1989. A note on global strategies. *Strategic Management Journal*, 10: 383–89.

———. 1990. International sequential advantages and network flexibility. In C. Bartlett, Y. Doz & G. Hedlund, editors, *Managing the global firm*. London: Routledge.

Lawrence, Paul R. & Jay W. Lorsch. 1967. *Organization and environment*. Boston, MA: Harvard University Press.

Leontiades, James. 1986. Going global-global strategies vs. national strategies. *Long Range Planning*, 19(6): 96–104.

March, James G. & Herbert A. Simon. 1958. *Organizations*. New York: John Wiley and Sons.

McCann, Joseph E. & Jay R. Galbraith. 1981. Interdepartmental relations. In P. Nystrom & W. Starbuch, editors, *Handbook of organizational design*. London: Oxford University Press.

Miles, Robert H. 1982. *Coffin nails and corporate strategies*. Englewood Cliffs, NJ: Prentice Hall.

Miller, Danny. 1987. Strategy making and structure: Analysis and implication for performance. *Academy of Management Journal*, 30: 7–32.

——— & Cornelia Dröge. 1986. Psychological and traditional determinants of structure. *Administrative Science Quarterly*, 31: 539–60.

——— & Jean-Marie Toulouse. 1988. Strategic process and content as mediates between organizational context and structure. *Academy of Management Journal*, 31: 544–69.

Mintzberg, Henry, Duane Raisinghani & André Theoret. 1976. The structure of unstructured decision processes. *Administrative Science Quarterly*, 21: 246–75.

Ouchi, William G. 1977. The relationship between organizational structure and organizational control. *Administrative Science Quarterly*, 22: 95–113.

Ouchi, William G. 1978. The transmission of control through organization hierarchy. *Academy of Management Journal*, 21: 173–92.

———. 1980. Markets, bureaucracies and clans. *Administrative Science Quarterly*, 25: 129–41.

Pfeffer, Jeffrey. 1978. *Organizational design*. Arlington Heights, IL: AHM Publishing Company.

Porter, Michael E. 1980. *Competitive strategy*. New York: The Free Press.

———. 1985. *Competitive advantage: Creating and sustaining superior performance*. New York: The Free Press.

———. ed. 1986. *Competition in global industries*. Boston, MA: Harvard Business School Press.

Prahalad, C.K. & Yves L. Doz. 1987. *The multinational mission. Balancing local demands and global vision.* New York: The Free Press.

Prahalad, C.K. & Richard A. Bettis. 1986. The dominant logic: A new linkage between diversity and performance. *Strategic Management Journal*, 7: 485–501.

Prescott, John E. 1983. Competitive environments, strategic types and business performance: An empirical analysis. Unpublished Ph.D. dissertation, The Pennsylvania State University.

Pugh, Derek, David J. Hickson, Christopher R. Hinnings & Christopher Turner. 1968. Dimensions of organization structure. *Administrative Science Quarterly*, 13: 65–105.

Pugh, Derek, David J. Hickson & Christopher Turner. 1969. The context of organization structures. *Administrative Science Quarterly*, 14: 91–114.

Quinn, James B. 1980. *Strategies for change: Logical incrementalism.* Homewood, IL: Richard B. Irwin.

Sheldon, Mary E. 1971. Investments and involvements as mechanisms producing commitment to the organization. *Administrative Science Quarterly*, 16: 143–50.

Snow, Charles C. & Lawrence G. Hrebiniak. 1980. Strategy, distinctive competence, and organizational performance. *Administrative Science Quarterly*, 25: 317–36.

Stopford, John M. & Louis T. Wells, Jr. 1972. *Managing the multinational enterprise.* London: Longmans.

Thompson, James D. 1967. *Organizations in action.* New York: McGraw-Hill.

Van de Ven, Andrew H., André L. Delbecq & Richard Koenig. 1976. Determinants of co-ordination modes within organizations. *American Sociological Review*, 41: 322–38.

Van Maanen, John & Edgar H. Schein. 1979. Toward a theory of organization socialization. In B. Staw, editor, *Research in organization behavior.* Greenwich, CT: JAI Press.

Venkatraman, N. & John E. Prescott. 1990. Environment-strategy coalignment: An empirical test of its performance implications. *Strategic Management Journal*, 11: 1–23.

Venkatraman, N. & Vasuderan Ramanujam. 1987. Measurement of business economic performance: An examination of method convergence. *Journal of Management*, 13(1): 109–22.

Victor, Bart & Richard S. Blackburn. 1987. Interdependence: An alternative conceptualization. *Academy of Management Review*, 12: 486–98.

Weber, Jacob. 1988. The effects of cultural differences on the implementation of mergers and acquisitions. Unpublished doctoral dissertation, University of South Carolina.

Yip, George S. 1989. Global strategy ... in a world of nations? *Sloan Management Review*, Fall: 29–41.

47

Exploiting Globalization Potential: U.S. and Japanese Strategies

Johny K. Johansson and George S. Yip

The emerging field of 'global strategic management' has many aspects, as witnessed by the eclectic collection of papers in the *Strategic Management Journal*'s special issue on global strategy (Bartlett and Ghoshal, 1991). One aspect concerns globally integrated competitive strategy: whether and how multinational companies (MNCs) should change their strategies to suit conditions in 'global' industries. Such global industries have been defined in various ways: Hout, Porter, and Rudden (1982) defined a global industry, in contrast to a multidomestic industry, as one in which a firm's competitive position in one country market is significantly affected by its competitive position in other country markets; Bartlett and Ghoshal (1989) defined a 'transnational industry' as being driven by simultaneous demands for global efficiency, national responsiveness, and worldwide learning; Morrison (1990) characterized a global industry as having intense levels of international competition, competitors marketing a standardized product worldwide, industry competitors that have a presence in all key international markets and high levels of international trade. These definitions have the common thread of the need or opportunity to integrate strategy across countries.

Most of the empirical work in this field of global strategy has focused on American and European MNCs, with relatively little systematic research about Japanese companies. But a great deal has been written on Japanese management in general (e.g., Yoshino, 1968; Ouchi, 1981; Abegglen and Stalk, 1985) and on Japanese approaches to competitive strategy (e.g., Pascale and Athos, 1981; Kotler, Fahey, and Jatusripitak, 1985). So this study seeks to partially integrate the fields of global strategy and of Japanese management and, in particular, to provide evidence on differences in American and Japanese approaches. To achieve this integration and comparison we review several of the

Source: *Strategic Management Journal*, Vol. 15, No. 8, 1994, pp. 579–601.

key constructs and issues in global strategy, and develop arguments as to how Japanese companies might differ from American ones in each regard. Because of the complexity of the issues and emergent stage of the field we develop research questions rather than specific hypotheses. Thus, this study takes a primarily exploratory approach in generating its theory and evidence.

Our ingoing assumption is that globalization strategy is multidimensional. Setting strategy for a worldwide business requires choices along a number of strategic dimensions. Some of these dimensions determine whether the strategy lies toward the multilocal end of the continuum or the global end. As summarized by Yip (1989, 1992), there are five such dimensions:

- *Market participation* – involves the choice of country-markets in which to conduct business, and the level of activity, particularly in terms of market share.
- *Products/services* – involves the extent to which a worldwide business offers the same or different products in different countries.
- *Location of value-adding activities* – involves the choice of where to locate each of the activities that comprise the entire value-added chain – from research to production to after sales service.
- *Marketing* – involves the extent to which a worldwide business uses the same brand names, advertising and other marketing elements in different countries.
- *Competitive moves* – involves the extent to which a worldwide business makes competitive moves in individual countries as part of a global competitive strategy.

Choices along these dimensions determine whether the strategy lies toward the multilocal end of the continuum or the global end. Intermediate positions are, of course, feasible. For each dimension, a multilocal strategy seeks to maximize worldwide performance by maximizing local competitive advantage, revenues or profits; while a global strategy seeks to maximize worldwide performance through sharing and integration.

Conceptual Model

The field of strategic management has four well-established analytical components or theoretical constructs: industry structure, strategy, organization/management, and performance (e.g., Chandler, 1962; Hofer and Schendel, 1978). These constructs can be, and have been, applied to the analysis of, and the need for, global strategy. In this section we discuss the existing literature on the role of these constructs in global strategy theory, consider how American and Japanese businesses might differ, and develop our own integrated model relating the constructs to the actual level of global strategy used and consequent performance.

Industry Structure

A central tenet of global strategy theory is that industries vary in globalization potential because of underlying industry structure or conditions (Porter, 1986; Morrison, 1990). This globalization potential means the opportunity to gain benefits from using globally integrated strategies in order to benefit from cost reductions (Kogut, 1985), improved quality of products or programs (Yip, 1989), enhanced customer preference (Levitt, 1983) or increased competitive leverage (Hout et al., 1982; Hamel and Prahalad, 1985). These industry globalization conditions can be summarized as market, cost, government and competitive drivers (Yip, 1989). Each set of drivers has its proponents, with market drivers (e.g., globally common customer tastes) being particularly associated with Levitt (1983), cost drivers (e.g., global scale economies) with Porter (1986), government drivers (e.g., absence of trade restrictions) with Doz (1979), and competitive drivers (e.g., cross-country subsidization) with Hamel and Prahalad (1985).

There is likely to be a somewhat different pattern of drivers facing Japanese and American companies. This is easiest to see in terms of *government drivers*. Japanese and American companies come from very different home countries in terms of trade barriers, and also face different trade barriers in major market areas such as the European Community. *Cost drivers* are also likely to differ perceptually, since the home country costs will differ. *Market drivers* may not be objectively so different, but looking at the world from Japan, rather than the United States, may change the subjective reality. In particular, the relatively wide global diffusion of many aspects of American culture, contrasted with almost no diffusion to-date of Japanese culture, may make customer tastes seem more globally homogenous to American eyes than to Japanese ones. The same may hold for perceptions of the transferability and viability of global marketing (e.g., global brand names and global advertising).

Competitive drivers may seem different, since Japanese companies are very focused on their compatriots (see Abegglen and Stalk, 1985, Ch. 3). There is, for example, a strong tendency for Japanese companies to pattern their overseas strategies on their Japanese competitors (e.g., Kotler et al. 1985). This means not necessarily a direct imitation, but rather that they pay close attention to the strategies employed by competition, and develop strategies that partly depend on the competitors' actual and anticipated moves (Hanssens and Johansson, 1991).

Strategy

A second central tenet of global strategy theory is that companies should respond to industry globalization potential with an integrated strategy. This strategy might include global market participation such as building major share in strategic countries (Ohmae, 1985), global product standardization (Levitt, 1983; Kogut, 1985; Walters, 1986), global activity concentration such as building a global value chain (Hout et al., 1982; Kogut, 1985; Bartlett and Ghoshal, 1989), globally uniform marketing such as global brand names or advertising (Takeuchi and Porter, 1986; Jain, 1989), and globally integrated competitive moves such as cross-subsidized competitive moves or sequenced moves (Hamel and Prahalad, 1985; Porter, 1986). But there is limited evidence on the use of global strategy. Morrison and Roth (1992) found that American businesses did not make much use of it, although their study uses only a limited number of measures and is also restricted to U.S.-located businesses.

Japanese corporations are well known for their flexibility and quickness of strategic adaptation (see, for example, Pascale and Athos, 1981; Kagono *et al.*, 1984; Stalk, 1988). One would expect, therefore, that given the recent general increase in globalization forces, Japanese corporations would, in most cases, be closer than American ones to the needed level of global strategy. Furthermore, using global strategy usually requires a longer term view (Yip, 1989), the ability to make sacrifices in some countries to benefit the worldwide business (Hamel and Prahalad, 1985), and the ability to implement centrally-determined decisions (discussed below). Japanese companies are well-known for exhibiting each of these characteristics (e.g. Kono, 1984; Brouthers and Werner, 1990). Thus, Japanese companies can be expected to exhibit a greater perceived need for a global strategy, and to be closer to optimum. On the other hand, their relatively recent emergence might lead to a lower actual level of global presence.

Organization/Management

For a worldwide business to develop and implement a global strategy, strong control and coordination mechanisms must exist between and among MNC headquarters and subsidiaries (Ghoshal, 1987; Bartlett and Ghoshal, 1989). An extensive literature (reviewed by Martinez and Jarillo, 1989) exists on the subject of MNC control and coordination mechanisms, although mostly predating the current debate on global strategy. Nevertheless, this literature clearly suggests the mechanisms that would apply to facilitating the use of global strategy. Which elements of organization are more important in facilitating the implementation of global strategy?

In terms of *organization structure* Bartlett and Ghoshal (1987, 1989) argue for a network structure that facilitates global learning. Ghoshal (1987) suggests that the tendency of global strategy toward a centralized global authority, and the potential corresponding erosion of global learning benefits, is one of the 'strategic tradeoffs' associated with pursuing a global strategy. According to this reasoning, the greater centralization of Japanese companies should help them to better implement global strategy. A special aspect of organization structure is whether control of a worldwide business is split between separate domestic and international divisions. Yip, Loewe and Yoshino (1988) argue that American MNCs are more likely than European and Japanese MNCs to have such a split, and that this split reduces the ability to implement a global strategy.

Prahalad and Doz (1987, Ch 8) down-play the role of organization structure in global strategy, emphasizing instead integrative *management processes* such as global information systems, global business teams, coordination committees, task forces and other cross-country coordination devices. Similarly, European-based research (e.g., Hedlund, 1980, and Edström and Lorange, 1984) has found evidence of more informal and subtler mechanisms as MNC control processes. Bartlett and Ghoshal (1989) also stress the importance of manage-ment processes that allow a balance between headquarters and subsidiary. Jaeger (1983) and Jaeger and Baliga (1985) found that Japanese MNCs employed a kind of cultural control (based on socialization) rather than control through more formal mechanisms. Egelhoff (1984) found that the cultural control described above was based on the use of expatriates, a high frequency of visits, a policy of transfer of managers, and a strong socialization process. At the same time, part of the Japanese centralization is achieved by the extensive use of newer communication devices, such as through the very heavy use of telefaxes. In consequence, one would expect the American business to be more dependent on formal periodic reporting. The Japanese, on the other hand, will be likely to rely more on informal, people-oriented coordination devices to manage their dispersing organizations.

Performance

The existence of industry globalization potential implies that companies can derive globalization-related benefits for the use of globally integrated strategy, and hence improve performance. Conversely, a strategy that is more global than warranted by industry globalization potential will yield drawbacks that result in worse performance. Previous studies have provided very limited evidence. Roth and Morrison (1990) found no significant difference in profit performance among businesses facing (1) global integration pressures, (2) local responsiveness pressures, and (3) both pressures. A narrower study, by Kotabe and Omura (1989) found that the market share and profit performance of 71 European and Japanese firms serving the U.S. market was negatively related to the extent to which products were adapted for the U.S. market, i.e., businesses with globally standardized products performed better.

In terms of American-Japanese differences, the well-known Japanese penchant for market share gains at the expense of short-term profits (Clark, 1979: 221; Kagono et al., 1984; Kono, 1984; Picken, 1987) suggests that a drive towards global strategy is viewed as a means to increasing share rather than profits. Japanese companies usually have, or at least report, significantly lower profitability on average than do American companies (Haar, 1989). Thus, the closer the Japanese get to the perceived optimal level of global strategy, the stronger the impact on market share, with no necessary impact on profits. In contrast, American firms should be more motivated by profit maximization goals, and can be expected to derive more direct profit benefits from an optimal global strategy (Abegglen and Stalk, 1985: 177). Odagiri (1990) conducted an extensive review of studies comparing American and Japanese profit rates, concluding that Japanese profitability is indeed lower on average even after various adjustments (e.g., for accounting methods and the cost of capital), and that the source of the difference arises from American companies emphasising the maximization of shareholder wealth, while the Japanese emphasize employee utility.

Relating the Constructs

We have discussed the roles of several constructs in globalization and global strategy:

- industry globalization drivers
- organization structure
- management processes
- globally integrated strategy
- performance
- national base

How do the constructs link up with each other? Alternative conceptual models are possible, each with a different combination of relationships. But, disregarding nationality for the moment, these different possible models fall into a limited number of categories. In particular, the models increase in complexity in terms of the number of *levels* of linkages. The alternative linkages are given in Figure 1.

Although necessary from an exploratory data analytical viewpoint, the simpler one- and two-level specifications need little discussion. Moving to models with three levels of effects allows more conceptual scope and incisiveness. For example, even though high industry globalization potential should lead to increased use of global strategy, organization structure and management processes might affect the ability to implement global strategy. Thus, one specification would hypothesize that industry globalization drivers should lead managers to change a company's organization structure and management processes in order to implement a particular type of global strategy. Specification 4 – *Strategy Follows Structure* – provides such a set of relationships, and requires three levels of effects. Industry Globalization Drivers is an exogenous construct that affects both Organization Structure and Management Processes. These in turn affect the choice and implementation of Global Strategy. Performance is then affected only by Global Strategy. The key assumption here is that the ability to use global strategy is determined by the existing state of organization structure and management processes. Such a view would fit with the argument that lags in organization and management have constrained firms' ability to implement global strategy (e.g., Bartlett and Ghoshal, 1989). In particular, the global strategy response to industry globalization conditions is very much affected by organization structure and management processes. In consequence, there may well be a lag or gap between the optimal global strategy indicated by industry structure and the actual global strategy achievable by the organization.

It could also be argued that global strategy changes precede organization and management changes, following Chandler's (1962) argument that structure follows strategy. This is depicted in Specification 5 – *Structure Follows Strategy*, which reverses the sequence of Specification 4. In particular, Organization Structure and Management Processes now mediate the effect of Global Strategy on Performance. In this model, companies implement a global strategy in response to industry globalization drivers, but the effectiveness, in terms of performance,

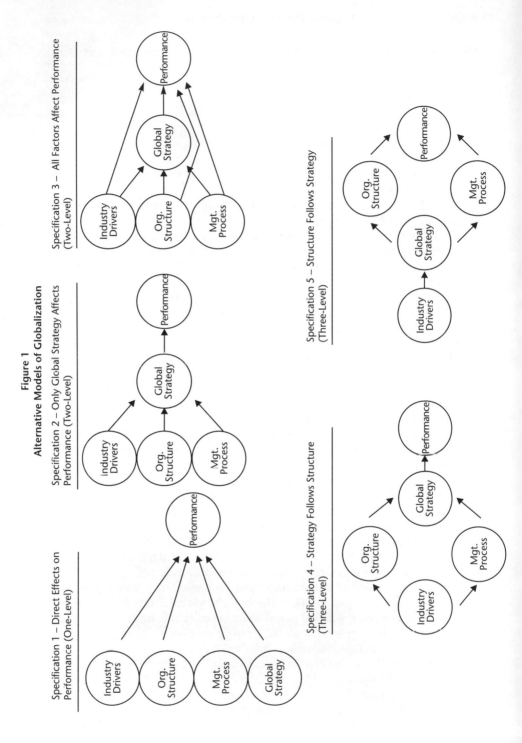

Figure 1
Alternative Models of Globalization

of the global strategy depends on whether a suitable organization structure and management process have also been instituted.

Lastly, as discussed earlier, nationality (being American or Japanese) can potentially affect several constructs, including performance. Rather than attempting to specify *a priori* where nationality has the greatest effect in our models, we will treat it as an empirical effect to be explored in the data collected.

Research Methodology

Choice of Research Method

Previous clinical studies (e.g., Bartlett and Ghoshal, 1989) have examined a large number of constructs but, inherently, did not do so in a systematic fashion with common measures across sites. Studies with large samples and short questionnaires (e.g., Kotabe and Omura, 1989; Morrison and Roth, 1992) on the other hand, are typically constrained to examine very few constructs. What seems particularly needed is a methodology that can fill the missing middle ground by examining a comprehensive number of constructs on a systematic basis. In addition, each of the constructs should be measured using the multiple indicators discussed above. It seems more important at this time to be able to examine *relationships* among the many different constructs than to generalize about the incidence or effects of a few constructs. Such a study should also include an open-ended element to allow the researcher to better learn about this highly complex topic. Given the complexity of the subject, a purely quantitative analysis is unlikely to yield a clear choice among the competing models postulated. Thus, this study uses semistructured personal interviews that cover a large number of topics in systematic fashion with a moderate size sample (36 businesses). Personal interviews with company management make it possible to explain concepts and measures, to help reveal problems in the measures and questions, and to allow unstructured discussion to elicit modifications of the framework. Although the limited sample prevents wide generalizability, this was enhanced by targeting one type of MNC: very large companies with a high proportion of international revenues. Similarly, even a limited sample can be designed to produce an eclectic sample of industries. Such differences are, a fortiori, desirable when investigating the linkages from industry globalization drivers to the differential use of global strategy.

Development of Data Gathering Instrument

From a measurement perspective, the broad theoretical constructs discussed are best viewed as 'latent' variables, not directly measurable on a single scale. To measure such latent constructs, it is necessary to identify multiple indicators. Measures of the industry globalization drivers and of the elements of global strategy, organization and management were developed by working with four multinational companies. In each company the researcher worked with both headquarters and local country management to formulate and scale the measures. A questionnaire was developed, using these measures, with slightly different versions for products and for services. Most of the questions used equal appearing intervals on a five-point scale for the response. The basic constructs were measured by the following multiple indicators:

Industry Globalization Drivers

- *Overall market drivers*
- *Overall cost drivers*
- *Overall government drivers*
- *Overall competitive drivers*

Organization Structure

- *One global head*
- *International division*
- *Business dimension of matrix*
- *Geographic dimension of matrix*
- *Functional dimension of matrix*

Management Processes

- *Cross-country coordination*
- *Global budgeting*
- *Global group meetings*
- *Global performance review*
- *Global strategy information system*

Global Strategy

- *Global share balance*
- *Standardized products*
- *Activity concentration*
- *Marketing uniformity*
- *Integrated competitive moves*
- *Overall global strategy*

Performance

- *Market share*
- *Relative profitability*

The Appendix details the above measures.

Data Collection

In each of the American companies, two managers were interviewed independently, and a researcher was present as the questionnaire was completed. This procedure was not feasible in Japan, with its more diffuse position descriptions and consensus-oriented decision-making style. To demand independent responses to the same question is impossible. Instead, the questionnaires were left with the designated respondent, who then polled the relevant people in the organization across the required functions, and reported their consensual responses. Because this process was time-consuming, the Japanese questionnaires were usually completed over the time span of several days, while the American interviews were completed in one session. The assistance with clarifications and explanations concerning the various questions had therefore to be done through return visits and via the telephone. In order to make questions about products and markets and competitors meaningful, the long (19 pages) questionnaire focused on the strategy of *one line of business, not on the corporation as a whole.* The English language form used was virtually identical between the U.S. and the Japanese companies. Since many of the English-language global strategy concepts are used also in the Japanese management vocabulary, no translation was attempted.

Response Bias

As with most cross-national questionnaires, there are possible biases. For example, the responses may be based on a misunderstanding of the meaning of the concepts covered, or a systematic response pattern (such as consistently overestimating one's achievements). If such aberrations occur, and if they are different between the Japanese and the Americans, there will be a systematic bias in their respective answers (see, for example, Douglas and Craig, 1983: 190–201). Despite our efforts to communicate the meaning of the various concepts to the respondents (see more on this below), we can not be entirely confident that in terms of absolute response values our data are completely clean. Also, because slightly different data collection approaches were used in the two countries, there is a possible method bias in direct comparisons of average levels of the variables.

But at another level of analysis, namely the relationships between variables, the response problem is not particularly damaging. Even if the mean levels of some variables might be incorrect, there is often less reason to mistrust the derived correlations between the variables. For example, even if the sample averages for the Japanese lie too low because they consistently underestimate their achievements, the same instinct will usually lead to lower averages on related variables, and the correlations between the variables may therefore be correct. Thus, by focusing mainly on the relationships between the variables, one can minimize the likelihood that response biases seriously distort the results.

There may also be bias inherent in self-reported and perceptual responses. This may be particularly strong for the measure of performance. But both Dess and Robinson (1984), and Venkatraman and Ramanujam (1986, 1987) have provided evidence supporting the general reliability of self-reported performance measures. Self-reports of performance and other measures have been used in a number of studies of global strategy, including Samiee and Roth (1992), and Morrison and Roth (1992).

Sample

The sampling was purposive, not random. To investigate the research questions a variety of industries needed to be included, so that the strategic drivers would show variation across businesses. The approach used was to identify international companies, in a broad cross-section of industries, matched as closely as possible across the two countries. We then recruited the companies based on letters of recommendations, past contacts, and similar networking approaches. We were able to recruit leading businesses in a wide variety of industries, approximately matched between the American and Japanese samples (Table 1).

Table 1
Industries in Sample

American Businesses	Japanese Businesses
financial service	financial service
toothpaste	toothpaste
detergent	toilet soap
beverage	beverage
fashion apparel	cosmetics
furnishing	watches
passenger automobile	cameras
automotive components	consumer electronics (1)
personal computers	consumer electronics (2)
business computers	passenger automobile
mainframe computers	tractors
specialized computers	floppy discs
industrial controls	photocopiers
electrical insulation	mainframe computers
specialty coatings	semi-conductors (1)
building supply	semi-conductors (2)
chemicals	control instruments
polyester/plastics	ball bearings

The study participants were some of the largest companies in their respective countries. For example, 56 percent of the American businesses and 67 percent of the Japanese businesses were the domestic market leaders in their industry. The American businesses averaged 42 percent of revenues as being international, and the Japanese 37 percent. These proportions are quite high for American and Japanese businesses, compared with, for example, the *Fortune* 500 as a whole. The American parent companies included Armstrong World Industries, Bausch & Lomb, Citicorp, Chrysler, Colgate-Palmolive, Eastman Kodak, E. I. Du Pont de Nemours, Honeywell, IBM and McDonnell-Douglas. Most of the Japanese companies declined to be named, but the list of industries should indicate that we were able to recruit many of the 'crown-jewels' of the Japanese economy. All of the Japanese companies were among the 200 largest in that country and included 5 of the top 15. The combination of high share of large domestic markets, and international revenues being less than half the total, may seem atypical when one thinks of global companies. But one of the facts of life for firms from both the United States and Japan is that they do have very large home markets, and that global leaders based in these countries almost inevitably have a large share in their home base. These are characteristics that do indeed affect their global strategies. Our sample merely reflects this reality.

Validity and Reliability

How well does our methodology capture the underlying phenomena? There are clearly likely to be variations in accuracy among companies, respondents and measures. But what is important is that the underlying patterns of relationships be reasonably true rather than the accuracy of individual observations. One way to examine for this trueness of patterns is to look for convergence within our data set between American and Japanese responses, and convergence with prior theory and observations. One such test is provided by examining the responses on the location of value-adding activities. Prior expectations are that upstream activities (e.g., R&D) would be more concentrated geographically while downstream activities (e.g., service) would be more dispersed. The pattern of concentration did indeed decline for more-downstream activities, for both the American and Japanese samples, thus providing convergence both between the American and Japanese data and between our data and prior expectations. So even if one or more businesses are measured imperfectly, the sample as a whole seems to converge into an average pattern that fits prior theory and evidence.

Analytical Method

The alternative models were evaluated using the PLS (partial least squares) method. This technique is now quite well established as a method for estimating path coefficients in causal models (see Fornell and Bookstein, 1982; Cool and Schendel, 1988; Cool, Dierickx, and Jemison, 1989; and Fornell, Lorange, and Roos, 1990). It has the advantage over LISREL of requiring less stringent assumptions about the randomness of the sample and the normality of the distribution of variables (Wold, 1982). Furthermore, it can accept smaller sample sizes, as each causal subsystem sequence of paths is estimated separately (Anderson and Gerbing, 1988). For example, Lohmöller (1982) demonstrates examples where a model with 27 variables is appropriately estimated with only 10 observations and a model of 96 indicators and 26 constructs is estimated on a sample of 100. Because of these characteristics PLS is particularly suitable for studies in the early stages of theory development and testing, and in dealing with comprehensive models.

Results

We initially estimated the different models using the full set of indicators for each latent construct (as listed earlier). Then for the sake of parsimony, and following standard practice (e.g., Fornell, 1982; Barclay, Duxbury, and Higgins, 1991) we reestimated the models using only the indicators with large weights for formative indicators or large loadings for reflective indicators. (The organization matrix measures fell out in this consolidation phase.) As one would expect, these more parsimonious models resulted in essentially the same path coefficients and levels of R^2 as the fuller models, and thus incurred little or no loss of information. The selected indicators are given in the model diagrams (Figure 2).

Including different versions for the location of the nationality construct, we estimated a total of eight models. The first five estimated models correspond to the conceptual specifications 1 to 5 discussed earlier. Models 6 to 8 add the Nationality construct in different positions to Specifications 4 ('Strategy Follows Structure') and 5 ('Structure Follows Strategy').

The Measurement Model

In PLS estimation the user needs to specify indicators as formative or reflective of their latent constructs. The formative specification is appropriate when the indicators directly help create the construct, while the reflective specification assumes that the indicators reveal various features of an underlying construct. Since the various aspects of strategy, industry conditions, management processes and organizational structure combine into broad factors, we treated the indicators as formative for these constructs. For performance we used reflective indicators (the formative and reflective conditions being indicated by the directions of the arrows in Figure 2). Performance is more of an abstract perceptual construct. For example, Japanese companies are often viewed as greater performers without making a lot of money. So superior performance is best viewed as reflected in different measures such as market share and relative profitability.

The PLS system estimates the weights and loadings for the indicators while trying to fit the entire model in an iterative fashion. Since all the alternative specifications (Models 1 to 8) are pointed towards Performance, it is not surprising that the indicator loadings and weights are very similar across the different models (Figure 2). Furthermore, the explained variance in the measurement is high and almost identical across the eight models estimated, ranging between 69 percent and 71 percent. These levels compare favorably with typical requirements (Fornell, 1982). Thus, in terms of reliability, the chosen indicators measure reasonably well the latent constructs. Given the similarity among models we will discuss here the loadings and weights for one model only.

In Model 6 the Industry Drivers construct shows the strongest influence from Overall Market Drivers (0.87 coefficient) and Overall Cost Drivers (0.32), while the Overall Government Drivers and Overall Competitive Drivers are much less important. The Organization Structure construct becomes defined by One Global Head (0.88) and International Division (–0.27), i.e., an organization structure that facilitates global strategy has unitary authority and does *not* have an international division that is separate from the domestic one. The Management Process construct is made up of Global Budgeting (0.74) and Global Group Meetings (0.60). The various other indicators (e.g., Cross-Country

Figure 2
Results of PLS Model Estimations

Model 1
Direct Effects on Performance

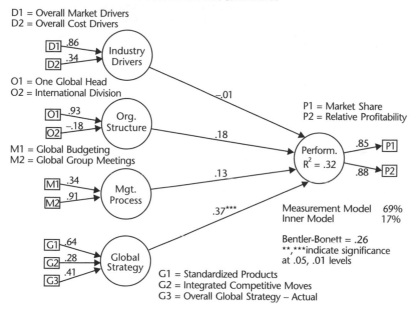

D1 = Overall Market Drivers
D2 = Overall Cost Drivers

O1 = One Global Head
O2 = International Division

P1 = Market Share
P2 = Relative Profitability

M1 = Global Budgeting
M2 = Global Group Meetings

Measurement Model   69%
Inner Model   17%

Bentler-Bonett = .26
,*indicate significance
at .05, .01 levels

G1 = Standardized Products
G2 = Integrated Competitive Moves
G3 = Overall Global Strategy – Actual

Model 2
Only Global Strategy Affects Performance

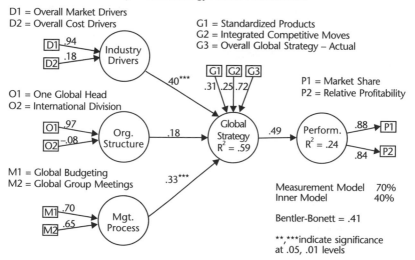

D1 = Overall Market Drivers
D2 = Overall Cost Drivers

G1 = Standardized Products
G2 = Integrated Competitive Moves
G3 = Overall Global Strategy – Actual

O1 = One Global Head
O2 = International Division

P1 = Market Share
P2 = Relative Profitability

M1 = Global Budgeting
M2 = Global Group Meetings

Measurement Model   70%
Inner Model   40%

Bentler-Bonett = .41

,*indicate significance
at .05, .01 levels

(Figure 2 continued)

(Figure 2 continued)

Model 3
All Constructs Affect Performance

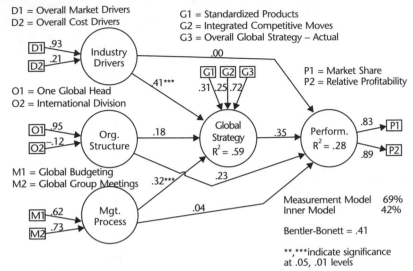

D1 = Overall Market Drivers
D2 = Overall Cost Drivers

G1 = Standardized Products
G2 = Integrated Competitive Moves
G3 = Overall Global Strategy – Actual

O1 = One Global Head
O2 = International Division

P1 = Market Share
P2 = Relative Profitability

M1 = Global Budgeting
M2 = Global Group Meetings

Measurement Model   69%
Inner Model   42%

Bentler-Bonett = .41

,*indicate significance
at .05, .01 levels

Model 4
Strategy Follows Structure

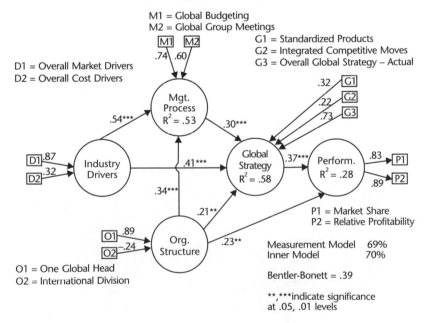

M1 = Global Budgeting
M2 = Global Group Meetings

G1 = Standardized Products
G2 = Integrated Competitive Moves
G3 = Overall Global Strategy – Actual

D1 = Overall Market Drivers
D2 = Overall Cost Drivers

P1 = Market Share
P2 = Relative Profitability

O1 = One Global Head
O2 = International Division

Measurement Model   69%
Inner Model   70%

Bentler-Bonett = .39

,*indicate significance
at .05, .01 levels

(Figure 2 continued)

(Figure 2 continued)

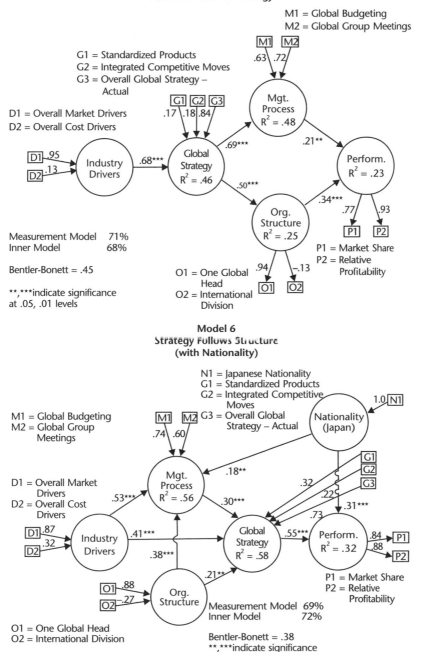

Model 5
Structure Follows Strategy

M1 = Global Budgeting
M2 = Global Group Meetings

G1 = Standardized Products
G2 = Integrated Competitive Moves
G3 = Overall Global Strategy –
         Actual

D1 = Overall Market Drivers
D2 = Overall Cost Drivers

Measurement Model   71%
Inner Model   68%

Bentler-Bonett = .45

,*indicate significance
at .05, .01 levels

O1 = One Global Head
O2 = International Division

P1 = Market Share
P2 = Relative Profitability

Model 6
Strategy Follows Structure
(with Nationality)

N1 = Japanese Nationality
G1 = Standardized Products
G2 = Integrated Competitive Moves
G3 = Overall Global Strategy – Actual

M1 = Global Budgeting
M2 = Global Group Meetings

D1 = Overall Market Drivers
D2 = Overall Cost Drivers

O1 = One Global Head
O2 = International Division

Measurement Model   69%
Inner Model   72%

Bentler-Bonett = .38
,*indicate significance
at .05, .01 levels

P1 = Market Share
P2 = Relative Profitability

(Figure 2 continued)

(Figure 2 continued)

Model 7
Structure Follows Strategy (Plus Nationality Affects Process)

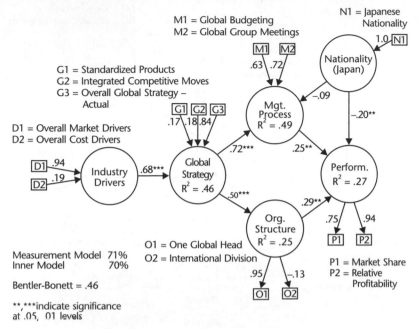

Model 8
Structure Follows Strategy (Plus Nationality Affects Strategy)

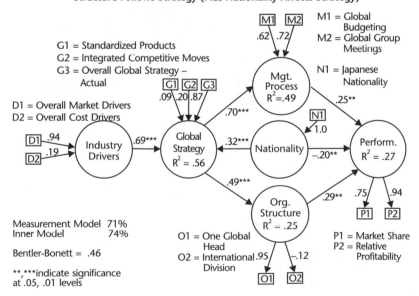

Coordination, Global Performance Review, Global Strategy Information System) were included as indicators in the earlier estimations, but yielded low weights. The Global Strategy construct is a combination of two of the five strategy elements that we used – Standardized Products (0.32) and Integrated Competitive Moves (0.22) having the largest impact, while Global Share Balance, Concentrated Activities and Uniform Marketing had lower weights. The weight of Overall Global Strategy (0.73) suggests that there are aspects of the strategy not captured by the five strategy elements. The individual global strategy elements, e.g., Standardized Products, can be considered to be more objective indicators of Global Strategy while Overall Global Strategy is more perceptual. The Performance construct is reflected in both Market Share (0.84) and Relative Profitability (0.88), both having very high loadings. It is worth noting that the measure of profitability is *relative* to leading compatititors, chosen so as to eliminate differences in average levels of industry profitability. Finally, the Nationality construct has only one indicator, which, therefore, has a full weight of 1.0.

With most indicators specified as formative, questions of validity and reliability take on a special meaning (see Fornell and Larcker, 1981). For example, the Integrated Competitive Moves variable has a relatively small contribution to make in creating the Global Strategy construct. But as a formative indicator it is a part of the global strategy, and to eliminate it – because of its low weight – would mean that we ignore this dimension of the strategy (the standardized weights are most usefully interpreted as multiple regression coefficients). The only justifiable omission concerns the indicators with very low – and thus insignificant – weights.

In the case of reflective indicators, however, one wants all indicators to show high loadings (i.e., high simple correlations with the construct). Since the construct (Performance, in our case) exists independently of the indicators chosen, one wants every one of the indicators to reflect the underlying concept. The high loadings for both Market Share and Relative Profitability are thus necessary (although not in and of themselves sufficient) to establish reliability and validity.

Path Linkages

Turning to the causal linkages between the latent constructs, Figure 2 also gives the relevant path coefficients and their associated significance levels. Because PLS makes no distributional assumptions, the significance levels cannot be based on standard t-statistics, which are unavailable. Rather, the algorithm provides jackknifed statistics, with a blindfolding routine rerunning the estimation for random subsamples (Lohmöller, 1982, Sec. 5.3). The results are generally robust and the approach has become standard practice (see, for example, Fornell and Barclay, 1983). As can be seen in the results in Figure 2, most of the paths are significant at generally accepted levels, and in the expected directions. The coefficients will be discussed first across all the models, and then we will focus on the model choice issue.

Comparing the coefficients for the Industry Drivers first, it is clear from Model 1 that there is no direct effect on Performance (as expected, since performance measures were relative to competition and thus controlled for industry differences). On the other hand, Industry Drivers, as hypothesized, affects the level of Global Strategy consistently across the different models and, as later models suggest, also influence the Management Processes employed by the firms.

As for Organizational Structure, the results are less clear. The linkages to Global Strategy, Management Processes and Performance are positive and mostly significant, but it is not very clear how the causal sequence is best viewed (compare Models 6 and 8, for example). The choice between the 'structure follows strategy' model vs. its opposite requires attention also to the goodness-of-fit of the different alternatives (see below).

Management Processes are clearly strongly related to the level of Global Strategy. There are also signs of a positive relationship to Performance (see Models 7 and 8, for example), but this linkage is less robust and contingent on the particular specification chosen.

Global Strategy is consistently associated with a higher performance level. The relationship is possibly mediated by Organizational Structure and Management Processes (see Models 7 and 8), but is clearly an empirical fact for these companies.

Nationality is introduced as an additional construct in the last four models, and its effect on Performance is consistently negative. Given the scoring, it is the Japanese companies that perform worse when the other global factors have been accounted for. But this significant linkage is perhaps best seen as an adjustment for scale levels. The Japanese firms in the sample, although top performers in many cases, have lower global market shares than their American counterparts, which have a much longer history of multinational operations. Coupled with the stronger American drive for profitability (a 'causal' factor) it is not surprising that the Performance scores for the Americans lie at a higher level. Introducing the Nationality construct allows us to correct for this difference, and avoids biasing the estimation of the strategy linkages.

The significant path coefficients from Nationality to Global Strategy and Management Processes suggest that the Japanese are more global and have stronger integration mechanisms than the Americans. These are expected results, and confirm our initial propositions. Furthermore, since both of these constructs have positive linkages to Performance, the Japanese get a positive performance boost from their globally integrated strategies.

The statistical findings are also very much supported by the comments made by the executives interviewed. A high proportion of the American businesses (78%) had an international division separate from the domestic division. But the American businesses respondents mostly saw this separate division as a hindrance to global strategy, and there was some trend toward disbanding international divisions. One business had recently shifted to three regions for the whole world. An executive in this business viewed the change of getting rid of the U.S. division, and breaking down regional barriers, as one of their greatest successes. The benefits included better allocation of resources and the recognition that business lost in one country need not necessarily be replaced in the same country, but could be recouped elsewhere. The international division structure also seemed to be losing its power. The head of another American business commented that the role of the country manager had changed a great deal – the country manager used to run the business in the country, but was now the titular head who represented the parent company in the country. In contrast, although all of the Japanese businesses had a separate international division, the Japanese respondents showed little concern about the role of these divisions.

It was also notable that American comments on managerial processes focused on difficulties in achieving global integration, while the Japanese comments complained about too much central coordination. For example, the head of international marketing and sales for an American industrial controls business viewed the lack of global performance review as a major problem. But that was somewhat offset now by basing on worldwide achievement a portion of incentive compensation for global team members. The head of business planning for an American company commented that the difficulty of getting product managers to think globally was exacerbated by the lack of global reward systems. So, it was all too common to not take the global job requirements as seriously as the domestic ones. Indeed, this executive believed that the product managers would like to be measured on a global basis, and were willing to take their chances on that. In the same business, the director of international strategic planning also viewed the lack of global compensation as a major weak spot. Of course, the Japanese businesses could not even try to use global compensation systems, as their compensation systems do not link to performance but to seniority. One Japanese respondent commented that his company's first attempt to open an office in the United States was not successful. But the staff were not fired, and were instead criticized and 'put by the window.' On the other hand some executives saw barriers to global processes. The executives in one American business were worried that if they created a global budget for strategic contingencies, the money would get appropriated by corporate 'the next day'.

Estimation on Split Sample

One question we had was whether our findings might differ by the level of globalization in each industry. Accordingly, we reestimated the final models, 6, 7 and 8 on two halves of the sample, representing higher and lower industry globalization. One possibility was to use Kobrin's (1991) classification (industries in which intrafirm trade accounts for less than 25 percent of international sales), but we preferred to use our own measures collected in the study, instead, in order to enhance the internal validity of our analysis. Accordingly, we split the sample using an index of industry globalization potential created by summing the scores on each of the four overall measures of globalization drivers (market, cost, government and competitive). The possible range for this index was 0–20, with an actual range of 9–18. As it happened, about half of both the American and Japanese samples fall below an index of 15. So we created a 'moderate globalization' sample for businesses scoring below 15, and a 'high globalization' sample for those scoring above. The lower subsample contained 8 American and 10 Japanese businesses, and the more global sample, 10 American businesses and 8 Japanese. The model reestimations on the split samples provided three notable results. First, the path from Industry Drivers to Global Strategy is consistently weaker, across Models 6, 7 and 8, in the *high* globalization than in the *moderate* globalization sample. Our interpretation is that this occurred because there is less variance in both the level of globalization drivers and the use of global strategy in the high sample. Second, in Model 6, in which Global Strategy has a direct path to Performance, there is no difference between the high and moderate samples, implying that a global strategy is superior irrespective of industry characteristics. Third, in Model 8, Nationality has a stronger path to Global Strategy in the high sample than in the moderate, implying that the Japanese respond more to high globalization drivers than to moderate, i.e., they respond appropriately. The same effect also holds in Model 6, where there is a direct path from Nationality to Management Processes (and little difference in Model 8).

We can conclude that our findings are reasonably robust even when splitting the sample into high and moderate globalization industries. Second, there are indications that the positive link between global strategy and performance holds irrespective of industry characteristics. Third, this additional analysis further supports the view of more appropriate Japanese response to globalization potential.

Checking the Effect of Parent Size

Given that the American parent companies were larger than the Japanese (mean of $19.5 billion vs. $11.5 billion), some of the nationality effects may be confounded by this difference in size. To check for this possible effect, we added parent company revenues (Parent Size) as an additional construct in Models 6, 7 and 8, using it both instead of Nationality, and with it (as a separate construct). The results are reassuring for the role of nationality. First, the addition of Parent Size had little effect on the paths from Nationality, when the latter were kept. Second, Parent Size had no significant paths to Performance. Third, in a couple of the models, Parent Size has a significant, negative path to Global Strategy slightly weaker than the positive path from Nationality to Global Strategy. Recall that the American parents are larger, while the Japanese businesses made more use of global strategy. So these two results are equivalent if Parent Size is acting as a proxy for Nationality in the effect on global strategy. Fourth, there are a couple of significant paths of conflicting signs from Parent Size to Management Processes in a couple of significant paths of conflicting signs from Parent Size to Management Processes in a couple of the models. Lastly, the R^2 levels were consistently lower when using Parent Size instead of Nationality. In conclusion, Parent Size does not affect the role of Nationality and is generally an inferior construct.

Model Choice

With the measurement linkages (the 'outer' model) so similar across the alternative specifications, the model choice can focus on goodness-of-fit measures of the 'inner' model (i.e., the relations between the latent constructs). The algorithm provides two fit measures. One is the Bentler-Bonett statistic (Bentler and Bonett, 1980), a normed (0–1) measure of the model's explained variance relative to a null model of complete independence. The second measure is the percent explanation of covariation among the latent constructs.

Since the number of indicators – the 'variables' in standard regression terminology – stays constant across Models 1 to 5, these goodness-of-fit indices can be readily interpreted. The simplistic Models 1 to 3 can be quickly dismissed in favor of the more informative Models 4 and 5. The simplest, one-level, model, Model 1 – Direct Effects on Performance, explains very little of the inner model, only 17 percent. Furthermore, only one of the paths from the exogenous constructs to Performance is significant. Next, the two-level models, Model 2 – Only Global Strategy Affects Performance and Model 3 – All Factors Affect Performance, provide a large improvement in the explained variance of the inner model, with values of 40 percent and 42 percent respectively. But few of the path coefficients are significant. When, however, we estimated the three-level models (Models 4 and 5) the explained variance of the inner model jumps from the 40 percent to the 70 percent range, and the Bentler-Bonett statistic makes a marginal improvement in some cases. Also notable is that all of the path coefficients become significant. Between Models 4 and 5, the 'structure follows strategy' specification in 5 seems slightly preferable with an increase in the Bentler-Bonett from 0.39 to 0.45 and a balanced shift in explained variation between the inner and the outer models.

The estimated Model 4 – Strategy Follows Structure worked best as an amalgam of Specifications 3 and 4. It differs from the conceptual models in a few ways:

- Industry Globalization Drivers has little effect on Organization Structure, so we dropped this path;
- Organization Structure has a direct effect on Management Processes as well as on Global Strategy and on Performance
- Management Processes has little effect on Performance, so we dropped this path.

The estimated Model 5 – Structure Follows Strategy has all its paths significant. Compared with Model 4, it achieves very similar levels of overall explained variance for the inner and outer models, and a slightly higher Bentler-Bonett statistic (0.45 vs. 0.39). With an additional endogenous construct (Organization Structure), the R^2 values for the endogenous constructs are somewhat lower than in Model 4. On the basis of these comparisons we cannot conclude that one model (4 or 5) is better than the other, although both these three-level models are significantly better than the one- and two-level models. So in our next stage of analysis we worked with both Models 4 and 5 to find the best placement for the effect of the Nationality construct.

The introduction of Nationality in the 'Strategy follows Structure' specification of Model 4, yielding Model 6, seems hardly worth it. Even though the paths to Performance and Management Processes are significant, the Bentler-Bonett drops fractionally (somewhat expected since the new construct adds a variable to account for), but the inner model explanation rises only slightly. But these results seem due to a misspecification of linkages. In the Chandlerian 'Structure follows Strategy' models 7 and 8, the Bentler-Bonett statistic is back up to 0.46, and when Nationality is linked directly to Global Strategy, the inner model explanation rises to 74 percent (Model 8). While a Bentler-Bonett value of 0.46 is relatively low in absolute terms, an explained covariation of 74 percent is quite respectable (Bentler, 1989: 93). Thus, even though this model does not explain the total variability in the constructs particularly well, the covariation ('communality' in factor analysis language) among the latent constructs is reproduced reasonably well. With Model 8 in addition showing everywhere significant coefficients, it becomes a strong candidate.

It is also necessary, however, to examine the R^2 values of the various endogenous constructs. As can be seen by comparing Models 6 and 8, the 'strategy follows structure' specification in 6 scores better on the explanation of the Performance construct. It is clear that when Global Strategy is related to Performance only indirectly (via organizational structure and management processes), its impact is somewhat attenuated (see Model 8). The reason can be gleaned from the weights of indicators. In Model 6, where the strategy links directly to performance, Global Strategy contains a stronger element of Standardized Products. This aspect of the Global Strategy generates stronger Performance. On the other hand, in the Model 8 specification, Global Strategy essentially consists of the perceptual measure only, which, translated into organizational structure and managerial processes, exhibits less of a Performance impact. Choosing Model 8 over Model 6 entails giving up a dimension of global Strategy – Product Standardization – which apparently has real Performance implications.

Direct and Indirect Effects

The path coefficients can also be used to determine the total influence of each determining construct on each affected construct, by multiplying all paths and summing. We present this analysis for Models 6 and 8 in Table 2. For the total influence on the actual use of global strategy it is notable that industry globalization drivers have easily the largest total influence in both models, but also that organization structure and management processes together add up the same total influence as drivers when these paths are added, as in Model 6. Nationality can have a large effect on Global Strategy, but this effect diminishes when the path is indirect via Management Processes.

In terms of the total influence on performance, the actual use of global strategy has the largest single influence in both models. Organizational structure

Table 2
Total Influences on Global Strategy and Performance

Model 6: Strategy follows structure

Total influence on global strategy

Industry drivers	= (0.53)(0.30) + 0.41	= 0.57
Organization structure	= (0.38)(0.30) + 0.21	= 0.32
Management Processes		= 0.30
Nationality (Japan)	= (0.18)(0.30)	= 0.05

Total influence on performance

Industry drivers	= (0.53)(0.30)(0.55) + (0.41)(0.55)	= 0.31
Global strategy		= 0.55
Organization structure	= (0.38)(0.30)(0.55) + (0.21)(0.55)	= 0.18
Management processes	= (0.30)(0.55)	= 0.17
Nationality (Japan)	= (0.18)(0.30)(0.55) + (−0.31)	= −0.28

Model 8: Structure follows strategy

Total influence on global strategy

Industry drivers	= 0.69
Nationality (Japan)	= 0.32

Total influence on performance

Industry drivers	= (0.69)(0.70)(0.25) + (0.69)(0.49)(0.29)	= 0.22
Global strategy	= (0.70)(0.25) + (0.49)(0.29)	= 0.32
Organization structure		= 0.29
Management processes		= 0.25
Nationality (Japan)	= (0.32)(0.70)(0.25) + (0.32)(0.49)(0.29) + (−0.20)	= −0.10

and management processes have larger total effects on performance when they have direct paths (Model 8) rather than indirect (Model 6). Chandler's 'structure follows strategy' model clearly places a premium on well aligned organizational structures and processes. Industry drivers have a moderate total influence on performance in both models.

Discussion

The data we collected provide strong support for our conception of the four globalization constructs: industry globalization drivers, globally integrated strategy, global organization, and global management processes. In particular, the quantitative data show a wide variation in the levels of each of these constructs, i.e., the phenomena exist. Of the four categories of industry globalization drivers, market and cost drivers showed a consistently strong association with the level of global strategy used. The data also illustrate the richness of industry globalization potential, with different types of drivers applying in different industries. Among the five major elements of globally integrated strategy, standardized products seem particularly representative of global strategy. At the same time, several dimensions are needed to fully represent the nature of global strategy. Global organization and global management processes are also found to vary greatly among the companies, and to have important effects on the ability of firms to implement global strategy. Lastly, the qualitative comments illustrate the importance of all these constructs to senior managers in these multinational companies.

The finding that the three-level models (Specifications 4 and 5 in Figure 1) provide the highest level of explained variance is important. It means that, at least in this sample, the various constructs do relate in the complex fashion indicated by the literature. Managers do need to concern themselves with how industry globalization drivers affect their choice of strategies, organization structure and management processes.

The findings also support a role for nationality. Even though as expected the perceptions of industry drivers varied between Japanese and American firms, we found the expected pattern in the responses to these drivers. We also found that the Japanese were better attuned to the global strategy requirements, also as expected since their history of centralized direction facilitates global integration. The study showed that it is in the development of smoother management processes that the Japanese arrive at a more effective global organization.

Trying to resolve the model choice question – including whether strategy follows or precedes structure, and what the exact influence of Nationality is – entailed running several alternative specifications. The versions presented here were the most promising ones – for example, the many additional options for Nationality linkages were all insignificant – but, as we have seen, a final choice is still difficult. The fact is, of course, that global strategy theory is not strong enough yet to avoid exploratory approaches in this type of empirical study. The models evaluated do not represent 'causal' structures but convenient ways of structuring the data analysis. Further conceptual development has to emerge, alternative testing instruments and scales have to be developed, and more rigorous data collection techniques are necessary to claim scientific validity for these results.

On the other hand, as an exploratory study, the results can stand some closer scrutiny. Face validity of both measurement and path linkages is reasonably high, given past research. Industry drivers, especially homogeneous markets and cost economies, seem to generate a force that makes firms opt for more global strategies. Where organizational structures and management processes are properly aligned to this strategy, whichever comes first, there is a pay-off in better performance. And the oft-quoted tendency of the Japanese to sacrifice profits for share again leads to better performance for the Americans.

Our new findings are thus given some credence. In the big picture, the Japanese have more of a global strategy than the direct influence of industry drivers would suggest. This is not only because the central coordination from Tokyo makes integration across the globe easier than for the multinational Americans, although the positive linkage between organizational structure and global strategy shows that this is an important factor. Rather, the linkage of nationality to management processes suggests that the Japanese have instituted more management mechanisms (global group meetings and global budgeting) that facilitate the implementation of global strategies.

As the consistently significant and positive linkage between global strategy and performance shows, firms with more global strategies do better. For the companies in the sample, globalizing their strategies further would make sense.

The Japanese managers who complained about too much central coordination apparently still outperformed their American counterparts. Thus, even though the Americans exhibit good performance due to their long presence in foreign markets and their focus on profitability, with more globalization they could have done even better. If the Japanese have established management processes that are more in tune with global strategies than those of the Americans, they have also gained a performance advantage.

In terms of further theory development, it is tantalizing to note that a global strategy by itself seems to lead to improved performance. This would seem to go counter to the contingency and 'fit' theories that the strategy has to fit the circumstances. It may of course be a purely empirical accident, with these 36 businesses happening to follow a peculiar pattern. One would still like to have some plausible theoretical explanation – could it be that the adoption of a global strategy serves as a stimulus to sharper managerial performance? a form of 'strategic intent' perhaps?

Another theory issue is the not-here-resolved question of structure following strategy or the other way around. The most fruitful path here would seem to be to recognize that the implicit time sequence involved – first strategy, then structure – is fundamentally dynamic. In a cross-section one would expect to find different businesses at different stages of adaptation to the desired (perhaps global) strategy, just as we found here. But to settle the 'which comes first' question one naturally has to await time series data. In the meantime, it is clear that a 'resource-based' perspective would suggest that an organizational structure helps define, delimit, but also enlarge organizational capability – just as the centralized Tokyo operations of many Japanese companies has enabled them to integrate faster globally. This does go counter to the Chandlerian notion of first formulating the appropriate (global) strategy and then develop the organizational capabilities to enable implementation.

The results encourage further research in several directions. One direction would be toward larger sample studies, probably with a smaller number of questions and using mail questionnaires rather than personal interviews. That would allow for more complex types of analysis and more confidence in the findings, thus avoiding some of the already-discussed limitations of this study's methodology. A second direction would be to add European multinational companies. Given their lengthy history of being multinational, European companies are likely to have a different pattern of globalization from both American and Japanese MNCs.

Acknowledgements

This research was sponsored and supported in part by the Marketing Science Institute. The authors thank MSI and the companies that participated in the study, and also Professor Ikujiro Nonaka, Institute of Business Research, Hitotsubashi University, and Professor Koji Tsubaki, School of Commerce, Waseda University, for their help with recruiting and interviewing companies in Japan. The authors are also grateful for the help of Sandra Burke, Elizabeth Cooper-Martin, José de la Torre, Bill McKelvey, Robert J. Thomas, Mary Ann von Glinow, and two anonymous referees.

References

Abegglen, C. and G. Stalk, Jr. (1985). *The Japanese Corporation*. Basic Books, New York.

Anderson, J. C. and D. W. Gerbing (1988). 'Structural equation modeling in practice: A review and recommended two-step approach', *Psychological Bulletin*, **103**(3), pp. 411–123.

Barclay, D. W., L. E. Duxbury and C. A. Higgins (June 1991). 'An introduction to the partial least squares approach to causal modeling', Working Paper Series no. 91–08, Western Business School, University of Western Ontario, London, Canada.

Bartlett, C. A. and S. Ghoshal (Fall 1987). 'Managing across borders: New organizational responses', *Sloan Management Review*, pp. 43–53.

Bartlett, C. A. and S. Ghoshal (1991). 'Global strategic management' *Strategic Management Journal*, **12**, Summer Special Issue, pp. 5–16.

Bartlett, C. A. and S. Ghoshal (1989). *Managing Across Borders: The Transnational Solution*. Harvard Business School Press, Boston, MA.

Bentler, P. M. (1989). *EQS: Structural Equations Program Manual*. BMDP Statistical Software, Los Angeles, CA.

Bentler, P. M. and D. G. Bonett (1980). 'Significance tests and goodness of fit in the analysis of covariance structures', *Psychological Bulletin*, **88**, pp. 586–606.

Brouthers, L. E. and S. Werner (Fall 1990). 'Are the Japanese good global competitors?', *Columbia Journal of World Business*, **25**,(3), pp. 5–11.

Chandler, A. D. (1962). *Strategy and Structure: Chapters in the History of the Industrial Enterprise*. MIT Press, Cambridge, MA.

Clark, R. (1979). *The Japanese Company*. Yale University Press, New Haven, CT.

Cool, K. and D. Schendel (1988). 'Performance differences among strategic group members', *Strategic Management Journal*, **9**(3), pp. 207–233.

Cool, K., I. Dierickx, and D. Jemison (1989). 'Business strategy, market structure and risk-return relationships: A structural approach', *Strategic Management Journal*, **10**(6), pp. 507–522.

Dess, G. C. and R. B. Robinson, Jr. (1984). 'Measuring organizational performance in the absence of objective measures: The case of the privately-held firm and the conglomerate business unit', *Strategic Management Journal*, **5**(3), pp. 265–273.

Douglas, S. P. and C. Craig (1983). *International Marketing Research*. Prentice-Hall, Englewood Cliffs, NJ.

Doz, Y. (1979). *Government Control and Multinational Management*. Praeger, New York.

Edström, A. and P. Lorange (Fall, 1984). 'Matching strategy and human resources in multinational corporations', *Journal of International Business Studies*, pp. 125–137.

Egelhoff, W. G. (Fall 1984). 'Patterns of control in U.S., U.K. and European Multinational Corporations', *Journal of International Business Studies*, pp. 73–83.

Fornell, C. (ed.) (1982). *A Second Generation of Multivariate Analysis: Methods*. Praeger, New York.

Fornell, C. and D. W. Barclay (1983). 'Jackknifing: A supplement to Lohmöller's LVPLS Program', Graduate School of Business Administration, University of Michigan, Ann Arbor, MI.

Fornell, C. and F. Bookstein (1982). 'A comparative analysis of two structural equation models: LISREL and PLS applied to consumer exit-voice theory', *Journal of Marketing Research*, XIX, pp. 440–452.

Fornell, C. and D. F. Larcker (1981). 'Structural equation models with unobservable variables and measurement error: Algebra and statistics', *Journal of Marketing Research*, **18**, pp. 382–388.

Fornell, C., P. Lorange, and J. Roos (1990). 'The cooperative venture formation process: A latent variable structural modeling approach', *Management Science*, Special Issue on State of the Art in Theory and Methodology in Strategy Research, **36**,(10), pp. 1246–1255.

Ghoshal, S. (1987). 'Global strategy: An organizing framework', *Strategic Management Journal*, **8**,(5), pp. 425–440.

Haar, J. (1989). 'A comparative analysis of the profitability performance of the largest U.S., European and Japanese multinational enterprises', *Management International Review*, **29**,(3), pp. 5–18.

Hamel, G. and C. K. Prahalad (1985). 'Do you really have a Global Strategy?' *Harvard Business Review*, **63**,(4), pp. 139–148.

Hanssens, D. M. and J. K. Johansson (1991). 'Rivalry as synergy? The Japanese automobile companies' export expansion', *Journal of International Business Studies*, Third Quarter, pp. 503–526.

Hedlund, G. (1980). 'The role of foreign subsidiaries in strategic decision-making in Swedish multinational corporations', *Strategic Management Journal*, **1**,(1), pp. 23–26.

Hofer, C. W. and D. E. Schendel (1978). *Strategy Formulation: Analytical Concepts*. West Publishing, St. Paul, MN.

Hout, T., M. E. Porter, and E. Rudden (September–October 1982). 'How global companies win out', *Harvard Business Review*, pp. 98–108.

Jaeger, A. M. (Fall 1983). 'The transfer of organizational culture overseas: An approach to control in the multinational corporation', *Journal of International Business Studies*, pp. 91–114.

Jaeger, A. M. and B. R. Baliga (1985). 'Control systems and strategic adaptation: Lessons from the Japanese experience', *Strategic Management Journal*, **6**(2), pp. 115–134.

Jain, S. C. (1989). 'Standardization of international marketing strategy: Some research hypotheses', *Journal of Marketing*, **53**, pp. 70–79.

Kagono, T., I. Nonaka, A. Okumura, K. Sakakibara, Y. Komatsu and A. Sakashita (1984). 'Mechanistic vs. organic management systems: A comparative study of adaptive patterns of American and Japanese firms'. In K. Sato and Y. Hoshino (eds.), *The Anatomy of Japanese Business*. M. E. Sharpe, New York, pp. 27–69.

Kobrin, S. J. (1991). 'An empirical analysis of the determinants of global integration', *Strategic Management Journal*, **12**, Summer Special Issue, pp. 17–32.

Kogut, B. (Fall 1985). 'Normative observations on the value added chain and stategic groups', *Journal of International Business Studies*, pp. 151–167.

Kono, Toyohiro (1984). *Strategy and Structure of the Japanese Enterprises*. M. E. Sharpe, New York.

Kotabe, M. and G. S. Omura (1989). 'Sourcing strategies of European and Japanese multinationals: A comparison', *Journal of International Business Studies*, **20**,(1), pp. 113–130.

Kotler, P., L. Fahey and S. Jatusripitak (1985). *The New Competition*. Prentice-Hall, Englewood Cliffs, NJ.

Levitt, T. (May–June 1983). 'The globalization of markets', *Harvard Business Review*, pp. 92–102.

Lohmöller, J. (1982). 'An overview of latent variables path analysis'. Paper presented at the Annual Meeting of the American Educational Research Association, New York.

Martinez, J. I. and J. C. Jarillo (1989). 'The evolution of research on coordination mechanisms in multinational corporations', *Journal of International Business Studies*, **20**,(3), pp. 489–514.

Morrison, A. J. (1990). *Strategies in Global Industries: How U.S. Businesses Compete.* Quorum Books, Westpoint, CT.

Morrison, A. J. and K. Roth (1992). 'A taxonomy of business-level strategies in global industries', *Strategic Management Journal*, **13**(6), pp. 399–418.

Odagiri, H. (Spring, 1990). 'Unravelling the mystery of low Japanese profit rates', *Business Strategy Review* (London Business School), pp. 25–36.

Ohmae, K. (1985). *Triad Power: The Coming Shape of Global Competition.* Free Press, New York.

Ouchi, W. G. (1981). *Theory Z: How American Business Can Meet the Japanese Challenge.* Addison-Wesley, Reading, MA.

Pascale, R. T. and A. G. Athos (1981). *The Art of Japanese Management: Applications for American Executives.* Simon and Schuster, New York.

Perlmutter, H. V. (January–February 1969). 'The tortuous evolution of the multinational corporation', *Columbia Journal of World Business*, pp. 9–18.

Picken, S. D. B. (1987). 'Values and value related strategies in Japanese corporate culture', *Journal of Business Ethics*, **6**(2), pp. 137–143.

Porter, M. E. (1986). 'Changing patterns of international competition', *California Management Review*, **28**,(2), pp. 9–40.

Prahalad, C. K. and Y. L. Doz (1987). *The Multinational Mission: Balancing Local Demands and Global Vision.* Free Press, New York.

Roth, K. and A. J. Morrison (1990). 'An empirical analysis of the integration-responsiveness framework in global industries', *Journal of International Business Studies*, **21**(4), pp. 541–564.

Samiee, S. and K. Roth (1992). 'The influence of global marketing standardization on performance', *Journal of Marketing*, **56**,(2), pp. 1–17.

Stalk, G., Jr. (1988). 'Time – the next source of competitive advantage', *Harvard Business Review*, 66,(4), pp. 41–51.

Takeuchi, H. and M. E. Porter (1986). 'Three roles of international marketing in global strategy'. In M. E. Porter (ed.), *Competition in Global Industries*. Harvard Business School Press, Boston, MA, pp. 111–146.

Venkatraman, N. and V. Ramanujam (1986). 'Measurement of business performance in strategy research', *Academy of Management Review*, 11, pp. 801–814.

Venkatraman, N. and V. Ramanujam (1987). 'Measurement of business economic performance: An examination of method convergence', *Journal of Management*, **13**(1), pp. 109–122.

Walters, P. G. P. (Summer 1986). 'International marketing policy: A discussion of the standardization construct and its relevance for corporate policy', *Journal of International Business Studies*, pp. 55–69.

Wold, H. (1982). 'Systems under indirect observation using PLS'. In C. Fornell (ed.), *A Second Generation of Multivariate Analysis*. Praeger, New York, pp. 325–347.

Yip, G. S. (1989). 'Global strategy ... In a world of nations?' *Sloan Management Review*, **31**(1), pp. 29–41.

Yip, G. S. (1992). *Total Global Strategy: Managing for Worldwide Competitive Advantage.* Prentice-Hall, Englewood Cliffs, NJ.

Yip, G. S., P. M. Loewe and M. Y. Yoshino (Winter 1988). 'How to take your company to the global market', *Columbia Journal of World Business*, pp. 37–48.

Yoshino, M. Y. (1968). *Japan's Managerial System, Tradition and Innovation*, MIT Press, Cambridge, MA.

Appendix: Measures of Globalization Used in Paper

All items are on a 5-point scale unless otherwise indicated

Industry Globalization Drivers

Overall Market Drivers. Overall strength of market factors favoring globalization in this product category today.
Overall Cost Drivers. Overall strength of cost factors favoring globalization in this product category today.
Overall Government Drivers. Overall strength of government factors favoring globalization in this product category today.
Overall Competitive Drivers. Overall strength of competitive factors favoring globalization in this product category today.

Organization Structure

One Global Head. Yes/no measure on whether there is one person whose primary job it is to be head of the worldwide business.
International Division. Yes/no measure on whether there is an international division that does not contain the domestic business.
Business Dimension of Matrix. Strength of business dimension of organization matrix.
Geographic Dimension of Matrix. Strength of geographic dimension of organization matrix.
Functional Dimension of Matrix. Strength of functional dimension of organization matrix.

Management Processes

Cross-Country Coordination. Extent to which the business has processes for coordinating strategy across countries.
Global Budgeting. Extent to which the business has global budgets that are used for global programs, as opposed to national budgets for national programs.
Global Group Meetings. Extent and frequency of meetings involving senior managers from around the world.
Global Performance Review. Extent to which senior managers are evaluated and compensated on the basis of global and not just regional or national performance.
Global Strategy Information System. Extent to which the business collects strategic information, such as market share and competitor data, from around the world in a consistent format on a regular basis.

Global Strategy

Global Share Balance. Extent to which the business's revenues are well spread compared with that of the worldwide market.

(Appendix continued)

(Appendix continued)

Standardized Products. Extent to which the business's products are globally standardized, i.e., as indicated by percent of cost of product or service that is in components that are standardized.

Activity Concentration. Location of each activity in relation to geographic markets where products are sold, ranging from mostly local to mostly central. Average of measures for Research, Development, Purchasing, Raw Material Processing, Subassembly, Final Assembly, Marketing, Selling, Distribution and Service.

Marketing Uniformity. Extent to which the business takes a different approach in each country or a uniform approach for each marketing element. Average of measures for Uniform Brands, Uniform Packaging, Uniform Absolute Pricing, Uniform Relative Pricing, Uniform Advertising, Uniform Promotion, Uniform Selling Approach, Uniform Distribution Approach.

Integrated Competitive Moves. Extent to which the business coordinates competitive moves across countries.

Actual Overall Global Strategy. How global the overall strategy is today.

Optimal Overall Global Strategy. How global the overall strategy should be today.

Overall Global Strategy Gap. Researcher-calculated difference between actual and optimal; overall global strategy.

Performance

Market Share. Extent to which the business was one of the largest competitors, medium sized competitors or smaller competitors.

Relative Profitability. Average profitability (return-on-investment) of the business over the previous 3 years compared with the worldwide category/major competitors.

48

The Performance Implications of a Global Integration Strategy in Global Industries: An Empirical Investigation Using Inter-Area Product Flows

Alfredo J. Mauri and Rakesh B. Sambharya

Introduction

Several International management scholars have focused on the role of global integration of activities for firms pursuing a global strategy (Bartlett/Ghoshal 1987, Hout/Porter/Rudden 1982, Roth 1995). The global integration of a company's operations is a response to the fundamental nature of global competition (Ghemawat/Spence 1986) and represents a key dimension of an international strategy (Kutschker/Baurle 1997, Prahalad/Doz 1987). Global integration indicates the importance given by the international firm to geographically disperse and specialize its operations with the intention of building sources of competitive advantage (Porter 1986).

Global competition is becoming commonplace in many industries. Host countries have liberalized regulations concerning the foreign control of assets and have reduced tariff barriers. By allowing the free movement of goods across borders, trade liberalization promotes the establishment of global integration strategies. Multinational enterprises (MNEs) are globalizing at a frantic pace to meet this increasingly global competition and achieve economies of scope and scale. MNEs are relocating operations globally in an unending search for cost efficiencies and location economies.

However, despite the theoretical and practical importance of global integration, surprisingly little empirical research has been done on this topic. This study investigates the performance implications of a strategy of global integration by constructing an index of global integration based on inter-area product flows

Source: *Management International Review*, Vol. 43, No. 2, 2003, pp. 27–45.

(Kobrin 1991, Mauri/Phatak 2001). Using a sample of US MNEs in four global industries for the period 1992–1997, empirical results show evidence of a curvilinear relationship between global integration and performance. For low and high levels of global integration, the global integration index is related negatively to MNE performance; however, at moderate levels of global integration a positive relation with performance is found.

Theoretical Framework

The MNE Network and Global Integration

Current theoretical developments in organizational theory consider the MNE as an interorganizational network (Andersson/Forsgren 2000, Ghoshal/Bartlett 1990, Ghoshal/Nohria 1989, Malnight 1996). The network view suggests that an MNE is a collection of differentiated units, operating in different parts of the world, and using various organizational modes (Ghoshal/Nohria 1989). The genesis of the network view lies in the seminal works by Emerson (1962), Pfeffer and Salancik (1978) and Thompson (1967), who examine various organizational issues based on an analysis of critical resources and resource linkages among network members. Their research explores power-dependency relations (Emerson 1962), a firm's adaptation and survival based on the access to scarce resources held by a limited number of external actors (Pfeffer/Salancik 1978), and the notion of resource interdependencies influencing the fit between an organization's administrative structure and the environment (Thompson 1967).

A highly interdependent network implies significant and frequent resource linkages and exchange across units. In an MNE, this resource exchange occurs between the parent company and the highly specialized subsidiaries, and among the subsidiaries themselves. As a result of the increasing network differentiation and integration needed to effectively compete internationally, the subsidiaries become interdependent nodes, and their outputs become inputs to other units located in other countries.

Consistent with the network view, a growing research stream in international management has attributed a more prominent role to the subsidiary (Andersson/ Forsgren 2000, Birkinshaw/Hood 1998, Malnight 1996). According to this literature, some foreign subsidiaries become centers of excellence (Andersson/ Forsgren 2000), that contribute key resources to the rest of the MNE by making use of subsidiary initiatives (Birkinshaw/Morrison 1995) or global mandates (Roth/Morrison 1992). Thus the subsidiary has a significant role in the MNE network since it possesses its own advantage and may even be an equal partner for headquarters (Andersson/Forsgren 2000, Birkinshaw/Hood 1998).

The integration of global operations can be gauged by the international resource exchange between interdependent MNE units (Bartlett/Ghoshal 1987, Ghoshal 1987, Gupta/Govindarajan 1991, Kobrin 1991). This exchange involves several types of resource flows: product and components, financial capital, and knowledge. Bartlett and Ghoshal (1987) and Kobrin (1991) underscore the importance of the product exchange compared to other resource flows. Bartlett and Ghoshal (1987, p. 48) suggest that product interdependence is the "most fundamental" among the resource exchanges. Product flows in globally integrated companies exhibit high frequency and lead to critical operational interdependencies requiring complex coordination processes.

Intra-firm trade statistics reveal the magnitude of the international product flows between units of MNE networks. Approximately 20 years ago, intrafirm shipments accounted for 24 percent of the entire US manufacturing trade (Hipple 1990). This fraction has become even more pronounced in recent years. The aggregate value of intrafirm exports has fluctuated between 32 and 40 percent of US exports in goods, and between 37 and 43 percent of US imports in goods, for the period 1982–1994 (Zeile 1997). The most recent statistics available from the US Bureau of Economic Analysis (Mataloni Jr/Yorgason 2002, Zeile 2001) show that intrafirm trade is currently at a level of 34 percent of US exports and 38 percent of US imports. This increase in magnitude over previous years indicates the importance accorded to global integration by US MNEs.

According to the network view, the globally integrating MNE faces two fundamental challenges: the geographic configuration of value-adding activities, and the coordination of those activities (Porter 1986). The configuration dimension involves arranging the overall system of MNE activities, including selecting the geographic location and defining the scope of responsibilities of each MNE unit; while coordination implies building the administrative mechanisms that enable the MNE to effectively organize its geographically dispersed units.

The Configuration of the Integrated Network in a Global Industry

Market structure and firm-specific factors affect the configuration of the integrated network for an MNE competing in a global industry. Market structure represents the technical and economic conditions that provide the context for industry competition, and which influence strategy choices and performance levels for the firms participating in an industry (Bain 1968, Scherer/Ross 1990). Porter (1986) suggests that global industries present converging patterns of competition "where a firm must in some way integrate its activities on a worldwide basis to capture the linkages among countries" (p. 19).

More specifically on the geographic configuration of global industries, Porter (1986) proposes that global competition is shaped by substantial upfront investments for creating new technologies and scale economies, as well as by the establishment of specialized subsidiaries in countries that offer the most attractive conditions. Another aspect of configuration lies in standardizing products and components to achieve cost reduction due to the convergence of consumer needs (Levitt 1983). Furthermore, Ohmae (1990) suggests that the expectations for building a global base provide strong incentives for an MNE to make large and specialized investments before it can take the products to their respective markets and generate revenues.

In contrast to the market structure explanations, firm-specific forces illustrate the influence of a firm's unique resources on the integration configuration of the MNE. Internalization theory (Dunning 1988) and transaction costs theory (Caves 1996, Hennart 1991, Teece 1986) suggest that firm-specific resources and location factors encourage the global firm to internalize value-adding activities abroad. The firm-specific resources provide an ownership advantage that enable the globally integrated company to develop and transfer knowledge and other resources internationally in a more efficient manner than if it used market transactions; while location factors influence where these value-adding activities are internalized.

Similarly, the resource-based view examines a firm's collection of specific resources to explain the sustainability of its competitive advantage. (Barney 1991, Conner 1991, Wernerfelt 1984). This resource advantage is difficult to imitate because of the long time periods required in developing firm-specific resource stocks (Dierickx/Cool 1989); the irreversible nature of the investments (Ghemawat 1991); and the uncertainty, complexity, and conflict that occurs while developing resources (Amit/Schoemaker 1993). The resource-based perspective suggests that the essence of a firm's competitive advantage resides in its ability to create, transfer and combine new knowledge efficiently across organizational units. Several authors have clearly illustrated the constant search for knowledge and technological developments in global industries (Ghoshal 1987, Ghoshal/Bartlett 1988, Kobrin 1991, Mauri/Phatak 2001, Roth/Morrison 1990). Consistent with this view, Kogut and Zander (1992) suggest that new knowledge and learning result from a firm's "combinative abilities" to generate new applications from existing knowledge and that these abilities are embedded in the social relations across members of the network.

In summary, configuring an integrated network requires arranging activities consistent with the characteristics of global industries, as well as with the internalization of firm-specific resources. While the industry forces call for convergent competitive patterns, firm-specific forces lead to the creation of competitive advantage.

Coordination of the Network

The information-processing theory of the MNE (Egelhoff 1982, Egelhoff 1991, Sambharya/Phatak 1990) provides a useful framework to examine the coordination demands of the dispersed and interdependent activities of the global MNE. Information-processing theory focuses on organizational adaptation to uncertainty. Galbraith (1973) defines uncertainty as "... the difference between the amount of information required to perform the task and the amount of information already possessed by the organization" (p. 5). The essence of information-processing theory is that the information-processing requirements due to uncertainty in the environment should be matched with the information-processing capacities created by the organization (Galbraith 1973, Tushman/Nadler 1978).

With respect to global integration, the coordination of interdependent activities is difficult because the global company operates in several countries in environments characterized by a high degree of rivalry. According to the information-processing theory (Egelhoff 1991, Tushman/Nadler 1978), globally interdependent activities call for the creation of coordination mechanisms able to handle the complexity inherent to a global strategy.

Several studies illustrate the increasing requirements for information processing associated with international integration. Empirical studies of MNE operations indicate the importance of balancing information processing requirements with information processing capacities in the form of establishing the appropriate organizational structure (Habib/Victor 1991, Stopford/Wells 1972). The headquarter-subsidiary literature (Ghoshal/Nohria 1989, Gupta/Govindarajan 1991, Martinez/Jarillo 1991) illustrates the process of establishing the requisite coordination capacity by adjusting other dimensions of organizational structure such as centralization, formalization, integrative mechanisms and socialization. Furthermore, other studies suggest that information-processing capacity can be increased by the simultaneous use of formal and informal control mechanisms, such as the creation of shared values (Baliga/Jaeger 1984), the use of information and career planning systems (Prahalad/Doz 1987), and the improvement of inter-unit communication patterns (Ghoshal/Korine/Szulanski 1994).

Hypotheses on the Influence of Global Integration on MNE Performance

This paper is based on the premise that the performance consequences of a global integration strategy can be examined by looking at the net balance between benefits and costs of global integration and coordination. We propose that for firms competing in global industries the performance implications of a global integration strategy differ for low, moderate, and high levels of global integration. As a result of these differences, the relation between global integration and performance follows a non-linear pattern.

Consistent with the previous discussion, firms with low levels of global integration have strong incentives to configure an integrated network by conforming to the market structure forces of global competition and by building firm-specific resources. This network configuration has the potential to increase profitability because of scale economies and learning, and because the investments in firm-specific resources can be leveraged across international markets. However, building a collection of firm-specific resources requires substantial investments and takes considerable time. While building these resources, the incremental costs are likely to outweigh the benefits because of the difficulties in the accumulation process when building firm-specific resources. In addition, inter-temporal trade-offs between the long-term benefits and current costs (Laverty 1996) for developing and deploying this ownership advantage contribute to a negative balance affecting firm performance in the short-term.

Several empirical studies have documented the strong links between investments in firm-specific resources in the form of intangible assets, and the international expansion of firms. Regarding global integration, studies by Kobrin (1991) and Mauri and Phatak (2001) showed evidence of the positive link between the development of intangibles assets, such as those produced by R & D and advertising, and the deployment of a global integration strategy. Similarly, Kotabe and colleagues (2002) and Morck and Yeung (1991) studied the moderating role of intangible assets in increasing the profitability of an MNE's international expansion. These studies suggest that investments in ownership advantage support the internationalization of firms. However, notwithstanding the long-term value of intangible assets, accounting rules treat the development of intangibles as current expenses with an immediate negative impact on firm profitability. This is particularly important for firms with low levels of global integration since as a consequence of the temporal tradeoff, the investments supporting the configuration of a globally integrated network may take years to become profitable.

According to information-processing theory, a firm's performance depends on its ability to build the appropriate organizational structures and effective coordination mechanisms to match the requirements for information processing. Firms may experience temporal setbacks during the initial phases of the global integration process. Kogut and Zander (1992, 1993) highlight the difficulties for creating an appropriate collaborative context for transferring tacit knowledge across MNE units. They argue that it takes considerable time and investments to build the combinative abilities between units of an MNE network to create and transfer new knowledge effectively. These delays may contribute to a negative balance between benefits and costs for firms willing to increase their commitment to become more global.

Consequently, for low levels of global integration the difficulties of developing the firm-specific resources required in a network configuration and the intertemporal tradeoffs when building such resources, as well as possible delays in building a collaborative network context are likely to result in a negative balance between benefits and costs. Hence, the following hypothesis is proposed:

> *Hypothesis 1 (HI)*. At low levels of global integration, global integration is negatively related to firm performance.

In contrast, at moderate levels of global integration, the benefits of an integrated network allow global firms to increase performance in relation to their rivals by the use of national differences, economies of scale and scope, and global learning and innovation (Ghoshal 1987, Porter 1986). Under these conditions, an MNE is likely to realize the benefits of the investments in firm-specific resources and reap the rewards of configuring an integrated network of geographically dispersed units. Regarding coordination, at moderate levels of global integration we expect that on average MNEs will be able to perform well given the moderate information-processing requirements and the availability of the several coordinating mechanisms outlined above. Furthermore, the larger exposure and longer experience at integrating the operations of interdependent units create a collaborative context encouraging innovations and entrepreneurial actions from employees operating within the network of subsidiaries. Therefore:

> *Hypothesis 2 (H2)*. At moderate levels of global integration, global integration is positively related to firm performance.

As global integration becomes high, the costs of managing and operating an integrated network of subsidiaries may begin to outweigh the benefits. Specifically, high levels of reciprocal interdependence (Thompson 1967) across the network produce strong demands for tightly coordinating activities and leave firms with a small margin of error. Under these demanding conditions it is likely that coordinating mechanisms may fail, and the firm's information-processing capacities are not up to the requirements of high global integration levels. In this case, the structural mechanisms are likely to be overwhelmed and lead to bottlenecks and breakdowns. This in turn will lead to delays and administrative problems that could disrupt operations and flows of information. Ultimately, any prolonged disruption could affect the firm's financial performance.

Levy (1995) developed a conceptual framework in which distance can reduce the advantages derived from the national differences owing to increases in inventory, high lead time, unfulfilled demand, and high transportation costs. Using a case study of a personal computer company and a subsequent simulation, Levy shows that these factors may have a significant effect on the costs of sourcing parts and components internationally. Consequently, the complex interdependencies are likely to lead to lower performance levels because the firm is likely to experience coordination problems.

As a result, a firm can handle global integration only up to a certain point; past that point, breakdowns occur due to overload in the system. The MNE is unlikely to succeed at building the appropriate information-processing capacities to match the overwhelming information-processing requirements at high levels of global integration. Consequently, we propose the following hypothesis:

Hypothesis 3 (H3). At high levels of global integration, global integration is negatively related to firm performance.

Methodology

Sample Selection

The sample of companies used to test the previous hypotheses was created from industries in which global integration may be assumed relevant for developing a competitive advantage. We selected the top four industries based on the Index of Transnational Integration reported by Kobrin (1991, p. 22). These include the computer equipment (SIC 357), communications equipment (SIC 366), electronic components (SIC 367) and motor vehicles (SIC 371) industries. Previous studies have also considered these industries to be of a global nature (Bartlett 1986, Birkinshaw/Morrison/Hulland 1995, Flaherthy 1986, Hout/Porter/Rudden 1982, Johansson/Yip 1994, Levy 1995, Porter 1986, Roth/Morrison 1990, Takeuchi/Porter 1986). Companies were included in the sample according to their participation in the selected industries, as indicated by the primary SIC code from COMPUSTAT. Only firms with annual revenues greater than $50 million were selected. In addition, the level of international exposure was controlled by only including companies that derive a minimum of 10 percent of sales from overseas operations (Daniels/Pitts/Tretter 1985, Habib/Victor 1991, Palepu 1985) and that explicitly disclose inter-area sales in their financial statements. Thus the sample resulted in 69 firms with a complete data series during the period 1992 to 1997 for a total of 414 firm-year observations.

Measurement of Independent and Dependent Variables

Global Integration Index

The index of global integration was based on intrafirm trade among corporate units in different geographic areas. Studies by Kobrin (1991) and Mauri and Phatak (2001) consider the inter-subsidiary product flows as an indicator of global integration. More specifically, the index of global integration was operationalized as follows:

$$GI_t = \sum_j IS_{jt} / (\text{Total company sales})_t,$$

– in which IS_{jt} refers to the inter-area sales reported in year t from subsidiaries located in area j to other geographic regions where the firm has operations. This index reflects the percentage of total sales that is within the firm and across geographic regions as an indicator for global integration of a company in year t. This information was collected from the financial statements of US companies. According to the Financial Accounting Standards No. 14 (FAS 14), companies are required to disclose information on their operations in geographic areas that represent sales or assets greater than 10 percent of the amounts presented in the consolidated financial statements. In addition to inter-area sales, sales to unaffiliated customers, identifiable assets, and operating income are disclosed. This information is usually included as a note to the financial statements.

The global integration index was created from sales of units directly or indirectly controlled by the parent company (the accounting criterion for consolidating sales of affiliated units is direct and indirect ownership by the parent company of more than 50 percent). Hence, sales from joint ventures or affiliates in which the parent company owns less than or equal to 50 percent are excluded from the index.

Control Variables

Several control variables that may have an impact on performance were included as controls: firm size, leverage, product diversification, level of internationalization, and industry effects. The data source for constructing all control variables was COMPUSTAT. Firm size was constructed to control for possible economies of scale at the corporate level, and was measured by calculating the log of sales for each year in the period 1992–1997. Leverage has been argued to be associated with financial performance (Jensen 1989) and has been used in previous studies examining the relation between internationalization and firm performance (Hitt/Hoskisson/Kim 1997, Tallman/Li 1996). Leverage was constructed using the fraction of total debt to total assets by firm and year. Similarly, product diversification was operationalized using an entropy index of diversification (Palepu 1985) from four-digit SIC segments sales. This index was calculated as:

$$ST_t = \sum_k S_{kt} \ln(1/S_{kt}),$$

– in which S_{kt} is the share of total company sales of each four-digit SIC industry segment k during year t. The diversification index was calculated for each year in the period 1992–1997. The level of internationalization was measured using the ratio of international assets to total assets for each year in the period 1992–1997. Industry effects were added as a control variable in the regression model using dummies for the industry groups.

Firm Performance

The dependent variable was measured using Return on Sales (ROS) for each year in the period 1992 to 1997 from COMPUSTAT. Return on sales was calculated as net income before extraordinary items divided by sales. The sales denominator reduces potential distortions while measuring firm performance because sales are generally expressed in more current monetary terms than total assets (Geringer/Beamish/daCosta 1989).

Statistical Methodology

We used the Prais-Winsten regression that corrects for serial correlations. The Prais-Winsten method uses a generalized least-squares estimator. The most common autocorrelated error process is the first-order auto-regressive process. Under this assumption, the linear regression can be written as $Y_t = \beta X_t + u_t$, where the errors satisfy $u_t = \varrho u_{t-1} + e_t$, and e_t is independent and identically distributed as $N(0, \sigma^2)$. The Prais-Winsten method provides a transformed Durbin-Watson statistic, useful in evaluating the removal of autocorrelation.

In the first model, we ran the regression using all control variables and the linear term of the global integration index. We then sequentially added the quadratic term of the global integration index in the second model. Finally we added the cubic term of global integration index in the third model. This methodology enables testing the proposed set of hypotheses. In particular, we expect negative regression coefficients for the linear and cubic terms of the global integration index, while the quadratic term should yield a positive coefficient.

Because of possible multicolinearity between the linear, quadratic and cubic terms of the global integration index, we followed the methodology developed by Jaccard, Turrisi, and Wan (1990). This procedure uses a "mean-centering" approach, originally proposed by Cronbach (1987), in which the linear variable is mean-centered before constructing its respective quadratic and cubic terms.

This procedure also requires testing whether adding the quadratic and cubic terms to the regression equation indeed increase the explanatory power of the base model using the linear global integration term, the control variables and the auto-regressive factor.

Results

Table 1 shows descriptive statistics of the variables used in the sample.

Table 1
Descriptive Statistics

Variable	Mean	S.D.	1	2	3	4	5
1. Size (log sales)	7.22	1.78					
2. Leverage	0.42	0.18	−0.01				
3. Product diversification	0.24	0.36	0.18***	0.02			
4. International assets	0.24	0.16	0.46***	0.18***	−0.23***		
5. Global integration index	0.16	0.22	0.22***	−0.05	−0.31***	0.43***	
6. Return on sales	0.05	0.08	0.09ψ	−0.45***	−0.02	−0.05	0.05

$N = 414$
ψ $p < 0.1$, ***$p < 0.001$

Table 2 shows the results of the Prais-Winsten regression models using return on sales (ROS) as the dependent variable. For the firms sampled, the regression coefficients for the "mean-centered" linear, quadratic and cubic terms of global integration were similar to those obtained using the original global integration variable. In order to facilitate the interpretation of the global integration regression coefficients, the results shown in Table 2 correspond to the original global integration index without the transformation.

As can be seen in Table 2, the regression results for Models 1 to 3 explain a considerable portion of the variation of performance for the companies sampled. The total R-squares, including both the regression model and first order auto-regressive error, range from 37.6 to almost 40 percent of the variation of firm performance. Of this total, the regression component explains between 13 to 16 percent of this variation, while the auto-regressive component represents the remaining 23 to 24 percent. The strong statistical significance of the auto-regressive coefficients across Models 1 to 3 confirms the relevance of this auto-regressive source. In addition, the Durbin-Watson coefficient in the three models showed a value close to 2, indicating the removal of the first-order serial auto-correlation.

Regarding the control variables, firm size was positively related to ROS, but only significant at the 0.10 level in model 2, and at the 0.05 level in Model 3. The leverage regression coefficient showed a negative and strongly significant association between leverage and performance for all regression models. This relation is consistent with previous studies (Hitt/Hoskisson/Kim 1997, Tallman/Li 1996) and indicates a tendency for highly leveraged firms to present lower performance levels. Neither product diversification nor international assets were significantly related to ROS.

Table 2
Results of Prais-Winsten Regression

Independent Variables	Dependent Variable: ROS		
	Model 1	Model 2	Model 3
Firm size (log sales)	0.005	0.006ψ	0.007*
	(1.56)	(1.92)	(2.17)
Leverage	-0.156***	-0.160***	-0.164***
	(-6.62)	(-6.83)	(-7.04)
Product diversification	0.007	0.004	0.000
	(0.44)	(0.25)	(0.00)
International assets	-0.015	-0.003	0.010
	(-0.42)	(-0.09)	(0.28)
Computer industry dummy	0.013	0.019	0.027ψ
	(0.97)	(1.40)	(1.94)
Communications industry dummy	-0.017	-0.007	0.003
	(-1.00)	(-0.38)	(0.17)
Electronic components industry dummy	0.028	0.033*	0.034*
	(1.91)	(2.25)	(2.35)
Global integration index	-0.0002	-0.090ψ	-0.330***
	(-0.01)	(-1.80)	(-3.53)
Global integration index square		0.088*	0.706***
		2.05	(3.38)
Global integration index cube			-0.336**
			(-3.02)
Constant	0.068**	0.063*	0.063*
	(2.72)	(2.52)	(2.55)
Auto-regressive coefficient	-0.419***	-0.412***	-0.412***
	(-9.27)	(-9.08)	(-9.07)
Regression R-square[/]	0.1319***	0.1426***	0.1617***
Total R-square	0.3755***	0.3817***	0.3955***
Change in Total R-square	–	0.0062*	0.0200**
Durbin-Watson	1.9651	1.9574	1.9489

t-statistic in parentheses
$\psi\ p < 0.1$, *$p < 0.05$, **$p < 0.01$, ***$p < 0.001$
[/]Includes the regression component of the model, excludes the first order auto-regressive error component.

Regarding global integration, the regression results show evidence supporting a non-linear relation between the index of global integration and firm performance. As can be seen in Model 1, the combination of the linear term of the global integration index, the control variables and the auto-regressive component are able to explain to 37.6 percent of the total variation of ROS. By adding the quadratic term of the global integration index to the regression equation in Model 2, the total R-square increases by 0.6 percentage points over the R-square of Model 1. This increment is statistically significant with a p-value of 0.0449 ($F = 4.05$; $df = 1,403$).

In Model 3, adding the quadratic and cubic terms of the global integration index, simultaneously, showed a much stronger increase in R-square. In Model 3, the total R-square increases 2 percentage points over Model 1. This change in total R-square is statistically significant with a p-value of 0.0015 ($F = 6.63$; $df = 2,402$). Furthermore, the comparison of Model 2 and Model 3 shows the individual contribution of the cubic term of global integration to the explanatory power of the regression model. In this case, R-square changes from 38.2 percent in model 2 to 39.6 percent in model 3. This increase of 1.4 percentage points has a p-value of 0.0027 (F = 9.14 df = 1,402), hence confirming the significant contribution of the cubic term.

Finally, in Model 3, the sign of the regression coefficients for the linear, quadratic and cubic terms of the global integration index are consistent with the proposed hypotheses. Both coefficients for the linear and cubic terms showed a significant negative association with firm performance. In contrast, the coefficient of the quadratic term of the global integration index was positive and highly significant. The signs of these coefficients provide evidence supporting the hypotheses that low and high levels of global integration are negatively associated with firm performance (*H1* and *H3*), while moderate levels of global integration are positively associated with firm performance (*H2*).

Figure 1 shows a graphical representation of the relation between global integration and firm performance according to the regression results of Model 3. This curve shows how the average level of ROS varies in relation to the global integration index in sampled firms.

Figure 1
Graphical Representation of the Relation between the Global Integration Index and ROS*

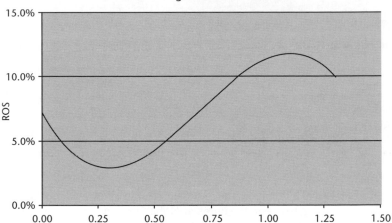

*Calculated from the regression results of Model 3 and using the Global integration index as the independent variable. The computer industry dummy variable was set to 1 and other dummy variables to zero, all other regression variables were held constant using their respective sample means.

Discussion and Conclusions

The Prais-Winsten regression results for Models 2 and 3 suggest the existence of a non-linear relationship between the global integration index and performance. The results of Model 3 show that low and high levels of global integration are associated negatively to firm profitability. In addition, the middle segment has a positive slope as suggested by the significance of the regression coefficient for the quadratic term of the global integration index. These findings support the view that the benefits derived from integrating operations globally (Ghoshal 1987, Porter 1986) may be offset by the costs of managing and coordinating distant international operations between the headquarters and subsidiaries and across subsidiaries themselves (Bartlett 1986, Davidson/Haspeslagh 1982, Levy 1995).

These results are consistent with the network view of the MNE. As can be seen in Figure 1, the left and negative portion of the curve represents the "threshold" to global integration. The negative slope in this section is consistent with the obstacles for developing and deploying the firm-specific resources that support the configuration of the integrated network. This negative segment also illustrates the efforts by the MNE for developing the necessary scale economies consistent with the market structure forces of global industries. The middle segment of the curve represents the "realization" of the global integration potential and suggests that moderate levels of intra-firm product flows result in an effective deployment of a global strategy across interdependent MNE units. This portion of the curve suggests that a global firm can achieve a competitive advantage by creating an integrated network of interdependent units.

Further, the right negative segment of the curve represents the "limits" of global integration. This negative section suggests the managerial boundaries for creating a network of specialized and geographically dispersed units. As illustrated in Figure 1, this negative segment represents a global integration index beyond 100 percent, and implies inter-area segment sales larger than a firm's annual sales to its external customers. At this level, the intra-firm product flows create excessive interdependencies that produce a tremendous strain on the organizational system. This segment highlights the dilemma faced by MNEs from the information-processing perspective. At very high levels of globalization, even mature and experienced MNEs have difficulty coping with the enormous information-processing requirements, and are likely to find their information capacities inadequate.

The managerial implication of integrating international product flows among MNE units is that global integration has costs as well as benefits. Firms are likely to start their internationalization process by exporting or serving local markets through local production. As firms become more internationalized, global integration becomes both feasible and profitable. Global integration allows companies to develop a competitive advantage by use of national differences, and economies of scale and scope. However, the integration of operations also brings coordination costs. The evidence found in this study clearly points in the direction of a non-linear relation between the index of global integration and performance. Managers should be aware of the difficulties of developing and coordinating their interdependent international operations. The negative relation between integration and performance at low levels of global integration implies that managers should realize that the firm needs to be prepared to sustain heavy costs before the benefits of the integration strategy are realized. Furthermore, at moderate levels of integration they should be aware that more integration is not necessarily better, and thus some activities may rather remain "decoupled."

This study has several limitations. One clear limitation refers to the issue of causality between global integration and performance. The Prais-Winsten regression is a cross-sectional methodology that permits correcting for serial autocorrelation. A more rigorous test would require examining how longitudinal changes in the global integration index affect changes in MNE performance. Another limitation is the selection of sampled firms from only four global industries. It may be interesting to evaluate the generalizability of the non-linear results by selecting firms from other industries in which global integration may have competitive relevance. One more limitation refers to the use of only one archival measure of global integration based on inter-area exchange of products. As the use of questionnaires is a common technique to collect data on the topic of global strategy, a methodology combining primary and archival sources can be used to validate the results of this study. This combined methodology may be applied to examine how other dimensions of global integration may affect MNE performance. Future research could continue to measure global integration as the inter-area product exchange disclosed in financial statements and enhance our understanding of the complex relation between global strategy and performance.

Acknowledgement

The authors thank Niels Noorderhaven and two anonymous reviewers for their insightful comments on earlier versions of this paper.

References

Amit, R./Schoemaker, P. J. H., Strategic Assets and Organizational Rent, *Strategic Management Journal*, 14, 1, 1993, pp. 33–46.

Andersson, U./Forsgren, M., In Search of Centre of Excellence: Network Embeddedness and Subsidiary Roles in Multinational Corporations, *Management International Review*, 40, 4, 2000, pp. 329–350.

Bain, J. S., *Industrial Organization*, New York, NY: Wiley 1968.

Baliga, B. R./Jaeger, A., Multinational Corporations: Control Systems and Delegation Issues, *Journal of International Business Studies*, 15, 2, 1984, pp. 25–40.

Barney, J., Firm Resources and Sustained Competitive Advantage, *Journal of Management*, 17, 1, 1991, pp. 99–120.

Bartlett, C. A., Building and Managing the Transnational: The New Organizational Challenge, in Porter, M. E. (ed), *Competition in Global Industries*, Boston: Harvard Business School Press 1986, pp. 367–401.

Bartlett, C. A./Ghoshal, S., Managing Across Borders: New Organizational Responses, *Sloan Management Review*, 29, 1, 1987, pp. 43–53.

Birkinshaw, J./Hood, N., Multinational Subsidiary Evolution: Capability and Charter Change in Foreign-Owned Subsidiary Companies, *The Academy of Management Review*, 23, 4, 1998, pp. 773–795.

Birkinshaw, J./Hood, N./Jonsson, S., Building Firm-Specific Advantages in Multinational Corporations: The Role of Subsidiary Initiative, *Strategic Management Journal*, 19, 3, 1998, pp. 221–241.

Birkinshaw, J./Morrison, A./Hulland, J., Structural and Competitive Determinants of a Global Integration Strategy, *Strategic Management Journal*, 16, 8, 1995, pp. 637–655.

Birkinshaw, J. M./Morrison, A. J., Configurations of Strategy and Structure in Subsidiaries of Multinational Corporations, *Journal of International Business Studies*, 26, 4, 1995, pp. 729–753.

Caves, R. E., *Multinational Enterprise and Economic Analysis*, Cambridge, MA: Cambridge University Press 1996.

Conner, K. R., A Historical Comparison of Resource-Based Theory and Five Schools of Thought Within Industrial Organization Economics: Do We Have a Theory of the Firm?, *Journal of Management*, 17, 1, 1991, pp. 121–154.

Cronbach, L. J., Statistical Tests for Moderator Variables: Flaws in Analyses Recently Proposed, *Psychological Bulletin*, 102, 3, 1987, pp. 414–417.

Daniels, J. D./Pitts, R. A./Tretter, M. J., Organizing for Dual Strategies of Product Diversity and International Expansion, *Strategic Management Journal*, 6, 3, 1985, pp. 223–237.

Davidson, W. H./Haspeslagh, P., Shaping a Global Product Organization, *Harvard Business Review*, 60, 4, 1982, pp. 125–132.

Dierickx, I./Cool, K., Asset Stock Accumulation and Sustainability of Competitive Advantage; Comment; Reply, *Management Science*, 35, 12, 1989, pp. 1504–1514.

Dunning, J. H., The Eclectic Paradigm of International Production: A Restatement and Some Possible Extensions, *Journal of International Business Studies*, 19, 1, 1988, pp. 1–31.

Egelhoff, W. G., Strategy and Structure in Multinational Corporations: An Information-Processing Approach, *Administrative Science Quarterly*, 27, 3, 1982, pp. 435–458.

Egelhoff, W. G., Information-Processing Theory and the Multinational Enterprise, *Journal of International Business Studies*, 22, 3, 1991, pp. 341–368.

Emerson, R. M., Power-Dependence Relations, *American Sociological Review*, 27, 1962, pp. 31–41.

Flaherthy, M. T., Coordinating International Manufacturing and Technology, in Porter, M. (ed), *Competition in Global Industries*, Boston: Harvard Business School Press 1986, pp. 83–110.

Galbraith, J. R., *Designing Complex Organizations*, Reading, MA: Adison-Wesley Publishing Company 1973.

Geringer, J. M./Beamish, P. W./daCosta, R. C., Diversification Strategy and Internationalization: Implications for MNE Performance, *Strategic Management Journal*, 10, 2, 1989, pp. 109–119.

Ghemawat, P., *Commitment: The Dynamic of Strategy*, New York, NY: The Free Press 1991.

Ghemawat, P./Spence, A. M., Modeling Global Competition, in Porter, M. (ed), *Competition in Global Industries*, Boston: Harvard Business School Press 1986, pp. 61–79.

Ghoshal, S., Global Strategy: An Organizing Framework, *Strategic Management Journal*, 8, 5, 1987, pp. 425–440.

Ghoshal, S./Bartlett, C. A., Creation, Adoption, and Diffusion of Innovations by Subsidiaries of Multinational Corporations, *Journal of International Business Studies*, 19, 3, 1988, pp. 365–388.

Ghoshal, S./Bartlett, C. A., The Multinational Corporation as an Interorganizational Network, *Academy of Management Review*, 15, 4, 1990, pp. 603–625.

Ghoshal, S./Korine, H./Szulanski, G., Interunit Communication in Multinational Corporations, *Management Science*, 40, 1, 1994, pp. 96–110.

Ghoshal, S./Nohria, N., Internal Differentiation Within Multinational Corporations, *Strategic Management Journal*, 10, 4, 1989, pp. 323–337.

Gupta, A. K./Govindarajan, V., Knowledge Flows and the Structure of Control Within Multinational Corporations, *Academy of Management Review*, 16, 4, 1991, pp. 768–792.

Habib, M. M./Victor, B., Strategy, Structure, and Performance of US Manufacturing and Service MNCs: A Comparative Analysis, *Strategic Management Journal*, 12, 8, 1991, pp. 589–606.

Hennart, J.-F., The Transaction Cost Theory of the Multinational Enterprise, in Pitelis, C. N./Sugden, R. (eds), *The Nature of the Transnational Firm*, New York, NY: Routledge 1991, pp. 81–117.

Hipple, F. S., Multinational Companies and International Trade: The Impact of Intrafirm Shipments on US Foreign Trade 1977–1982, *Journal of International Business Studies*, 21, 3, 1990, pp. 495–504.

Hitt, M. A., Hoskisson, R. E. and Kim, H., International Diversification: Effects of Innovation and Firm Performance in Product-Diversified Firms, *Academy of Management Journal*, 40, 4, 1997, pp. 767–798.

Hout, T. M./Porter, M. E./Rudden, E., How Global Companies Win Out, *Harvard Business Review*, 60, 5, 1982, pp. 98–108.

Jaccard, J./Turrisi, R./Wan, C. K., *Interaction Effects in Multiple Regression*, Newbury Park, CA: Sage 1990.

Jensen, M. C., Eclipse of the Public Corporation, *Harvard Business Review*, 67, 5, 1989, pp. 61–74.

Johansson, J. K./Yip, G. S., Exploiting Globalization Potential: US and Japanese Strategies, *Strategic Management Journal*, 15, 8, 1994, pp. 579–601.

Kobrin, S. J., An Empirical Analysis of the Determinants of Global Integration, *Strategic Management Journal*, 12, Summer Special Issue, 1991, pp. 17–31.

Kogut, B./Zander, U., Knowledge of the Firm, Combinative Capabilities, and the Replication of Technology, *Organization Science*, 3, 3, 1992, pp. 383–397.

Kogut, B./Zander, U., Knowledge of the Firm and the Evolutionary Theory of the Multinational Corporation, *Journal of International Business Studies*, 24, 4, 1993, pp. 625–645.

Kotabe, M./Srinivasan, S. S./Aulakh, P. S., Multinationality and Firm Performance: The Moderating Role of R & D and Marketing Capabilities, *Journal of International Business Studies*, 33, 1, 2002, pp. 79–97.

Kutschker, M./Baurle, I., Three Plus One: Multidimensional Strategy of Internationalization, *Management International Review*, 37, 2, 1997, pp. 103–125.

Laverty, K. J., Economic "Short-Termism": The Debate, the Unresolved Issues, and the Implications for Management Practice and Research, *Academy of Management Review*, 21, 3, 1996, pp. 825–860.

Levitt, T., The Globalization of Markets, *Harvard Business Review*, 61, 3, 1983, pp. 92–102.

Levy, D. L., International Sourcing and Supply Chain Stability, *Journal of International Business Studies*, 26, 2, 1995, pp. 343–360.

Malnight, T. W., The Transition from Decentralized to Network-Based MNC Structures: An Evolutionary Perspective, *Journal of International Business Studies*, 27, 1, 1996, pp. 43–65.

Martinez, J. I./Jarillo, J. C., Coordination Demands of International Strategies, *Journal of International Business Studies*, 22, 3, 1991, pp. 429–444.

Mataloni Jr, R. J./Yorgason, D. R., Operations of US Multinational Companies: Preliminary Results from the 1999 Benchmark Survey, *Survey of Current Business*, 82, 3, 2002, pp. 24–54.

Mauri, A. J./Phatak, A. V., Global Integration as Inter-Area Product Flows: The Internalization of Ownership and Location Factors Influencing Product Flows across MNC units, *Management International Review*, 41, 3, 2001, pp. 233–249.

Morck, R./Yeung, B., Why Investors Value Multinationality, *Journal of Business*, 64, 2, 1991, pp. 165–187.

Ohmae, K., *The Borderless World: Power and Strategy in the Interlinked World Economy*, New York, NY: Harper Business 1990.

Palepu, K., Diversification Strategy, Profit Performance and the Entropy Measure, *Strategic Management Journal*, 6, 3, 1985, pp. 239–255.

Pfeffer, J./Salancik, G. R., *The External Control of Organizations: A Resource Dependency Perspective*, New York: Harper and Row 1978.

Porter, M. E., Competition in Global Industries: A Conceptual Framework, in Porter, M. E. (ed), *Competition in Global Industries*, Boston, MA: Harvard Business School Press 1986, pp. 15–60.

Prahalad, C. K./Doz, Y. L., *The Multinational Mission: Balancing Local Demands and a Global Vision*, New York: The Free Press 1987.

Roth, K., Managing International Interdependence: CEO Characteristics in a Resource-Based Framework, *Academy of Management Journal*, 38, 1, 1995, pp. 200–231.

Roth, K./Morrison, A. J., An Empirical Analysis of the Integration-Responsiveness Framework in Global Industries, *Journal of International Business Studies*, 21, 4, 1990, pp. 541–564.

Roth, K./Morrison, A. J., Implementing Global Strategy: Characteristics of Global Subsidiary Mandates, *Journal of International Business Studies*, 23, 4, 1992, pp. 715–735.

Sambharya, R. B./Phatak, A., The Effect of Transborder Data Flow Restrictions on American Multinational Corporations, *Management International Review*, 30, 3, 1990, pp. 267–289.

Scherer, F. M./Ross, D., *Industrial Market Structure and Economic Performance*, Princeton, NJ: Houghton Mifflin 1990.

Stopford, J. M./Wells, L. T., *Managing the Multinational Enterprise: Organization of The Firm and Ownership of the Subsidiaries*, New York, NY: Basic Books 1972.

Takeuchi, H./Porter, M. E., Three Roles of International Marketing in Global Strategy, in Porter, M. E. (ed), *Competition in Global Industries*, Boston: Harvard Business School Press 1986, pp. 111–146.

Tallman, S./Li, J., Effects of International Diversity and Product Diversity on the Performance of Multinational firms, *Academy of Management Journal*, 39, 1, 1996, pp. 179–196.

Teece, D., Transactions Cost Economics and the Theory of the Multinational Enterprise, *Journal of Economic Behavior and Organization*, 7, 1986, pp. 21–45.

Thompson, J. D., *Organizations in Action*, New York: McGraw-Hill 1967.

Tushman, M. L./Nadler, D. A., Information Processing as an Integrating Concept in Organizational Design, *Academy of Management Review*, 3, 3, 1978, pp. 613–624.

Wernerfelt, B., A Resource-Based View of the Firm, *Strategic Management Journal*, 5, 2, 1984, pp. 171–180.

Zeile, W. J., US Intrafirm Trade in Goods, *Survey of Current Business*, 77, 2, 1997, pp. 23–38.

Zeile, W. J., US Affiliates of Foreign Companies: Operation in 1999, *Survey of Current Business*, 81, 8, 2001, pp. 141–158.

49

To Kill Two Birds with One Stone: Revisiting the Integration–Responsiveness Framework

Masaaki Kotabe

Introduction

Marketing products and services around the world, transcending national and political boundaries, is a fascinating phenomenon. The phenomenon, however, is not entirely new. Products have been traded across borders throughout recorded civilization, extending back beyond the Silk Road that once connected East with West from Xian to Rome. What is relatively new about the phenomenon, emerging with large US companies in the 1950s and 1960s and with European and Japanese companies in the 1970s and 1980s, is the large number of companies with interrelated production and sales operations located around the world. The emergence of competitive European and Japanese companies gave the notion of global competition a touch of extra urgency and significance in the 1980s.

Against this backdrop, Bartlett and Ghoshal wrote *Managing Across Borders* in 1989. They popularized the Integration-Responsiveness (IR) framework. In a way, global integration represents a supply-side argument that economies of scale and economies of scope practiced on a global basis are beneficial to a company. However, local responsiveness characterizes a demand-side argument that, as markets are different from country to country, a company should be responsive to differing market needs and conditions.

Source: Michael Hitt and Joseph Cheng (eds), *Managing Transnational Firms*, New York: Elsevier, 2002, pp. 59–69.

Regionalization of Global Strategy

Two Opposing Forces at Work

Combining supply-side and demand-side factors into a conceptual framework is nothing new. In fact, as early as 1969, Fayerweather wrote emphatically:

> What fundamental effects does (the existence of many national borders) have on the strategy of the multinational firm? Although many effects can be itemized, one central theme recurs, that is, their tendency to push the firm toward adaptation to the diversity of local environments which leads toward fragmentation of operations. But there is a natural tendency in a single firm toward integration and uniformity which is basically at odds with fragmentation. Thus the central issue . . . is the conflict between unification and fragmentation – a close-knit operational strategy with similar foreign units vs. a loosely related, highly variegated family of activities (Fayerweather, 1969, pp. 133–134).

Indeed, we still debate the very issue raised more than 30 years ago: counteracting forces of "unification vs. fragmentation" in developing operational strategies along the value chain. Over the years, two fundamental counteracting forces have shaped the nature of business in the international arena. The same counteracting forces have been revisited by many other authors in such terms as "standardization vs. adaptation" (1960s–1970s), "globalization vs. localization" (1970s–1980s), and then Bartlett and Ghoshal's "global integration vs. local responsiveness" (1980s–1990s). And if I were to add another contemporaneous description, I would say "scale vs. sensitivity." If the recent explosive growth of the Internet and e-commerce is considered, I could suggest an even fancier one, "online scale vs. offline sensitivity," to the litany of the supply-side and demand-side counteracting forces.

My point is that, although terms have changed, the quintessence of the strategic dilemma that globally operating companies face today has not changed and will probably remain unchanged for years to come. Are these terms just fashionable dichotomous (either/or) concepts of the time without some deep meanings, or has something inherently changed in our society? What has happened since the 1980s? Indeed, what Bartlett and Ghoshal (1989) drove home is the notion that these counteracting forces are no longer an either/or issue. That is how Bartlett and Ghoshal differentiated their work from their predecessors. Forward-looking, proactive firms have the ability and willingness to accomplish both tasks simultaneously.

The IR Framework

Bartlett and Ghoshal focused their effort on identifying how companies develop and manage an internal organization or organizations to address integration and local responsiveness. Their study was based on their in-depth clinical study of three US (General Electric, Procter & Gamble, and ITT), three European (Philips, Unilever, and Ericsson), and three Japanese (Matsushita, Kao, and NEC) companies. Each company studied had a very different strategic position, organizational structure, and management process. ITT, Philips, and Unilever were referred to as being *multinational* (or, more commonly, multidomestic) companies that developed a strategic position by being responsive to local differences. Kao, Matsushita, and NEC operated as *global* companies that developed strategic positions more focused on global efficiency. Procter & Gamble, General Electric, and Ericsson were *international* companies primarily interested in transferring and adapting the parent company's knowledge to foreign subsidiaries.

Unfortunately, while all of the companies studied might have understood the necessity to manage efficiency, responsiveness and knowledge simultaneously, they tended to rely on their existing internal capability or administrative heritage to develop such strategic change. Administrative heritage refers to a company's way of doing things. A company's heritage can be its greatest asset or greatest liability. It is shaped by the three factors of organizational inertia: (1) key executive founders; (2) national culture; and (3) organizational history.

Their thesis is that no firm can sustain a competitive advantage today by following just one of these unidimensional strategies. However, a generation of managers grew up believing that there was one right strategy-structure fit. The problem with this mentality is that companies ended up concentrating on only one key variable – formal structure. Today, companies must respond flexibly to changes and must achieve all three goals simultaneously. According to the authors, companies need to transform themselves. Because of increasing global competition and the convergence of customer preferences worldwide, among other things, companies must be flexible to meet local and worldwide demands.

The percentage changes in the stock prices of these companies in two points in time (1991 and 2001) are presented in Table 1. Most of their stock prices appreciated until around 1997 but have since depreciated significantly. Thus, although the percentage change in their stock prices over two time points may not necessarily represent their overall corporate performance, they may still be illustrative of their ultimate market tests in the 1990s. Only General Electric (an international company) and Philips (a multinational/multidomestic company) enjoyed a spectacular stock performance in the 1990s. The lackluster performance of the Japanese companies is attributed mostly to the decade-long recession in Japan and the Asian financial crisis of the late 1990s (discussed later).

Table 1
Changes in Stock Prices between 1991 and 2001
(Change = End-of-Year Stock Price in 2001/Beginning-of-Year Stock Price in 1991)

Industry/Company	US	European	Japanese
Consumer Electronics	General Electric	Philips	Matsushita
	10.4 times	8.7 times	1.3 times
Branded Packaged Goods	Procter & Gamble	Unilever	Kao
	3.3 times	2.6 times	3.3 times
Telecommunications Switching	ITT	Ericsson	NEC
	(split)	2.5 times	1.4 times

The common limitation of the traditional models is that the subsidiary's role is local. Thus, Bartlett and Ghoshal proposed the Transnational Model. The distribution of the corporate assets and capabilities is best handled through an integrated network. This configuration must include a portfolio of coordinating processes that include centralization, formalization, and socialization if the organization is to be flexible and responsive enough to make local as well as worldwide changes.

The transnational model recognizes that the transnational company centralizes some resources at home and some abroad, and distributes others among its many national operations. The result is a complex configuration of assets and capabilities that are specialized but also dispersed.

In a way, the transactional prescriptions are similar to Porter's (1986) general approach to understanding global competition based on the value-chain concept. Porter, among others, introduced the value-chain concept for students of international business to understand what it takes to manage the interrelated value-adding activities of a corporation on a global basis. Value-adding activities include materials procurement, technology development and engineering (R&D), manufacturing, marketing, finance, personnel management, and so on. Thus, a global strategy is one in which a company seeks to gain competitive advantage on a global basis by an optimal arrangement of value-adding activities, coordinating among those dispersed value-adding activities, or both.

Let me willingly take a risk of oversimplification by summarizing these two important works of the 1980s. Bartlett and Ghoshal examined the inner workings of the transnational company that could satisfy its needs for both global integration for economies of scale and scope and responsiveness to different market needs and conditions in various parts of the world, thus killing two birds with one stone. However, Porter emphasized the external configuration of value-adding activities on a global basis.

For both Bartlett and Ghoshal's IR framework and Porter's value chain, the starting point of discussion, and thus the focus of their work, was that of the firm (supply-side). However, marketers examined the same issue to address specifically how companies could address market diversity (demand-side). First, let me address marketers' interpretation of the IR framework. Second, let me explore the test of time on it, in particular, in relation to the Asian financial crisis of the late 1990s that reverberated throughout the world economy.

Marketers' Interpretation of the IR Framework

International marketers interpreted the IR framework to suit their needs. Let me offer marketers' explanation and application of the IR framework in examining global marketing strategies by which to exploit the benefits of both global integration and local responsiveness.

As Bartlett and Ghoshal made us fully aware, one thing that has changed since the 1980s is the ability and willingness of many companies to integrate various activities along the value chain on a global basis in an attempt either to circumvent or to nullify the impact of differences in local markets to the extent possible. It may be more correct to say that these companies have been increasingly compelled to take a "transnational" view of their businesses, owing primarily to increased competition particularly among the Triad regions of the world: namely, the USA, Western Europe, and Japan. "If you don't do it, somebody else soon will to your disadvantage" epitomizes a contemporary view of competitive urgency shared by an increasing number of executives of multinational firms, irrespective of nationality.

While national boundaries have all but lost their significance both as a psychological and as a physical barrier to international business, the diversity of local market environments still plays an important role not as a facilitator, but rather as an inhibitor, of optimal global marketing strategy development. Now, the question that global marketers raise is: to what extent companies can circumvent the impact of local market diversity?

This issue can be understood best if we examine marketing's interfaces with product development (engineering and manufacturing) activities. Let me explain these interfaces from the transnational perspective.

Marketing and Product Development Interfaces: Transnational Solutions

There exists a continual conflict among engineering, manufacturing, and marketing divisions. It is to the manufacturing division's economies-of-scale advantage if all the products and components are standardized to facilitate for standardized, low-cost production. The marketing division, however, is more interested in satisfying the diverse needs of customers, requiring broad product lines and frequent product modifications adding cost to manufacturing. How have successful companies coped with this dilemma?

Recently, there has been an increasing amount of interest in the strategic linkages between product policy and manufacturing long ignored in traditional considerations of global strategy development. With aggressive competition from European and Japanese companies emphasizing corporate product policy and concomitant manufacturing, many US companies came to realize that product innovations alone cannot sustain their long-term competitive position without an effective product policy linking product and manufacturing process innovations. So, the strategic issue is how to design a robust product or components with sufficient versatility built in across uses, technology, and situations. This is consistent with Bettis and Hitt (1995), who argue that the robustness of strategic response capabilities – the potential for success under varying future circumstances or scenarios – is a possible organizational response to rapid technological and market changes and resultant inability to forecast.

Four different ways of developing a global product policy are generally considered an effective means to streamline manufacturing, thus lowering manufacturing cost, without sacrificing marketing flexibility (Takeuchi & Porter, 1986). They are:

(1) core components standardization;
(2) product design families;

(3) universal product with all features; and
(4) universal product with different positioning.

Core Components Standardization

Successful global product policy mandates the development of universal products, or products that require no more than a cosmetic change for adaptation to differing local needs and use conditions. A few examples illustrate the point. Seiko, a Japanese watchmaker, offers a wide range of designs and models, but they are based on only a handful of different operating mechanisms. Similarly, the best-performing German machine tool companies have a narrower range of products, use up to 50% fewer parts than their less successful rivals, and make continual, incremental product and design improvements, with new developments passed rapidly on to customers.

Product Design Families

This is a variant of core component standardization. For companies marketing an extremely wide range of products owing to cultural differences in product-use patterns around the world, it is also possible to reap economies-of-scale benefits. For example, Toyota offers several car models based on a similar family design concept, ranging from Lexus models to Toyota Avalons, Camrys, and Corollas. Many of the Lexus features well received by customers have been adopted in the Toyota lines with just a few minor modifications (mostly downsizing). In the process, Toyota has been able to cut product development costs and meet the needs of different market segments. Similarly, Electrolux, a Swedish appliance manufacturer, has adopted the concept of "design families," offering different products under four different brand names, but using the same basic designs. A key to such product design standardization lies in the standardization of components, including motors, pumps, and compressors. Thus, White Consolidated in the USA and Zanussi in Italy, Electrolux's subsidiaries, have the main responsibility for components production within the group for worldwide application.

Universal Product with All Features

As just noted, competitive advantage can result from standardization of core components and/or product design families. One variant of components and product standardization is to develop a universal product with all the features demanded anywhere in the world. Japan's Canon has done so successfully with its AE-1 cameras and newer models. After extensive market analyses around the world, Canon identified a set of common features that customers wanted in a camera, including good picture quality, ease of operation with automatic features, technical sophistication, professional looks, and reasonable price. To develop such cameras, the company introduced a few breakthroughs in camera design and manufacturing, such as the use of an electronic integrated circuitry brain to control camera operations, modularized production, and standardization and reduction of parts.

Universal Product with Different Positioning

Alternatively, a universal product can be developed with different market segments in mind. Thus, a universal product may be positioned differently in different markets. This is where marketing promotion plays a major role to accomplish such a feat. Product and/or components standardization, however, does not necessarily imply either production standardization or a narrow product line. For example, Japanese automobile manufacturers have gradually stretched out their product line offerings, while marketing them with little adaptation in many parts of the world. This strategy requires manufacturing flexibility. The crux of global product or component standardization, rather, calls for proactive identification of homogeneous segments around the world, and is different from the concept of marketing abroad a product originally developed for the home market. A proactive approach to product policy has gained momentum in the last two decades, as it is made possible by intermarket segmentation (Levitt, 1986). In addition to clustering of countries and identification of homogeneous segments in different countries, targeting different segments in different countries with the same products is another way to maintain a product policy of standardization.

For example, Honda has marketed almost identical Accord cars around the world by positioning them differently in the minds of consumers from country to country. The Accord has been promoted as a family sedan in Japan, a relatively inexpensive sports car in Germany, and a reliable commuter car in the USA. In recent years, however, Honda has begun developing some regional variations of the Accord for the US, European, and Japanese markets. None the less, Honda adheres to a policy of core component standardization such that at least 50% of the components, including the chassis and transmission, are shared across the variations of the Accord (*Business Week*, 1997).

As is clear from the above discussion on marketers' interpretation, the IR framework has been a very useful tool in explaining these transnational solutions to dealing with inevitable market diversities in the 1980s to mid-1990s around the world. Bartlett and Ghoshal, as well as Porter, assumed in their respective frameworks that *globally scattered business functions* could be managed. This assumption was reasonable, since exchange-rate fluctuations were either relatively stable or predictable, and the world economy experienced an unprecedented growth through the mid-1990s.

Then, unexpectedly, the Asian financial crisis in the latter half of the 1990s escalated into the wild exchange-rate fluctuations and the greatest threat to global prosperity since the oil crisis of the 1970s. In the following section, let me explore some issues facing the IR framework.

The IR Framework in an Unstable World Economy

As a result of the Asian financial crisis, the region's once-booming economies are still fragile, liquidity problems are harming regional trade, and losses from Asian investments are eroding profits for many Japanese companies. Similarly, among Western companies, quite a few US companies that have large invest-ments in Asia have reported less-than-expected earnings. Others fear that the Asian crisis would wash ashore to the seemingly unrelated regions of the world, including the USA and Europe. For example, the unsettling ups and downs of the Dow Jones Industrial Average reflect the precarious nature of US investments in Asia. Economists blamed Asia for nipping the world's economic growth by one percentage point in 1998–1999. The Asian financial crisis and its ramifica-tions could not only have far-reaching economic consequences, but also force many companies to adopt new business views and practices for competing around the world at the dawn of the new century.

Bartlert and Ghoshal's Transnational Model is predicated on a complex configuration of assets and capabilities that are specialized but also dispersed. Indeed, many foreign companies operating in Asian countries tend to procure certain crucial components and equipment from their parent companies. Now that Asian currencies had depreciated precipitously, those foreign companies are faced with those imported components and equipment whose prices have in-creased enormously in local currencies. In other words, the more dispersed the company's assets and capabilities are, the more difficult it is for them to manage wild currency fluctuations.

Companies that have localized procurement do not have to be affected easily by fluctuating exchange rates. As a result, many companies are also scurrying to speed up steps toward making their operations in Asian countries more local. Suffering from the recession in their domestic market as well as being most seriously affected by the Asian financial crisis, Japanese companies seem to stay one step ahead of US and European competitors in this *localization* strategy. Since the yen's sharp appreciation in the mid-1980s, Japanese manufacturers have moved to build an international production system that is less vulnerable to currency fluctuations, by investing in local procurement and more recently have begun to transfer R&D activities to local markets (*Nikkei Weekly*, 1998, 2001).

When financial hedging has not been able to cope with the extensive currency fluctuations, companies have been known to resort to operational hedging. *Operational hedging* is to shift production and procurement abroad to match revenues in foreign currency. For example, by producing abroad all of the product that a company sells in foreign markets, the company could create an operational hedge by shielding itself from fluctuating exchange rates (Bodnar & Marston, 2001).

This localized production and marketing strategy is fundamentally different from local responsiveness, as originally envisioned by Bartlert and Ghoshal. Current localization movement is to address the wild, and sometimes unexpected, currency fluctuations rather than local market needs per se. However, as a result of constant cost pressures from many competitors, the need for global inte-gration still remains strong for the sake of cost efficiency. How could the benefits of global integration be achieved in a localization strategy? Could the results of home-grown R&D activities be transferred easily to local subsidiaries or affiliates for local product development? How could a transnational company manage increasingly localized production and marketing without relinquishing too much autonomy to local subsidiaries and affiliates? Or, simply, can such a localization strategy be explained in the spirit of the IR framework?

Future Directions

The IR framework drove home *why* it is imperative for globally operating companies to develop an organizational mechanism by which to benefit from both global integration and local responsiveness. Depending on dispersed assets, specialized operations, and interdependent relationships among the units of a company, Bartlett and Ghoshal described the plausible parent-subsidiary relationships for "peace-time" transnational solutions. However, they fell short of offering specific solutions as to *how* to cope with a world market that is not so peaceful, characterized by wild and unpredictable currency fluctuations. Bartlett and Ghoshal are not to blame. They developed a very useful conceptual framework to address the *climate of the time* of the 1980s through to the mid-1990s. The climate has changed since the Asian financial crisis that wreaked havoc over what otherwise could have been a stable and growing world economy.

Although it is beyond the scope of this paper, one broad solution may be found in modular production, or the application of modular design capabilities in product development (Bettis & Hitt, 1995; Sanchez, 1999; Schilling, 2000). Again, this view is consistent with global marketers' four alternative specifications on global product policy. Modular production generally refers to the process of assembling final products from a number of predetermined and interchangeable modules. The fundamental difference, however, is that modular production could reduce the inherent difficulty in technology transfer, in particular, that of tacit knowledge, between units of a company, thereby making decentralized/localized production feasible without losing the benefits of global integration.

Clearly, more research is needed. One thing is clear from Bartlett and Ghoshal's contribution. Globally operating companies need to be in constant search of methods to "kill two birds with one stone," or meeting supply-side and demand-side counteracting forces head on for their sustainable competitive advantage.

References

Bartlett, C. A., & Ghoshal, S. (1989). *Managing Across Borders*. Boston, MA: Harvard Business School Press.

Bettis, R. A., & Hitt, M. (1995). The New Competitive Landscape. *Strategic Management Journal, 16* (Special Issue), 7–19.

Bodnar, G. M., & Marston, R. C. (2001). A simple model of foreign exchange exposure. University of Pennsylvania. A Working Paper.

Business Week (1997). Can Honda build a world car? September 8, 100–108.

Fayerweather, J. (1969). *International Business Management: Conceptual Framework*. New York: McGraw-Hill.

Levitt, T. (1986). *The Marketing Imagination*. New York: The Free Press.

Nikkei Weekly (1998). Manufacturers Reshape Asian Strategies. January 12, 1 and 5.

Nikkei Weekly (2001). Japanese R&D Trickling Overseas: Skilled, Cheap Work Forces in Other Asian Nations Attracting Japanese Firms. June 18, http://www.nni.nikkei.co.jp/.

Porter, M. E. (Ed.) (1986). *Competition in Global Industries*. Boston, MA: Harvard Business School Press.

Sanchez, R. (1999). Modular Architecture in the Marketing Process. *Journal of Marketing, 63* (Special Issue), 92–111.

Schilling, M. A. (2000). Towards a General Modular Systems Theory and Its Application to Inter-Firm Product Modularity. *Academy of Management Review, 25*, 312–334.

Takeuchi, H., & Porter, M. E. (1986). Three roles of international marketing in global strategy. In: M. E. Porter (Ed.), *Competition in Global Industries* (pp. 111–146). Boston, MA: Harvard Business School Press.

50

Regional Strategy and the Demise of Globalization

Alan M. Rugman

1. Introduction

The evidence is in and it shows that globalization is a myth. At an aggregate level, the intraregional trade of each of the "triad" regions of Europe, North America, and Asia is the majority of trade for each of these economic blocks. For 2000, intraregional exports were 62% for the European Union (EU), 56% for NAFTA, and 56% for Asia. Furthermore, there is a growing trend towards regionalism over the last 25 years.

Perhaps even more interesting is that the lack of globalization can now be shown at firm level. Across the world's 500 largest companies, a startling 72% of all sales are within their home region. Representatives of a stunning lack of global sales activity are as follows:

Wal-Mart	94% in North America
General Motors	81% in North America
Kingfisher	98% in Europe
Vodafone	93% in Europe
Sumitomo Metal	95% in Asia
Mitsubishi Heavy Industries	93% in Asia

Indeed, across the 500, for the 380 firms for which geographic sales data are available, it is only possible to classify 9 firms as truly "global." In contrast, 320 of the 380 firms are home region bound, and these 320 firms have an average of 80% of their sales in their home region. Thus, we need to examine the regional strategies of these 380 firms as globalization does not exist.

Table 1 reports data on the largest 50 multinational enterprises (MNEs) according to *Fortune* (data on all 500 MNEs are available upon request). Of the

Source: *Journal of International Management*, Vol. 9, 2003, pp. 409–417.

Table 1
The 50 Largest Companies with Triad Percent Sales, 2001

500 Rank	Company	Region	Revenues in Billion US$	F/T Sales	Percentage of Intraregional	NA Percentage of Total	EUR Percentage of Total	AP Percentage of Total
1	Wal-Mart Stores (q)	North America	219.8	16.3	94.1	94.1	4.8	0.4
2	Exxon Mobile	North America	191.6	69.6	37.5	37.5[a]	8.9[b]	10.4[c]
3	General Motors	North America	177.3	25.5	81.1	81.1	14.6	na
4	BP	Europe	174.2	80.4	36.3	48.1[d]	36.3	na
5	Ford Motor	North America	162.4	33.3	66.7	66.7[d]	21.9	na
6	Enron	North America	138.7	na	na	na	na	na
7	Daimler Chrysler	Europe	136.9	na	29.9	60.1	29.9	na
8	Royal Dutch/Shell Group	Europe	135.2	na	46.1	15.6[d]	46.1	na
9	General Electric	North America	125.9	40.9	59.1	59.1[d]	19.0	9.1
10	Toyota Motor	Asia-Pacific	120.8	50.8	49.2	36.6	7.7	49.2[c]
11	Citigroup	North America	112.0	na	na	na	na	na
12	Mitsubishi	Asia-Pacific	105.8	13.2	86.8	5.4[d]	1.7[b]	86.8[c]
13	Mitsui	Asia-Pacific	101.2	34.0	78.9	7.4	11.1	78.9
14	Chevrontexaco	North America	99.7	56.5	43.5	43.5[d]	na	na
15	Total Fina Elf	Europe	94.3	na	55.6	8.4	55.6	na
16	Nippon Telegraph and Telephone	Asia-Pacific	93.4	na	na	na	na	na
17	Itochu	Asia-Pacific	91.2	19.1	91.2	5.5	1.7	91.2
18	Allianz	Europe	85.9	69.4	78.0	17.6[e]	78.0	4.4[f]
19	International Business Machines	North America	85.9	64.8	43.5	43.5[e]	28.0[g]	20.0
20	ING Group	Europe	83.0	77.3	35.1	51.4	35.1	3.4
21	Volkswagen	Europe	79.3	72.3	68.2	20.1	68.2	5.3
22	Siemens	Europe	77.4	78.0	52.0	30.0[c]	52.0	13.0
23	Sumitomo	Asia-Pacific	77.1	12.7	87.3	4.8[d]	na	87.3[c]
24	Philip Morris	North America	72.9	42.1	57.9	57.9[d]	25.8	na
25	Marubeni (q)	Asia-Pacific	71.8	28.2	74.5	11.6[d]	na	74.5
26	Verizon Communications	North America	67.2	3.8	96.2	96.2[d]	na	na
27	Deutsche Bank	Europe	66.8	69.0	63.1	29.3	63.1	6.5

(Table 1 continued)

(Table 1 continued)

500 Rank	Company	Region	Revenues in Billion US$	F/T Sales	Percentage of Intraregional	NA Percentage of Total	EUR Percentage of Total	AP Percentage of Total
28	E.ON	Europe	66.5	43.4	80.1	9.4[d]	80.1	na
29	U.S. Postal Service (q)	North America	65.8	3.0	97.0	97.0[d]	na	na
30	AXA (q)	Europe	65.6	77.3	51.2	24.1[d]	51.2	19.9
31	Credit Suisse	Europe	64.2	73.3	60.9	34.9[e]	60.9	4.1[f]
32	Hitachi	Asia-Pacific	63.9	31.0	80.0	11.0	7.0	80.0
33	Nippon Life Insurance	Asia-Pacific	63.8	na	na	na	na	na
34	American International Group	North America	62.4	na	59.0	59.0[a]	na	na
35	Carrefour	Europe	62.2	50.8	81.3	na	81.3	6.6
36	American Electric Power	North America	61.3	12.3	87.7	87.7[d]	11.8[b]	na
37	Sony	Asia-Pacific	60.6	67.2	32.8	29.8[d]	20.2	32.8[c]
38	Royal Ahold	Europe	59.6	85.0	32.8	59.2	32.8	0.6
39	Duke Energy	North America	59.5	13.1	96.5	96.5	na	na
40	AT&T	North America	59.1	na	na	na	na	na
41	Honda Motor	Asia-Pacific	58.9	73.1	26.9	53.9	8.1	26.9[c]
42	Boeing	North America	58.2	33.3	66.7	66.7[d]	14.5	16.3
43	El Paso	North America	57.5	2.8	97.2	97.2[d]	na	na
44	BNP Paribas	Europe	55.0	na	na	na	na	na
45	Matsushita Electric Industrial	Asia-Pacific	55.0	35.1	64.9	12.4[e]	6.9	64.9
46	Home Depot	North America	53.6	6.2	100.0	100.0	–	na
47	Bank of America	North America	52.6	na	92.9	92.9[a]	3.5[g]	2.7
48	Aviva	Europe	52.3	na	na	na	na	na
49	Fiat	Europe	51.9	65.6	73.3	13.0	73.3	na
50	Assicurazioni Generali (q)	Europe	51.4	67.2	91.4	1.7[a]	91.4	na

Sources: Braintrust Research Group, *The Regional Nature of Global Multinational Activity*, 2003. (http://www.braintrustresearch.com).
[a] Refers to Canada and the United States only.
[b] Refers to the United Kingdom only.
[c] Refers to Japan only.
[d] Refers to the United States only.
[e] Refers to the Americas.
[f] Includes Africa.
[g] Refers to the EMEA region Europe, Middle East, and Africa.

380 firms in the top 500 for which geographic sales data are available, 58 firms have zero foreign sales, i.e., 100% of their sales are in their home region and 262 firms have extraregional sales but derive over 50% of their sales in their home market. These firms include the following: Kroger, Allstate, Bank One Corporation, U.S. Bancorp, Circuit City, Safeway, Cathay Life, Kyushu Electric, and so on. Of the 380 firms with data, 320 are home region based. These firm-level data are discussed in detail in Rugman and Verbeke (2004). This work builds on Rugman (2000). I shall now discuss these data in more detail and then comment on the three papers.

2. Multinationals are Not Global, but Regional

Today, MNEs largely operate within their home region of the triad or at best are biregional (competing only across two of the triads of the EU, NAFTA, and Asia). Few MNEs are "global," and thus few MNEs are really good case studies of globalization. Instead, today, most of the largest 500 MNEs are interested in the deepening of regional trade and investment agreements in Europe, the Americas, and Asia.

The data to support the regional nature of MNE activity are now becoming better understood. At an aggregate level, it shows that the majority of trade of the triad is intraregional (62% in the EU, 56.7% in NAFTA, and 56% in Asia) (Rugman, 2000). The trend towards intraregional trade has been increasing over the last 20 years. In addition, foreign direct investment (FDI) is mainly undertaken between the EU and NAFTA or is intraregional within each region of the triad. There is relatively little FDI on a multilateral basis. The economic picture is one of increasing regionalization, not "globalization" (Rugman, 2000; Rugman and Verbeke, 2003). This indicates that there is an increasing economic interdependence within each region of the triad, but not between the regions of the triad.

At the microlevel, the evidence of regionalism is even stronger. Of the largest 500 corporations in the world, 320 of the 380 for which geographic sales data are available have, on average, 80% of their sales in their home region of the triad. For example, the world's largest company, Wal-Mart, has 94% of its sales in NAFTA. Of the other top 50 companies ranked by size, General Motors has 81% in NAFTA; Mitsubishi has 87% in Asia; Mitsui has 79% in Asia; TotalFinaElf has 56% in Europe; Allianz has 78% in Europe; VW has 68% in Europe; Deutsche Bank has 63% in Europe; and Credit Suisse has 61% in Europe.

Of the 380 companies for which data are available, only 9 are "global" in the sense of having at least 20% of their sales in each region of the triad. These are mainly MNEs in electronics such as IBM, Sony, Philips, Nokia, Intel, Canon, and Flextronics. The others are Coca-Cola and LVMH. There are also a score of "biregional" MNEs with at least 20% of sales in two of these regions of the triad. These include Toyota, Nissan, DaimlerChrysler, Honda, AstraZeneca, GlaxoSmithKline, Ericsson, Diageo, Michelin, etc. Overall, there are incredible few truly global firms and most MNEs operate mainly in their home region of the triad, (Rugman and Verbeke, 2004).

The regional nature of multinational business was demonstrated in Table 1. It reports the intraregional sale of the 50 largest MNEs. The world's largest company is Wal-Mart. It has 94.1% of its sales in North America; it is not a global company. There are six companies with even more sales in their home region than Wal-Mart, as shown in Table 1. The rest of the table is interesting reading; most of the world's largest companies are not global but home region based.

For the 380 firms for which data are available, the 320 home region based show an average 80% of intraregional sales, whether these are North American, European, or Asian. Of the world's largest 500 firms, there are no geographic sales data for 120, leaving 380 with data. Of these, 320 form this group of home region firms. A set of 25 are biregional, with 20% of sales in two regions of the triad and less than 50% in their home region. Only 10 firms out of the top 500 are remotely global, with at least 20% of their sales in each region of the triad. An additional 14 MNEs have insufficient data for categorization. These data are reported in Table 2.

Table 2
Classification of the Top 500 MNEs, 2001

Type of MNE	No. of MNEs	Percentage of 500	Percentage of 380	Weighted Average Percentage of Intraregional Sales
Global	9	2.0	2.6	38.2
Biregional	25	5.0	6.6	42.0
Host region oriented	11	2.2	2.9	30.9
Home region oriented	320	64.0	84.2	80.3
Insufficient data	15	2.8	3.7	40.9
No data	120	24.0		NA
Total	500	100.0	100.0	71.9

Source: Braintrust Research Group, *The Regional Nature of Global Multinational Activity, 2003.* (http://www.braintrustresearch.com).
Weighted averages were calculated by assuming the lowest point in intraregional sales (i.e., > 90 = 90).

3. The Regional Triad

The importance of economic-based regionalization and the triad and the lack of globalization is now being reflected in political alignments. Following the definitive change of U.S. political attitudes towards national security after the September 11, 2001 terrorist attacks, a new world political system is emerging. This is based on the triad reality of regionalization.

The United States already has economic security on a regional basis. This was affirmed by the NAFTA agreement of 1994, (Rugman, 1994). Now Canada and Mexico supply energy and other natural resources to the United States in exchange for the enhanced business access to the world's single largest and richest market. The NAFTA does not provide the depth of economic integration of the EU, and it has none of its political and currency integration (Rugman and Kudina, 2002). Yet it ties together these three economies in a gigantic and highly successful free trade area to the mutual economic benefit of all three partners.

So successful is NAFTA that it is in the process of being expanded to the FTAA in 2005. This will lock in all 34 countries of the Americas into an extension of NAFTA. The U.S. economy will serve as the regional regime for growth and renewed prosperity for Latin America and the Caribbean, just as NAFTA has done for Mexico.

The economic data on NAFTA show ever increasing interdependence in trade and FDI. Table 3 shows that intraregional trade has increased from 49% to 57% between 1997 and 2000. Today, the United States has 22.6% of its exports going to Canada and 14.1% to Mexico, for a total of 36.7%. It only has 21.3% to all 15 member states of the EU. The United States is now a regional player in terms of trade. Similar data exist for FDI. In addition, at firm level, the 169 U.S. firms in the list of the world's largest 500 firms have an average of 77.3% of all their sales within NAFTA. Of course, Canada and Mexico are more than pulling the weight on intraregional trade. Canada has 87% of its exports to the United States; Mexico has 88.7%.

Table 3
Intraregional Trade in the Triad, Intraregional Exports (%), 1980–2000

Year	EU	NAFTA	Asia
2000	62.1	55.7	55.7
1997	60.6	49.1	53.1
1980	52.1	33.6	35.3

Source: IMF, *Direction of Trade Statistics Yearbook, 1983–2001*, and OECD, *International Direct Investment Statistics Yearbook, 2001*.

Table 3 also demonstrates that Europe and Asia are becoming increasingly regionalized. Intraregional trade in the EU increased from 60.6% to 62% over the 1997–2001 period. In Asia, even without a formal trade agreement across the region, the intraregional trade increased from 53.1% to 55.7%. Intraregional FDI increases from 36% in 1986 to 46% in 1999 in the EU. In Asia, intraregional FDI increased from 20.5% in 1986 to 26.2% in 1999.

Regionalism is the dominant economic force. As a direct corollary to this trend, there is even less trade between the triad blocks. Elsewhere, I have shown that the blocks are closing and becoming more inward looking and less global (Rugman, 2000). This economic reality should now be reflected in analysis of MNE strategy.

4. Comments on Papers

Given the evidence about the lack of globalization, what relevant comments can be made on the three papers in *Journal of International Management* (Volume 9, 2003). Sadly, these papers would not have been necessary if the authors had done their homework. There is very little added value in discussing a concept that does not exist. All three papers need to be rethought and made relevant by linking them to the data showing an absence of globalization and an abundance of triad activity. I shall now make some brief suggestions as to how to rethink each of these papers. Overall, these papers help the debate about globalization to the extent that they represent current attitudes about globalization by leading international business researchers. Even in textbooks, the same thinking applies. For example, Charles Hill's best-selling text in international business takes "the global grocer" as its first case. Yet, Wal-Mart has 94% of its sales in North America – not a good example of anything global.

First, Clark and Knowles make the point that writers on globalization define the issue from the viewpoint of their home discipline. They also complain that there is more to globalization than an economic perspective. To illustrate why both points are technically correct but misleading, let us focus on one of their prime suspects, Anthony Giddens, the sociologist who was director of the London School of Economics until recently. In his major statement on globalization, Giddens (1999) indeed uses a sociological definition to the effect that globalization leads to an increased commonality, i.e., cultural integration, based especially on U.S. values. He argues that

> Globalization is political, technological and cultural, as well as economic. It has been influenced above all by developments in systems of communications, dating back only to the late 1980s (p. 10).

Giddens (1999) also says that "many of the most visible cultural expressions of globalization are American – Coca-Cola, McDonald's, CNN; most of the giant multinational companies are based in the U.S. too" (p. 15).

As will be obvious to any empirically literate professor of international business, Giddens (1999) has the numbers wrong. Of the world's largest 500 companies in 2000, only 185 were from the United States. Another 141 were from the EU and 104 from Japan. The "triad" accounted for 430 of the top 500. Giddens (1999) is incorrect to state that most of the giant MNEs are American. Further, he is wrong to see globalization as American – it is triad based, as all the data reveal. Indeed, U.S. firms are more intraregionally oriented than their European and Asian counterparts.

The criticism of economic procrusteanism is also unfounded. As Giddens (1999) makes clear, there is a clear connection between perceived cultural commonality and the global economic drivers of free trade, FDI, and MNE activity. Indeed, the usual argument is that the economic drivers lead to cultural commonality. My point is that whatever the sequencing, there is neither cultural commonality nor economic-led globalization. Instead, the data constantly reveal triad-based economic activities and a remarkable lack of cultural homogenization. All MNEs know the need to "think global, act local," i.e., to be nationally responsive in order to be successful. To conclude, the authors' statistical myopia clouds their analysis and it calls for major rethinking.

Allan Bird and Michael Stevens argue that there is an emerging global culture of high-living professionals with common values. This is a high-end "niche" of the commonality viewpoint in which they argue that "the world is clearly becoming more unified and homogeneous." However, basically every aspect of their arguments is wrong. Instead of one language, one thirst, one food, one car, etc., there are strong regional differences within each part of the triad. Even Nestlé has found that it needs regional brands. Even Coca-Cola needs to act local (according to its own CEO) and be nationally responsive. Toyota has almost no presence in Europe, with only 7.7% of its sales there; it is a biregional MNE with 36.6% of its sales in North America but half still in Asia. A more serious study of such data would negate the need for this paper; we have triad effects not global ones.

Lyn Amine's paper is even easier to deconstruct to a triad level – it is pretty obvious that environmental regulations do not exist on a multilateral basis, but there are some regionally. The EU "ecolabels" and other European environmental regulations are quite different from NAFTA's. The latter only extends the principle of national treatment to FDI and applies trade-related environmental arbitration panels. There is not even a regionally agreed upon set of NAFTA regulations, just the national ones with national treatment. There are no commonly accepted environmental regulations in force in Asia. Stakeholders are best analyzed at a national level, possibly regionally but not globally. The so-called civil society is mainly a North American- and Western European-led set of activists, many of whom join their national governments as "insiders" to influence policy. There is no future in multilateralism for them. The MNEs can indeed develop green capabilities as shown in Rugman and Verbeke (1998), but at a regional level not globally.

5. Conclusions

The evidence is that the world economy is now a triad one; the economic regions of North America, the EU, and Asia dominate international business. Both aggregate data and disaggregated data on the sales of the world's largest MNE show the regional pattern of economic activity. What does this mean for globalization? The lack of globalization means that scholars of international business need to be careful in distinguishing regional triad strategies from true global strategy. Above all, before rushing to write about globalization, it is necessary to look at the evidence.

References

Giddens, A., 1999. *Runaway World: How Globalization is Reshaping Our Lives*. Profile Books, London.

Rugman, A., 1994. *Foreign Investment and NAFTA*. University of South Carolina Press, Columbia, SC.

Rugman, A., 2000. *The End of Globalization*. Random House, London.

Rugman, A., Kudina, A., 2002. Britain, Europe and North America. In: Fratianni, M., Savona, P., Kirton, J. (Eds.), *Governing Global Finance*. Ashgate, Aldershot, pp. 185–195.

Rugman, A., Verbeke, A., 1998. Corporate strategy and environmental regulations. *Strateg. Manage. J.* 19 (4), 363–375.

Rugman, A., Verbeke, A., 2003. Regional multinationals: the location-bound drivers of global strategy. In: Birkinshaw, J., et-al. (Eds.), *The Future of the Multinational Company*. Wiley, Chichester, UK, pp. 45–57.

Rugman, A., Verbeke, A., 2004. Regional and global strategies of multinational enterprise. *Journal of International Business Studies* 35 (1) (in press).

51

Geographic Scope of Operations by Multinational Companies: An Exploratory Study of Regional and Global Strategies

B. Elango

Global operations have continued to be increasingly important to companies operating in the current business environment. Affiliate companies' sales revenues are estimated at $19 trillion, accounting for a tenth of world GDP and a third of world exports. In addition, employees of foreign affiliates of these firms jumped from 24 million in 1990 to 54 million in 2001 (United Nations, 2002). Given the importance of global operations, firms can no longer afford to ignore globalization of their markets. From a strategic perspective, the trend toward globalization requires firms to operate beyond their national boundaries to remain competitive. A significant body of literature has been published which presents ideas as to how companies can capitalize in a world with falling trade barriers, under the notion of global strategy (e.g., Yip, 2003). The phenomenon of internationalization and its underlying relationship with performance has been a topic of interest to scholars in the field of international strategy. In general, the numerous studies generated by this interest have reinforced the belief that internationalization is related to a firm's performance, although significant debate exists as to the exact nature of this relationship (Annavarjula and Beldona, 2000).

In recent years, however, there has been an emerging stream of studies that challenge the notion of global strategies. One such study even calls the common assumptions of globalization a "myth" (Rugman, 2000). The main proposition of these studies is that few multinationals are truly global and most multinational firms are regionally-oriented, and therefore strategic management of MNCs should be regionally-focused (Rugman and Brain, 2003). This line of thought

Source: *European Management Journal*, Vol. 22, No. 4, 2004, pp. 431–441.

calls for an approach referred to as regionalization, wherein firms operate primarily in geographically proximate markets (i.e., countries located close to the home country), as opposed to truly global markets. While this view is a radical departure from the prevalent understanding of this topic, one cannot deny the inherent logic of its premise. Recent work by Ghemawat (2003) indicates that the degree of economic integration of global markets has increased in recent years, but most markets fall between the extremes of integration and isolation, a state he refers to as "semiglobalization". The formation and expansion of trade blocs such as NAFTA, EU, and ASEAN, the increasing likelihood of newer trade zones being formed (e.g., FTAA – Free Trade Area of the Americas), and the recent failure of GATT talks all lead one to expect that regional trade blocs will become a fixture of global trade. If trade blocs allow greater and easier access to regional markets that are closer to home, one could propose that firms would be better off seeking regional markets, rather than global markets, to gain the benefits of international operations.

The above perspective has generated a significant amount of interest and debate. Therefore, this study seeks to review the regionalization strategies of the world's largest MNCs, with the goal of answering the following two empirical questions: *What is the relationship between regionalization and non-regional operations and performance?* and *What are significant differences across MNCs that are regionalized in their operations relative to those that are not?* This study will contribute to the international strategy literature in two important ways. It will be the first to test the relationship between regional strategies and financial performance of firms. Additionally, a comparison of regional and global (i.e., non-regional) firms will allow for a greater understanding of the characteristics that differentiate the firms which follow regional strategies versus global strategies. Needless to say, such a study has significant implications for firms planning and implementing international strategies. It is also of great interest to researchers and public policy practitioners, due to the importance of the domination of MNCs in international trade and the prevalence of regional trade blocs worldwide. The following section will expand on the underlying theory and develop hypotheses for the study.

Theory and Hypothesis

Regional Strategies

Internationalization refers to the degree to which a firm's sales revenue or operations are gained from outside its home country. Researchers have traditionally argued that internationalization offers significant benefits for a firm. These include new market opportunities (Buhner, 1987); economies of scale and scope (Porter, 1985); factor advantages; exploiting distinctive capabilities (Hymer, 1976); learning (Ghoshal, 1987); flexibility (Kogut, 1985a, b); risk reduction (Shaked, 1986); crosssubsidization (Hamel and Prahalad, 1985), as well as many other competitive benefits such as foreclosing entry by rivals, avoidance of intense competition in home markets, etc. (Elango, 2000). If these benefits accrue to a firm seeking international markets, the underlying assumption is that internationalization will result in higher performance.

Studies testing for the relationship between internationalization and performance have reported an inverted U-shaped relationship (Daniels and Bracker, 1989; Geringer *et al.*, 1989; Hitt *et al.*, 1997; Gomes and Ramaswamy, 1999; Mauri and Sambharya, 2001; Caper and Kotabe, 2003). Even though these findings have been subjected to significant debate in the literature, theoretical expositions have been presented to support the inverted curvilinear relationship between internationalization and performance (Hitt, Hoskisson and Ireland, 1994). It is argued that while internationalization brings increases in performance (explaining the positive slope), the benefits of internationalization tend to decline after a certain point, as the costs of internationalization increase much faster than the benefits, resulting in declining returns for the firm (explaining the negative slope).

International operations could result in increased operational costs and risks to firms for several reasons. These increased operational costs and risks are commonly referred to as liability of foreignness (Hymer, 1976). According to Zaheer (1995), liability of foreignness arises from four sets of factors: 1. Costs associated with travel, transportation, coordination, and time zones, wherein firms face increased setup, coordination, and monitoring costs due to operations being spread across large distances (Hitt *et al.*, 1994). 2. The lack of roots of being in an unfamiliar environment due to changing political situations in the host countries, economic risks, and fluctuations in currency exchange values (Bae and Jain, 2002). 3. Costs due to the lack of legitimacy and economic nationalism in the host country. 4. Home country restrictions on host country operations which reduce freedom of operation for foreign firms (Zaheer, 1995). These risks and the alien environment for foreign firms can increase the likelihood and cost of managerial mistakes (Hymer, 1976).

One way for a firm to minimize this negative impact of internationalization is by seeking markets that are close to their home country. One can argue several reasons why operations in regional markets will be less costly and risky compared to global operations (i.e., non-regional markets). For instance, by locating in regional markets, firms can reduce the costs of coordination, as compared to globally dispersed operations. By definition, regional markets are located at a more proximate distance and have lesser time zone differences, thereby allowing for relatively closer monitoring of changes within and outside the organization. It is also likely that for a firm operating in regional markets, the degree of learning that needs to take place would be lower due to reduced 'psychic distance' (Johanson and Vehlne, 1977; Vermeulen and Barkema, 2002). Operation in regional markets (within trade blocs) also significantly reduces the restrictions a host or home country can place on business transactions by firms, due to the many anti-competitive and pro-trade clauses in free trade agreements.

Another factor that could encourage regionalization strategies is the difficulty in implementing a global strategy. Baden-Fuller and Stopford (1990), in their study of the washing machine industry, show the difficulties and pitfalls involved in the creation of a global product suitable for many countries. Regional markets may offer several other advantages for international operations in this regard. In a study on the exposition of international strategy, Prahalad and Doz (1987) present managerial choice in terms of two options: integration and responsiveness. The integration option offers many of the benefits of globalization while allowing the firms to be responsive to national country needs. The responsiveness option, on the other hand, does not allow for benefits of globalization. Assuming commonality in some market characteristics, regionalization may serve to be a good compromise between the two choices of integration and responsiveness. Evidence of this trend is apparent in the automobile industry, wherein customers' needs are not necessarily unique to a nation, while at the same time, these needs are far from globally similar (Schlie and Yip, 2000). In such instances, regionalization could serve as a 'middle' or 'third' way for multinationals (Verdin and Heck, 2001), where at least some of the benefits of globalization are gained, and at the same time, they can remain responsive to local market needs.

Evidence of the viability and importance of a regional approach to current world trade is well documented by Rugman (2000), who points out that a majority of the trade and foreign direct investment during the last twenty years took place within each of the triad regions of the world. Rugman and Brain (2003), based on their analysis of Fortune Magazine's list of 500 global companies, claim that even the most international companies are home region-based in their activities. The importance of this regional approach to enhance competitiveness of firms has also been noted by other scholars (e.g., Morrison *et al.*, 1991; Segal-Horn, 1996) as being due to the inherent limitations of standardization required to implement a truly global strategy.

Based on the benefits of a regionalization approach argued above, the explanation for the positive slope could be that initially, firms may seek to internationalize through regional markets, thereby increasing performance, whereas as the firm expands its geographic scope, the benefits of internationalization decrease. While this assertion needs to be tested empirically, previous studies testing for the relationship between internationalization and performance do not control for the influence of regionalization. Most studies operationalize international operations as a single unitary dimension (e.g., foreign sales or foreign assets), or at best as diversification across various geographic regions. In this study, we differentiate international operations into a regional component and a global component, allowing a better understanding of the relationship. Hence, it is proposed:

Hypothesis 1a: *Other things remaining equal, the extent of regionalization of operations by a firm will be positively related to its performance.*

Hypothesis 1b: *Other things remaining equal, the extent of non-regional operations by a firm will be marginally related to its performance.*

Product Diversification

The practice of dual strategies of international and product diversification by multinational firms has been reported in the literature (Sambharya, 1995). While many studies have been conducted on the topic of product diversification, scholars concur on the fact that there is no agreement on the precise nature of the relationship between diversification and performance (see Hoskisson and Hitt, 1990; for a review). The interactive and direct influence of product diversification on international operations has also been elaborated in many previous studies (e.g., Buhner, 1987; Kim et al., 1989; Geringer et al., 1989; Grant et al., 1988; Hitt et al., 1994; Sambharya, 1995; Hitt et al., 1997). Overall, these studies indicate that significant interactive effects exist between international diversification and product diversification. While it is hard to link the findings of these studies, as each of them measure product and international diversification differently compared to the current study, we can make the following assertion: Firms will be able to handle moderate or low levels of international or product diversification effectively, but will find high levels of diversity in products and markets constraining for effective performance. For example, a firm with higher levels of product diversity will be able to handle and coordinate regional operations within the existing structure and systems of the company. The same cannot be said for global operations which are spread out in many regions of the world. Therefore, extensive diversification in markets and products will lead to increased costs and/or ineffective control of the MNC, resulting in poor performance. One would assume managers of firms that are diversified in varied markets and products may find it increasingly difficult to give proper attention to diverse markets that are unfamiliar and all aspects of business that are dissimilar (Grant et al., 1988). Therefore, it may be proposed,

Hypothesis 2a: *Other things remaining equal, the relationship between regionalization of operations and performance will be positively moderated by the extent of product diversification by the firm.*

Hypothesis 2b: *Other things remaining equal, the relationship between globalization of operations and performance will be negatively moderated by the extent of product diversification made by the firm.*

Geographic Scope

One of the central assumptions in the notion of international strategy is that different industries offer different potentials for the globalization of firms (Yip, 2003). According to Porter (1986), an industry can be classified as global or multidomestic in nature. In a global industry, "a firm's competitive position in one country is significantly affected by its position in other countries or *vice versa*" (p. 18). In contrast, a multidomestic industry is defined by competition taking place on a country-by-country basis and is bound by national boundaries (Porter, 1986; Kim et al., 2003). Therefore, in global industries, it is suggested that a company integrates its international operations with linkages across leading countries to gain competitive advantage (Hout et al., 1982). Considering that MNCs operate in different industries with differing scope for global, regional, or home country-based operations, it is likely that they will follow differing approaches to geographic scope for international operations (Yip, 2003). Apart from industry characteristics, a MNC's institutional heritage, country characteristics, and its own product diversification strategy are likely to create specific preferences for operating in differing geographic regions. Since one of the goals of this study is to explore differences of MNCs in their geographic scope of operations, the following hypothesis is stated in an open-ended manner:

Hypothesis 3: *MNCs will follow distinct strategies and differ in the extent of operations across geographic markets and product diversification.*

The data collection procedure used in this study as well as the operationalization of variables is described in the following section.

Research Methodology

Data Collection

The starting point of the data collection process was the Directory of Multi-nationals (2001) published by Caritas Data. According to its publishers, this directory provides data on the 500 largest MNCs who have consolidated sales of over US $1.5 billion and overseas sales in excess of US $750 million during 1999/2000. We chose this source for our sample because it is one of the few publicly available sources which offer sales of MNCs by geographic region in a useable manner. Firms who focus exclusively on banking, insurance, and commodity brokering are not included in this directory, even though other service firms are. Informal inquiries in academic circles on the relative quality and accuracy of this source were very positive, encouraging us to use this directory for our sample. We also randomly crosschecked the data with other sources of information when possible and found them to be consistent with one another. Even though this directory lists 500 MNCs, we were limited to using 136 MNCs for which data was available on geographic scope of operations. We also had to drop many MNCs wherein the data on geographic scope was available but who reported intra-firm transfer separately. In such instances, the geographic sales of the MNC (when added to the intra-firm transfer) was significantly higher than 100%. While it is understandable that the total segment sales of all reported regions will not add up to 100% all the time, due to rounding errors and other approximations inherent with a large MNC, we felt it would be better to drop firms wherein we lacked confidence in the numbers. We felt this would preserve the integrity of the data, though the resultant outcome would be a reduced sample size. Data availability is an inherent limitation for a study of geographic scope of operations because of the considerable leeway in accounting requirements, which results in differing ways companies are allowed to define and report information on their geographic operations. Once we collected information on geographic scope, we used the WorldScope database to find additional information on other firm-specific data which was unavailable in the Directory of Multinationals. In this step, we lost six companies due to missing values, further limiting our sample size to 130 firms.

Operationalization of Variables

Previous studies in the literature on internationalization indicate a variety of ways to measure international operations, one of which is widely practiced: the percentage of foreign sales to total sales (the foreign sales ratio) [e.g., Grant, 1987; Grant et al., 1988; Kim et al., 1989; Tallman and Li, 1996; Geringer et al., 2000; and Caper and Kotabe, 2003]. Hence we operationalize Regional Sales Ratio as sales within the home geographic region (excluding home country sales) divided by the total sales of the firm. For a U.K.-based multinational, the Regional Sales Ratio would be computed as total firm sales in Europe (excluding sales in the U.K.) divided by the total firm sales. For a U.S. MNC, home region would be defined as North America,[1] for a Japanese MNC, home region would be defined as Asia, and so on. This definition of Regional Sales Ratio is a significant modification to the approach used by Rugman and Brain (2003), in which their measure captures home-triad operations of MNCs. We feel the approach chosen in this paper is more appropriate for the research question undertaken by this study, which attempts to capture the relationship between degree of international sales in the home region (by definition, this will not include home country sales) and performance. However, we use the operationalization of Rugman and Brain (2003) in developing clusters based on geographic scope of operations. The reasons for this will be elaborated in the next section. We also developed a new measure called Global Sales Ratio, wherein we capture the sales outside the home-triad region of the multinational. For instance, for a multinational based in Japan, the Global Sales Ratio would be computed as firm sales that took place outside Asia divided by its total sales.

The addition of Regional Sales Ratio and Global Sales Ratio will result in the total foreign sales ratio (Internationalization) of the firm.

The dependent variable performance is operationalized as gross profit margin (GPM). For a crosscountry study of this nature, the usage of GPM offers two benefits compared to the other traditional measures (like ROA or ROS) used to measure performance. First, the use of GPM allows for the capture of profit margins undiluted by other firm-related expenses and accounting treatments and artifacts, which vary significantly across countries. Second, use of a ratio such as GPM avoids distortions created by taxation and currency conversion. Needless to say, GPM is of significant interest to managers and investors alike, and is highly related to ROA and ROS. Based on past research findings, this study will also incorporate three control variables (firm size, firm growth rate, and debt ratio) in the testing of the relationships. The operationalization of the variables and the sources of information for the various elements in the study are described in Table 1. Descriptive statistics of the variables along with correlation values is presented in Table 2. A review of the correlation tables indicates that the likelihood of multicollinearity issues influencing or biasing the results of the regression models used in this study to be minimal.

The sample of firms used in this study came from a broad spectrum of industries. To control for industry effects, each of the major categorical industry types was dummy coded. Two procedural issues in the coding process deserve

Table 1
Variable Definition & Data Sources

Variable	Definition	Data Source
Dependent Variables		
Financial Performance	Gross Profit Margin	WorldScope
Independent Variables		
Regional Sales Ratio	Sales within the Home Geographic Region (excluding home country sales)/Total Sales	Directory of Multinationals
Global Sales Ratio	Sales Outside the Geographic Region (i.e., sales outside Home-Triad)/Total Sales	Directory of Multinationals
Internationalization	Regional Sales Ratio+Global Sales Ratio	Directory of Multinationals
Product Diversification	$1 - \Sigma p_i^2$, where p represents the percentage of a firm's sales on product line I (Herfindahl Index)	Directory of Multinationals
Research Expenditure	Research & Development Expenditures/Sales	WorldScope
Firm Debt Ratio	Long Term Debt/Assets held by the Firm	WorldScope
Firm Growth Rate	Percentage Change in Firm Size	WorldScope
Firm Size	Natural log of Total Employees	WorldScope
Foreign Asset Ratio	Foreign Assets/Total Assets	WorldScope
Administrative Ratio	Administrative and Selling Expenditures/Sales	WorldScope

Note: Firm Sales=[Home Country Sales + Regional Sales + Global Sales]

mention. First, some firms operated in too many industries, making it difficult to categorize into a single industry. In such cases, firms were coded as "conglomerate", meaning that no single industry could be associated with the firm. Second, the remaining firms were coded into six groups: "primary manufacturing", "secondary manufacturing", "food", "service", "consumer goods", and "utility". Appendix A provides a distribution of firms across industries and the geographic home region of the MNC. The following section discusses the findings reported in the Tables and concludes with implications of this study.

Discussion of Results

Regression models were used to test the first two hypotheses, and the results of these models are presented in Table 3. Taken independently, the results of Model 1 indicate very limited support for the notion that regional sales ratio is positively related to performance (Hypothesis 1a). This model explains about 37.3% ($p < 0.01$) of the variance, but the regional sales ratio (beta=0.114) is supported only at the 1 level. Model 2 tested for the interactive effect of product diversification and regionalization wherein an additional element, the interactive (multiplicative) term (product diversification * regional sales ratio), was added to the equation in Model 1. This model explained about 41.5% ($p < 0.01$) of the variance, but interestingly, the regional sales ratio beta value reduced to –0.070 from 0.114, which is statistically insignificant. In Model 2, the interactive term was characterized by relatively large beta loading (beta=0.305, $p < 0.01$), coupled with a marginally significant negative loading for product diversification (beta=–0.174, $p < 0.1$). This finding lends support

Table 2
Means, Standard Deviations and Correlations ($N = 130$)[a]

Variables	Mean (STD. DEV.)	1	2	3	4	5	6	7	8	9	10
1. Regional Sales Ratio	27.59 (17.83)	1									
2. Global Sales Ratio	37.41 (18.24)	0.169	1								
3. Internationalization	59.96 (25.22)	0.784**	0.651**	1							
4. Product Diversification	0.5141 (0.2499)	-0.237*	-0.129	-0.132	1						
5. R & D Expenditures	3.55 (4.12)	0.201	0.127	0.162	-0.139	1					
6. Debt Ratio	61.25 (110.23)	-0.076	-0.190*	-0.205**	0.005	-0.155	1				
7. Sales Growth	10.27 (19.74)	0.249*	0.011	0.157	-0.164	0.116	0.012	1			
8. Employees	69503 (79567)	0.020	0.042	0.086	0.046	0.122	0.164	0.152	1		
9. Administrative Ratio	17.64 (11.21)	0.014	0.308**	0.154	-0.065	0.257*	-0.035	-0.041	-0.088	1	
10. Foreign Asset Ratio	28.42 (19.38)	0.269*	0.498**	0.476**	0.059	-0.096	-0.148	0.098	0.058	0.317*	-

***=$p<0.01$
**=$p<0.05$
*=$p<.10$
[a]Due to missing values, the sample size for Regional Sales was 105, R & D Expenditures was 102, Administrative Ratio was 100, Foreign Asset Ratio was 73. To avoid sampling losses, pairwise comparison procedure was used. Therefore the addition of Regional Sales Ratio and Global Sales Ratio will not approximate Internationalization

Table 3
Regression Results between Internationalization and Performance

	Model 1	Model 2	Model 3	Model 4
Independent variables				
Global Sales Ratio × Product Diversification				0.052
Regional Sales Ratio × Product Diversification		0.354***		
Global Sales Ratio			0.226***	0.204***
Regional Sales Ratio	0.114*	−0.081		
Product Diversification	0.046	−0.237*	−0.037	−0.076
Sales Growth	−0.082	−0.085	−0.027	−0.032
Firm Size	−0.013	−0.079	−0.076	−0.083
Debt Ratio	−0.174*	−0.145*	−0.078	−0.075
Conglomerate Effect (Dummy)	−0.038	−0.078	−0.058	−0.060
Consumer Goods Sector Effect (Dummy)	0.569***	0.516***	0.513***	0.520***
Food Sector Effect (Dummy)	0.181	0.145	0.140	0.143
Primary Manufacturing Sector Effect (Dummy)	−0.001	−0.055	−0.060	−0.057
Secondary Manufacturing Sector Effect (Dummy)	0.057	−0.017	−0.015	−0.013
Service Sector Effect (Dummy)	−0.102	−0.196	−0.196	−0.198
R-Square	0.373	0.395	0.440	0.436
F Value	6.616***	6.737***	10.219***	9.317***
Sample *N*	105	105	130	130

***=$p < 0.01$
**=$p < 0.05$
*=$p < 0.1$
Seven sectors were included in all of the above models (the Utility Sector is the baseline sector for the dummy effect)

to Hypothesis 2a, which proposed that the regional approach to international markets coupled with product diversification is positively related to performance.

Model 3 tested for the relationship between global sales ratio and performance. In contrast to Hypothesis 1b, this regression model had the highest *R*-Square among the models tested (*R*-Square = 0.440, $p<0.01$) indicating a strong positive relationship between global sales ratio and performance. Model 4 tested for the interactive effect of product diversification and globalization wherein an additional element, the interactive (multiplicative) term (product diversification * global sales ratio), was added to the equation in Model 3. Despite the presence of the interaction term in Model 4, it had a much lower *R*-Square value than Model 3, indicating that the interactive term did not contribute to explaining the variance. It should also be noted that, unlike the regional sales ratio in Model 2, the global sales ratio beta loading increased while remaining statistically significant, thereby indicating no support for Hypothesis 2b.

Study findings indicate a weak link between regionalization and performance and a strong link between globalization and performance, which is quite contrary to the proposed hypothesis. Upon reflection, one can think of several reasons as to why this may be the case. First, this study operationalized performance as gross profit margin. It could be the case that firms, when operating in global markets, may seek a higher return or margins than firms operating in regional markets, in order to compensate for the greater risk involved in global operations. Second, one would presume that firms operating in global market segments could be facing less intense competition compared to regional markets.

For instance, a firm operating in global markets would be able to choose markets wherein the competitive conditions are more suitable for its resource-profile compared to being forced to operate in home regions where it might not possess the greatest advantage *vis-à-vis* its rivals. Third, it is also likely that firms with global operations are able to gain the benefits of the multinational network effectively. Global operations allow a firm to optimize on the cost and changes in prices of goods, interest rates, labor, and raw materials by shifting operations across nations (Kogut, 1985; Pantzalis, 2001). This flexibility to reduce risks and gain synergies in operations may not be available to firms with international operations that are regional in nature. Therefore, despite the existence of the large number of firms whose geographic scope is largely regional, this finding would call for firms to undertake global operations to maximize their profits.

The strong showing of the interaction term of regional sales ratio and product diversification is indicative of the importance of managing diversification of markets and products effectively. It seems that large MNCs who are diversified in product markets are better off seeking regional markets and capitalizing on the opportunities offered. Based on this study's findings, one may say the regional approach to international operations allows firms to integrate product and international diversification to exploit interdependencies to gain synergies as argued by Hitt *et al.* (1997). It can also be argued that firms with diversified product lines will be able to use existing managerial capabilities and systems to gain economies of scale and scope with greater ease in regional markets. However, it should be noted that when the interaction term is added to the model, both regional sales ratio and product diversification show negative beta loading, thereby indicating the inherent risk in such an approach. This, however, is consistent with previous findings reported in the literature wherein international operations and product diversification do not have an effect on performance, but have strong interactive effects with performance (Sambharya, 1995).

In testing Hypothesis 3, cluster analysis was used to develop empirical grouping of geographic strategies of firms. We initially attempted to use four variables in the development of clusters. However two of them (home country sales and regional sales ratio) were highly correlated (correlation$=0.717$, $p<0.01$) with one another. Therefore, we combined these two variables into a single variable, similar to the approach by Rugman and Brain (2003). This resulted in three variables along with global sales ratio and product diversification. The K-Means cluster procedure was used to generate three clusters representative of three approaches to internationalization (i.e., home-based, regional, and global). The statistical significance of these tests across the three clusters for the three variables was supported at a 0.001 level of confidence. To better understand the differences across MNC clusters, we also conducted one-way analysis of variance on various organizational characteristics of the MNC. To illustrate the differences, the results of these tests are reported in Table 4 along with the sample means.

The first cluster represented 30 of the 130 firms (23%) in our sample. These firms, on average, had about 20% of the sales in their home country, 26% of the sales in their home region, and 63% of the sales outside their home region. We designated these firms in this cluster *global*, since a majority of their sales came from outside their home region and were truly international in scope (77%).

Table 4
Mean Comparison of Clusters

Variable	Full Sample (N = 130)	Global Cluster (N = 30)	Multinational Cluster (N = 36)	Regional Cluster (N = 64)	F-Test Results Comparing Cluster Means
Home Country Sales[a]	40.62	19.86	65.24	30.77	9.04***
Regional Sales Ratio	27.59	26.18	19.30	33.00	47.09***
Global Sales Ratio	37.41	62.90	16.06	37.47	6.84***
International Sales	59.96	77.73	33.75	66.38	324.42***
Financial Performance	27.20	37.32	21.16	25.85	51.75***
Product Diversification	0.5141	0.388	0.5109	0.5787	2.05***
Research Expenditure	3.55	3.88	2.100	4.05	7.05*
Firm Debt Ratio	61.25	30.29	96.78	55.78	3.24**
Firm Growth Rate	10.27	8.90	5.86	13.38	1.790*
Firm Size (Employees)	69503	76598	74205	63531	0.359
Administrative Ratio	17.64	24.19	14.08	16.65	6.15***
Foreign Asset Ratio	28.41	38.29	17.04	30.55	8.06***

***=$p<0.01$
**=$p<0.05$
*=$p<0.1$
[a]Home country sales is the extent of sales generated by the firm in the country where it is based

Firms in the global cluster are relatively more focused on their products' markets and have lower debt ratios. They also have higher administrative expenditures, foreign asset ratios, and profit margins. As argued earlier in the hypothesis, global firms may be better off with fewer products, as their managers are already dealing with greater geographic diversity. The high administrative sales ratio of the global cluster relative to the other two clusters indicates that globalization is an expensive process, in spite of the existence of its many benefits. Similarly, these firms' lower debt ratios will allow them to invest in international projects which take longer to pay off, albeit with higher returns.

The second cluster of 36 firms represented about 27% of our sample. These firms had a majority of the sales in the home country (65%) and about 19% regional and 16% global sales. We called the firms in this cluster *multinational*, as they pass the traditional test (10~20% international sales) of being multi-national in operations. Firms in the multinational cluster are home country focused and are characterized by high debt ratios, low research and development expenditures, and moderate levels of diversification. Due to these factors, these firms may not want to be exposed to international markets for reasons quite opposite to global firms. For instance, the average debt ratio of firms in this cluster was about three times (3.12) that of global firms, indicating that firms in this cluster have relatively higher leverage.

The third cluster was the largest, with 64 firms, representing about 49% of the sample. These firms had a higher level of home country sales (31%) than global firms, but a lower level than multinational firms. In contrast, they had a higher level of global sales than multinational firms but a lower level of global sales compared to the firms in the global cluster. Their regional sales were the highest (33%) compared to the other groups, leading us to call the firms in this cluster *regional*. Firms in the regional cluster are relatively more diversified, have higher growth rates, and have marginally higher amounts of investment in research, compared to global firms. In many ways, regional firms fit in between the continuum of global and multinational firms, offering a third alternative argued in the literature (Verdin and Heck, 2001). This largest of the three clusters validates the importance of this regional approach to international strategy as argued by its proponents (e.g., Rugman and Brain, 2003). The limitation and implications of this study's findings will be discussed in the following section.

Study Limitations and Implications

A cross-sectional study of this nature has limitations by virtue of its design. First, the study sample was limited to the largest MNCs for which data was available. Second, as this study was crosssectional in nature, it does not capture the dynamics that are characteristic of the phenomena studied. Future studies may want to test the same hypotheses with a much wider variety of firms, also incorporating time series data. Replication of this study's hypotheses through diverse samples and multiple time-periods will help increase the validity and relevance of the reported findings. Despite these limitations, this study offers many implications for the field of international business strategy.

First, the presence of a large number of MNCs which are regional in nature confirms the call by Rugman for the need to pay greater attention to regional strategies of MNCs. Anecdotal conversations with many senior executives of relatively smaller firms (compared to the study sample) with international operations also confirmed the prevalence of regional strategies. Barring the handful of studies cited in the paper, we generally found a dearth of studies on this topic in the literature. Needless to say, this study's findings posit the need for more research to be conducted on the regionalization of operations by firms. To help students in their careers, instructors teaching International Business courses may want to spend greater time on this topic. To our knowledge, few books on international strategy (barring notable exceptions like Yip, 2003) discuss regional strategy, and those that do, do so very briefly. At a public policy level, the findings strongly support the need for trade blocs. Governments interested in facilitating free trade should encourage trade blocs (which are regional in nature), as they reduce barriers and facilitate the day-to-day operations of these MNCs in regional markets. Trade blocs could help regional multinationals set up facilities which are global in scale (when possible), giving them a better opportunity to compete with global firms and potentially bring the benefits of competition (such as lower prices).

The relationship between internationalization and performance has always been a topic of interest to researchers in IB. This study proposed that one of the reasons for the inverted U-shaped curve reported in the literature could be due to the geographic scope of operations by a firm. In the hypothesis section, we had attributed the positive slope in the internationalization-performance relationship to regionalization benefits. However, the evidence found was quite contrary and shows that non-regional operations are characterized by a positive slope. Despite this contradiction in the empirical findings compared to the proposed argument, the importance of control for geographic scope of operations while testing the international-performance relationship is quite evident. Study findings offer two interesting implications for managers who seek to maximize performance. First, global operations offer higher profit margins compared to regional operations, thereby making it worthwhile for firms to operate in alien environments despite the risks involved. Second, a regional approach to international operations may be a viable option for MNCs who are diversified in many product segments.

Lastly, the results indicate the presence of three distinct but viable approaches to international operations: Global, Multinational, and Regional. Even though the comparison of the means in Table 4 were done without formal hypotheses (i.e., by post-hoc rationalization) the importance of "fit" (Venkatraman, 1989) between the strategy chosen and organization characteristics is apparent when one reviews the profiles of firms and the strategy followed. For instance, many studies reviewed in the earlier section indicate that a firm that has high levels of diversification in both products and markets has a negative relationship with performance. The multinational and regional clusters are highly diversified and less internationalized relative to the global cluster, thereby serving as a positive validation to this notion. Therefore, to a certain extent, practitioners may want to recognize that the requirements of various international strategy choices differ from one another. Additionally, it should be noted that even though firms in the global cluster reported the highest gross profits, from a transaction cost perspective, it also appears that global strategies are more costly to implement in terms of administrative costs.

Concluding Comments

This study sought to review the regionalization strategies of the world's largest MNCs. Study findings support the existence of regional orientation in operations among the largest multinationals in the world. More interestingly, the study's findings indicate that a MNC's global scope of operations has a direct effect on performance and a MNC's regional scope of operations has interactive effects through product diversification with performance. Therefore, the importance of managing geographic scope and product diversification strategies is a significant contribution by this study to the literature, as is the presence of three distinct approaches to international operations. An interesting finding in this regard is that firms with each of these approaches have a differing profile allowing them to be successful in the marketplace. We hope this exploratory study's findings will serve as an important stimulus to further research on this topic.

Appendix A

See Table A1.

Table A1
Table Showing Sample Distribution of Firms across Industries and Continents

Industry	Continent of Origin				
	Europe	North America	Japan	Other Countries	Total
Conglomerates	7		1	2	10
Consumer Goods	12	6	3		21
Food	9	2	1		12
Primary Manufacturing	15	4	3	1	23
Secondary Manufacturing	20	11	4		35
Service	23		2		25
Utility	4				4
Total	90	23	14	3	130

Note

1. This rule was relaxed marginally (North America operations was defined as U.S. and Canadian operations alone, since data on Mexican sales was unavailable) for 10 of the 23 U.S.-based firms in the sample. Separate statistical models were used to ensure that this operationalization did not confound the study findings.

References

Annavarjula, M. and Beldona, S. (2000) Multinationality-performance relationship: A review and reconceptualization. *International Journal of Organizational Analysis* **8**(1), 48–67.

Baden-Fuller, C.W. and Stopford, J. (1990) Globalization frustrated: The case of white goods. *Strategic Management Journal* **12**, 493–507.

Bae, C.S., Jain, V., 2002. Multinationality, R & D intensity, and firm performance: Evidence from U.S. industrial firms. Paper presented at the 2002 Academy of International Business Meetings, June 28–July 1, Puerto-Rico.

Buhner, R. (1987) Assessing international diversification of West German corporations. *Strategic Management Journal* **8**, 25–37.

Caper, N. and Kotabe, M. (2003) The relationship between international diversification and performance of service firms. *Journal of International Business Studies* **34**(4), 345–355.

Daniels, J.D. and Bracker, J. (1989) Profit performance: Do foreign operations make a difference? *Management International Review* **29**, 46–56.

Elango, B. (2000) An exploratory study into the linkages between corporate resources and the extent and form of internationalization. *American Business Review* **XVIII**, 12–26.

Geringer, M.J., Beamish, P.W. and daCosta, R.C. (1989) Diversification strategy and internationalization: Implications of MNE performance. *Strategic Management Journal* **10**, 109–119.

Geringer, M.J., Tallman, S. and Olsen, D.M. (2000) Product and international diversification among Japanese multinational firms. *Strategic Management Journal* **21**, 51–80.

Ghemawat, P. (2003) Semiglobalization and international business strategy. *Journal of International Business Studies* **34**, 138–152.

Ghoshal, S. (1987) Global strategy: An organizing framework. *Strategic Management Journal* **8**, 425–440.

Gomes, L.K. and Ramaswamy, K. (1999) An empirical examination of the form of the relationship between multinationality and performance. *Journal of International Business Studies* **30**(1), 173–188.

Grant, R.M. (1987) Multinationality and performance among British manufacturing companies. *Journal of International Business Studies* 18(3), 79–89.

Grant, R.M., Jammine, A. and Thomas, H. (1988) Diversity, diversification, and profitability among British manufacturing companies, 1972–84. *Academy of Management Journal* **31**, 71–81.

Hamel, G. and Prahalad, C.K. (1985) Do you really have a global strategy? *Harvard Business Review* **64**(4), 139–148.

Hitt, M.A., Hoskisson, R.E. and Kim, H. (1997) International diversification: Effects on innovation and firm performance in product diversified firms. *Academy of Management Journal* **40**, 767–798.

Hitt, M.A., Hoskisson, R.E. and Ireland, R.D. (1994) A midrange theory of the interactive effects of international and product diversification on innovation and performance. *Journal of Management* **20**, 297–326.

Hoskisson, R.E. and Hitt, M.A. (1990) Antecedents and performance outcomes of diversification: A review and critique of theoretical perspectives. *Journal of Management* **16**, 461–509.

Hout, T., Porter, M.E. and Rudden, E. (1982) How global companies win out. *Harvard Business Review* **60**(5), 98–108.

Hymer, S.H. (1976) *The International Operations of National Firms: A Study of Foreign Direct Investment*. MIT Press, Cambridge, MA.

Johanson, J. and Vehlne, J.E. (1977) The internationalization process of the firm: A model of market knowledgement and increasing foreign market commitments. *Journal of International Business Studies* **8**, 23–32.

Kim, W.C., Hwang, P. and Burgers, W.P. (1989) Global diversification strategy and corporate profit performance. *Strategic Management Journal* **10**, 45–57.

Kim, K., Park, J.-H. and Prescott, J.E. (2003) The global integration of business functions: A study of multinational businesses in integrated global industries. *Journal of International Business Studies* **34**(1), 1–18.

Kogut, B. (1985a) Designing global strategies: Comparative and competitive added value chains. *Sloan Management Review* **26**(4), 15–28.

Kogut, B. (1985b) Designing global strategies: Profiting from operational flexibility. *Sloan Management Review* **27**(1), 27–38.

Mauri, A. and Sambharya, R. (2001) The impact of global integration on MNC performance: Evidence from global industries. *Management International Review* **10**, 441–454.

Morrison, A., Ricks, D. and Roth, K. (1991) Globalization versus regionalization: Which way of the multinational? *Organizational Dynamics* **19**, 17–29.

Pantzalis, C. (2001) Does location matter? An empirical analysis of geographic scope and MNC market valuation. *Journal of International Business Studies* **32**, 133–155.

Prahalad, C.K. and Doz, Y. (1987) *The Multinational Mission: Balancing Local Demands and Global Vision*. Free Press, New York.

Porter, M.E. (1985) *Competitive Advantage*. Free Press, New York.

Porter, M. (1986) Competition in global industries: A conceptual framework. In *Competition in Global Industries* ed. M.E. Porter, pp. 15–60. HBS Press: Boston, MA.

Rugman, A. (2000) *The End of Globalization: Why Global Strategy is a Myth & How to Profit from the Realities of Regional Markets*. Amacom, New York.

Rugman, A.M. and Brain, C. (2003) Multinational enterprises are regional, not global. *Multinational Business Review* **11**(1), 3–12.

Sambharya, R.B. (1995) The combined effect of international and product diversification strategies on the performance of U.S.-based multinational corporations. *Management International Review* **35**(3), 197–218.

Schlie, E. and Yip, G. (2000) Regional follows global: Strategy mixes in the world automotive industry. *European Management Journal* **18**, 342–354.

Segal-Horn, S., (1996). The limits of global strategy. Strategy & Leadership November/December 12–17.

Shaked, I. (1986) Are multinational companies safer? *Journal of International Business Studies* **17**, 83–106.

Tallman, S. and Li, J.T. (1996) Effects of international diversity and product diversity on the performance of multinational firms. *Academy of Management Journal* **39**, 179–196.

United Nations (2002). *World Investment Report 2002: Transnational Corporations and Export Competitiveness*. New York and Geneva: United Nations.

Verdin, R. and Heck, N.V. (2001) *From Local Champions to Global Masters*. Palgrave, New York.

Vermeulen, F. and Barkema, H. (2002) Pace, rhythm, and scope: Process dependence in building a profitable multinational corporation. *Strategic Management Journal* **23**, 637–653.

Venkatraman, N, (1989) The concept of fit in strategy research: Toward verbal and statistical correspondence. *Academy of Management Review* **14**, 423–444.

Yip, S.G. (2003) *Total Global Strategy II*. Prentice Hall, New Jersey.

Zaheer, S. (1995) Overcoming the liability of foreignness. *Academy of Management Journal* **38**, 341–363.